AF600284

DANTE'S IDEA OF FRIENDSHIP

The Transformation of a Classical Concept

Dante's Idea of Friendship

The Transformation of a Classical Concept

FILIPPA MODESTO

UNIVERSITY OF TORONTO PRESS
Toronto Buffalo London

Toronto Buffalo London
www.utppublishing.com

ISBN 978-1-4426-5059-6

Toronto Italian Studies

Library and Archives Canada Cataloguing in Publication

Modesto, Filippa, 1957–, author

Dante's idea of friendship : the transformation of a classical concept / Filippa Modesto.

(Toronto Italian studies)

Includes bibliographical references and index.

ISBN 978-1-4426-5059-6 (bound)

1. Dante Alighieri, 1265–1321. Divina commedia. 2. Friendship in literature. I. Title. II. Series: Toronto Italian studies

PQ4432.F75M63 2015 851'.1 C2015-902339-4

University of Toronto Press acknowledges the financial assistance to its publishing program of the Canada Council for the Arts and the Ontario Arts Council, an agency of the Government of Ontario.

Canada Council for the Arts
Conseil des Arts du Canada

Funded by the Government of Canada
Financé par le gouvernement du Canada

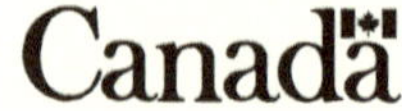

Contents

Acknowledgments

I wish to take this opportunity to thank the various scholars who have helped to inspire, inform, and shape my ideas on Dante. In particular, I thank Robert Hollander of Princeton University, Giuseppe Mazzotta of Yale University, John Freccero of New York University, and Teodolinda Barolini of Columbia University for their solid contributions to Dante scholarship. For this study I have used Robert and Jean Hollander's translation of the *Inferno*, *Purgatorio*, and *Paradiso*. In addition, the value of Robert Hollander's commentary at the end of each canto is inestimable. At the City University of New York, I thank Paul Oppenheimer of The Graduate Center and Luigi Bonaffini of Brooklyn College for their support. I thank also Jill Cirasella at the Mina Rees Library, The Graduate Center, for her assistance.

I am indebted to the late Ron Schoeffel, who believed in this project in its early stages, and to Suzanne Rancourt at the University of Toronto Press, for their dedication and professionalism. I am grateful to Abby Egerter, for her incisive suggestions.

Finally, I dedicate this book to my son, Antonio Alexander, in gratitude for his love and friendship.

Abbreviations

Conf.	Augustine. *Confessions*. Trans. William Watts. Cambridge: Harvard University Press, 1989. Citations show book and chapter numbers.
Conv.	Dante. *Convivio*. Ed. Giorgio Inglese. Milano: Biblioteca Universale Rizzoli, 1999.
DA	Cicero. *De Amicitia*. Trans. William A. Falconer. Cambridge: Harvard University Press, 1992.
De Consol.	Boethius. *The Consolation of Philosophy.* Trans. V.E. Watts. New York: Penguin Books, 1969.
EE	Aristotle. *Eudemian Ethics,* in *The Complete Works of Aristotle.* Ed. Jonathon Barnes. Princeton: Princeton University Press, 1984.
Epistle	Dante. *Dantis Alagherii Epistolae: The Letters of Dante.* Ed and trans. Paget Toynbee. Oxford: Clarendon Press, 1966.
Inf.	Dante. *Inferno*. Trans. Robert Hollander and Jean Hollander. New York: Anchor Books, 2002.
NE	Aristotle. *Nicomachean Ethics*. Trans. Terence Irwin. Indianapolis: Hackett Publishing Company, 1985.
Par.	Dante. *Paradiso*. Trans. Robert Hollander and Jean Hollander. New York: Anchor Books, 2008.
Purg.	Dante. *Purgatorio*. Trans. Robert Hollander and Jean Hollander. New York: Anchor Books, 2004.
ST	Aquinas. *Summa Theologiae*. 61 vols. New York: McGraw-Hill, 1964–80.

DANTE'S IDEA OF FRIENDSHIP

The Transformation of a Classical Concept

Chapter One

Introduction

The next topic … is friendship … it is a virtue, or involves virtue, and besides is most necessary for our life. For no one would choose to live without friends even if he had all the other goods.

(Aristotle, *Nicomachean Ethics*, 8.1 1155a1–5)

The purpose of these pages is not to offer a comprehensive study of the history of friendship but rather to address a more focused area of inquiry by examining Dante's ideas of friendship as exemplified in the *Vita Nuova*, *Convivio*, and *Commedia*. Dante's conception of friendship is complex, and this study will show it to be the synthesis of a classical notion grounded in human reason and virtue and a medieval Christian notion grounded in the love of God. Friendship in the *Commedia* will be viewed in relation to the interplay between reason and faith, philosophy and theology, the human and the divine. It will here be shown that classical friendship, a relationship grounded in human reason and virtue, serves both as an illuminating point of origin and deviation for Dante. His notion of friendship, as will also be seen, is compatible with the classical notion of friendship. To the extent that it concerns Dante's belief that humans should seek both secular and spiritual perfection, friendship in the *Commedia* bridges the human and the divine. Far from being a mere extra or addendum, friendship thus constitutes an integral part of Dante's journey, a handmaiden to his spiritual perfection and complete happiness. Particular attention will therefore be paid to Virgil and Beatrice as benevolent and compassionate friends, and their union will be shown to mirror the relationship between secular and spiritual happiness, flesh and spirit, philosophy and theology.

The ancients viewed friendship as a noble subject, one worthy of the highest respect and serious consideration. Friendship thus acquired a special significance and was understood to have powerfully ethical dimensions. In its intrinsic link to a person's highest good, friendship became a bridge that led beyond particularity into universality. In the *Nichomachean Ethics*, Aristotle defines *philia* as a virtue, a relationship intrinsically linked to a person's ultimate happiness and perfection.[1] Friendship is seen as the highest external good (*NE* 9.9 1169b10). That friendship is necessary for human life and that no one would willingly choose a life without friends (*NE* 8.1 1155a3, 1155a5) are claims that remain difficult to refute. In Plato's *Lysis,* Socrates praises friendship above all other virtues, telling Menexenus of his long-lasting desire for this kind of companionship:

> Now it happens that since I was a boy I've desired a certain possession, just as others desire other things. For one desires to acquire horses, another dogs, another gold, and another honors. Now me, I'm of a gentle disposition regarding these things, but when it comes to the acquisition of friends I'm quite passionately in love; and I would like to have a good friend rather than the best quail or cock to be found among humans, and indeed, by Zeus, for my part, rather than a horse or a dog. And I suppose, by the Dog, that I would much rather acquire a companion than the gold of Darius, and rather than Darius himself – that's the kind of lover of companions I am. (Plato, *Lysis,* 211e–212a)

The desire to seek comfort and assistance from others of the same species was understood by the ancients as a natural and distinctively human attribute.[2] While other species may seek the comfort of their own kind, a person's passionate refuge to his own is unique in its frequent reliance upon reason. Human friendship alone seems to aim at the highest possible end of moral perfection. For both Plato and Aristotle, all forms of association, including various types of friendship, acquire significance and are to be understood within and in relation to that most encompassing of human associations, the *polis*. As humans are social and political beings, a person's friendships seem to presuppose a natural union with others within a particular kind of socio-political reality.[3] For the ancients, friendship was thus linked to the active life, and the Latin *amicitia,* for example, also implied the notion of being active together. While noting how Horace identifies himself as Maecenas's companion not merely in private life but also in the professional and political realms, David Armstrong observes that "indeed, there is hardly such a thing to the ancient mind, whether Greek or Roman, as friendship separate from the idea of acting together in the world."[4] In an attempt to contrast the attitudes of the ancients with the general apathy towards politics that is more common in the present day, H.H. Joachim draws attention to their depth of commitment to the political life of the state:

> Citizenship – the being a member of the polis – meant far more to Plato and Aristotle than it means to us. The whole of the man was, so to say, absorbed in the

> association: his interests all found their fulfillment in his civic life – his duties all had their basis in his civic position.[5]

Friendship, like justice, therefore belonged within the political community: "For in every community there seems to be some sort of justice, and some type of friendship also ... The proverb 'What friends have in common' is correct, since friendship involves community" (Aristotle, *NE* 8.9 1159b26–32). The intrinsic value of friendship is to be found in no source other than itself. The truth perhaps is that friendship, whether as topic or experience, remains as significant today as ever:[6] in place of disparity, it brings accord; in place of chaos, order; of many, it creates one. Cicero notes that for Empedocles, all things in the universe are either united by friendship or disbanded by discord.[7]

Despite its numerous benefits in both private and public life, friendship seems to remain an enigma, its definition and worth shaped within specific historical, social, and political realities. Like other types of social constructs, the language of friendship mirrors to a great extent the socio-political and socio-cultural reality within which it takes shape. Cultural differences often translate to hermeneutic discrepancies and confusion regarding language and sense and these discrepancies between the Greek and Latin terminology for friendship and our modern terminology adds to the confusion regarding correspondence.[8] The fact that cultures are not homogeneous and that definitions of friendship have evolved over time adds to the complexity. Despite certain confusions regarding terms used to describe it, a core idea of friendship – discussed below – dating from the ancient world and running through the Middle Ages has somehow managed to transcend the existing discrepancies, so in some essential ways, the concept of friendship remains continuous.[9] A common ground for all forms of friendship is a person's natural tendency, as a socio-political animal, to form bonds with others of the same species (Aristotle *NE* 9.9. 1169b17–19).

Notwithstanding cultural and hermeneutic discrepancies, this text will assume an essential core of friendship, one worth investigating. Such a core is here understood as a personal, mutual,[10] active,[11] and loving relationship that is grounded in reason, virtue, and excellence of character, rather than on external goods.[12] Unlike contractual relations, friendship is to be understood as a union that is essentially acquired and not imposed. It is a relationship grounded in voluntary and rational choice[13] rather than in obligatory reciprocity, political factions, economic alliance, or ties to one's family, ethnic group, or nation. Acquired relationships, to be sure, may not always result from personal decisions. As David Konstan observes, there are instances when one meets people by accident, feels some attraction, and through time develops a friendship with them.[14] In such instances, the friendship is rooted in incidental circumstances. Arranged marriages may, for good reasons, be seen as imposed relationships;

nonetheless, these individuals may grow to love each other and become friends. Beyond these examples, friendship is here understood as an intimate union that results from a free, rational, and ethical choice.

It is important to note that friendship also acquires significance in relation to its opposite: enmity. Above all, friendship is ineluctably joined with reason, virtue, constancy, and harmony, while enmity is linked with emotions, vice, fickleness, and disparity. Friendship leads to concord; evil to civil conflict.[15] At the centre of enmity there is malevolence, disaccord, and pride.[16] At the centre of the experience of friendship, there is benevolence, accord, and humility. For Aquinas, evil results from a defect in the way one shares in the supreme good.[17]

Christ taught that friendship is rooted in humility. By means of humility, the Word became flesh. By contrast, because of his pride, Satan rejected the Word, became an enemy of God (*e contra 'l suo fattore alzò le ciglia* – and raised his brow in scorn of his creator [*Inf.* 34, 35]),[18] and was forever condemned to silence in a place marked by its distance from Him, in ice.[19] As the epitome of evil, Satan is a parody of the love that is at the centre of Christian friendship. Note that in the *Commedia*, friendship and the harmony it bears are evoked by a reference to the enmity and chaos that afflict and disrupt the city.[20] If, as Mazzotta observes, enmity is what destroys the garden and continues to pose a threat to the safety of its inhabitants, friendship is what establishes order, stability, and harmony in the city.[21]

It is puzzling that, despite its importance, friendship has not until recently been seen as a topic of interest to scholars. One wonders why even today there exist relatively few comprehensive studies of classical friendship.[22] It is fair to note that the bulk of work on friendship examines it from a philosophical point of view, and along these lines, Aristotle's *Nicomachean Ethics* receives the most attention.[23] Among classical studies, the most crucial texts are Plato's *Lysis*, Books 8 and 9 of Aristotle's *Nicomachean Ethics*, and Cicero's *De Amicitia*. Decent modern surveys also exist, but none of them are in English except David Konstan's *Friendship in the Classical World* (1997). Pizzolato's *L'idea di amicizia nel mondo antico classico e cristiano* (1993) explores the theme of friendship in classical antiquity up to the ancient Hebrew and Christian period in Italian, while J. Fraisse's French-language text *Philia: La notion d'amitie' dans la philosophie antique* (1974) presents a philosophical study of friendship from ancient to modern times. Fitzgerald's *Greco-Roman Perspectives on Friendship* (1996), though not a survey, presents a collection of studies on friendship in ancient authors. Additionally, a number of good studies of the relationship between the classical and Christian traditions are available.[24]

As noted above, one illuminating study on friendship is David Konstan's *Friendship in the Classical World*, which is to my knowledge the only history of friendship in classical antiquity written in English. Its value is inestimable. Konstan sets out to examine the entire scope of friendship, tracing its development from ancient Greece and Rome into the Holy Roman Empire (or from the eighth century BC up to the fourth and fifth centuries AD). His study remains enlightening and innovative for challenging the conventional conception of classical friendship as a union grounded in political and economic alliances and obligatory reciprocity, a relationship that is essentially devoid of the emotive element. Konstan provides ample evidence to support his thesis that, for the most part, classical friendship denotes a personal union that is rooted in affection and altruism or that exists separate from ties of kinship, citizenship, and other ascribed unions.[25]

In contrast to popular opinion, Konstan argues that as a noun, *philos* is to be restricted to indicating a personal friend.[26] He rejects the views of scholars such as Paul Millett,[27] Malcolm Heath, and Simon Goldhill,[28] who too-readily equate the wide range of relationships encompassed by the Greek term *philia* with political obligation and duty. The insistence on reciprocity seems to contribute to the common misunderstanding of classical friendship as a union grounded in political obligation, economic transactions, and personal advantage. Konstan argues against the dominant conception of ancient friendship as a union devoid of personal and emotive aspects. He understands the ancient concept of friendship as a relationship that is personal and affectionate.[29] In doing so, he refutes the strictly political interpretation of Roman friendship that has been offered by such scholars as Ronald Syme and Wilhelm Kroll,[30] who posit *amicitia* as a relationship devoid of the emotional and reduce it to political factions and social alliances. That there may be personal advantages to friendship is obvious, but these advantages in no way diminish friendship to a utilitarian union grounded in calculated self-interest and obligation.[31] The truth is that one of the necessary conditions for classical friendship is disinterested love; as Aristotle states, "to a friend, however, it is said, you must wish goods for his own sake" (*NE* 8.2 1155b31).

Throughout this study, the terms used for "friend" will be *philos* (Greek), *amicus* (Latin), and *amico* (Italian). The terms for "friendship" will be *philia* (Greek), *amicitia* (Latin), and *amicizia* (Italian). It is worth noting that the Latin word for friendship, *amicitia*, is most often restricted to the distinct relationship between *amici*, rather than embracing the wide range of meanings indicated by the Greek word *philia*. As Konstan observes, the Latin term that corresponds to *philia* in the sense of love in general is *amor*.[32] These terms will be used to address several themes that recur throughout this book. One theme concerns an understanding of friendship as a union grounded in moral excellence, character, reciprocity, compassion, love, and benevolence; another concerns the set of relations between friendship and each of love, virtue, happiness, and perfection. The conflict between self-love and the love of another individual, egoism and altruism, will be addressed as well.

Within the scope of this study on friendship, the following key issues need to be addressed: What is the precise nature of classical friendship, and how does it relate to human virtue, reason, happiness, and perfection? What is the nature of Christian friendship, and how does it relate to *caritas*, divine grace, wisdom, and revelation? What are the relations between classical and Christian friendship? Is friendship a relation between a select few who are similar in virtue, or is it a union of opposites? Is it a union rooted in similarity or in difference, or both? Does it involve abundance or deficiency in that it is either a relation between good people who selflessly give of themselves from a surplus of moral goodness, or a relation between good people and people who have moral, material, psychological, emotional, or intellectual deficiencies? Is it a union involving equality or inequality? Why do we become friends with some people and not with others? And finally, what is the nature and function of friendship in Dante, and in the *Commedia* in particular?

The importance of the study to follow thus lies, first, in its offering a new interpretation of friendship in Dante as a synthesis of the ideas of classical and Christian friendship, and, second, in its proposing a novel understanding of his journey towards God as a movement intrinsically linked to friendship. This study proposes to investigate the role of friendship in the *poema sacro* in relation to Dante's ascent to ultimate perfection and complete happiness. My research indicates that, as vast as it is, Dante scholarship rarely deals with friendship of any kind, and there is nothing that corresponds to the claims that will be elaborated in the following chapters. In consulting the *Enciclopedia dantesca*, edited by Umberto Bosco and others (1970–8), and *The Dartmouth Dante Project* (1982–1988), one comes across various entries for "friendship," "*amicizia*," and "*amicitia*," but no entry that addresses topics important to this study.

Friendship is one of the most important themes in Dante's work and can be traced back to his earliest rhyme: *Guido I'vorrei che tu e Lapo Ed Io, Deh ragionamento, Sonar bracchetti, and Volgeti gli occhi* (Guido, I wish that Lapo, thou, and I, Could be by spells conveyed, as it were now, Upon a barque).[33] It is a theme that occurs frequently in Dante's lyric poetry. Teodolinda Barolini points out that in Dante, there seems to be a link between "making poetry and making friends."[34] In the *Commedia*, the link between poetry and friendship is consolidated through the various encounters and discourses of poets. Dante is welcomed by the ancient poets as "*sesto tra cotanto senno*" (the sixth amidst such wisdom [*Inf.* 4, 102]). Barolini notes that in the *Commedia*, conversing is a favourite activity that unites both poets and friends.[35] Dante walks with Virgil and with the ancient poets in Limbo conversing, or *parlando cose che 'l tacere è bello* (speaking of things that here are best unsaid [*Inf.* 4, 104]). Following Virgil and Statius (*Purg.* 21), Dante is listening to their discourse (*ascoltava i lor sermon / ch'a poetar mi davano intelletto* – listening to their discourse, / which gave me understanding of the art of verse [*Purg.* 22, 128–30]). The importance of discourse in relation to friendship will be explored further in the chapters that follow.

It may even be argued that the *Commedia* is itself a gift of friendship. As Dante asserts in his letter to Cangrande, one intention of the *Commedia* is "to remove those living this life from the state of misery and to lead them to the state of happiness."[36] Dante's journey becomes a universal journey through an act of friendship. The first two of its 14,233 lines place the poem within the interplay of the particular and the universal, between the "I" and the "you": *Nel mezzo del cammin di nostra vita / mi ritrovai per una selva oscura* (Midway in the journey of our life / I came to myself in a dark wood [*Inf.* 1, 1–2]). It is precisely by means of friendship that the distance between the particular "I" and the universal "you" is bridged. An individual is not an isolated being. One arrives at truth by means of one's interaction with others. Along these lines, Simone de Beauvoir has argued that "if it is true that every project emanates from subjectivity, it is also true that this subjective movement establishes by itself a surpassing of subjectivity. Man can find a justification of his own existence only in the existence of other men. Now, he needs such a justification; there is no escaping it."[37] As will be proposed below, Dante's "surpassing of subjectivity" occurs by means of his acts of friendship, first with Virgil and then with Beatrice. By embracing their friendship, Dante's "subjective movement" toward universal truth leads to "a surpassing of subjectivity."

The following chapters will focus on friendship in the *Vita Nuova*, the *Convivio*, and the *Commedia*. In particular, they will focus on those parts of the *Commedia* in which Dante's transmutation of the ideas of classical friendship is most evident: *Inferno* 2, *Purgatorio* 30, and *Purgatorio* 31. I argue that Dante's transmutation of classical friendship is not a case of a mere transference from the secular to the spiritual realm; rather, it involves a shift in focus from the particular and finite (the human) to the universal and eternal (the divine). While the focus in classical friendship is on a person *qua* person, the focus in Christian friendship is on a person's relation with God. Along these lines as well, Dante's union with Beatrice will be considered in relation to the love of God. Once a woman of flesh and blood, Beatrice becomes for the poet the bridge between the human and the divine, the finite and the infinite, and particular and universal truth. Ultimately, Dante learns to love Beatrice not merely for herself in accordance with a classical notion of friendship, but for the sake of his love of God. That an individual should reach ultimate happiness by means of his union with a woman will be shown to be revolutionary, as inconceivable for the poets and thinkers of antiquity as for Dante's contemporaries.

The role assigned to Beatrice in relation to Dante's redemption will also be seen as elevating friendship to new heights. It is Beatrice, both as woman and friend, who leads Dante to God. Dante does not hesitate to embrace the friendship of a woman, understanding and valuing it as a union of equals. The introduction of Beatrice marks a revolutionary modification of both the classical and Christian ideas of friendship. To those who wish to object by pointing to the Christian cult of Mary, it may be replied that as the mother of God, she belongs in a different category of relationships altogether than does Beatrice, an ordinary woman of flesh and blood whose experiences are also ordinary. That Dante's ultimate perfection and happiness is attained by means of his friendship with Beatrice is thus unusual if conceivable from a Christian point of view. Through Beatrice, friendship is transported to a higher level. Dante learns to love himself and the Other through his love of God.

Ultimately, friendship as it is developed by Dante is to be understood as a union that overcomes duality and opposition, life and death, the particular and the universal. In Dante, friendship is no longer the union conceived of by the ancients and grounded in human reason and virtue, nor is it the Christian union grounded in divine love. Friendship as understood by Dante is both of these and more: it is a union grounded in both human virtue and divine grace, philosophy and theology, particular and universal truth. It is through his friendship, first with Virgil and then with Beatrice, that Dante transcends his human self to reach God. In this sense, friendship may be understood as an activity whose purpose is to transcend humanity to join divinity while encompassing both.

I will thus argue that in the classical notion of friendship, Dante finds the seeds for his own notion of friendship. By means of human reason and virtue, one experiences earthly perfection and happiness; by means of divine grace and revelation, one experiences spiritual perfection and happiness. The earthly and the divine do not interfere with each other. Nonetheless, autonomy does not exclude cooperation. Like Aquinas before him, Dante accepts a distinction between faith and reason without interpreting it according to an Averroistic concept of opposition.[38] Human reason alone cannot lead to ultimate perfection, for that role belongs to revelation. Giovanni Gentile observes that in Dante, theology reaches an individual through the assistance of reason, but since it remains limited, reason leads one only to a certain point, after which faith must take over.[39] Gentile refers to particular points of the journey, such as in *Purgatorio* 6 and *Purgatorio* 15, in which Virgil openly admits to his own limitations with regard to certain issues, pointing out that Beatrice alone can provide answers to all his questions.[40] While Virgil points to Beatrice as one who is more knowledgeable than himself, she in turn looks to Virgil for help. Because of his imperfection, Dante is unable to experience blessedness directly without assistance of human virtue and reason. In all of her blessedness, Beatrice cannot reach Dante directly and needs the assistance of Virgil. For Gentile, Virgil's intervention is to be understood as "thomistic rationality," a place where theology is to a certain extent subjected to reason.[41] While Gentile is right in stressing the importance of philosophy and rationality, he ends up subscribing to Averroes's opposition between the two. In short, by implying that Dante has Averroistic leanings, Giovanni Gentile misses Dante's sense of the constant, vital interplay between philosophy and theology. Considering the necessary interaction of philosophy and theology, I propose that Dante's transmutation of classical friendship be placed within the positions adopted by Virgil and Beatrice, or between the secular and the spiritual, the human and the divine.

Through an exposition of Aristotle's ideas in the *Nicomachean Ethics*, Cicero's ideas in *De Amicitia*, and Dante's ideas in the *Convivio*, the second and third chapters of this book arrive at an understanding of the nature of classical friendship and its influence on Dante. The discussion here is limited to Aristotle and Cicero since, as is maintained, both philosophers had a singular and profound impact on the formation of Dante's philosophical thought. It may thus be seen that within the ideas of Aristotle and Cicero, Dante discovered the seeds of his own understanding of friendship. In considering Aristotle's influence on twelfth-century Europe, especially in philosophy and theology, chapter two explores how and in what form Aristotle's thought reached Dante, chiefly by tracing its arrival, transmission, and prominence in the West. This should provide sufficient evidence of Dante's direct knowledge of Aristotle via Latin translations from the Arabic and as influenced by Thomistic Aristotelianism.

In contrast to earlier Christian thinkers who aimed at reconciling Aristotle with Augustine and stressing the Platonic elements in both, the proponents of the new Aristotelianism known as Orthodox Aristotelianism worked to reconcile the pagan-Greek rational world view with their Christian faith.[42] It will be argued that it is precisely within the context of this new type of Aristotelianism that Dante's ideas of friendship are to be understood as leading into a relationship that attempts to reconcile opposition with duality, a relationship that aims to fulfil a person's dual goals to achieve both secular and spiritual perfection or happiness. While taking into consideration important Aristotelian and Ciceronian influences, this exploration is not intended to diminish the richness of Dante's originality. It is simply a fact that Dante refuses to adhere to a single position, and that he is both a critic and a follower of Aristotle and Cicero. The evidence shows that, indeed, Dante tailors his authorities to suit his plan and uses their ideas so that they elaborate his vision.

In an attempt to comprehend classical friendship, chapter two thus examines Aristotle's three types of friendship as it is discussed in the *Nicomachean Ethics*, as it is reflected in Dante's *Convivio*, and as it corresponds to his three classifications of motivation – utility, pleasure, and virtue (*NE* 8.2 115b20). Aristotle argues that since people are pleasant or useful coincidentally, and since only the good are good in and for themselves, friendship grounded in virtue alone is of the highest order, while the other two types of friendship are incomplete and coincidental (*NE* 8.3 1156b6–30; 8.4 1157a20–35). Friends of the type that Aristotle has in mind are united by emotion and not a mental state, so each wishes the other the sort of benevolence that only the friend can provide him with: pleasure or utility (*NE* 8.4 1157a5–25). Aristotle thus defines a complete friendship as the union between good people, while a friend is to be understood as one who loves his friend for himself (*NE* 8.3 1156b6–10). Bad people cannot enjoy a complete friendship, for bad people find no enjoyment in one another without profit (*NE* 8.3 1156a11–20; 8.4 1157a15–35). Aristotle concludes that only among good people is friendship experienced in its full and best form (*NE* 8.4. 1157a30) and that only primary friendship is all-inclusive, since it encompasses the other two types, as the good are also useful and pleasurable to each other (*NE* 8.3 1156b20–4).

While offering a lucid and comprehensive understanding of classical friendship, Aristotle's notion of friendship in Books 8 and 9 of the *Nicomachean Ethics* and in Book 7 of the *Eudemian Ethics* is – like the ancient Greek notion of *philia* – broader than the modern English usage of the term implies. The English word "friendship" is far more restricted in its meanings and does not offer an accurate rendition of the Greek term *philia*. Unlike *philia* – a term encompassing a wide spectrum of associations, including relationships of a personal, political, social, and religious nature – the English word "friendship" denotes a mutual and loving bond existing outside of familial, political, or religious affiliations, or a relationship free of impositions and obligations. For the sake of clarity, chapter two goes on to describe the Aristotelian distinction between erotic love and friendship. Friendship is defined as a virtue and a state of mind, and since it is rooted in reason it remains an option. By contrast, love is an emotion that refuses choice. The contrast between love and friendship is of concern to Plato and Aristotle. In Plato's *Phaedrus*, Phaedrus observes:

> A lover more often than not wants to possess you before he has come to know your character or become familiar with your general personality, and that makes

> it uncertain whether he will still want to be your friend when his desires have waned, whereas in the other case, the fact that the pair were already friends before the affair took place makes it probable that instead of friendship diminishing as a result of favors received, these favors will abide as a memory and promise of more to come. (233a1–8)

Constancy in friendship, a union rooted in character and thereby a state of mind, is contrasted with the instability of love, a union rooted in passion and desire, thereby an emotion. A bit later in this dialogue, it is Socrates who defines love in relation to the desire for pleasure and the enjoyment of beauty:

> It is plain to everyone that love is some sort of desire ... When irrational desire, pursuing the enjoyment of beauty, has gained the mastery over judgment that prompts to right conduct, and has acquired from other desires, akin to it, fresh strength to strain toward bodily beauty, that very strength provides it with its name – it is the strong passion called love. (Plato *Phaedrus*, 237e–238c)

If the guiding principle in love is passion, the guiding principle in friendship is reason. Friendship is a virtue, and it is a state that has roots in the best part of us, in reason (*NE* 8.1 1155a1–3; 8.5 1157b30). In taking stock of the similarity between love and friendship in their mutual desire for physical proximity, Aristotle observes that in love, the desire for physical proximity and intimacy is guided by sensation rather than by reason: "Love [*eros*] seems to resemble friendship; for the lover desires a life together, although not in the most proper way but according to sensation [or perception, termed *aesthesis*]" (*EE* 7.12 1245a24–6).[43] Moreover, while friendship originates in goodwill, love originates in the pleasure of perception: "In fact goodwill would seem to originate friendship in the way that pleasure coming through sight originates in erotic passion" (*NE* 9.5 1167a3–5). The interplay between love and friendship is indeed too significant to ignore. Friendship is to be understood in relation to virtue, reason, and the Good. By contrast, love is to be understood in relation to physical beauty, passion, and the sublime. In taking stock of Plato's and Aristotle's understanding of love and friendship, friendship is to be placed within the realm of ethics and love within the realm of aesthetics. A friend is loved for his virtuous character and moral goodness, while a lover is loved for his aesthetic beauty.[44] Beauty changes, while moral excellence remains constant. It is within the context of ethics and virtue that Aristotelian friendship is studied in the next chapter.

The understanding of friendship in relation to ethics extends to the classical understanding of a friend as another self. In reflecting on his friendship with

Maecenas as the most valued treasure in life – for instance, as that which most sustains him – Horace refers to Maecenas as his other half:

> Your friendship is the thing my life most glories in. It is what most sustains me. Ah, if some unexpected event should happen one day, and carry you off who are the half of what I am, what would the other half do, going on living, neither as dear as it used to be, nor able to be by itself? That fatal day would be the ruin of us both. (*Odes*, II, 17)

Horace cannot envision a life without Maecenas, his "other half." The understanding of a friend as another self is not limited to the Greeks or to the ancients: it is a notion that seems to have transcended time and place.[45] To be sure, a friend is a sort of image of oneself.[46] By means of friendship, the duality of opposing wills is bridged, and one learns to know and love another as a mirror of oneself. Individuals who are alike in moral goodness are drawn to each other, so in this sense, a friend is an extension of oneself. By looking into the eyes of a friend, one sees a reflection of oneself. It is within the context of the understanding of a friendship as a moral and intellectual relation that the subject of friendship is explored.

Following the analysis of Aristotelian friendship, chapter three explores friendship in *De Amicitia* and the *Convivio*. Cicero's influence on Dante is considered in light of Gilson's remark that "for here at any rate in *De Amicitia*, the men of the twelfth century found much they felt to borrow; either as it stood or adapted to their need."[47] In the *Convivio*, it is Dante himself who insists on Cicero's philosophical influence. He cites Cicero's *De Amicitia* along with Boethius's *Consolation of Philosophy* as valuable guides and manuals of instruction both on love and philosophy (Dante *Conv.* II, xli, 3–5). It would be erroneous to interpret Cicero's ideas on friendship in *De Amicitia* as merely derivative of Aristotle's, but it would be equally erroneous to overlook their similarities. Both philosophers understand complete friendship as a disinterested relationship, the union of good people who are similar in their virtues, each of whom wishes the other well for that person's sake. Both share the belief that friends love each other for themselves and their character, rather than for external goods, and understand complete friendship as a union ineluctably grounded in virtue.[48] Friends, they believe, are willing to sacrifice their own lives for each other.[49]

Ultimately, both Aristotle and Cicero hold friendship in the highest regard. Friendship supplies all that is denied by life: in it the poor find wealth; the needy and disconsolate, solace; and the weak, strength. Friendship is understood by both as the offspring of plenitude and affluence, rather than of need and deficiency. Only those who are good and sufficient in themselves can love others for themselves. Their accord in matters of friendship is never clearer than in their mutual understanding of the friend as "another self." This claim of *allos autos* (another self) is found in both Aristotle's works on ethics (*NE* 8.12 1161b28–9, 9.9 1166a32, 9.91169b6–7, 9.91170 b6–7; *EE* 7.12 1245a34–5) and in the *Magna Moralia* (2.15 1213a23–4); Cicero uses the term *alter idem*.[50] The argument will be made that Aquinas's use of the expression *alter ipse* in his interpretation of Aristotle's *allos autos* must be placed and understood within a Christian understanding of a friend as "another self" in relation to God. A Christian friend is not merely another self, he is another self in the love of God. In this manner, a friend is to be loved for God.

Following the discussion on classical friendship, chapter four attempts to explain how classical friendship was transformed by Christian writers. To this end, it studies the ideas of Christian writers who acted as bridges between Aristotle and Cicero on the one hand and Dante on the other. The ideas of Boethius, Augustine, and Aquinas will be explored and related to Dante's notion of friendship. It will be shown that Dante seems to draw on the classical idea of friendship and its association with human virtue, and on Christian friendship understood as *caritas*, the mutual love of an individual and God. As Konstan notes, "Christians outdid the classical tradition in recognizing the possibility of friendship between mortals and God or angels."[51] Aristotle rejected the possibility of friendship between mortals and god because of the degree of inequality between the two.[52] By contrast, in embracing inequality, Christianity embraces a friendship between mortals and God. In his *Epistle*, Dante attempts to ingratiate himself with Cangrande della Scala by reflecting a Christian understanding of friendship as a relationship that encompasses the union between superiors and inferiors, humans and God:

> And if our attention be directed to true friendship for its own sake, shall we not find that the friends of illustrious and mighty princes have many a time been men obscure in condition but of distinguished virtue? Why not? Since even the friendship of God and man is in no wise impeded by the disparity between them. But if any man consider this assertion unseemly, let him hearken to the Holy Spirit when it declares that certain men have been partakers of its friendship.[53]

Friendship between superiors and inferiors finds equality in reciprocity, and "therefore, since it is a doctrine of ethics that friendship is equalized and preserved by reciprocity, it is my wish to preserve due reciprocity in making a return for the bounty more than once conferred upon me."[54] In an effort to reciprocate the good he has received from Cangrande, Dante dedicates the *Paradiso* to his patron.

As Konstan observes, the notion of friendship with God has roots in the Bible; in the Old Testament when Moses asks for the forgiveness of his people, he is described as "a friend to God" (Ex 33:11; Gn 18:17; Ws 7:27).[55] When Abraham argues for the lives of the residents of Sodom and Gomorrah, he is called God's friend (Is 41:8; Jas 2:23). At the last supper, Jesus called his Apostles his friends: "Ye are my friends, if ye do whatsoever I command you" (Jn 15:14). Jesus identifies self-sacrifice as the greatest sign of friendship: "Greater love hath no man than this, that a man lay down his life for his friends" (Jn 15:13). By means of self-sacrifice, Christ proclaimed friendship grounded in a spiritual community.

In the early Church, monastic ideas of brotherhood and universal love begin to replace the classical notion of friendship as a personal relationship grounded in the mutual love of human virtue. The ideas about Christian friendship were in fact shaped and influenced by theological principles and by the Monastic life.[56] St Ambrose, for example, understood friendship as a spiritual bond of brotherhood grounded in faith; when discussing the topic, he would often be addressing priests.[57] With the rise of spiritual communities – cloisters, monasteries, and seminaries – more emphasis was placed on a universal sense of charity and spiritual brotherhood, and less on the individual and personal relationship.[58] In this manner, the classical notion of friendship was gradually transformed from a particular union between individuals to a broader faithful community of Christ. At the same time, the traditional vocabulary associated with friendship also began to change. The term *caritas* began to permeate the language of friendship and gradually displaced *amicitia*.[59] In the fourth century, for example, Paulinus of Nola generally reserves the term *caritas* for friendships grounded in Christ and *amicitia* for unions strictly grounded in human affection.[60] As Konstan notes, even St Jerome, Augustine, and Basil of Caesarea, who adopt the classical terminology of friendship, commonly substitute *caritas* or *agape* for *amicitia* or *philia*.[61] Often in the writings of Venantius Fortunatus, the language of *amor* becomes interchangeable with that of *amicitia*, and the distinction between love and friendship becomes less marked than it was for the ancients.[62] Unlike classical friendship, which emphasizes a certain degree of equality, Christian friendship seems more willing to embrace inequality regarding moral goodness.[63] It is a union less grounded in personal merit and moral excellence than on divine grace and faith. While rejecting the classical conception of friendship, which at best was grounded in moral excellence and personal merit, Christianity welcomes friendship between mortals and God.[64] This notion may seem less paradoxical if one considers the fact that from a Christian standpoint, human virtues are imperfect and limited. For Augustine, virtues that are not referred to God are incomplete and deceptive.[65]

Consequently, Augustine notes "he truly loves a friend who loves God in his friend, either because He is in him, or so that He be in him."[66] Since God's love is taken to be above human affection, secular friendship as an end in itself is less than perfect: "the friendship of this world is the enmity of God" (Jas 4:4).[67]

After a discussion of Christian friendship, chapter five studies friendship in the *Vita Nuova* in light of the juxtaposition presented in that work between love and friendship, between Guido, who is the friend, and Beatrice, the beloved. The premise to be argued here is that in reconceptualizing the nature of love, the *Vita Nuova* moves closer to a Christian understanding of friendship as a relationship that encompasses the love of God, or as *caritas*. Chapter five also studies Dante's encounters with Brunetto Latini, Forese Donati, Casella, Statius, Farinata, and Cavalcante, Guido's father, in the *Commedia*. Particular attention is given to the interplay between poetry and friendship and between discourse and friendship.

Chapter six examines the relationships between *amor* (love) and *amicizia* (friendship) and between Virgil and Beatrice as distinct types of friends. This chapter also explores the importance of friendship in relation to Dante's spiritual salvation. Similar to classical friendship, the poet's relation with Virgil is a loving and disinterested union grounded in reason, moral excellence, virtue, and common interest – their mutual love of poetry.[68] Dante loves and admires Virgil for his "magnanimous spirit," an essential feature of classical friendship. While it is true that nowhere in the *Commedia* does Dante call Virgil his "friend," Virgil's magnanimous spirit, his active benevolence, constant guidance, and tender affection are signs of friendship. In friendship, actions are equally as important as titles and names, if not more so, and Virgil acts in a benevolent, tender, and loving manner towards Dante. I would remind any who may wish to point to the degree of inequality between the two poets that Aristotle, Cicero, and Dante consider friendship between those of unequal ranks. As will be seen in chapter two, the conception of *philia* held by the ancients covers a wide range of relationships and is thus more encompassing than the English definition of "friendship." In Books 8 and 9 of the *Nicomachean Ethics*, Aristotle considers friendship between people of unequal ranks, including the natural union between parents and children. Aspasius, who commented on Aristotle in the second century AD, noted that despite the element of reciprocity, *philia* can and does exist between people of unequal rank.[69]

To be sure, Dante benefits from his friendship with Virgil, who leads him to moral perfection and to Beatrice, who in turn leads him to divine grace. Nonetheless, the friendship between Dante and Virgil is primarily grounded in character, virtue, and reason, rather than in incidental attributes. Their friendship is not static: it develops and grows through time. Dante learns to trust

Virgil and places himself under Virgil's care. Virgil does everything within his powers to lead Dante out of the dark wood and along the path towards salvation. By means of his noble speech, and through his compassion and guidance, Virgil instils in Dante energy, courage, strength, and a renewed desire to begin the journey (*Tu m'hai con disiderio il cor disposto/ sì al venir con le parole tue,/ ch' i' son tornato nel primo proposto* – Your words have made my heart / so eager for the journey / that I've returned to my first intent [*Inf.* 2, 136–8]). It is by means of Virgil's assistance and benevolence that Dante overcomes alienation and loneliness (*e io sol uno* – and I, alone [*Inf.* 2, 3]). The restorative power of friendship is never more evident than at the end of *Inferno* 2 when, having found *allos autos* (another self), Dante and Virgil proceed joined together as one (*Or va, ch'un sol volere è d'ambedue* – Set out then, for one will prompts us both [*Inf.* 2, 139]).

Chapter six continues to explore the centrality of discourse in friendship. The premise to be argued here is that the changes and movement that occur in *Inferno* 2 occur through the intercession, compassion, and discourse of friends. By means of discourse, Mary moves Lucy, who then moves Beatrice, who in turn moves Virgil to compassion and then to action. Compassion for Dante's perilous state moves the three blessed ladies to orchestrate and facilitate his spiritual journey back home to the Father. No doubt, by means of discourse, friends are led to activity and change. By means of discourse, friends arrive at a better understanding of the self, the Other, and the universe. Along these lines, Virgil and Beatrice are seen as benevolent and active friends as they do not merely wish Dante well, but participate in his attainment of well-being, or goodness, and are essential to it. Nonetheless, it is worth noting that their senses of their relations with Dante are very different.

Chapter seven examines the transmutation of classical friendship in relation to the disappearance of Virgil and the appearance of Beatrice at the summit of *Purgatorio.* It is suggested that the transition from Virgil to Beatrice in *Purgatorio* 30 parallels the transition from a lower to a higher type of friendship. It is argued that with the disappearance of Virgil and the appearance of Beatrice at the top of *Purgatorio* classical friendship is transmuted to a higher and more perfect form: a union that transcends humanity to encompass divinity. The awakening of Dante to God occurs through Beatrice, who arrives both as divine grace and as a friend in Christ. In her dual nature – in her humanity and in her divinity – Beatrice teaches Dante how to love her in God. With the return of Beatrice in the poem, friendship manifests itself as a spiritual union that acquires significance in relation to God.[70]

Dante's friendship with Virgil, though finite and imperfect, is understood as preparation for Beatrice, or for divine grace. In turn, Dante's friendship with Beatrice is understood as the epitome of Christian friendship. Singleton's remarks are pertinent: "Virgil's guidance in the *Comedy* is that of '*praeparatio ad gratiam*' while Beatrice is '*lumen gratiae*.'"[71] In the garden, Dante's journey under Virgil's guidance comes to an end even as a new journey begins under the instruction of Beatrice. Mazzotta interprets this section of the poem as a "Pauline *rite de passage*," noting that:

> In the garden the pilgrim's journey under Virgil's guidance ends and the new journey led by Beatrice starts; moreover, this is the place where the Pauline *rite de passage* from the condition of the old man occurs and, at the same time, it appears as a veritable garden of love where the fall of man took place.[72]

Without disputing Mazzotta's interpretation, it may be suggested that the pilgrim's rite of passage from a lower to a higher and more enlightened self parallels a passage from finite and imperfect friendship (human friendship with Virgil), to a more complete and perfect friendship (spiritual friendship with Beatrice). Dante's passage to his higher self occurs through his union with two compassionate and benevolent friends – first with Virgil and then with Beatrice, a friend in Christ. In her own love for God, Beatrice intervenes on his behalf. With the disappearance of Virgil and the appearance of Beatrice as grace in *Purgatorio* 30, friendship acquires its proper significance in the realm of Augustinian theology.[73] In the end, friendship in Dante is to be understood in relation to the Word that has become flesh. It is to be understood in relation to the words of Christ in John 15:

> Greater love has no one than this, than to lay down one's life for his friends. You are my friends if you do whatever I command you. No longer do I call you servants, for a servant does not know what his master is doing; but I have called you friends, for all things that I have heard from my Father I have made known to you. (Jn 15:13–15)

Friendship reveals a loving bond among those united in one purpose, of love of God.

Chapter Two

Classical Friendship: Aristotle and Dante's *Convivio*

For centuries, Aristotle's work was virtually unknown in the West except for the Latin translation of the *Categories* and *On Interpretation* with commentaries by Boethius (c. 480–525).[1] Boethius's translation of the *Categories, On Interpretation,* and his commentary on Porphyry's *Isagoge* were well known in Northern Europe from the ninth century forward. These works formed what became known as the Old Logic (*logica vetus*)[2] and the basis for the dialectical movement in theology, which culminated at Paris with Peter Abelard (1079–1142).[3] Aristotelian categories were used as a means of understanding problems of universals, the Eucharist, and the Trinity.[4] In the late twelfth and early thirteenth centuries, translations of Aristotle from Arabic to Latin appeared primarily in Spain and Sicily.[5] While only portions of Aristotle's texts were known in the early Middle Ages, a great deal more reached the universities of Europe in the twelfth and thirteenth centuries. These works extensively influenced the fields of philosophy and theology, particularly between 1250 and 1350. This rediscovery of Aristotle in the West thus occurred within a time span of about one hundred years (1200–1300), which also marked a turning point in European history.[6] By 1265, about fifty-five of Aristotle's works had already been translated into Latin,[7] and even those critical of the secular limitations of Aristotelianism eventually ended up adopting his doctrines and terminology.

After 1230, with the Latin commentaries of Averroes, a new kind of Aristotelianism appeared.[8] In contrast to earlier Christian thinkers who aimed at reconciling Aristotle with Augustine while stressing Platonic elements in both, the proponents of this new Aristotelianism worked to reconcile the pagan Greek rational world view with Christian faith. Its foremost representatives were the two Dominicans, Albertus Magnus (1200–80) and his student Thomas Aquinas (1225–74).[9] Albertus and Aquinas, who were the leading interpreters of Aristotle,[10] were both instrumental in the diffusion of Aristotle in the West[11] and influential for Dante, particularly Albertus.[12] Like Albertus, Aquinas professes adherence to Aristotelian thought, but unlike his predecessor, he ends by adopting Aristotelian ideas and at times even moulding them so that they conform to Christian doctrine. Influenced by Albertus, Aquinas recognized the importance of both reason and faith in relation to the entire body of knowledge, human and divine.[13] Accordingly, a person's understanding of the material world also yields knowledge of God as the creator of all creation. Notwithstanding its importance in relation to truth, however, natural reason is limited, particularly concerning religious mysteries; to fully examine religious truth, human reason requires the assistance of divine revelation. Rather than rejecting Aristotelian philosophy, Aquinas shapes it so that it becomes a handmaiden to theology. Both the *Summa contra Gentiles* and the *Summa Theologiae* present an interpretation of Aristotelian thought that concurs with Christian truths.[14]

Dante's thought was shaped within the intellectual fervor of Thomistic Aristotelianism, with its synthesis of faith and reason, flesh and spirit. It is within the rich philosophical background of classical and Christian thought that Dante's own ideas grow and develop.[15] For Dante, as for Aquinas, human happiness begins in the here and now, though in its complete form it may be said to be found in the Hereafter, for the path towards happiness and the Good is a progressive upward movement.[16] Like Aquinas, Dante values the importance of human reason and philosophy in relation to divine wisdom. Given the intellectual fervor of his time, his understanding of Aristotle was influenced by the various sources and interpretations from Albertus, Aquinas, and Averroes. Aquinas's commentaries on Aristotle and the *Summa contra Gentiles* as primary sources were particularly important to Dante.[17] He was well acquainted with the scriptures and the Latin writers Seneca, Orosius, and Boethius. Dante was familiar with the Arabian commentaries on the works of Aristotle, most likely through the references of others. His familiarity with the Greek philosopher arrived through the Arabian commentators and indirectly through the references in works such as Augustine's *Confessions,* Albertus Magnus's *De meteoris*, the *De coelo et mundo*, and other works, and Egido Colonna's *De regimine principium.*[18] Which of Aristotle's works did Dante know? In his own works he makes specific references to the Greek philosopher's works on ethics, as well as *Metaphysics, Physics, De anima, De meteoris, De caelo et mundo, De sensu et sensato, De generatione et corruptione, De iuventute et senectute, De animalibus, Organon, Rhetoric*, and *Politics.*[19] For the *Nicomachean Ethics*, Dante most likely consulted Robert Grosseteste's translation from the Greek and the *Compendium Alexandrium*, also known as the *Liber ethicorum*, a digest compiled by Brunetto Latini in his *Tresor* (2.1, 39).[20]

Influences from Aristotle are easily ascertained, but what about influences from Plato and specifically from the *Lysis,* his dialogue on friendship? Vossler insists that while Dante had no direct knowledge of Plato, indirectly he was also Plato's student.[21] Apart from the Latin translation of the *Timaeus,* Dante's knowledge of Plato was obtained indirectly through Aristotle, Cicero, Augustine, Albertus Magnus, and Aquinas,[22] although Dante was likely not aware of this. For example, in his *Nicomachean Ethics* and *Eudemian Ethics,* Aristotle demonstrates a thorough knowledge of Plato's *Lysis,* and H.H. Joachim and A.W. Price suggest that the *Lysis* served as a point of departure for Aristotle. Joachim traces Aristotle's formulation of the three types of friendship to Plato's *Lysis,* stating that "Aristotle formulates his own theory of the types of friendship by starting from (and rendering more precise) popular views, and particularly the views of Plato's *Lysis.*"[23] Similarly, Price argues that Aristotle possessed a detailed and complete familiarity with Plato's *Lysis* and took it as a point of origin for his *Nicomachean Ethics* and *Eudamian Ethics.*[24] While citing specific passages in Aristotle that either concur with or diverge from Plato's ideas, Price notes that the *Lysis* serves as the groundwork for Aristotelian friendship[25] and provides a valuable background for future discussions on friendship by raising crucial questions and setting the tone. According to Price, "despite its failure to define or to explain friendship, the *Lysis* succeeds in setting the scene for a genuine understanding; as Plato no doubt intended, it therefore constitutes a limited achievement under the guise of a fiasco."[26]

The most immediate issue raised in the *Lysis,* one that is addressed by Aristotle himself, is whether friendship is a union arising from need and deficiency, or a union grounded in one's love of another's goodness.[27] It seems that Socrates simultaneously accepts and rejects this higher type of union. At first he seems to adhere to the Homeric view that friendship is a union among likes, and thus concludes that only among good people can friendship so much as exist. Soon after, he argues that the good are self-sufficient, and thus they neither desire nor need anything or anyone and are incapable of friendship.[28] The *Lysis* leaves the reader to wonder about the precise nature of friendship and to seek his or her own definition, in a manner that is true to the Socratic method.[29]

That the ideas explored in Plato's *Lysis* reached Dante indirectly, via his knowledge of Aristotle, is evidenced by the numerous direct references to the pagan philosopher. As Giovanni Gentile notes, Dante possessed a thorough knowledge of nearly all current philosophical and scientific trends.[30] Given his command of a wide body of knowledge, his creative complexity, and his intellectual depth, tracing Dante's philosophical thought to one particular source is probably impossible, at least in many instances. Instead, it may be more fruitful to consider the general intellectual and cultural ambience within which he worked, keeping in mind a predominant influence of Aristotelianism. While the issue of originality and influence is crucial, one should not make light of Dante's power of imagination and ability to establish connections among the various threads of knowledge or, to use Auerbach's expression, to synthesize traditional trends of ideas and to invent links where previously there were none:

> Thus the question of whether Dante was an original philosopher is poorly formulated. He was original in the same sense as most scholastic thinkers, whose significance resides less in any freeborn thought than in their striving for a systematic synthesis of differential bodies of traditional thought. Just as Thomas Aquinas sought to combine Aristotelianism with the Christian Platonism of Augustine, so Dante tried to reconcile the Thomistic system with the mystical ideology of the *cor gentile.*[31]

Regardless of whether one agrees or disagrees with Auerbach's claims, what can be ascertained is Dante's unique capacity to assimilate past and contemporary ideas, at times even opposing ones, giving them an innovative spin and thereby making them his own. Notwithstanding his creative genius, crucial influences from Aristotle, Cicero, St Thomas Aquinas, and others are scattered throughout the body of his work.

All available evidence points to the fact that like most of his contemporaries, Dante thus held Aristotle in high regard. Numerous references to and compliments bestowed upon Aristotle throughout the body of his work confirm his direct familiarity with the philosopher,[32] and Dante hails him as the one philosopher who, more than any other, upholds truth as the loftiest of friends (*Conv.* IV, vi, 15–16). He admires Aristotle for having perfected moral philosophy and for having posited the attainment of earthly happiness by means of virtue, *il preceptor morum* (*Monarchia,* III, i, 3), *cuncta moralia dogmatizans* (*Epistola,* XI, ii). Aristotle is deemed worthy of the highest trust, faith, and obedience,[33] and his authority worthy of the highest respect.[34] Dante refers to the Greek philosopher as *maestro e duca della ragione umana,* (teacher and lord of human reason [*Conv.* IV, vi, 8]) and as the *glorioso filosofo al quale la natura più aperse li suoi segreti* (the glorious philosopher to whom more than any other nature revealed its secrets [*Conv.* III, v, 7]).

Vossler recognizes Aristotelian influence in the *Commedia* regarding the overall plan, terminology, scholastic division, virtue and sin. Nonetheless, he argues that Dante "never took seriously the doctrine that makes of action the source of happiness and the condition of virtue."[35] As accurate as Vossler's observations may be, he fails to consider the value that Dante places on action guided by reason in relation to earthly happiness. Vossler does not consider the interplay between reason and theology, earthly happiness and celestial bliss. Like Aquinas before him, Dante accepts the distinction between faith and reason without interpreting it in Averroistic opposition.[36] Reason alone cannot lead one to ultimate perfection, for that role belongs to revelation. Nonetheless, as Giovanni Gentile observes, reason does not hinder theology but aids it.[37] Despite its limitations, reason is the means by which theology reaches an individual and saves him or her.[38] In the dark wood, Beatrice does not meet Dante directly; rather, she implores the assistance of Virgil. While it is true that complete happiness in Dante occurs by means of vision, it is equally true that earthly happiness is attained by means of human reason and virtue. In embracing Aristotelian philosophy, Dante embraces earthly happiness as a preparation for and a prefiguration of celestial happiness. It is precisely because Dante embraces Aristotelian philosophy, grounded as it is in human reason, that he can use classical friendship as a point of departure for his own understanding of friendship.

In the *Commedia,* the importance assigned to Aristotle is further evidenced by the privileged position he holds in Limbo amongst the ancient philosophers. Dante looks up, raises his brow in awe, and hails Aristotle as *'l maestro di color che sanno* (the master of those who know [*Inf.* 4, 131–3]). The honour bestowed upon Aristotle equals the honour bestowed upon philosophy. As Gentile notes, the scene is rich with symbolic meaning: light standing for human reason, the seven doors for the seven liberal arts, and the green meadow for all knowledge available to man through the use of his reason.[39] Dante wonders why these souls hold such a privilege position (*O tu ch' onori scïenzïa e arte, / questi chi son c'hanno cotanta onranza, / che dal modo de li altri li diparte?* – O you who honor art and knowledge, / why are these so honored they are set / apart from the condition of the rest [*Inf.* 4, 73–5]). As Virgil makes clear, their fame on earth gains them preference in Heaven (*Inf.* 4, 76–8). The intellectual wisdom that was the cause of *l'onrata nominanza* (their honorable fame [*Inf.* 4, 76]) on earth is the cause for their privileged position among the dead. Intellectual wisdom is honoured in the world of the living as it is in the world of the dead.

Just as honour is bestowed upon Aristotle in Limbo on account of his wisdom, honour is also bestowed upon Virgil by *la bella scola* (the fair school [*Inf.* 4, 94]). Homer, Horace, Ovid, and Lucan welcome back their fellow poet with words denoting the greatest kind of admiration and honour: *Onorate l'altissimo poeta; / l'ombra sua torna, ch'era dipartita* (Honor the loftiest of poets! / His shade returns that had gone forth [*Inf.* 4, 80–1]). Interestingly, Gentile argues that in choosing Virgil as guide and master, Dante intends to vest himself in a poetry that is capable of leading its prospective readers to the attainment of Aristotelian knowledge, that is, to philosophy in general.[40] Gentile's analysis is particularly significant, for it brings to the foreground the close link between philosophy and poetry, philosophy and wisdom. The interplay between philosophy and revelation, human reason and divine wisdom, is central to an understanding of friendship in the *Commedia*. If one is to accept what Gentile here proposes, friendship in Dante is to be understood within the context of a synthesis of reason and revelation, philosophy and theology, a synthesis of a person's two ends – earthly happiness and heavenly bliss. This is a theory that will be further examined in the chapters that follow. For now, a discussion of classical friendship, as presented first by Aristotle and then by Cicero, is appropriate.

Books 8 and 9 of Aristotle's *Nichomachean Ethics* present a lucid and comprehensive treatise on the topic of friendship. David Konstan observes that "as a window onto Greek ideas of friendship, this material is invaluable, but it has also been the cause of misunderstanding."[41] As John M. Cooper points out, it is unfortunate that these two books have received little attention from scholars and philosophers.[42] At the centre of Aristotle's discussion of friendship in the *Nicomachean Ethics* stands his ethical theory. It is here that Aristotle directly addresses the notion of active benevolence towards others, merely for their own well-being.[43] Aristotle's theory of friendship is to be understood in relation to his ethical theory, and his ethical theory must be understood in light of his theory of friendship.[44] Friendship is directed towards the attainment of our highest good, the acquisition of which results in happiness. To the extent that a person's highest good consists in the perfection of his character as a rational and moral being, Aristotelian friendship may be said to stand at the core of human perfection and happiness.

Aristotle begins his discussion of friendship in Books 8 and 9 of the *Nicomachean Ethics* with the assertion first, that it is a virtue, or more precisely, that it "involves virtue"; second, that it is necessary for a morally good life and for the life of the *polis*; and last, that no one would choose a life without friends even if it were possible to have all other good things.[45] As a political animal, it is natural for a human being to want to form ties with others of the same species; accordingly, Aristotle argues, no one in his right mind would choose a life without friends.[46] Friendship is natural among members of the same species and it creates peace and harmony (*homonia*) among citizens.[47] For all of these reasons friendship is both necessary and noble (*NE* 8.1 1155a28–31). Everyone – rich, poor, young, and old – needs friends. The wealthy need friends to share their prosperity and to help them guard it, the poor need friends with whom to share their misfortune, the young need friends for guidance, and the old need friends to take care of them (*NE* 8.1 1155a12–17).

Having established the worth of friendship, Aristotle goes on to discuss its essential features and the necessary conditions for its proper development and growth. He accepts the popular understanding of friendship as reciprocal benevolence grounded in one of the three objects of love, but adds to it the element of awareness, or recognition.[48] Friends reciprocate benevolence, and they are aware of this reciprocal benevolence (*NE* 8.2 1155b32–5). Reciprocity of goodwill and a mutual recognition of moral goodness are essential attributes of friendship. It is through shared activities and time spent together that reciprocity and mutual recognition of goodwill can be ascertained (*NE* 8.5 1157b19–22), and it is vital that friends spend time together, for with prolonged absence, friendship may be destroyed (*NE* 8.5 1157b10–12). Since it is natural to escape that which is a source of pain and seek that which provides pleasure (*NE* 8.5 1157b16–17), it is quite natural for individuals to desire the company of those friends who are source of both pleasure and comfort (*NE* 8.5 1157b22–4). Friendship grounded in virtue is friendship essentially and not incidentally; hence, the pleasure aspect in this type of union is intrinsic to the relationship and not accidental (*NE* 8.3 1156b8–10, 1156a11, 1156b10; 8.4 1157b3).

It is worth noting that the Greek word *philia* encompasses a wide spectrum of associations, to include bonds of a familial type, relationships outside the family, as well as those of a political, social, and religious nature. Aristotle's study of friendship takes into account the bond between friends (*philoi*), the familial bond between child and parent and between siblings, as well as the bond among citizens. The union among fellow citizens (*politai*) acquires significance in relation to political interests; it is understood primarily as a political association (*politikè philia*). All of these associations ultimately acquire significance within and in relation to the political association that is the *polis* (*NE* 8.9 1159b25–1160a35; 8.11 1161a1–1161b10). They are all grounded in a common purpose, which may stem from political or communal interest, familial ties, or the love of a good and virtuous character. Friendship exists within a community. The common ground for this broad range of relationships is the individual's desire as a political and social being to connect, or unite with others of the same species (*NE* 8.1 1155a20–3).

Since the word *philia* encompasses a wide range of relationships, scholars have erroneously concluded that there is no Greek equivalent for the present-day personal notion of friendship. Contrary to common belief, as Konstan notes, Aristotle distinguishes between the *philia* that takes into account a wide range of relationships and the *philia* that corresponds to friendship in the more contemporary sense – referred to here as friendship proper.[49] Aristotle uses the noun *philos* to refer to a friend in the more general sense, but reserves the term *philoi* for the unique bond between personal friends; for example, when speaking of the bond between parent and child, Aristotle does not use *philoi.* While he applies the verb *philein* (to love) to the more broad and abstract *philia,* he also draws a distinction between the more encompassing *philia* and *philia* proper, which is the distinct union between *philoi.* Konstan thus argues that Aristotle does in fact give serious consideration to friendship proper, the affectionate and disinterested union between friends, *philoi.*[50] One distinguishing factor may be that while other types of relationships may involve love, they may not necessitate requital, a prerequisite for *philia* proper.[51]

While the desire for complete friendship is most natural to humans, its enjoyment is unique and uncommon (*NE* 8.3 1156b25–30). Not only are good people scarce, but there is often no time for people to truly get to know and trust each other. Since only the very few are truly good, primary friendship is a union for the very few rather than for the many. Moreover, it is infinitely more difficult to be good and selflessly loving and devoted towards many people simultaneously, since this requires excessive time and self-commitment. On the contrary, it is easier to please many if the friendship is based on utility and pleasure, since the majority of people do not aspire to a higher type of relationship (*NE* 8.6. 1158a11–15).

Friendship does not belong to inanimate existence; rather it belongs to the rational being capable of mutual goodwill (*NE* 8.2. 1156b27–30). While it is possible to love soulless objects, reciprocal loving is a result of a conscious decision. Perfect friendship is the result of a rational decision to love the good present in the other (*NE* 8.6. 1158a30–5). What unites friends is a decision and, as Aristotle explains, a decision comes from a mental "state" (*NE* 8.5 1158a30). Love is an essential part of friendship, but they are not one and the same thing: love is a feeling while friendship is a state. Complete friendship is a foreign phenomenon to the irrational beast lacking self-awareness and rational thought, the beast whose actions are dictated by the instinctual predisposition towards self-preservation. Those lacking in reason also lack the ability to consider the good of others; hence, brutes are necessarily antisocial, their only goal and primary concern being the satisfaction of primary needs and desires, at least as they perceive them. Complete friendship is thus the companion of rational thought, self-consciousness, and moral rectitude.

Central to Aristotle's discussion of friendship in the *Nicomachean Ethics* is his classification of friendship according to three types, depending on the object of love: the pleasant, the useful, and the good (*NE* 8.3 1156a6–1156b30). Joachim argues that in formulating three types of friendship grounded in three objects of love, Aristotle adheres to the same popular view that is expounded in Plato's *Lysis.*[52] According to a widespread belief, the object of love can be pleasant, useful, or good; hence, some unions are grounded in pleasure, others in interest or advantage, and others still in a person's moral goodness. In agreement with the popular notion, Aristotle states "now since these causes differ in species, so do the types of loving and types of friendship. Hence friendship has three species, corresponding to the three objects of love" (*NE* 8.3. 1156a3–5). The three types of friendship are further classified as complete and incomplete: utility and pleasure friendships are incomplete since they are grounded in coincidental qualities, while virtue friendship alone is complete since it is grounded in essential attributes. Accordingly, complete friendship is defined as "the friendship of those who are good and alike in virtue" (*NE* 8.3 1156b6–8); furthermore, "only good people can be friends to each other because of the other person himself" (*NE* 8.4 1157a20). These friends love each other for their own sake or for their virtuous character, which is constant; thus their friendship is enduring (*NE* 8.3 1156b6–10). Since it is grounded in character, complete friendship is inclusive and permanent. Primary friendship alone is all-encompassing since it also incorporates the other two types – good people are also pleasurable and useful. Only among the good or virtuous is friendship experienced in its fullest (*malista*) and best (*ariste*) form (*NE* 8.3.1156b21–4). Complete friendship is a union of equals who are similar in virtue (*NE* 8.8.1159b4–5).

In contrast to virtue friendship, which is constant since it is grounded in character, utility and pleasure friendships are unstable and finite since they are grounded in mutable realities such as advantage and pleasure (*NE* 8.3. 1156a19–20; 8.4 1157b5). These friends are coincidental since "the beloved is loved not in so far as he is who he is, but in so far as he provides some good or pleasure" (*NE* 8.3. 1156a16–19). Often these unions are capricious since they are subjugated to the whims of fortune and external conditions. The relationship will last so long as each friend provides some good for the other and will dissolve as soon as the one stops being useful or pleasant to the other (*NE* 8.3. 1156a20). There are palpable elements of exploitation and superficiality in these types of unions. Each friend treats the other as a means to his own end rather than as an end in himself. Joachim succinctly identifies the business-like nature of these types of friendship: "There is something sordid, mercantile, vulgar – some trace of a definite bargain – in this type, which is the most common type of friendship."[53] These relationships are friendship only to the extent that they resemble the primary type. Pleasure friendship and utility friendship resemble complete friendship, but because they focus on incidental properties rather than on the whole person, friendships of these sorts are not inclusive and they are subject to dissolution.

Of the two incomplete forms, it is pleasure friendship that most resembles complete friendship (*NE* 8.6 1158a20). Pleasure friends tend to want to spend time with one another and derive pleasure from one another's company; to the extent that their union is less mercantile and more humane, they seem to come closer to ideal friendship. While the worth of the useful friend stands outside of himself, that of the pleasant is intrinsic to the friend. It would seem that of the two, it is pleasure friendship that is less incidental. Friendship grounded in utility arises from difference, since we normally seek that which we lack and repay with some other thing.[54] These friends seek each other coincidentally and not in themselves,[55] and neither loves the other for who he is but for what he can provide, so the relationship is easily dissolved as soon as the profit or pleasure disappears (*NE* 8.3 1156a20, 1156b10). For all of these reasons, it must be concluded that only the friendship of good people is friendship in the primary and most complete sense; the others are friendship by analogy (*NE* 8.4 1157a31).

Although virtue is a prerequisite of complete friendship, it is not a sufficient condition. While it is possible to be virtuous and yet lack friendship, it is impossible to have friendship in the absence of virtue. This leads Aristotle to conclude that friendship might be even more desirable and rare than moral virtue as it is capable of providing a greater happiness. Although virtue ought to be sought and praised for itself, it is always more rewarding and enjoyable when it is mutually shared among friends. As friends mutually recognize and appreciate each other's virtuous character, virtue itself ceases to exist as an abstract concept and is rendered a living reality. In applying one's virtue for the well-being of a friend, one becomes an active good for that friend. Through friendship, potential good transforms into active and actual good. Through the mutual and reciprocal exchange of benevolence, the particular good that exists to a lesser degree in each friend joins and becomes one with the universal good.

The question arises as to whether friendship changes or ceases to exist under certain conditions. Aristotle envisions circumstances when friendship may change, diminish, or dissipate. Life's misfortunes can become obstacles to both friendship and happiness, and even in virtue friendship, pain, suffering, and unfavourable conditions may push the elderly and the ailing to withdraw from others' company. The happiness that is derived from friendship is thus to a certain degree contingent upon external and uncontrollable forces. When a good person becomes incurably vicious, a friend can no longer love him, since the ground for the original bond no longer exists; on the other hand, if there is a slim possibility that a friend may be steered towards the right path, one must do everything possible to rescue his character from corruption (*NE* 9.3 1165b15–30). In the event that one friend remains the same while the other becomes more virtuous and excels morally, the better person has a moral obligation to dissolve the friendship, because the gap between the things that each approves and finds agreeable becomes so great that it would be impossible to continue the friendship (*NE* 9.3 1165b21–30). Nonetheless, the dissolution of the friendship by the better person should not result in the mistreatment of the other as though he had never been a friend. Some recognition and respect should be reserved for past friendship, unless the disbandment is due to extreme lack of virtue (*NE* 9.3 1165b31–5). Since perfect friendship is grounded in character, major changes in character would seem to result in the mutation or total disintegration of the relationship. Of course, while it is possible for complete friendship to disintegrate, it is more common to witness the disintegration of utility or pleasure friendship. It is logical that these less perfect type of unions dissolve as soon as they cease to be pleasant or useful (*NE* 9.3 1165a1–4). Since passion, self-interest, and instability is of their nature, these unions are short lived as compared to those grounded in character.

In an attempt to shed light on Aristotelian friendship, Price addresses the important distinction between *praxis,* action which has intrinsic value, and production or *poiesis,* which has only instrumental value.[56] It would seem that of the three types of Aristotelian friendship, virtue friendship alone belongs to *praxis,* while pleasure and utility friendship fall under the category of *poiesis.* Virtue friendship is the union of good individuals who love each other for their intrinsic value, each loving the other *qua* himself, or *qua* his virtuous character. By contrast, pleasure and utility friends love each other *qua* their instrumental good.

When discussing virtue friendship, Aristotle envisions a complete friendship, or a union of good people (*NE* 9.3 1156b7–8). But if virtue is the determining factor in this kind of friendship, then why are we not attracted to all those possessing such moral attribute? To be sure, one does not become friends with all virtuous individuals, however excellent their character may be. Moreover, in loving a friend for his virtue, does one love the abstract attribute or the individual himself? And does the importance placed on virtue diminish the role of individuality in this friendship? According to Suzanne Stern-Gillet, there is a certain degree to which Aristotle takes into account the importance of individuality, but on the whole, individuality is not at the forefront of his discussion.[57] Konstan argues that the object of love in Aristotle is the individual.[58] Accordingly, one does not merely love virtue; rather one loves the virtuous friend on account of his virtue.[59] That the object of love is the individual bearer of each quality can be deduced from Aristotle's own definition of complete friendship: "But complete friendship is the friendship of good people similar in virtue; for they wish goods in the same way to each other in so far as they are good, and they are good in themselves" (*NE* 8.3 1156b6–9). It would seem that for Aristotle, complete friendship is a relationship concerning individuals rather than abstract qualities. The good person loves the virtue present in his friend insofar as that virtue is related to the essence and character of who the friend is as an individual.

After categorizing the lovable as good, pleasant, or useful, Aristotle goes on to consider the requirement of reciprocity in friendship. Friendship is an activity that requires reciprocated goodwill and an awareness of the reciprocated goodwill (*NE* 8.2 1155b31–5). While it is possible to love a soulless object, it is not possible to establish friendship with it (*NE* 8.2 1155b28–30). Aristotle's claim must be understood in relation to the distinction he makes between love and friendship: love is a feeling while friendship is a state and the result of a conscious and rational choice. One freely and consciously enters into a union with another as a result of a rational decision to love the other for himself and for his virtuous character (*NE* 8.5 1157b30–5). Moreover, while friendship requires reciprocity, love does not. One may envision a situation when someone or something is loved without being aware of the love or reciprocating it, and abstract qualities are capable of neither reciprocating love nor exercising reason. From all that has been said, it would seem that the object of love in complete friendship is the individual and not the abstract quality. Since good people are good in themselves and not coincidentally, it follows that each loves the other for his individual self (*NE* 8.3 1156a5–15). On the other hand, utility and pleasure friends love one another instrumentally and not intrinsically (*NE* 8.3 1156a10–20; 8.8. 1159b20). These friends love one another for the sake of gain and interest (*NE* 8.3 1156a11–15), so the object of love in these types of unions would seem to be the abstract quality. These individuals love neither themselves nor their friends (*NE* 8.4 1157a15).

Another point of contention in Aristotle's works is the relationship between self-love and friendship. The relation between self-love and friendship, as that between virtue and friendship, is to be understood within and in relation to Aristotle's theory of ethics. He argues that the same features that are to be found in friendship are also to be found in self-love (*NE* 9.4 1166a1–10). Since the relationship to the self precedes all other relationships, a person's relation with others mirrors his relationship to himself: the decent person loves himself for his own sake, for his virtuous and rational parts (*NE* 9.4 1166a12–13, a15–20; 9.8 1168b4–7, 1169a4–5), and likewise, he loves his friend for his friend's sake and for his virtuous character (*NE* 9.8 1168b1–4). By contrast, the base person does not love himself, nor is he friendly towards himself because there is nothing lovable or admirable about him (*NE* 9.4 1166b26–7). Being incapable of truly loving himself, the base person is incapable of experiencing loving and friendly feelings towards others (*NE* 9.4 1166b1–25). Friends feel and act most benevolently towards each other when in agreement about the good. Good people lack internal contradictions: they are of one mind (*NE* 9.4 1166a14–18).

The decent person, thus, relates to himself as he does to his friend and has the same features in relationship to oneself and to one's friend (*NE* 9.4 1166a30–1).

Rather than being an expression of selfish egoism, the Aristotelian notion of self-love constitutes an ideal of moral excellence. Suzanne Stern-Gillet observes that for Aristotle, self-love is unattainable by individuals who are not virtuous.[60] Reason is the element with which the good person most identifies, the most authoritative part with which an individual most associates; the treatment of friends as "other selves" encourages a consideration of their well-being as primary.[61] Hardie notes that, since Aristotle's virtuous individual is not hedonistic, his self-love cannot be egoistic.[62] Aristotle's theory of self-love is consistent with self-sacrifice (*NE* 9.8 1169a18–35). Good people are willing to sacrifice all else, even life itself, for the sake of their friends and country.[63] Since it is easier to study the behavior and character of others (*NE* 9.9 1169b23–1170a4), and since a friend is a mirror of oneself, it is in loving a friend that the good person learns to know and love himself best (*NE* 9.9 1169b25). In benefiting friends, the happy person is also attaining his ultimate goal, the fulfilment of his own supreme good (*NE* 9.9 1169b11–15).

Aristotle's theory of self-love acquires significance in relation to his notion of the friend as another self. For Aristotle, a friend is indeed ever another self (*allos* or *heteros autos*) (*NE* 9.4. 1166a30; 9.9 1170b5; *EE* 7.12 1245a30), and the attributes that characterize friendship derive from the attributes of friendship as expressed to oneself (*NE* 9.4 1166a1–30). A friend spends time with his friend, sharing in her suffering and joys (*NE* 9.4 1166a15). A friend wishes and does good for his friend's sake and in complete accord, makes the same choices (*NE* 9.4 1166a14); additionally, the good person lives in complete accord with himself, wishing and doing good for the sake of the best part of himself – his thinking self (*NE* 9.4 1166a15–19; 9.8 1168b30–5). Since a virtuous person relates to himself in the same way as he relates to his friend, the friend may be seen as an extension of himself. Aristotle concludes: "The excellent person is related to his friend in the same way as he is related to himself, since a friend is another himself" (*NE* 9.9 1170b6). In other words, the good are drawn towards the good.

A.W. Price gets to the heart of the matter as he identifies an ethical conception of the self that is central to Aristotle's account of friendship.[64] It is in the understanding of oneself as an ethical being that the notion of a friend as another self acquires significance. In loving a friend for his own sake and in himself, one loves him for his character (*NE* 8.3 1156b9–10; 8.4 1156b10, 1157a20). From all that has been said, it would seem that complete friendship is grounded in similarity and not difference. Since a friend is another self, and since "similar is a friend to similar" (*NE* 9.3. 1165b15; *EE* 7.1. 1235a6), friendship is a union grounded in similarity (*NE* 8.8 1159b3–5).

While focusing on the uniqueness of the individual, the modern age has distanced itself from the ancients' conception of the self. Aristotle, as did all the ancients, had no conception of an isolated self. An individual was understood in relation to the civic life, to the socio-political community, and to the life of the *polis*. Perhaps H.H. Joachim is correct in arguing that being a citizen was far more important to Plato and Aristotle than it may be to many of us.[65] For the ancients, a person's life seems most often to have acquired meaning in relation to the life of the *polis*, which encompassed within itself the various and best forms of human nature,[66] and the essence and good of an individual were to be fully comprehended and realized only in relation to the other citizens within a community. Within the various types of political associations, there were various types of friendship; friendship, like justice, is found in the political community (*NE* 8.9 1160a31; 8.12 1162a33). Ultimately, friendship was understood in relation to the most encompassing association of all – that of the *polis*. The Aristotelian conception of a person as a political being justifies the need for friendship: "For no one would choose to have all [other] goods and yet be alone, since a human being is political, tending by nature to live together with others ... Hence the happy person will need friends" (*NE* 9.9 1169b16–22). Solitude cannot be conducive to happiness. For Aristotle, the happy life is a life that promotes the sharing of intellectual discussion and pursuit of knowledge together with friends (*NE* 9.9 1170b8–10). The solitary life is not conducive to continuous activity and pleasant experiences (*NE* 9.9 1170 a5–10), but an individual is alive most of all insofar as he is thinking; thinking is the essence of human life. And if one perceives, one is aware that he is perceiving, which is the same as perceiving that one exists (*NE* 9.9 1170a30). Friendship encourages virtue through shared activity and conversation and thought, the mark of human life (*NE* 9.9 1170a11, 1170b9–14). Aristotle thus concludes: "Anyone who is to be happy, then, must have excellent friends" (*NE* 9.9 1170b18).

Proximity plays a crucial role in friendship. To be sure, it is important that friends live together. Living together, however, is much more than the mere sharing of physical space and the sharing of food and drink, as animals might be expected to do, but consists in "the sharing of words and thought" (*NE* 9.9. 1170b11–12). Beasts merely share food and drink; people share thoughts and deeds. The relation of friendship is built on free speech and open discourse. By means of open discourse, friends – as active and rational beings – arrive at a mutual knowledge of themselves, each other, and the universe. Living together entails cooperation and learning. Friendship leads to wisdom and moral perfection. Through the mutual sharing of thoughts, words, and deeds, friends of similar character improve themselves and each other: friendship encourages development and growth (*NE* 9.12 1172a10–14; 9.9 1170a11–12; 10.9

1180a31–2). Since a friend is more directly visible to me than my own self, it follows that in observing my friend, I discover my own perfection (*NE* 9.9. 1169b34). To the extent that each friend is a conscious and active being who exists, acts, and reacts within a particular socio-political reality, he is involved in a dynamic and reciprocal relation with his friends and with the world around him.

As A.W. Price notes, "cooperation" plays an important role in Aristotelian friendship.[67] It is through the cooperation and the sharing of activities that a friend's actions become one's own (*NE* 9.9 1169b30, *NE* 9.9 1170a3). Compatibility of character is tested over time and by means of shared experiences and thoughts.[68] Through cooperation and the exchange of thoughts and deeds, friends get to know each other and themselves. Of course, one may envision situations in which a refusal to cooperate might be a sign of friendship, such as when a friend requires another friend to brings harm to one's country or to another individual. Nonetheless, it is through my interaction with another that I become aware of myself as a thinking person with a particular character, so that by means of interacting with my friends, I obtain self-knowledge.[69] By means of cooperation, by sharing ideas and activities, friends are simultaneously moved inwardly towards themselves and outwardly towards each other. In this double movement of two independent self-consciousnesses, each friend sees the other acting as he does and each does what he expects of the other.[70] The identity of one is influenced by the identity of another. Aristotelian friendship is thus to be understood as a becoming, an activity by means of which the duality of opposing wills is resolved in cooperation and in knowledge.

In the same way that self-love and virtue are essential components of primary friendship, goodwill and active benevolence are essential attributes of friendship. While an essential aspect of goodwill is wishing for the friend's good, that alone does not equal friendship, as it is possible to have goodwill towards someone unknown to us or in cases when the person is unaware of our goodwill. In addition to mutual goodwill, it is necessary that friends be aware of their goodwill. Aristotle goes on to clarify the distinction between love and goodwill. In contrast to love, goodwill lacks intensity and desire, and it may also lack familiarity (*NE* 9.5 1166b30–5). While it is a necessary attribute of friendship, it does not necessarily presuppose friendship because it is possible to desire good for one who is a stranger or a mere acquaintance. Aristotle defines goodwill as inactive friendship, a relationship that can be transformed into friendship with shared experience and with the passage of time (*NE* 9.5 1167a11). Friendship is thus equated with activity. Benevolence requires more than merely wishing a friend his good – it requires that one does all that is humanly possible to bring about that good. In this sense, friendship is to be understood as an activity by means of which potential good is transformed into actual good. Friendship is an activity that leads to happiness (*NE* 9.9 1169b30), and since the actions of virtuous people are good and their activity is of the highest sort, it follows that their happiness is most perfect.

Along these lines, Aristotelian friendship should be understood in relation to ethics and to the philosophic life. Friendship consists in living together and sharing in discussion and thought, which is the mark of the philosophic life.[71] Price notes the close relation between Aristotelian friendship and philosophy: "Aristotle's ideal friendship, at once rich in its philosophic content and pregnant in its practical implications, represents his moral philosophy at its best and most distinctive."[72] In an effort to reach beyond particularity and arrive at universal truth, philosophy aims at the transcendence of self-consciousness. Jaffa also remarks on the interplay between friendship and the philosophic life: "this is the mark of the true work of a philosophic life."[73] He observes that, like philosophy, friendship is the means by which an individual's self-consciousness transcends itself.[74] Through intellectual wisdom, individuals learn to love themselves in relation to universal truth; similarly, through friendships individuals learn to know and love themselves not as isolated entities but in relation to others within a community. In the same way that the philosophic life – the perfection of wisdom – is the highest internal good, friendship – the perfection of self-love – is the highest external and internal good.

Any study of Dante's transmutation of classical friendship would in fact not be complete without considering Dante's friendship with Philosophy in the *Convivio* (ca.1303–5), a work that in many ways mirrors Aristotle's notion of friendship as defined in the *Nicomachean Ethics*. An examination of Dante's friendship with Philosophy reveals the extent to which Dante's ideas on friendship grew and were transformed from what they were in the *Convivio* to what they became in the *Commedia*. By Dante's time, Aristotelian ideas and terminology, particularly from *De Anima* and the *Nicomachean Ethics*, had permeated works of the Arabs, Albertus Magnus, and Aquinas,[75] and scholars have good reasons to believe that Dante had read Aristotle's works on ethics with the assistance of Aquinas's commentary.[76] What Dante seemed to have appreciated in Aquinas's commentary on Aristotle's works was his sense of causality and ordering, a concept that directs all things towards God. As Dronke observes, Dante focuses on Aquinas's notions that "ethics orders us towards the other forms of knowledge,"[77] and that "to know the order of one thing in relation to another is the specific act of reason."[78] Accordingly, ethics aids man's ascent towards God.

In celebrating the virtue of Philosophy in the *Convivio*, Dante seems to celebrate Aristotelian friendship. He echoes Aristotle's classification of friendship according to three types: utility, pleasure, and virtue (*per onestade*).[79] The difference among the three types lies in the object of love and in its origin. For both Dante and Aristotle, the friendship that is grounded in accidental attributes such as pleasure and utility is incomplete and imperfect.[80] In the same way that perfect friendship is grounded in the love of virtue (*per onestade*) philosophy is grounded in the love of truth and of the rational life.[81] The object of love and the efficient cause of this love in perfect friendship is virtue, and its form is a desire for that virtue. Similarly, the object of love in philosophy is knowledge, its form is love of the intellect, and its efficient cause is truth.[82] Just as the end of friendship is the happiness resulting from a life lived together and ordered according to reason, so also is the end of philosophy the happiness resulting from the contemplation of truth.[83]

Aristotle's notion of *generatio* left its definitive mark on Christian theology by influencing a wide spectrum of thinkers, from theologians such as Philippe le Chancelier (1230), to Albertus Magnus and Aquinas, to poets such as Guido Guinizelli and Dante himself. These Christians found a useful explanation for divine grace in the Aristotelian theory of *generatio*.[84] For Aquinas, *generatio* is a change from matter to form.[85] Similarly, in the *Convivio* Dante interprets Aristotle's process of *generatio* as a movement from matter into form.[86] In both the Aristotelian and in the Christian senses, *generatio* is movement towards perfection. However, for a Christian, a person's natural desire for happiness and perfection requires that he move beyond humanity to unite with God, who is his original source for being. Through grace, God moves humans towards Him. In his study of Dante's experience of happiness at the top of the mountain in *Purgatorio* 30,[87] Singleton refers to both the *Convivio* and the *Monarchia* as proof that Dante knew and agreed with Aristotle's definition of happiness as "operation according to perfect virtue," the inner activity of the soul's virtues by means of which an individual achieves his own perfection. For Aristotle, happiness is to be sought and valued for its own sake, and it is to be obtained from the pursuit of knowledge. Since creation desires its own perfection above all else, all individuals strive after happiness. Like Aristotle, Dante believes that happiness is to be sought for its own sake and that all creation ultimately desires its perfection. However, the Aristotelian parallel of happiness and knowledge represented in the *Convivio* is superseded in the *Epistle* and in the *Commedia* by the Boethian subordination of secular knowledge to the source of ultimate truth and happiness – God. In contrast to Aristotle, Dante locates ultimate perfection and happiness in Heaven, and his own voyage towards happiness is necessarily an ascent towards God. For both Dante and Aristotle, friendship is an activity that leads to happiness and perfection.

In contrast to Aristotle, however, the Christian poet locates ultimate perfection and happiness in God.

As in Aristotle's *Ethics*, friendship in the *Convivio* is understood as analogous to a person's desire for truth and happiness. For Aristotle, any person who is to be happy must have friends,[88] and the link between friendship and happiness underscores a mutual concern for the morally virtuous life.[89] In the *Convivio*, Dante cites Aristotle's definition of happiness as *operazione secondo virtude in vita perfetta* (a life lived according to perfect virtue [*Conv*. IV, xvii, 8]). Aristotle's understanding of happiness rests on the principle that all individuals desire their own perfection above all things, and that perfection lies in operation according to perfect virtue. In the *Convivio*, Dante refers back to Aristotle's principle that all individuals desire to know.[90] Dante recognizes that while all individuals desire to know, not all individuals are privy to knowledge. The *Convivio* is a gift offered in a spirit of benevolence for all those whose natural desire for knowledge has been impeded because of a physical or emotional ailment, because of familial or civic obligations, or because of the place where they were born or reared (*Conv*. I, i, 2–12). Precisely because of his intent to educate the many, Dante writes the *Convivio* in the Italian vernacular rather than in Latin, a language understood by few.[91] All individuals desire to know because all individuals naturally desire happiness, which resides in the perfection of the soul and which is achieved through knowledge; true happiness is an activity of the soul that results in complete virtue.[92] The perfection of the rational soul, together with the happiness that results from that perfection, seems to lie more in *agere* (drive, set in motion) than in *facere* (to do, make).[93] The inner activity of the rational soul, similar to *agere*, is to be understood as a driving force, an urging, that is absent in mere mechanical making. Indeed, the inner activity of one's soul toward perfection implies much more than mechanical production: it implies consciousness, an awareness of one's choices and decisions, the ability to discern right from wrong, true from false; it is a learning process. Yet, learning and growing are impossible in the absence of rational consciousness. While all individuals may naturally desire happiness as the ultimate goal of their actions, disagreement arises regarding the meaning of happiness (*NE* 1, 1095a 20).[94]

For both Dante and Aristotle, happiness is the inner movement of the soul towards its own good and its own perfection. Dante's journey towards happiness and perfection is *generatio* – it is a movement or a becoming from potentiality to actuality, from matter to form.[95] No doubt, for Aristotle *agere* and *generatio* concern a person *qua* person in an earthly existence. As such, happiness is attained through the subservience of one's lower powers to his reason.

For both Aristotle and Dante, the interplay between philosophy and friendship was vital in facilitating and promoting one's movement towards perfection and happiness, or towards the moral good. One crucial difference seems to be that for Dante, as for Aquinas, *agere* and *generatio* begin in the here and now, but in their most perfect and complete form they reside in the Hereafter. Dante's journey towards perfection and happiness, like his journey towards perfect friendship, is by necessity an ascent towards divinity.[96] For Aristotle, happiness is an activity grounded in secular reason and virtue; for Dante, it is an activity grounded in divine wisdom and love.

In the third book of the *Convivio*, Dante draws an analogy between friendship and philosophy and then refers to Book 9 of Aristotle's *Nicomachean Ethics*.[97] If the efficient cause of true friendship is virtue, then the efficient cause of philosophy is truth. And if the end of true friendship is the joy of living the rational life surrounded by friends, the end of philosophy is the happiness attained in the perception of truth. In the same manner as a friend must be loved for virtue rather than for utility or pleasure, so must philosophy be loved for itself, for the love of truth (*Conv.* III, xi, 7–11). This analogy is crucial, for it presents friendship in relation to the activities of knowing and loving. The *Convivio* treats *sì d'amor come di vertù* (both of love and of virtue [*Conv.* I, i, 14]). Knowing and loving are both at the centre of friendship. The natural bond of human love moves one to feel compassion for a friend who is suffering (*Conv.* I, i, 8–9).[98] While the efficient cause of friendship is the love of a friend's virtuous character, the efficient cause of philosophy is the love of truth (*Conv.* III, xi, 13–15). The uniting force in both instances is love. Love strengthens the bond of friendship, for it is the spiritual union of the soul with the object of love.[99] In his love of truth, the knower unites and becomes one with what he knows. The lover becomes one with what he loves.[100] In both cases, happiness is experienced as a result of both knowing and loving and as a consequence of living the virtuous and rational life. A friend unites and becomes one in spirit with his virtuous friend that he knows and loves.

In the *Commedia*, the relationship between knowing and loving acquires particular significance in *Paradiso* 10 as Beatrice and Dante move together into the sphere of the Sun. The link between knowledge and love is exemplified in the presentation of the holy trinity: the Father (Power), the Son (Wisdom), and the Holy Spirit (Love).[101] The link is further represented by the circle of twelve lights, or twelve bright souls who encircle Beatrice and Dante.[102] Later, it will become clear that Beatrice's eyes and smile are manifestations of divine Wisdom, but for now, it is sufficient to say that through his friendship with Beatrice, Dante partakes in a celestial *convivium* where *lo pane degli angeli* (the bread of the angels) is served.[103] In the *Commedia*, the "bread" is no longer the intellectual food that was shared in the *Convivio*.[104] The intellectual "bread" that sustains man on earth cannot entirely satisfy his hunger for ultimate truth.[105] Through Dante's union with Beatrice, he begins to taste the food that simultaneously satiates and causes more hunger[106] – he tastes the bread of life.

Looking back at the *Convivio* from the prospective of the *Commedia*, one notices that Dante's transmutation of classical friendship parallels the journey from philosophy to revelation, from human reason to divine grace, from earthly happiness to celestial bliss. Dante's friendship with Philosophy in the *Convivio* is a preparation and a prefiguration of the return of Beatrice in the *Commedia*. Philosophy and morality encourage and prepare a person's ascent towards God; they teach a person how to distinguish good from evil, right from wrong. Human reason and philosophy are means by which man reaches secular truth, moral goodness, and earthly happiness (*Conv*. IV, xxii, 1–18). The study of philosophy is the path towards the moral good,[107] and through philosophy and morality, an individual is made happy in this life. Though incomplete and imperfect, earthly happiness prefigures perfect happiness in the heavens; similarly, Philosophy finds completion and fulfilment in Beatrice. When Dante writes of *amore* (love) and *virtù* (virtue) in the *Convivio* and in the *Commedia*, the difference seems to lie in the object of love and in the direction of the movement towards that object. The journey in the *Commedia* is an ascent towards divine love and wisdom, attainable through divine grace with assistance from the theological virtues. The journey in the *Convivio* leads to secular truth, attainable by means of philosophy and human natural reason with assistance from the cardinal virtues.

In the *Convivio*, Dante's friendship with Philosophy is grounded in love of wisdom and a need for consolation.[108] In an effort to console himself after the death of Beatrice, Dante immersed himself in the study of philosophy, particularly the study of Boethius's *Consolation of Philosophy* and Cicero's *De Amicitia*.[109] He began to attend the religious schools where philosophy is taught.[110] Like one who goes looking for silver but finds gold instead, Dante finds much more than just a source of consolation in the works of these authors.[111] The love and virtue of the noble lady was of such power that within a period of thirty months all thoughts of his previous love dissipated.[112]

The debate over the *donna gentile* as the object of Dante's affection in the *Convivio* and in the *Vita Nuova* has been a topic of interest among *dantisti*.[113] It centres on a discrepancy between the description of the *donna gentile* in the two works and Dante's conflicted attitude towards her. Dante is asking the reader to believe that the *donna gentile* in the *Vita Nuova* is not a real lady and that she is none other than Philosophy, the daughter of the emperor of the universe.[114]

Should the reader accept Dante's claim that the *donna gentile* in the *Convivio* is one and the same lady as she is in the *Vita Nuova* and that she is always an allegory of philosophy? This is an issue that has crucial ramifications for the *Commedia*, and more particularly for *Purgatorio* 30 and 31. If the *donna gentile* is always an allegory of philosophy, the fact remains that in *Purgatorio* 30 and 31 she is presented as a real woman. How does one account for the apparent contradiction and how does one justify Beatrice's accusations against Dante in *Purgatorio* 30, 124–6?[115] On the other hand, if the *donna gentile* in the *Vita Nuova* is indeed a real lady, then Dante's love for Beatrice is questionable, his friendship with her less than perfect, and the scolding that he receives from her is merited.

Undoubtedly, the appearance of Beatrice in *Purgatorio* 30 announces her triumphal return in the life and work of Dante.[116] The question that remains to be answered is whether we should interpret Beatrice's return in the *Commedia* as a correction of erroneous ideas presented in the *Convivio*.[117] Some scholars have interpreted the return of Beatrice in the *Commedia* as Dante's admission that he committed a blunder in the *Convivio*. According to Robert Hollander, the readers are so happy to witness Beatrice's return in Dante's work, if not his life, that they fail to recognize that this "is a sort of *rifacimento* of *Convivio*," or an attempt to counter and modify ideas earlier expressed in the *Convivio*. Accordingly, readers fail to recognize that in the *Commedia*, Dante is also "countering or modifying particular ideas or attitudes expressed [there]."[118] Perhaps, rather than a "*rifacimento* of *Convivio*," Beatrice's triumphant return in the *Commedia* signals *un adempimento* (a fulfilment). For as Hollander himself observes, although Philosophy herself is absent in the *Commedia*, she is represented by the ancient philosophers in Limbo and by Virgil, Marco Lombardo, and Aquinas.[119]

What is here maintained is that the return of Beatrice in the *Commedia* is in fact less a contradiction than a completion and a fulfilment of Dante's friendship with Philosophy in the *Convivio*. Dante's friendship with Philosophy, a union grounded in natural reason and the love of secular truth, finds fulfilment and completion in his reunion with Beatrice at the summit of Purgatory. Through the incarnation of Christ, reason is fulfilled in faith, love in *caritas*, philosophy in theology.[120] With the appearance of Beatrice, philosophy is fulfilled in faith and grace. Dante never stops loving philosophy nor thinks of her as unimportant.[121] Philosophy both prefigures and leads to ultimate Wisdom.[122] Beatrice transcends and fulfils both Virgil and the *donna gentile*.

Through philosophy and reason, an individual reaches secular truth and earthly happiness, which are less perfect and less complete than divine truth, and the eternal happiness granted through revelation and grace. In the *Convivio*, the limitations of philosophy are clearly set forth. Humans are imperfect and limited, and the secular happiness they attain is also imperfect and limited (*Conv.* III, xv, 6–10; III, iv, 9; *Par.* 4, 40–2).[123] By living a moral and virtuous life in accordance with reason, humans experience a happiness that at best is incomplete. Dante draws a distinction between the natural life, which is imperfect and finite, and the supernatural, which is eternal. He draws a distinction between the active and the contemplative life.[124] Each leads one to a distinct form of happiness and to a particular type of vision. Philosophy leads to finite happiness and a limited vision. Perfect happiness and perfect vision belong to the supernatural life, when humans may experience the beatific vision of God. In contrast to Philosophy, Beatrice leads Dante into a perfect vision, divine wisdom and into divine love as the ultimate origin of all things. Beatrice knows who she loves, and loves whom she knows in God. According to Kenelm Foster, Beatrice is "essentially … the same ideal wisdom whom we met in the *Convivio*."[125] The secular wisdom present in the *Convivio* is transmuted into divine wisdom in the *Commedia*. Like Aristotle, Dante knows that by its very nature the mind seeks to attain truth because in it rests its perfection.[126] While divine wisdom is above secular wisdom, philosophy is important and necessary.[127] Philosophy can help a person to know God, and Dante is well aware of this. Even in the *Commedia* where Philosophy is not directly present, she is represented by each of Virgil, the ancient philosophers of Limbo, Boethius, and the virtuous pagans.[128]

Often scholars overlook the importance of philosophy in relation to salvation. In the *Commedia*, philosophy is a handmaid of theology.[129] In the *Convivio*, philosophy is *la bellissima e onestissima figlia de lo Imperadore de lo universo, a la quale Pittagora pose nome Filosofia* (the most beautiful and most dignified daughter of the emperor of the Universe whom Pythagoras called Philosophy [*Conv.* II, xv, 12]). In her physical aspect, she is linked both to faith and spiritual salvation, and her physical beauty mirrors the beauty of her soul, which in turn reflects divine goodness.[130] Similar to the miraculous body of Christ, her own body is linked to man's salvation.[131] The beauty reflected in her eyes and smile echo the divine beauty reflected in the eyes and smile of Beatrice,[132] and like Beatrice, Lady Philosophy is intrinsically linked to Paradise.[133] Her beauty mirrors divine beauty and light; it mirrors God's greatness.[134] By looking into her eyes and at her smile, which are the demonstrations and persuasions of *Sapienza*, Dante experiences both perfection and happiness.[135] That her physical aspect is linked to the moral virtues and to moral philosophy[136] emphasizes the importance of philosophy and ethics in relation to man's salvation. That her physical aspect is linked to faith and salvation underscores the interplay between philosophy and theology, morality and spiritual salvation, earthly happiness and heavenly bliss. More importantly, that her physical beauty mirrors heavenly beauty highlights the relation between a person's two ends: earthly happiness and celestial bliss. It is precisely in relation to a person's dual ends that friendship in *Purgatorio* 30 will be studied in the last chapter. However, first we will study Cicero's notion of friendship in *De Amicitia* and its influences on Dante's *Convivio.*

Chapter Three

Cicero's *De Amicitia* and Dante's *Convivio*

E misimi a leggere quello non conosciuto da molti libro di Boezio, nel quale, cattivo e discacciato, consolato s'avea. E udendo ancora che Tullio scritto avea un altro libro, nel quale, trattando de l'Amistade, avea toccate parole de la consolazione di Lelio, uomo eccellentissimo, ne la morte di Scipione amico suo, misimi a leggere quello ... E sì come essere suole che l'uomo va cercando argento e fuori de la 'ntenzione truova oro, lo quale occulta cagione presenta, non forse sanza divino imperio; io, che cercava di consolarme, trovai non solamente a le mie lagrime rimedio, ma vocabuli d'autori e di scienze e di libri...

And I set myself to read that Book of Boethius, not known to many, in which, when a captive exile, he had consoled himself. And, again, hearing that Tullius had written another book, in which, treating of Friendship, he had spoken words for the consolation of Laelius, a most excellent man, on the death of his friend Scipio, I set myself to read it ... And as it wont to be that a man goes seeking for silver, and beyond his purpose he finds gold, whose hidden cause appears not perhaps without the Divine Will; I, who sought to console myself, found not only a remedy for my tears, but words of authors and of sciences and of books...

(Convivio, II, xii, 3–5)

Unlike Greek, Latin has a specific word for friendship: *amicitia*. Although the word *amicitia* may encompass some of the wider sense of the Greek *philia*, for the most part it denotes a personal bond between friends (*amici*), rather than love in general.[1] Konstan argues that contrary to popular belief, *amicitia* did not designate party relationships[2] and that it was used to designate personal and sentimental relationships. The Latin word corresponding to *philia* in the broader sense is *amor*, while the verb *amare* is equivalent to the Greek verb *philein*. As Konstan notes, the common misconception of Roman *amicitia* as a union devoid of personal intimacy and emotion may be a reaction to the various Roman political factions and alliances that were grounded in private favor and known as *amici*. The Roman preoccupation with reciprocity may be another reason for this misconception. The term *gratia* refers to the payback that is due for a service (*officium* or *beneficium*) received and to the moral sense of gratitude, debt, and obligation imposed on the beneficiary. This sense of moral obligation, especially prevalent among friends, paralleled the more pragmatic reciprocity among political alliances.[3] Thus there is the assumption that all *amicitia* is devoid of emotional and personal ties. It may be useful to draw a distinction between the *gratia* found in political alliance and the reciprocity that is essential to friendship. Reciprocity found in political alliance seems to arise from a sense of duty, debt, and obligation, and it is grounded in the demand for recompense (*gratia*) and in the desire for profit. In friendship reciprocity is free of all imposition; it is grounded in generosity, love, and the mutual and free exchange of benevolence.[4] Like Konstan, Brunt challenges the common assumption that *amicitia* implied political alliance and that "if a Roman called a man *amicus*, it meant that he was a political ally." Brunt argues that in fact "complex personal relationships could cut across political discords."[5] To be sure, close personal bonds among individuals often survived political disagreements.[6] He refers to the various passages in Cicero's writings in which *amicitia* is not restricted to a connection founded solely on mutual services and common interests, and still less to membership of the same faction. In an attempt to strengthen his argument, Brunt notes that the Latin word for friendship (*amicitia*) derives from the verb meaning "to love" (*amare*).[7] Cicero himself establishes the necessary link between love and friendship: *Amor enim, ex quo amicitia nominata est, princeps est ad benevolentiam coniungendam* (For it is love, from which the word friendship is derived, that leads to the establishing of goodwill [*DA*, VIII, 26]). Brunt concludes that "the range of *amicitia* is vast ... it covers every degree of genuinely or overtly amicable relation."[8] An understanding of *amicitia* (friendship) as a union that transcends political affiliations to encompass personal ties between *amici* (friends) will henceforth be assumed. Of course, during the political instability that leads up to and follows Caesar's assassination, Cicero associates friendship with matters of honour and loyalty to the state.[9] But even during such unstable times when he is most aware of the interplay between friendship and politics, Cicero never reduces friendship to a union grounded in mere utilitarianism. This is made evident in his most serious and complete meditation on friendship, *De Amicitia* (44–3 BC), a work that coincides with the assassination of Julius Caesar and the outbreak of civil war (44–3 BC).[10]

I limit my discussion of *amicitia* to the term defined by Cicero's discourse on friendship, *De Amicitia*, for it is here that Dante finds the seeds of his own understanding of friendship (*Conv.* II, xii, 3).[11] The goal Cicero sets for himself is to write on the topic of friendship: *sic hoc libro ad amicum amicissimus scripsi de amicitia* (in this book I have written as a most affectionate friend to a friend on the subject of friendship [*DA* I, 5]). The fictional frame that he creates for his work is as follows: a few days after the sudden death of Scipio Minor (129 BC), Laelius and his two sons-in-law, Quintus Mucius Scaevola and Gaius Fannius, discuss the topic of friendship. It is a dialogue that Cicero, while still a young man, had heard around the year 90 BC from the elder Roman lawyer Scaevola, his mentor and instructor in Roman law. The unexpected death of Scipio Africanus provides the opportunity for Laelius to remember his friend's noble character and to reflect on the merits of friendship. Laelius considers himself most fortunate to have known Scipio both in private and public (*DA* IV, 14–16).

Critics differ on the Greek influences and sources for the composition of *De Amicitia*. For Diogenes Laertius and Aulus Gellius, the primary Greek influence is Theophrastus's treatise *On Philia*.[12] There is no doubt that Aristotelian influences permeate *De Amicitia*. Whatever its sources and influences, *De Amicitia* is unique in its own right. The thought, style, and form of the work is highly original and presents a clear and comprehensive study of friendship. Fritz-Arthur Steinmetz, who insists that Cicero's primary source for his treatise on friendship was the Stoic Panaetius, recognizes that the discussion of violence against the state (*DA* 36–44) is unique.[13] A discourse on friendship is seen as a most noble endeavor, one that should be reserved for the most skilled philosophers (*DA* V, 17). Laelius urges Scaevola and Gaius Fannius to value friendship above all other good things, for it is a natural human experience and it is indispensable for one's happiness in troubled times as well as during fortunate moments (*DA* V, 17).[14] Similar to Aristotelian friendship, Ciceronian friendship is grounded in virtue: *sed haec ipsa virtus amicitiam et gignit et continet, nec sine virtute amicitia esse ullo pacto potest* (but this very virtue is the parent and preserver of friendship, and without virtue, friendship cannot exist at all [*DA* VI, 21]). Friendship exists among good people who are loyal, just, and generous (*DA* V, 19). Their actions are dictated neither by passions nor whims, but by what their nature dictates as good.

Cicero's letters and political speeches provide insight into his friendships. In his letters and political speeches, Cicero stresses the importance of virtue, character, benevolence, and self-sacrifice in friendship. In a letter addressed to his friend Atticus, Cicero acknowledges Atticus's love for him, manifested in the form of support given and in sacrifices made on Cicero's behalf.[15] In the letter, Cicero continues to stress the importance of character, self-sacrifice, and shared conversation in friendship. The importance of conversation is also stressed in his treatise *On the Orator*, where Cicero asks, "What leisue activity can be more delightful or more suitable to mankind than witty and broadly cultivated conversation?"[16] If Cicero's relationship with Atticus was an intimate friendship, his relationships with Quintus Metellus Celer and Marc Antony were more distant relationships, amicable associations grounded in public life, in the mutual exchange of services, in *beneficium* and *gratia*. As a Roman, Cicero was well aware of the difference between personal friendships and amicable, useful associations. In a letter addressed to Atticus he notes:

> ... those politicking and powdered-up friendships of mine have a certain brilliance in the forum but are profitless at home. Though my house is quite full [of greeters] in the morning, though I go down to the forum hemmed in by droves of "friends," I can find no one out of that great crowd with whom I can freely make a joke or sigh familiarity. That's why I am waiting for you, longing for you, even beckoning you now.[17]

To be sure, Cicero's relationship with Atticus was of a personal nature. It was an intimate friendship grounded in familiarity, moral uprightness, integrity, virtue, and benevolence. Cicero and Atticus were not drawn to each other by hopes of profit; rather, they were drawn to each other because of love itself. As Cicero notes in *De Amicitia*: *sic amicitiam non spe mercedis adducti, sed quod omnis eius fructus in ipso amore inest, expetendam putamus* (so we believe that friendship is desirable, not because we are influenced by hope of gain, but because its entire profit is in the love itself [*DA* IX, 31]).

For Cicero, as for Aristotle, friendship is linked to his system of ethics: *Virtus, inquam, C. Fanni, et tu, Q. Muci, et conciliat amicitias et conservat* (Virtue, my dear Gaius Fannius, and you, my dear Quintus Mucius, Virtue, I say, both creates the bond of friendship and preserves it [*DA* XXVII, 100]). One way in which friendship can thus be distinguished from other types of relationships is to determine whether it marks the union between good and morally upright individuals. Complete friendship is desired for itself. It is a union grounded in virtue, and it arises from an altruistic desire to give of oneself selflessly and completely (*DA* XXII, 83). Accordingly, friends value and seek each other's company because they love and admire the other's virtuous character. Friendship among good individuals is stable and constant since it is grounded in character – and such friendship will outlive even death: *Mihi quidem Scipio, quamquam est subito ereptus, vivit tamen semperque vivet; virtutem enim amavi illius viri, quae exstincta non est* (For me, indeed, though he was suddenly snatched away, Scipio still lives and will always live; for it was his virtue that caused my love and that is not dead [*DA* XXVII, 102]). By contrast, friendship grounded in pleasure, profit, or power is unstable and short-lived since it relies on changing realities: *Nam si utilitas conglutinaret amicitias, eadem commutata dissolveret; sed quia natura mutari non potest, idcirco verae amicitiae sempiternae sunt* (For on the assumption that advantage is the cement of friendship, if advantage were removed, friendship would fall apart; but since nature is unchangeable real friendships are therefore eternal [*DA* IX, 32]).

The question arises whether friendship is a union of similarity or difference. Nature is such that it attracts and desires that which is like itself. For Cicero, as for Aristotle, good individuals are necessarily attracted to other good individuals in a spirit of mutual goodwill and affection,[18] and each person seeks to unite with another in a bond that is both good and natural. Complete in themselves, virtuous individuals seek each other from a natural desire to love and to give of themselves; advantage and material gain are foreign to complete friendship (*DA* XIV, 51). Laelius hopes that his sons-in-law value virtue: *vos autem hortor ut ita virtutem locetis (sine qua amicitia esse non potest) ut ea excepta nihil amicitia praestabilius putetis* (I exhort you both so to esteem virtue (without which friendship cannot exist) that, excepting virtue, you will think nothing more excellent than friendship [*DA* XXVII, 104]). Since virtue is the parent of friendship, in valuing virtue one also values friendship above all other goods.

Apart from virtue, an essential attribute of Ciceronian friendship is goodwill. While other types of relationships may exist in the absence of goodwill, friendship cannot (*DA* V, 20). If goodwill is removed from friendship, the very nature of friendship is altered. Moreover, in contrast to other types of natural human relationships, friendship always unites two or, at most, a few people (*DA* V, 20). Cicero echoes Aristotle in his claim that good people are few, and since time is needed to grow familiar with each other, friendship of good people is rare.[19] While it is difficult to feel affection and goodwill towards a multitude of people, it is more difficult to establish close contact with a great number and be in accord with them about crucial matters both of a secular and the spiritual nature.

These preliminary remarks concerning the attributes and conditions of friendship lead Laelius to define friendship as *nihil aliud nisi omnium divinarum humanarumque rerum cum benevolentia et caritate consensio* (nothing else than an accord in all things, human and divine, conjoined with mutual goodwill and affection [*DA* VI, 20]). Here again, one hears an echo of Aristotelian friendship. Both stress the importance of goodwill and virtue in relation to friendship, and both note the innumerable advantages of friendship, whether during fortunate or unfortunate times. Each values friendship as the highest form of good. All other forms of the good – riches, power, good health, and sensual pleasure – are unstable and shortlived. Friendship alone remains stable since it is grounded in the virtuous character of the friends. While all other goods are devoted to a single end – riches to wealth, public position to power, health to the freedom of physical pain, and pleasures to sensual gratification – friendship alone encompasses a multitude of ends. Cicero concludes that a life without friends is a life not worth living, for friendship makes prosperity all the more pleasurable and lessens the pains of misfortune by "dividing and sharing" (*DA* VI, 22).

Friendship must be valued for itself. It alleviates the most painful calamity and enriches the most rewarding experience. Friendship provides all that is denied to us by life itself. With friendship the poor find wealth, the needy find solace, and the weak find strength. Friends are good people who are similar in virtue and who love and treasure each other for their character. Friends place the well-being and interest of their friends before and above their own, and revel in each other's successes and share in each other's misfortune. Similar in virtue, friends share similar values regarding important matters. In this sense, a friend is a reflection of oneself. The bond between friends is such that death itself cannot destroy it, for a friend though absent or deceased lives in the loving memory and sweet recollection of a friend (*DA* VII, 23). Because of its crucial role in the private and public realm, friendship may be understood as a primary good in the universe. Order and stability are often accepted as the necessary components of a civilized and cultured society, and both are established by means of friendship. Single households and entire cities are quick to surrender and even crumble under the duress of conflict and animosity (*DA* VII, 23). Friendship establishes stability and brings accord to households, cities, and the universe.

After reflecting upon the various benefits of friendship, Laelius begins to reflect on whether it arises from need and weakness or from plenitude and strength. Do friends seek each other from some form of deficiency or weakness so that each takes from the other what he lacks while providing that which the other needs? Or, do they seek each other from a surplus of good and from a natural desire to share and give of themselves? (*DA* VII, 26). He concludes that the desire for friendship arises from a person's natural inclination to unite in a loving bond with friends, rather than from a self-centred concern for profit: *Quapropter a natura mihi videtur potius quam indigentia orta amicitia, applicatione magis animi cum quodam sensu amandi, quam cogitatione quantum illa res utilitatis esset habitura* (Wherefore it seems to me that friendship springs rather from nature than need, and from an inclination of the soul joined with a feeling of love rather than from calculation of how much profit the friendship is likely to afford [*DA* VIII, 26–7]). In addition to this natural desire to love, friendship is grounded in a person's desire for virtue. Both animals and humans have a natural impulse to provide for and protect their offspring (*DA* VIII, 27). In contrast to animals, however, a person's natural impulse to virtue inspires him to seek the company of others similar to himself in character, since *nihil est enim virtute amabilius, nihil quod magis alliciat ad diligendum* (there is nothing more lovable than virtue, nothing that more allures us to affection [*DA* VIII, 28]). In instances where a person's natural instinct to love the good is received with mutual affection, goodwill, and recognition, the bond is strengthened and flourishes into friendship (*DA* IX, 29).

Cicero goes on to consider the conditions or circumstances under which friendship may change or cease to exist. It is his belief that a friendship which continues till the end of life is truly a rare occurrence (*DA* IX, 33). Often, friendship ceases to exist when the relationship ceases to be mutually advantageous or when the friends no longer share similar political viewpoints. It may be the case that a friend's character changes as a result of adversity, tribulations, and old age (*DA* IX, 33). In such an instance, the friendship may also vanish. In considering the circumstances under which friends have both the right and the obligation to dissolve their relationship, Laelius is unequivocal. When a friend implores one to commit dishonourable deeds and particularly those against the state, then one is obliged to sever ties of friendship (*DA* XII, 40). Under no circumstance should one commit an unjust or evil deed on behalf of a friend, particularly if the deed is directed against the republic: *ut ne quis concessum putet amicum vel bellum patriae inferentem sequi* (so that no one may think it permissible to follow even a friend when waging war against his country); accordingly, one has the moral obligation to withdraw from friends who are plotting against the republic (*DA* XII, 42–3). A friend must dare to give advice with frankness and, if the occasion demands it, even with sternness, and having the friend's well-being in mind, one should do for a friend and ask of him only what is honourable (*DA* XIII, 44). Committing an immoral deed in the name of friendship means forsaking the friendship itself, because in committing a dishonourable deed, one is forsaking the virtue upon which the friendship itself was founded and thus asking the friend to dismiss the very foundation upon which the friendship was built (*DA* XI, 38).

This idea that one ought not to expect anything bad from friends can be traced to Aristotle.[20] The element of patriotism in friendship, however, is unique to Cicero. In considering those circumstances that may alter or destroy friendship, Cicero, like Aristotle,[21] identifies change in character, in interest, in fortune, and old age. However, unlike Aristotle, Cicero adds disagreement over political sides and disloyalty to the republic.[22] Konstan remarks that "the most telling indication, however of Cicero's concern with patriotism is the vigor with which he denies that loyalty to friends can ever justify rebelling against the state."[23] Laelius is shocked that Gaius Blossius Cumanus would have been willing to set fire to the Capitol on the request of his friend Tiberius Gracchus (*Nulla est igitur excusatio peccati, si amici causa peccaveris* – Therefore, it is no justification whatever of your sin to have sinned in behalf of a friend."[24] For Cicero, one of the most serious crimes is a crime against one's own country. No one should plead defense of evil deeds against the republic on account of friendship (*DA* XII, 40), and loyalty towards one's friend is never an excuse for waging war against one's country (*contra patriam*). If one is to account for Cicero's politicized definition of friendship, one must look at the civil and political turmoil of his time, civil wars, and tyrranicide.[25] Cicero lived in a time of political instability and social disorder. He could not afford to rule out the possibility that friends demand dishonourable deeds from each other.[26]

It is clear that in many ways Cicero's understanding of friendship echoes that of Aristotle. For both, friendship is a unique bond grounded in goodwill, virtue, and reason, and is a union by means of which an individual reaches happiness, actualization, and perfection of self. Both understand friendship as a union between individuals who are alike in virtue and love each other for their virtuous character. Both understand friendship in relation to the morally upright character and the rational life. Life without friends is understood as a life not worth living. The failure to rush to a friend's assistance, particularly in times of need, is interpreted by both as the absence of goodwill. Finally, both understand friendship as an activity that leads to the moral and rational life. Notwithstanding these similarities, there are major points of divergence worth noting, particularly Cicero's emphasis on patriotism, which may be the most crucial difference. Another difference is what Karl Vossler views as a difference regarding their respective notion of righteousness and justice. Vossler argues that, while Aristotle and Cicero both link justice to the political and social community, Cicero adds a personal and metaphysical aspect to Aristotle's political interpretation:

> It was Cicero who gave to the political and social ideal of righteousness of Aristotle a personal, metaphysical, and essentially Stoical foundation. This is, as it seems to me, the most valuable contribution made by Cicero, and is contained in his concept of duty (*officium*).[27]

Clearly, for both Aristotle and Cicero, the righteous person is the good citizen who extends himself towards his neighbour, coming to his assistance with affection and selfless benevolence. Cicero's conception of justice, however, seems more encompassing, for it extends outside of the political community to embrace even the non-citizen and slave:

> So Cicero's conception of justice includes more than the modern one, but it also embraces more than Aristotle's definition. The latter insists on justice only within

> the political community. Toward those who stand outside of it, gods and slaves, there can, strictly speaking, be no injustice. Cicero, on the other hand, expressly demands justice not only for his enemies, and, in a certain sense, for the gods, but even for the slaves.[28]

It is precisely in this extension of justice to the entire human community that Cicero may come a step closer to the Christian notion of friendship, understood as a form of brotherly affection:

> Let us not forget that even toward the humblest members of human society, justice must be observed. It is a sound principle that they are to be regarded as hirelings; that is, we are to require their service, and must also give them due recompense.[29]

According to Vossler, with the assistance of Cicero the Aristotelian concept of justice finds fulfilment and completion in Dante:

> Dante completed, with the aid of Cicero, the Aristotelian conception of justice. From Aristotle he accepts the division of all acts of injustice into two classes: those which are committed in passion (*incontinenza*) and those inspired by malice (*malizia)* ... When he further assumes, as we recalled above, that human violence and even to some extent human deceit, may offend not only our fellow men but also God, Nature, and our own reason – he then comes much closer to Cicero's conception of justice than to Aristotle's.[30]

Accordingly, in his morality Dante is indebted to Cicero for having "distinguished what is ethically *good* from that which is politically *profitable* by inserting between them legal right as the *political good*."[31] Whether it be the Aristotelian justice, understood in relation to the political good and well-being of the political community, or the more encompassing Ciceronian justice, the truth is that a common ground for both is the association between virtue and friendship. The ideal of moral excellence is what links justice to friendship. A friend is a just person, someone who lives according to the norms of the moral life. A friend does not deceive, nor does he bring harm to himself or to another. While it is true that one can imagine cases where the presence of justice excludes friendship, it is never the case that friendship proper precludes justice. Where there is friendship there is also justice, so in this manner, friendship can become the means by which justice is actualized.

When Aristotle discusses friendship in relation to the morally good life, he is linking friendship to justice as it relates to the *polis*. Friendship is a unifying force within the political community that is the *polis*. Cicero also links friendship to justice and to the morally good life but, unlike Aristotle, he is more willing to extend it outside of the *polis*. He envisions a more encompassing and perhaps a more universal notion of justice, one that would extend friendship to one's enemy, to a non-citizen, even to a slave (*De Officiis* I, xiii, 41). As with Aristotle, Cicero's notion of justice bears great weight on his notion of friendship, but for Cicero, friendship is possible even among the humblest members of human society. Cicero's influence on the Christian notion of friendship would seem to lie in his extension of justice and benevolence towards all individuals. In this manner, Ciceronian friendship bridges distances of rank. In *De Amicitia*, Cicero asserts that in a friendship it is most important that one be a peer to one's inferior. This notion is conveyed by Laelius as he notes that a superior friend must be a peer to the inferior friend, as it was the case with Scipio's relationship with friends of lower rank (*Sed maximum est in amicitia superiorem parem esse inferiori* – But it is of the utmost importance in friendship that superior and inferior should stand on equality).[32] The superior friend must place himself on the same level as the inferior friend (*DA* XX, 71), and at times even lower himself in order to lift up the inferior to his level (*Quam ob rem, ut ei, qui superiores sunt, submittere se debent in amicitia, sic quodam modo inferiores extollere* – As, therefore, in friendship, those who are superior should lower themselves, so, in a measure, should they lift up their inferiors [*DA* XX, 72]). In the same way that the superior friend places himself on the level of his inferior, the inferior friend must not be resentful that they are surpassed in intellect, fortune, or position (*DA* XX, 71]). As Konstan notes, in *De Amicitia*, Cicero tells stories of princes who even after their true identity had been revealed, continued to show *caritas* towards the shepherds who had raised them as their own.[33] What is refreshingly new in Ciceronian friendship is this desire to transcend political barriers and bridge social distances through the extension of generosity (*humanitas*) and fraternal affection, even to the most unfortunate and humble members of society.

It may be worth noting that Cicero's notion of nobility echoes his notion of justice. For Cicero, as for Boethius and the Stoics, nobility has its origin in character, rather than in birth or social or political rank. As Aristotle and Cicero before him, Boethius places nobility neither in lineage nor in material possession.[34] Boethius diverges from both Aristotle and Cicero, however, not in the definition but in its source, as he traces the originating source of nobility to God and not to the individual.[35] For Boethius, that which is good and noble in a person – his soul – is linked to its source – God. While virtue and nobility reside in the soul, the origin of both resides outside of the person and instead comes from God. Accordingly, it is no longer sufficient to love a friend in himself; instead, he must be loved in God. And God lies at the centre of Christian friendship. The classical understanding of friendship as a union grounded in virtue and character, is transformed as a union that is grounded in the love of Christ. In this way, friendship transcends the limits of human reason and virtue to embrace divine wisdom and love, or *caritas*.

Vossler argues that it is from the Stoics, Cicero, Seneca, and Boethius, "that Dante borrows the weapon with which to oppose the human, all too human, value set on riches, noble birth, and good fortune."[36] Arguing against the value placed on riches, in the *Convivio* Dante resorts to a passage from Cicero's *Paradoxa*.[37] Dante echoes Cicero's sentiment that wealth can never lead to happiness: the thirst for wealth is never quenched (accumulation of wealth generates a desire for more wealth), and wealth leads to anxiety and fear of loss. The third *canzone* of the *Convivio* and the commentary on it expound the nature of true nobility (*Conv*. IV, i). In the first part of the *canzone* (stanzas 2–4) and in his commentary, Dante argues against the opinion of those who erroneously believe that nobility or *gentilezza* resides in wealth or in birth.[38] In the second part (stanzas 5–7) Dante proceeds to define the nature of true nobility, while referencing Aristotle's works on ethics as a source of authority. For Dante, as for Aristotle, Cicero, and Boethius, true nobility resides in the soul and inner worth, rather than in birth or wealth. Nobility is grounded in virtue, which renders a person happy.[39] Where there is virtue, there is nobility.[40] Nobility adds to a person's virtue, while vileness makes him bad.[41] For Vossler, Dante perceived a "natural bridge" between the classical notion of virtue and Christian morality.[42] If Vossler is correct in his assertion, it follows that Dante would perceive a natural link between classical friendship, which is a union grounded in virtue, and Christian friendship, which is a union grounded in *caritas*. This point will be explored further in the chapters that follow. For now let us return to Cicero's influence on Dante, as evidenced in the *Convivio*.

Given that *De Amicitia* was a work well known to twelfth-century thinkers, Dante's direct knowledge of Cicero's treatise on friendship is not surprising. As Etienne Gilson observes, "for here at any rate in the *De Amicitia*, the men of the twelfth century found much they felt to borrow; either as it stood or adapted for their need."[43] All facts point to a direct knowledge of Cicero in the original Latin. Between the end of 1291 and 1295, Dante had fully immersed himself in the study of philosophy taught by the Franciscans at Santa Croce and by the Dominicans at Santa Maria Novella.[44] His knowledge of both Aristotle and Cicero can be traced to these religious schools. In the second *tractate* of the *Convivio*, he tells us that shortly after 1290, in an effort to console himself after the death of Beatrice, he began to devote himself to the study of philosophy.[45] He read Boethius's *Consolation of Philosophy* and Cicero's *De Amicitia*, and in these works he found much more than consolation (silver), he found philosophy, or wisdom (gold).[46] He began to frequent the religious schools where philosophy was taught and within thirty months his new love of philosophy erased all prior thoughts of his first love:

> *E imaginava lei fatta come una donna* gentile ... *E da questo imaginare cominciai ad andare là dov'ella si dimostrava veracemente, cioè ne le scuole de li religiosie a le disputazioni de li filosofanti. Si che in picciol tempo, forse di trenta mesi, cominciai tanto a sentire de la sua dolcezza, che lo suo amore cacciava e distruggeva ogni altro pensiero* (And I perceived her as a gentle lady ... And from this perception, I began to frequent the schools of the disputations of those who teach philosophy, so that, in a short time, perhaps thirty months, I began to be so keenly aware of her sweetnes that the love of her drove away and destroyed every other thought [*Conv.* II, xii, 6–8]).

Dante imagined philosophy in the allegorical figure of a noble and beautiful lady, the daughter of God.[47] The *Convivio* (ca.1303–5) abounds with direct references to both Aristotle and Cicero. In the first *tractate*, while tracing the origin of his friendship with the Italian vernacular, Dante makes reference to both philosophers.[48] He then traces his definition of friendship directly to Aristotle and Cicero, linking the ideas of one philosopher to that of the other. In addition to the references to Aristotle and Cicero, Dante makes an implicit reference to Aquinas through the example of the union between father and son as two who are most alike while discussing the causes of his friendship with the vernacular.[49] Dante echoes Aquinas's understanding of friendship as a union grounded in similarity, as a son is similar to his father,[50] while simultaneously mirroring Cicero's belief that likeness draws and attracts people to one another in a union of friendship; the theme that like loves like is also shared by Aristotle.[51]

In the *Convivio*, while expounding the origin of his friendship with his vernacular, Dante embraces many of Cicero's ideas. In the begininning of the fourth book, he echoes Cicero's definition of friendship as an accord in all things, united in mutual benevolence and love.[52] Like Cicero, Dante defines friendship as a natural union grounded in the love of the good and in similarity, a union that grows with proximity, through time and shared activities.[53] Like Cicero and Aristotle, Dante identifies the original causes of love as virtue and similarity. He became a friend to his vernacular because it was closer to him than any other language and because of its innate goodness.[54] By introducing Dante into the path of both knowledge and Latin, his mother tongue has been his friend and benefactor.[55] Dante's friendship with the vernacular grew and was strengthened and perfected through familiarity, long study, conversation, and mutual benevolence.[56] By means of his friendship with his mother tongue, he was made more perfect in goodness.[57]

In addition to the emphasis placed on love, virtue, benevolence, philosophy, and wisdom, the *Convivio* seems to mime Cicero's notion "that even to the humblest members of society, justice must be observed" (*De Officiis*, I, xiii, 41). As seen earlier in this chapter, Cicero extends justice outside of the *polis*. Unlike Aristotle, he seems more willing to extend friendship and justice to a non-citizen, to one's enemy, and to a slave (*De Officiis*, I, xii, 41). Both the *Convivio* and the *Comedy* stress the importance of justice in relation to the peace and harmony of the city. Like friendship, justice strengthens and builds relationships within the community. If friendship and justice establish order and stability, enmity and fraud destroy the natural bonds of friendship and trust, thereby creating disaccord and chaos within a society. Under the guise of friendship, treachery veils its true nature that is enmity (*Conv.* IV, xii, 3). Dante's opposition to fraud becomes even more clean in the cantos of lower Hell. Treachery, a subcategory of fraud, is regarded as a more serious sin since it severs all bonds of trust within a community. In his opposition to fraud, particularly to treachery, Dante mimes Cicero's sentiment: "While wrong (*iniuria*) may be committed, then, in two ways – either by force or by fraud – fraud seems to belong to the fox, force to the lion; both are most alien to man, but fraud is the more odious."[58] By manipulating reality, the traitor appears as a friend when in actuality he is an enemy. The world of fraud is a world of simulation in which concealment, appearances, and seeming become all important: seeming friendly becomes more important than being friendly. In its distortion of reality and in its reliance on trickery and imitation, fraud and treachery (in contrast to justice and friendship) creates chaos, instability, and disorder within a community.

Cicero's influence on Dante's notion of friendship resides in his extension of benevolence and justice towards all individuals, regardless of rank. In this manner, benevolence bridges disparity of rank. As Dante himself explains in the first *tractate*, he writes the *Convivio* in the vernacular from a sense of benevolence and justice towards "even the humblest member of society." As Cicero does, Dante extends justice to all citizens – to the poor and wealthy, to the uneducated and the erudite, to women and men. Through the use of his "*maternal locution*" (mother tongue), Dante intends to educate the many, particularly the less erudite.[59] Latin would have served the few, but his mother tongue is more useful since it is understood by many more people. Dante knows, as Aristotle before him knew, that "... *tutti li uomini naturalmente desiderano di sapere*" (... all men by nature desire to know); all individuals desire to know because all individuals desire happiness, and true happiness resides in the perfection of the soul acquired by means of knowledge.[60] Dante writes the *Convivio* in the vernacular (*Conv.* I. x, 6), the language understood by ordinary people, precisely because he adheres to the Aristotelian *dictum* that all individuals, regardless of socio-political status, desire to know and be happy. Dante's intent is to share knowledge with those who have been excluded from it (*Conv.* I, x, 10).

Dante's generosity is a testament of his affinity with Cicero's *humanitas.* Dante's *humanitas* acquires significance in light of his notion of nobility. In *Convivio* IV, Dante refutes the generally held opinion that nobility is grounded on genealogy and social rank (*Conv.* IV, iii, 7; xiv–xv). He points to Emperor Frederick II (1194–1250) as one who supported the erroneous view that nobility acquires significance in relation to riches and high birth (*Conv.* IV, *canzone* 21–4; IV, iii, 6). In contrast to Frederick, Dante offers a more democratic definition of nobility. Whether or not Frederick in fact subscribed to this opinion,[61] what matters is that Dante understands nobility in relation to virtue. And since Dante understands virtue in relation to the rational mind, his concept of nobility is to be understood in relation to the autonomous will, the mind, and character. The close link between nobility and virtue in Dante brings to mind Boethius, who deemed "noble birth" to be an "empty and worthless title," understanding it as a sort of "borrowed nobility," since it is grounded in the status and deeds of one's parents rather than on one's own deeds (*De Consol.* III, vi). Like Cicero and Boethius, Dante proposes an understanding of nobility as a quality that resides in moral excellence, an attribute that is independent from wealth, social rank, and familial ties (*Conv.* IV, xvii, 1–2, 7–8; IV, xx, 5).

As the title itself makes clear, the *Convivio* is a banquet where intellectual food is being served to all people, the learned and the unlearned, men and women, wealthy and poor. More particularly, the *Convivio* is a gift offered in a spirit of friendship for the less fortunate members of society, whose natural hunger for knowledge has been impeded because of their place of residence, physical ailments, inner turmoil, or familial and civil obligations.[62] Blessed are the few who are privy to *lo pane de li angeli* (the bread of angels) that is being served at this banquet, he tells us, and wretched are those who feed as the sheep in pastures.[63] Since individuals are naturally drawn to each other in bonds of friendship, it is natural that friends grieve for each other's misery. In a spirit of friendship, the privileged few who partake in the banquet where the bread of angels is being served must show mercy on the less fortunate who feed on the grass and acorns.[64] Here Dante seems to follow Cicero in the belief that "… friendship lessens the burden of adversity by dividing and sharing it" (*DA* VI, 22). He also mirrors Cicero's sentiment that in friendship the superior must lower themselves so as to lift up their inferior (*DA*, XX, 72).[65] Similar to

Cicero's *humanitas*, Dante's *humanitas* drives him to show charity towards all people, and in particular towards the less fortunate. Dante's extension of goodwill towards the less fortunate mirrors Cicero's understanding of friendship as a union that springs from a feeling of love, rather than from a calculated desire for profit (*DA* VIII, 27). To the extent that compassion is the mother of benevolence, and to the extent that benevolence is a primary attribute of friendship, the *Convivio* is none other than a gift of friendship.[66] Dante's desire to educate all people, particularly the less fortunate, stems from a feeling of benevolence and affection towards others (*Conv.* I, i, 10). At the heart of the *Convivio* lies a feeling of charity and *misericordia* (mercy) towards others. In point of fact, Dante writes the *Convivio* because he is is *misericordievolmente mosso ... per li miseri alcuna cosa ho riservata* (compassionately moved towards the less fortunate [*Conv.* I, i, 10]).

All who are hungry for the bread of angels are welcomed to sit at the table, particularly those who have been oppressed by civil and domestic obligations, but those who have been enslaved by sloth and other bad habits will sit at their feet and eat from Dante's plate.[67] The food offered at this banquet is composed of "meat" (fourteen songs of love and virtue) and "bread" (expositions). The explanation of the songs is "*lo dono di questo commento*" (the gift of the commentary [*Conv.* I, IX, 7]). Dante seeks to "*inducere li uomini a scienza e a vertù*" (to lead men to wisdom and to virtue [*Conv.* I, ix, 7]), and as he notes in the first treatise, the *Convivio* treats "*sì d'amor come di vertù*" (both of love and of virtue [I, i, 14]). Love and virtue are the same two themes found in Cicero's *De Amicitia*. Both Cicero's *De Amicitia* and Dante's *Convivio* are gifts of friendship offered in a spirit of benevolence on the themes of virtue and love. The understanding of friendship in relation to both *amor* (love) and *vertù* (virtue) leads us to a discussion of Christian friendship understood as *caritas*.

Chapter Four

Christian Friendship

... beatus qui amat te, et amicum in te, et inimicum propter te. solus enim nullum carum amittit, cui omnes in illo cari, qui non amittitur.

Blessed is the man that loves Thee, O God, and his friend in Thee, and his enemy for Thee. For he alone loses no one that is dear to him, if all are dear in God, who is never lost.

(Augustine, *Confessions*, IV, ix)

Following the earlier discussion of classical friendship, it remains to be shown how classical friendship was transformed in the work of Christian writers. With this goal in mind, what follows is a discussion of Christian writers who acted as bridges between Aristotle and Cicero on the one hand, and Dante on the other. The ideas of Boethius, Augustine, and Aquinas will be explored and related to Dante's notion of friendship. In the same way that in the classical notion of virtue Dante finds the foundation of Christian morality,[1] in the classical notion of friendship he finds the foundation of his own theory of friendship.

It is convenient to begin with Anicius Boethius, the Roman philosopher who occupies a central position at the crossroads between the classical and medieval worlds. As V.E. Watts maintains, Boethius belonged to an era in which ancient classical culture had become somewhat integrated into Christianity but was still in many ways a distinct phenomenon, not completely immersed in it.[2] The historical importance of Boethius is great: the spread and survival of Aristotle in the West was in large part due to Boethius's translation of Aristotle's logic, and his own commentaries on it and others of Aristotle's works. In his application of Aristotelian logic and methods to theological questions, Boethius may be seen as a precursor of Scholasticism,[3] or as "the divine popularizer."[4]

That the *Consolation* inspired writers, translators, and commentators of the Middle Ages is a well established fact.[5] It was Boethius who perhaps more than any other philosopher influenced Medieval writers. Richard Morris correctly observes that "no philosopher was so bone of the bone and flesh of the flesh of Middle-Age writers as Boethius. Take up what writer you will, and you find not only the sentiments, but the very words of the distinguished old Roman."[6] Boethius more than any other thinker provided medieval philosophers and theologians with a comprehensive world view.[7] There are those who attribute the popularity of the *Consolation* to its broad philosophical nature and to Boethius's attempt to escape a strict and formal philosophical inquiry.[8] Scholars such as Bruno of Corvey and John of Salisbury have seen the *Consolation* as the fruit of a pagan world view, while others choose to focus on Christian influences. A "philosophical protreptic" towards God,[9] the *Consolation* is unique in its attempt to synthesize pagan structure and Christian context. Whether one chooses to focus on pagan or Christian influences in the *Consolation*, the fact remains that in the presence of death, Boethius turns to reason rather than faith for assistance. It is to philosophy, rather than divine grace, that Boethius entrusts his salvation. While true good and happiness is found in God alone, the ascent to God occurs through philosophy. Perhaps it is precisely in his attempt to reach God by means of philosophy that Boethius is drawn both close to and away from Christianity. In his reverence for God and philosophy, faith and reason, and in the distinction he draws between these last two, Boethius both defends pagan culture and prefigures Christianity. While the basic scheme of the *Consolation* has been seen as Platonic, with comparisons made to the ascent of the soul in Plato's allegory of the Cave,[10] the soul's ascent to God and the doctrine of recollection are indicative of Christian influences. For instance, it is not far-fetched to draw an analogy between the doctrine of recollection in Book III, understood as the inward turning of the soul to its inner light, and the Christian belief of the soul's natural desire to reunite itself with its source of origin, which is God. Men may have a natural desire for the good, but while the pagan understands the good in relation to reason and virtue, the Christian understands it in relation to God. Ultimately, whether pagan or Christian, it is a moral error that leads an individual away from the good.[11] The notion that a moral error leads one astray is a crucial theme in Dante's *Commedia.* Both Boethius and Dante are initially sidetracked and their minds clouded by false goods.

That Dante had first-hand knowledge of Boethius is a fact that he himself establishes in the *Convivio.* He asserts that after the death of Beatrice, Boethius's *Consolation* along with Cicero's *De Amicitia* were sources of comfort and inspiration for him as he took up the study of philosophy (*E misimi a leggere quello non conosciuto da molti libro di Boezio, nel quale, cattivo e discacciato, consolato s'avea. E udendo ancora che Tullio scritto avea un altro libro, nel quale, trattando de l'Amistade ... misimi a leggere quello* – I set myself to read that book by Boethius, in which he consoled himself about his anxiety and punishment. And then, hearing that Cicero had written another book on 'Friendship' ... I set myself to read that too [*Conv.* II, xii, 3, 5]). In addition to the references found in the *Convivio*, the *Commedia* abounds with echoes from Boethius. Virgil's discourse on the nature of Fortune in *Inferno* 7, for instance, is reminiscent of the first two chapters of Book 2 of the *Consolation*. The Lady Philosophy explains to Boethius that while those who suffer tend to blame Fortune for their misfortune, the truth is that they bring misfortune upon themselves by loving false goods: in other words, fallible and fleeting things. In *Inferno* 7, Dante echoes and accepts Philosophy's message as mere facts of life.[12] In the *Convivio* (IV, xi 6–8), Fortune is presented in negative light: she acts randomly and distributes goods among humans according to her whim. By contrast, in the *Commedia*, Fortune is provident.[13] She turns her "wheel" in bliss.[14]

That Dante held Boethius in high regard is also made clear by Boethius's privileged position among the twelve lights in the heaven of the Sun and as he is referred to (*l'anima santa che 'l mondo fallace / fa manifesto a chi di lei ben ode* – the holy soul who makes quite plain / the world's deceit to one who listens well).[15] It has not gone unnoticed that the *Paradiso* ends with an echo of Boethius's *caelo imeritans amor – l'amor che move il sole e l'altre stele* (the love that moves the sun and all the other stars [*Par.* 33, 145; *De Consol.* II poem 8 l.29]). There are parallels in both journeys, understood as the soul's ascent homewards to God.[16] A resemblance in scheme is evident in both works, with the gradual ascent of the soul from darkness to light, from false good to supreme good, from misery and suffering to complete happiness. In both cases, vision and love descend from on high in the figure of a woman who leads her friend to perfection and happiness. Philosophy and Beatrice both descend from on high and lead Boethius and Dante respectively to truth. Their souls turns to witness the inward light that is a reflection of the true light – God.[17]

If the importance placed on philosophy in Boethius's *Consolation* mirrors pagan thought, the emphasis on love mirrors Christian dogma. In its exaltation of love as the ultimate moving force in the universe, the *Consolation* mirrors Christian ideology. Needless to say, the exposition of love in the *Consolation* is vital for the the ideas of friendship. In Book II, while singing its praises, Philosophy links friendship to love. Love strengthens the bond of friendship and bridges the gap between the human and the divine. "Love who rules the sky" promotes peace and unity among nations; it joins people in marriage and solidifies friendship.[18] Love establishes order and unity in the universe. Boethius's notion of love as the original cause of all things and as that phenomenon to which all creation wishes to return[19] is the seed of Dante's ideas on love. In his presentation of love as the ultimate moving force of the universe, Dante seems to echo Boethius. This influence is evident in the first and last lines of the *Paradiso*: *La gloria di colui che tutto move* (the glory of Him who moves all things [*Par.* 1, 1]) and *l'amor che move il sole e l'altre stelle* (Love that moves the sun and the other stars [*Par.* 33, 145]). For both Boethius and Dante, ascent occurs because of the love, compassion, and friendship of a lady of sublime beauty and worth. However, while Lady Philosophy is an allegorical figure, Beatrice is a blessed lady, once a woman of flesh and blood, thus both human and divine. Notwithstanding this difference, it is love that moves both ladies from on high to bring healing and assistance to their respective friends.[20] Each lady descends so that her friend may ascend to God; each guides her friend towards true vision and light, and delivers him out of his state of "amnesia."[21] Both ladies are moved to show compassion for the friend's suffering and come to share in it, thereby lessening the burden.[22] It is out of love that Philosophy chides Boethius and Beatrice chides Dante for having abandoned the right path towards God for the sake of false goods.[23]

While similarities and influences between the *Consolation* and the *Commedia* abound, the differences are equally if not more significant. Boethius chooses reason over faith: the ascent of the soul to God occurs directly by means of philosophy. He relies on the compassion of Lady Philosophy for his consolation. To the extent that it is grounded in the love of secular wisdom and of moral goodness, Boethius's friendship with lady Philosophy is reminiscent of *philia*. Indeed, Boethius's thought closely adheres to the ancients whose doctrines he respected and upheld. According to V.E. Watts, "Boethius had not undergone the inner conversion of a Sidonius or an Ennodius: the ancient learning still preserved its hold upon him unimpaired."[24] In contrast to Boethius, the medieval Christian thinker turns to faith, belief, and trust in God. The same importance that is assigned to philosophy in the *Consolation* is assigned to grace in the *Commedia*, where ascent is a gift of grace achieved by means of revelation. Moreover, while Boethius's experience of divinity is direct, Dante's experience of divinity necessitates the mediation of friends such as Virgil and Beatrice, except at the end, when he has earned the right to a direct experience of it.

In light of these similarities and differences between Boethius and Dante, it may be pertinent to ask what precisely were Boethius's ideas on friendship and how they influenced Dante's thought. As did Plato and Aristotle, Boethius distinguishes those unions grounded in extrinsic attributes, such as power, wealth, and pleasure, from those unions grounded in the intrinsic moral worth of a person when he says "as for friendship, the purest kind is counted as a mark not of good fortune, but of moral worth, but all other friendship is cultivated for the sake of power and pleasure" (*De Consol.* III, 2). And like Plato and Aristotle, Boethius understands that in most cases, friendship is grounded in a person's desire for mutable goods, in the desire for power, riches, and pleasure. While all individuals have a natural desire for happiness, most are sidetracked by their attraction to false goods (*De Consol.* III, 8). Since power, riches, and pleasure are mere shadows of the true good, it is impossible to find perfect happiness in them.[25] Like his pagan predecessors, Boethius posits perfect friendship in relation to virtue and moral worth,[26] with the exception that he takes the pagan and Stoics' emphasis on virtue back to its source of origin, God.[27] He diverges from their conception of virtue not in definition but in source. Like Aristotle and Cicero, he takes nobility and moral excellence to reside neither in lineage nor in possession, but unlike them he looks to God rather than to man for the source of both nobility and virtue.[28] While virtue and nobility are seen to reside in the human soul, the origin of both lies with God. Since God is the source of all creation and since reason shows us that he is perfect good, true good and ultimate happiness reside in God.[29]

If happiness equals divinity, the happiness of mortals is to be found in divinity.[30] While God is divine, mankind becomes divine by means of its proximity and participation in divinity.[31] Of course, while Boethius participates in divinity through philosophy, Dante participates in divinity through faith, grace, and revelation. In contrast to Boethius, whose philosophizing leads him straight to God, Dante's experience of divinity is achieved through the mediation of friends such as Virgil and Beatrice. If in the *Convivio* one's experience of divinity is posited in the secular world attainable through moral excellence, in the *Commedia*, the experience of divinity transcends humanity and is attainable through divine grace.[32] While philosophy aids mortals in their journey towards God, it cannot on its own take them to God, for that is the work of grace and revelation. The *donna gentile* in the *Convivio* leads Dante to the perfection of his character; in the *Commedia*, Dante's friendship with Beatrice leads him to the perfection of his soul. As noted earlier, the *Convivio* adheres to the conception of happiness adopted in the *Nicomachean Ethics*, which was the active life lived according to virtue.[33] In the *Commedia*, complete happiness is understood in relation to spiritual perfection and is experienced in the heavens through the beatific vision of God. The perfection of the Christian soul lies in a sanctifying grace that is attained with the aid of the divine virtues. Through grace and with the assistance of faith, hope, and charity, mortals rise above their human selves and attain perfection: "Faith, hope, and charity transcend the human virtues, for they are virtues of a man insofar as he is made a sharer in divine grace."[34] In a manner similar to the ideas of classical friendship described earlier, Christian friendship aims to move beyond narrow particularity to reach perfection in universality. The difference is that in Christian friendship, the movement beyond particularity is a movement beyond humanity and into divinity.

It is proper that a consideration of the classical literature of friendship take into account Augustine's *Confessions*, and to better comprehend Augustine's influence on Dante's thought, particular attention must be given to the ideas found in its fourth book, in which a comprehensive study of friendship is enunciated. Undoubtedly, Augustine had an overwhelming impact on Christian attitudes towards friendship. As Peter Brown notes, "no thinker in the Early Church was so preoccupied with the nature of human friendship."[35] Crucial to Augustine's notion of friendship is the belief that God is the creator of all things and the source of all good, as a result of which all things must be loved in God. Augustine's notion of friendship is directly linked to the belief that God is the supreme good, ultimate truth, and love. In Book IV of his *Confessions*, Augustine defines friendship as the union of two souls in a common goal in search of perfection and wisdom: a union of two hearts in the Holy Spirit, who is God. Since God is true love, a friend must be loved in God "and he who abides in love abides in God."[36] Friendship is a good and noble thing, but for Augustine, any friend who loves his friend in and for himself loves in a perverse way; it is a love that is bound to fail. Since all earthly beings are transient and since God alone is immutable, complete friendship is a relationship that takes into consideration the love of God.

Augustine's recollection of his childhood friend and of their union brings to mind the idea of classical friendship. Theirs was a union rooted in their common interests, a friendship that was sweeter to Augustine above all else in life.[37] The untimely death of his childhood friend brings inconsolable grief, and he begins to hold his very existence in disdain.[38] That which once was the cause of much merriment is now the source of much suffering. His only recourse is inconsolable despair and a desire and fear of death.[39] In a real sense, a part of himself dies with his friend, for as he explains, they were one soul in two bodies.[40] Augustine's description of his friend as his other half mirrors the classical understanding of a friend as "another himself."[41]

After his conversion, Augustine regards this same friendship from an entirely new perspective, and he concludes that his friend was not a friend in the true sense of the word.[42] Through faith, Augustine comes to realize that there is no friendship in the absence of God. He now understands that to place one's happiness in the hands of an imperfect and finite being is a foolish blunder[43] and comes to regard his past grief as the result of his own fallacious reasoning, which led him to rely on the transient world for his happiness.[44] He now understands that a friend who is loved through God can never be lost, for God is eternal.[45] Friendship is a noble and good thing, provided that the friends love one another in God,[46] as God alone is immutable, and he alone deserves to be loved as an end. Moreover, since the source of the good that is loved in the friend is God, to love one's friend in himself is a misplaced love.[47] Augustine understands that his misery stemmed from having mistaken the source of good as man rather than God.[48] Through faith, he comes to understand that all good originates in and returns to God, and that in loving the good in the other person, one loves God. Since earthly virtues are mutable and unreliable, an attempt to trace the origin of virtue and the good to man rather than to God is a faulty decision that opens the door to vices.[49] Christians become ever so sceptical of the classical conception of friendship grounded in virtue. Human virtues are deceptive and unreliable (*City of God* 19.25).

From the Christian perspective, friendship is a good to be enjoyed for its own sake, but it is finite and imperfect unless it looks and moves towards God. Only in *caritas* can a friend be truly loved.[50] *Caritas* universalizes love, directing it to a community of individuals united in faith and solidarity in Christ (*In illo ergo amentur, et rape ad eum tecum quas potes* – In him, therefore, let them be loved; and draw unto him along with thee as many souls as though canst [*Conf.* IV, IV]). *Caritas* leads to a higher and clearer vision, one grounded in humility.[51] Humility is understood in relation to Christ, who died on the cross for the sake of humanity. Humility is also understood in relation to humans, as they accept their own limitations in the face of ultimate truth. In its most profound form, *caritas* was manifested by Christ himself, who descended to Earth so that mortals could ascend to the Father.

A study of Augustine's ideas on friendship would not be complete without a consideration of his great friend, Alypius, who plays a central role in the *Confessions*. Alypius studied under Augustine, both in their native town and at Carthage, and became attached to Augustine because of his mentor's kindness and breadth of knowledge. Augustine became attached to Alypius for his virtue, his integrity, and his morally upright character (*Conf.* VI, VII). Their union resembled classical friendship in the importance it placed on virtue, wisdom, and character. As friends do, they shared good times and bad times together, each serving as a source of inspiration for the other. In pursuit of a career in law, Alypius went to Rome. While in Rome, he became Augustine's close friend. Also while in Rome, Alypius became passionate about the bloody games at the Coliseum. It was through Augustine, through a passage he was expounding to his students, that Alypius became cured of his thirst for the pastimes of the games and the circus. Alypius applied the passage to himself, thinking that Augustine had intended it for him, although this was not the case. Instead of being angry with Augustine, as another young man might have been, he became angry with himself for having wasted his good mind and valuable time on frivolous pursuits (*Conf.* VI, VII). Understanding this incident as an opportunity for growth, he became closer and more attached to Augustine.

In his desire to be closer to Augustine, Alypius followed him to Milan. What type of person was Alypius? From all that Augustine tells us, he was a morally upright human being, a person of deep integrity. In Rome, as Assessor to the Chancellor of the Italian Treasury, he carried out his obligations with the highest respect for justice and the law. Alypius was moved neither by bribes, even those offered by powerful officials, nor by threats to his own person. Instead, he treated both bribery and threats with contempt. He neither sought the friendship nor feared the enmity of powerful people. Everyone was amazed by his deep sense of righteousness, and he, in turn, was amazed that any person would choose wealth over honesty. Such then was the person who was Augustine's close friend (*Conf.* VI, X). In his desire to live in proximity and share wisdom with Augustine, Alypius tried to dissuade his friend from marrying. He feared that if Augustine should marry, they would no longer be at leisure to pursue wisdom. In his lust and need of the flesh, Augustine rejected his friend's advice by giving examples of those who, although married, remained faithful to the pursuit of wisdom, to their friends, and to God. Being chaste himself, Alypius was amazed at the degree to which Augustine was enslaved by lust. Gradually, however, amazement transformed into curiosity. Alypius himself began to desire marriage, not because of lust, but out of curiosity: he wanted to fully comprehend the object of his friend's desire (*Conf.* VI, XII). In their mutual pursuit of wisdom and in their desire to escape the chaos of everyday existence, the two friends, along with several other friends, set up one common household where, in a spirit of friendship and trust, all possessions were shared and used equally by each and all (*Conf.* VI, XIV). Augustine loved his friends for themselves, for their sake. And they, in turn, loved him in the same way, for his own sake (*Conf.* VI, XVI).

Interestingly, Augustine's conversion occurred in the presence of Alypius. Over the years, the two friends had shared many trials and tribulations, but they had never shared an experience as distinctively miraculous, deeply intimate, and apocalyptic as this one. The interlocking of friendship, discourse, and truth becomes clear in this case, and their friendship was solidified through Christian conversion. As Augustine shared his experience with Alypius and showed him the passage that was instrumental in his conversion,[52] Alypius confesses that he, too, experienced a similar conversion by reading further into the passage (*Conf.* VIII, XII). He reads the line that Augustine himself had not read, but that was instrumental in his own conversion: "Now him who is weak in faith take unto you" (Rom 14:1). By means of the Word, both friends were led to Truth, from blindness to new vision. As Augustine began to know and love himself in relation to God, he began to know and love Alypius not merely for Alypius's sake, but for his love of God. This new vision allowed Augustine to transcend the bounds of his own spirtitual abyss. Through faith he learns to face and transcend his limited self. The two friends learn to love each other in their love of God. In Milan, Augustine is baptized together with his son, Adeodatus, and with his friend, Alypius (*Conf.* IX, VI).

The ascent of the soul to God, from the transient to the intransient, is one of the major themes running throughout the *Confessions.*[53] For Augustine, love is understood as a weight that pulls the soul upward towards its resting place, *pondus amoris.*[54] If earthly concerns are weights that pull downward and away from God, love is a flame that pulls upward, towards Him. In contrast to the Aristotelian theory of *generatio,* or the proper activity of the soul's virtues towards perfection through reason, the movement of the Christian soul towards perfection is achieved beyond the visible world, by means of grace and with the aid of the theological virtues.[55] Looking up towards God, Christian friendship is a union grounded in *caritas* – the love of God. While a person's final goal is the experience of supreme happiness and spiritual perfection in the heavens, his union with others will support and guide him on this journey. For the Christian thinker, reason by itself cannot lead one to ultimate truth: assistance from faith and divine revelation are also necessary.[56] While most individuals seek friendship as a path toward happiness, not all share the same definition of friendship and happiness. For Augustine, all moral issues, including friendship, rest on faith, or on those things that are unseen. By contrast, for Aristotle and for Cicero, friendship is a matter of reason. Accordingly, for the ancients, trust in friendship was to be placed in the material world where things are seen, namely virtuous actions.[57] For Aristotle and Cicero, friendship is strengthened by shared activity in the secular world.

Throughout the fourth century, more and more one notes a distinction being drawn between Christian friendship and the classical notion of friendship, with a preference given to the term *caritas* to denote Christian affection.[58] St Jerome, Augustine, and Basil use *caritas* and *agape* for the traditional *amicitia* and *philia.* They come to understand friendship as a union of brotherhood grounded in faith in Christ.[59] In the late fourth century, in an effort to draw such a distinction, Paulinus of Nola applies the term *caritas* when speaking of the union among Christians and reserves *amicitia* mostly for relationships of a strictly secular nature. Konstan notes that, even when using *amicitia* to denote Christian friendship, Paulinus goes to great lengths to differentiate it from its classical predecessor. In a letter written to Pammachius, Paulinus defines

Christian friendship as a "brotherhood of souls."[60] He further defines Christian friendship in relation to Christ and exalts its merits of divine origin and eternal nature. Unlike classical friendship, Christian friendship defies time limits. It introduces a new type of union, one grounded less in reason, personal merit, and moral excellence than in charity and divine grace.[61] If classical friendship is a union grounded in human virtue and moral excellence, Christian friendship is a union grounded in *caritas*. It was Augustine who first attempted to provide a systematic understanding of the term *caritas*, understood as the third and most important of the three theological virtues.

It is proper that a discussion on Christian friendship take into consideration the ideas of Aquinas, as all evidence points to Dante's direct knowledge of Aquinas. Dante was already studying Aquinas's works at the time of the *Vita Nuova*, around 1292 AD, and in all probability, he studied Aristotle with the aid of Aquinas's commentaries.[62] In both the *Convivio*[63] and in the *Monarchia*,[64] Dante quotes from the *Contra Gentiles*, even referring to Aquinas's work by name.[65] The fourth book of the *Convivio* addresses the nature of true nobility. And in his commentary, Dante requests that the poem be cited by the first words of the *tornata*, *Contra gli erranti*, and then explains that the name is "chosen after the example of the good friar Thomas Aquino, who gave the name 'Against the Gentiles' to a book of which he made to the confusion of all those who depart from our faith."[66] Given the extent of Aquinas's influence on Dante, what here follows is an analysis of Aquinas's understanding of friendship as *caritas*.

Like Augustine, Aquinas understands *caritas* as the essence of spiritual perfection.[67] Accordingly, Aquinas insists that "charity is not a virtue insofar as he is a man but rather insofar as he is divinized and made a son of God."[68] The question arises whether *caritas* is a friendship. In the *Summa Theologiae*, Aquinas identifies friendship with *caritas*. He does not equivocate on this point – *caritas* is not simply love, it is friendship.[69] In an attempt to clarify matters and strengthen his argument, he addresses foreseeable objections to his claims. The first point of concern is the importance of dwelling together in friendship. Since, as Aristotle asserts, nothing so marks friendship as dwelling together, and since human charity is directed towards God and the angels, who do not dwell among humans, it would seem that *caritas* is not friendship (*ST* 2a2ae.23.1). The second point in question is the attribute of reciprocity in friendship. According to Aristotle there is no friendship without reciprocal goodwill, but since *caritas* requires us to love even our enemies, it would seem that *caritas* is not friendship (*ST* 2a2ae.23.1). The third point concerns Aristotle's three kinds of friendship: for utility, for pleasure, for worth. According to Aquinas, charity is none of these: charity is neither useful nor pleasurable (*ST* 2a2ae.23.1), and it is not like Aristotle's conception of complete friendship, for that is restricted to the virtuous, whereas charity is directed to the wicked also (*ST* 2a2ae.23.1). At first glance it would seem that charity is not friendship (*ST* 2a2ae.23.1). But after playing devil's advocate, Aquinas proceeds to argue that *caritas* is indeed friendship. In an attempt to strengthen his argument, he refers to the words of Christ ("no longer will I call you servants but my friends") and claims that they can only be explained as charity, which therefore is friendship.[70]

Concerning the importance of reciprocity in Aristotelian friendship (*NE* 8.2 1155b 32–35), Aquinas notes that Aristotle's reciprocal goodwill is rooted in fellowship or in something that friends share or have in common (*ST* 2a2ae.23.1). In *caritas*, the sharing of mortals with God occurs through the sharing of His son, and so friendship with God is grounded in this sharing of Christ.[71] Of an individual's double life, secular and spiritual, his friendship with God and the angels belongs to the life of the spirit.[72] Though impefect in this life, a person's friendship with God will become perfect in heaven, as *caritas* is imperfect in our present state, but will reach perfection in heaven.[73] Aquinas further argues that friendship extends to another in two ways: when a person is loved in himself and when he is loved because of someone else.[74] In the first instance friendship is grounded in the love of the friend himself, whereas in the second it is grounded in the love of another person. The friendship of charity extends to our enemies, who are loved for the sake of loving God (*caritas, quae maxime est amicitia honesti, se extendit ad peccatores quos ex caritate diligimus propter Deum* – charity, which above all is friendship, reaches out to sinners whom we love for God's sake [*ST* 2a2ae.23.2]). From all that has been said, it would seem that *caritas* is indeed friendship. But is *caritas* a friendship in the Aristotelian sense? To be sure, *caritas* is friendship, but it is also the greatest of the theological virtues, which have no place in Aristotle's philosophy.[75] For this reason and because Aristotelian friendship is a strictly human relationship, *caritas* is not friendship in the Aristotelian sense.

Is *caritas* a virtue? And is it a virtue in the Aristotelian sense of the word? While in the *Nicomachean Ethics* Aristotle defines moral virtue *according to correct reason*,[76] Aquinas considers *caritas* to be a virtue because it extends to God and because it joins an individual to Him.[77] In an attempt to strengthen his argument Aquinas refers to Augustine, who asserts that charity is a virtue by means of which humans are united with God.[78] Without refuting Aristotle's claim that friendship is *a virtue or with a virtue*,[79] Aquinas distinguishes the moral virtue that extends to other persons from the virtue that is charity, which is grounded in divine goodness.[80] It would seem that charity is a special kind of virtue since its proper object of love is divine goodness, which is the final object of a person's beatitude.[81]

Of all the virtues, *caritas* is the greatest and most encompassing since its object is the ultimate goal of human life, eternal happiness.[82] *Caritas* is a friendship between a person and God, but it includes friendship towards one's neighbour.[83] Aquinas returns to the words of St John: "This commandment we have from God, that he who loves God should love his brother also."[84] While encompassing the human and the divine, charity remains a single virtue for the primary object of love is one, God.[85] It is for the sake of God that we love our neighbours.[86] Charity thus extends mutually and in one act to the love of God and to the love of our neighbour.[87] In friendship, a person loves two things: his friend himself for whom he wishes good things and the good itself which he wishes his friend.[88] Charity would seem to belong to the second category.[89] A person loves and forms friendships with both God and with his neighbour, but his love for them also includes a love of charity itself, God.[90]

Caritas originates and culminates in God himself: *Deus caritas est* (God is love). It is the love that God bestows upon humanity in the figure of Christ. Since God himself is ultimate love and perfect good, and since He essentially is complete in Himself, in loving humans He seeks only their greatest good.[91] That which is unique in Christian friendship is this notion of friendship between mortals and God. In its journey towards divinity, Christian friendship transcends the particular and embraces the universal. In the beatific vision of God, the particular and the universal coexist as one. Christian friendship thus is a union that aims to transcend duality: it aims to resolve the opposition between the human and the divine, the finite and the infinite. While looking upward towards God, *caritas* simultaneously looks downward towards mortals. Accordingly, it simultaneously encompasses the love of God and the love of one's neighbour. Christ calls each person to love God with all his heart, and he also calls him to love his neighbour as he loves himself: "Thou shalt love thy neighbor as thyself" (Mt 29:39).[92]

Self-love is both just and necessary, and it is the basis for the love of one's neighbours. It is impossible for any individual truly to love God and not to love himself and the rest of humanity.[93] As Etienne Gilson notes, there exists no real contradiction between loving another and loving oneself: "To love another as oneself cannot be a contradiction because love tends to unity and there can be no division within something which is one."[94] One is not forbidden to love his friend so long as he does not love him in the way he loves God, without restrictions, as if he were the highest good.[95] Since God alone is the highest good, He alone deserves to be loved without reservation.[96] Friendship that is not grounded in *caritas* is a coincidental union. In such instances the friend is not loved in so far as who he is essentially; he is not loved for the love of God.

While God alone is the supreme good and the object of perfect love, *caritas* is mutually the love of God and the love of humans. It includes the love of self and the love of one's neighbour. For Aquinas, as for Augustine, there are two kinds of self-love: one is a well-ordered love of self whereby an individual guided by reason and faith seeks his true good; the other type is a misguided love of self where a person is guided by his emotions rather than by his reason and the love of God. This second type of self-love seeks to gratify sensual appetites, or the desire for power or pleasure without concern for one's true good.[97] Similar to this notion, in Aristotle bad self-love seeks to gratify the passionate part of one's soul, causing an individual to desire false goods such as power, pleasure, and money. Good self-love seeks to gratify the rational part of the soul, and desires a constant good: virtue.[98] Guided by his reason, the good person will do whatever is best for both himself and others. By contrast, he who is guided and ruled by his passions will bring harm to himself and others.[99]

Although ultimate perfection and happiness reside in the beatific vision of God, human friendship is to be understood as a preparation and prefiguration for perfect bliss.[100] The love I have for my neighbour, it is believed, will prepare and guide me towards the ultimate object of love – God.[101] One friend seeks the company of another friend for the sake of reaching God. Although our ultimate object of love and final end is God Himself, *caritas* embraces the entire Christian community (*ST* 2.2.23.1). God commands us to love Him and love each other, it is assumed, as he has loved us. He commands that we love each other in *caritas*.[102] *Caritas* thus embraces all of humanity, even our enemies. It is thought that Christ, while knowing that Judas would betray him, did not stop loving him and allowed him to receive communion.[103] By means of his own example, Christ teaches a crucial lesson about *caritas* as the path away from death towards spiritual life and perfection. It is precisely in relation to descent and ascent that Christian friendship acquires a unique meaning. In the *Confessions*, Augustine calls on believers to accept Christ's descent as an invitation to ascent (*numquid et post descensum vitae non vultis ascendere et vivere?* – Will ye not now after that life is descended down to you, will not you ascend up to it and live?).[104] By means of his death and resurrection, Christ called his followers to new life. As he states, "anyone who loves me will be true to my word, and my Father will love him; we will come to Him and make our dwelling place with Him" (Jn. 14:23).[105] Though it may in some respects parallel Cicero's notion of *amicitia*, Christian friendship is grounded in the Scriptures.[106]

For Aquinas, as for Aristotle, the essence of friendship is abundance and similitude, rather than deficiency and difference. Imperfect unions are grounded in deficiency: one enters into a relationship with others to receive from them what one lacks. But in complete friendship, one enters into a relationship with others who are like himself in goodness, that he may share and communicate with them the abundance of his goodness:

> In the love of concupiscence, we draw to us what is extraneous for us, for we love other things by the love in so far as they are useful of delectable for us. But in the love of friendship, it is otherwise. For we draw ourselves to that which is outside of us. Since to whom we love by that love, we behave ourselves just as to ourselves and communicate ourselves to them in a certain manner. Therefore, in the love of friendship, similitude is the cause of love, for we do not love someone in this way unless we are one with him, and similitude is a kind of unity.[107]

For Aquinas the goodness present in mortals originates in divine goodness and in divine abundance. God created the universe from an abundance of goodness.[108] Humans, in varying degrees, share in His divine goodness and are a representation of His goodness. Mortals participate in divine goodness and by nature desire to communicate his goodness to others.[109] Friendship is thus the union of good people who are alike in goodness. In friendship, one wishes good things for his friend as one does for oneself. A friend thus becomes another self, *alter ipse*.[110] Moreover, friendship is a mutual relationship.[111] By means of love, reciprocity, and shared experiences, each friend influences the other, without losing their own identity.[112] In Aquinas, one finds a close link between existence and action. By the very fact that something exists, it is active.[113] In this manner, friendship is to be understood as an active relationship: a union that bridges the distance between the self and the other. An individual establishes his individuality not in isolation, but through his relations with others who are different from himself. A person's identity is established through his interaction with someone other than himself.[114] The relation between friends is dynamic and reciprocal. By means of discourse and shared activities, each friend changes the other and each becomes a source of comfort, love, and good.

Before proceeding to a discussion of friendship in *Inferno* 2, it is appropriate, if not essential, to summarize and arrive at a clear understanding of the basic distinction between classical and Christian friendship. A fundamental difference between the two seems to lie in the object of love and in the movement implied by that love, either an ascent towards God (*caritas*) or descent towards humankind (*philia* or *amicitia*). For ancients and Christians alike, friendship is an activity that leads to happiness and perfection of the soul. While not all humans love the same good and not all seek perfect "goodness,"[115] insofar as all humans have a natural inclination towards happiness and perfection, all strive towards what they perceive to be their good. Disagreement arises in regards to the particular doctrine of happiness and knowledge, which is closely connected to the notion of being. While happiness seems to be sought by all individuals, it seems, its definition shifts so that it means different things to different people at different points in history. As Singleton notes, "happiness is that which all desire as something for its own sake, the final goal of all striving. Yet, while this is true, while all agree that happiness is that object, there are many differing conceptions of what happiness actually is."[116] Singleton refers to Virgil's discussion of happiness in the *Commedia*, where he states *quel dolce pome che per tanti rami / cercando va la cura de' mortali, / oggi porrà in pace le tue fami* (that sweet fruit which mortals seek / and strive to find on many boughs / today shall satisfy your carvings [*Purg.* 27, 115–17]). As Virgil here makes clear, a person's natural thirst for happiness manifests itself on different planes. While the Christian conceives of happiness as a transcendent reality, the pagan conceives of it as part of the secular world. For both, the object of love is the good, but while the pagan places the essential good in the individual, the Christian believes that it resides in God. Thus, the discrepancy in the definition of happiness extends to friendship. For ancients and Christians alike, friendship is understood as a union that has origin in a surplus and an abundance of a good, however, the abundance of good in Christian friendship is traced back to God, who alone is seen as ultimate Good. Since it is believed that God is the ultimate good, and that He neither lacks nor needs anything, it is believed that He creates and loves from an abundance of goodness.

As F.C. Copleston notes, Aristotle conceives of a universe that is existentially independent of a god.[117] As such, he is concerned with what things are and how they become what they are; thus, his theory of becoming. In contrast to Aristotle, Aquinas concerns himself with why things exist at all or with the origin of things; thus, his theory of existence.[118] While adopting much of Aristotelian philosophy, Aquinas transforms Aristotle's notion of being. For Aristotle truth is to be found in the essence of things; for Aquinas it is found in the existence (*esse*) of things.[119] Aristotle understands being primarily as form and potentiality. Aquinas understands it as existence that must be traced back to its source or creator. Their understanding of being was to have important influences on their notion of happiness, the good, knowledge of the universe, and ultimately on their notion of friendship. Aquinas views friendship, as he does all human experiences, from a human prespective. For Augustine, however, friendship, ultimately acquires significance in relation to God, who is the ultimate original cause.[120] Aquinas incorporates Aristotelian virtue, elevating it from the realms of natural ethics and philosophy to the realms of spiritual truth and theology. He begins with the Aristotelian notion of happiness in the here and now and ends with Christian happiness found in the beatific vision of God in the heavens. Similarly, he begins with earthly virtues and ultimately arrives at the theological virtues of faith, hope, and charity.[121] For Aquinas, human reason can reinforce the need for faith, but it cannot on its own merits arrive at ultimate truth. Accordingly, complete happiness and goodness are attained through revelation and grace.[122] Still, the goodness found in the visible world, though finite and imperfect, is seen as an anticipation of the supreme good found in the heavenly sphere.[123] In this sense then, friendship yields a foretaste of the heavenly bliss that humans so desire.[124] The love of God is *caritas*, the highest of the theological virtues. The more a person partakes of *caritas*, the greater his chances of experiencing complete happiness. For both Aquinas and Dante, charity is understood as a preparation for spiritual perfection.[125] The distinction between classical friendship and Christian friendship is to be placed within the interplay between reason and faith, philosophy and theology. Classical friendship is a union grounded in human reason and virtue, while Christian friendship is a union grounded in *caritas* and faith in Christ.[126] While reason and revelation are distinct means of arriving at the truth, both acquire significance in relation to the one truth.[127] Augustine also believed, however, that while reason alone can never yield complete truth, there is no faith without reason.[128]

Following in the footsteps of Aristotelian and scholastic philosophy, Aquinas's quest for truth begins in the material world. Since humans are part of the secular world, by necessity, all knowledge begins in sense perception.[129] In his search for truth, Aquinas ascends from the material to the transcendent. As finite beings living in the sensible world, individuals by necessity deduce the existence of God from the world in which they live.[130] By means of philosophy, humans arrive at the realization that the world is existentially related to the creator – God – and that all things are related to him causally. Through reason and philosophy they come to realize that empirical reality is causally dependent upon a transcendent reality and that all things are causally related to the creator.[131] Unlike other thirteenth-century thinkers – such as Albertus Magnus and St Bonaventura – who drew a distinct line between reason and faith, Aquinas seeks to resolve the opposition between the two. He places each within its proper context and order, thereby creating a synthesis of both.[132] For Etienne Gilson, "the historical significance of St. Thomas Aquinas rests with the fact that he was the first medieval thinker to go to the root of the difficulty."[133] The root of the difficulty that Gilson here refers to is the duality between faith and reason. Aquinas posits the relation between faith and reason as one of coexistence and harmony, rather than opposition. While both are distinct types of knowledge aiming at distinct truths, their distinction does not translate to a conflict.[134] Aquinas is of the belief that while certain truths are accessible to human reason, truths of revelation are not. In the third book of the *Contra Gentiles*, he attempts to show that complete beatitude is unattainable to mortals solely by means of his human faculties.[135] While the highest form of vision belongs to revelation, a person's complete beatitude is to be found in the beatific vision of God and in the direct knowledge of his essence.[136] While truths of revelation are inaccessible to reason, they are not necessarily opposed to it.[137] Religious truths are inaccessible to philosophy, but philosophy can be useful in shedding light on religious truths.[138] Along these lines, Vossler poses a reasonable question: if reason can rise to faith then why the need of revelation?[139] For Aquinas, revelation leads to a more complete and direct knowledge of God. Nonetheless, Aquinas stands firm on the harmonious relation between reason and revelation, philosophy and theology.[140] As Vossler notes, for Aquinas humans hold a central position in the universe, serving as a bridge between material and spiritual reality:

> Since Thomas's philosophy fixes man's place between beast and angel, matter and God, as the most important middle link, and finds in the soul of the individual the iron ring that holds together the terraced structure of the universe ... and, in short, sets man and his reason in the center of all things.[141]

If humans are truly the "middle link" between matter and God, human friendship would seem to be a necessary first step towards divinity. From a Christian vantage point, the love that one person feels for another inspires and encourages that person to love God, thereby promoting his spiritual perfection and happiness.[142] In this manner Christian friendship is universalized. It is an activity by means of which an individual is first drawn towards another individual from a love of the good present in him and then ultimately drawn to God, who is the source of all good.

After having explored friendship in some of the Christian writers who influenced Dante's thought, we may now proceed to a study of friendship in the *Vita Nuova*, a work that contains a reflection on the relationship between *amor* (love) and *amicizia* (friendship), between Cavalcanti, the friend, and Beatrice, the beloved.

Chapter Five

The *Vita Nuova*: Dante's Friendship with Guido Cavalcanti and Others

This chapter proposes a study of Dante's friendship with Guido Cavalcanti and others, as seen in the *Vita Nuova* and in the *Commedia*. Given the fact that friendship is a social construct that flourishes within a particular socio-political reality, it seems proper to place and understand Dante's friendships within and in relation to the historical and socio-political reality of his times. Indeed, Dante's friendships with his fellow poets and scholars acquire significance in relation to the wider intellectual and political spectrum of his times. His discourses with friends must be understood as the expression of both personal and social relations deeply rooted in historical circumstances. One needs to remember that Dante lived in a world where political leaders, merchants, poets, and aristocrats often mingled in the same circles, and we know that Dante was involved in the turbulent political life of Florence. Involvement in public life meant access to prominent intellectual and social circles. It meant friendship with prominent scholars and poets such as Brunetto Latini, Guido Cavalcanti, Cino da Pistoia, and acceptance into the prestigious social circles of Nino Visconti and Guido da Polenta.[1] Dante's dedication to politics and his love for poetry were influential forces in his friendships. If Aristophanes was correct in claiming that "poets make better people in their cities," Dante's friendships are to be understood in relation to poetry and politics within the city.

During the thirteenth century, daily life in Italy was marked by the strife between church and state, family feuds, and party affiliation. During such volatile times friends were indispensible. The Italian city-states were divided along the lines of friends and enemies. The line between personal friendship and socio-political affiliation was not always well defined. Often, the personal and the political crossed paths so that personal relationships had political and social implications and vice versa. At times friendships even crossed party lines. The conflict between the Emperor (followed by the Ghibellines) and the

Pope (followed by the Guelfs) ignited a family feud. At the battle of Montaperti (1260), the Guelfs were defeated. Daily life in Florence consisted of constant battles between the Guelfs and Ghibellines. To complicate matters further, in 1300, the Guelfs divided into the Blacks (headed by the Donati) and Whites (headed by the Cerchi).

The conflict between the Whites and Blacks and their allied families escalated to warfare. In 1300, Corso Donati, a leader of the Blacks and a relative of Dante's wife, Gemma, was banished from Florence. A year later, Corso returned to Florence and defeated the Whites. At the same time a disjunction between the *popolo* (trading and shopkeepers community) and the magnates (great men) was growing. After the split of the Guelfs into Whites and Blacks, the dividing line between Guelfs and Ghibellines became obscured. There were instances when the White Guelfs found themselves siding with the political cause of the Ghibellines.[2] Dante had friendships and connections with political leaders on both sides. As a Guelf he was on the side of the Church, but as a White Guelf he opposed the corruption of Boniface VIII and of the Church. He was exiled from Florence in 1302 and later was condemned to be burned at the stake (if he re-entered Florence) for failure to appear in court.

In the *Inferno*, Dante gives further insight into the political strife dividing Florence. In *Inferno* 10, Dante's confrontation with Cavalcante de' Cavalcanti (Guido's father and a Guelf) and with Farinata (leader of the Ghibellines) dramatizes Dante's precarious position in a world in which poetry, politics, and friendship were interlocked. The scene sheds light on the intricate complexities between political alliance and personal relationships. The two heretical Florentines and in-laws, Farinata and Cavalcante, are occupying the same tomb, yet they do not speak to one another since they are divided along party loyalty. The episode in *Inferno* 10 exposes the extent to which friendship, politics, and poetry were interwoven into the very fabric of the city. If Dante's Tuscan dialect gives Farinata reason to rejoice, Dante's lineage gives him reason to lament. As a fellow compatriot, Farinata feels a certain affinity towards Dante (*Inf.* 10, 22–4), but as a Guelf, Dante is Farinata's enemy (*Inf.* 10, 46–8). While united in common speech and patriotism, the two are divided along party and familial loyalties.

As Dante reveals his ancestors, Farinata recognizes them as enemies and proudly recalls his victorious defeat of the Guelfs (*Fieramente furo avversi / a me e a miei primi e a mia parte, / sì che per due fiate li dispersi* – They were most bitter enemies / to me, my forebears, and my party / not once, but twice, I had to drive them out [*Inf.* 10, 46–8]).[3] Dante, in turn, eagerly informs the Ghibelline leader of his party's eventual defeat by the Guelfs (*"S'ei fur cacciati, ei tornar d'ogne parte," / rispuos'io lui, "l'una e l'altra f'iata; / ma i vostri non appreser ben quell'arte*" – "If they were banished," I responded, "they returned / from every quarter both the first and second time, / a skill that Yours have failed to learn as well" [*Inf.* 10, 49–51]). Dante's conversation with Farinata is interrupted by the appearance of Cavalcante de' Cavalcanti (died ca. 1280), father of Guido, Dante's first friend.[4] The political theme of Farinata's episode offsets the theme of friendship referenced through Dante's encounter with Cavalcante, Guido's father. The juxtaposition between Farinata and Cavalcante, Dante and Farinata, and Dante and Guido, is to be understood in light of the juxtaposition between the two themes of politics and friendship: each permeates the other, and acquires significance in relation to the other. Poetic discouse is the means by which both worlds – the private and public – confront one another and merge. The two narratives, Farinata's political narrative and Cavalcanti's private narrative, must be understood within the inescapable interlocking of opposing themes of friendship and politics. Farinata's narrative is immersed in political significance; it mirrors a world of political disorder and violence. Cavalcanti's narrative is immersed in familial affection; it is the story of a father's love and concern for his son. What joins the two worlds and the seemingly divergent themes is "love from which the word friendship takes its name" (*Amor enim, ex quo amicitia nominate est* ... (*DA*, VIII, 26]). The disjunction between politics and friendship finds resolution in love: Farinata's love for Florence, and for his party and family; Cavalcanti's fatherly love for Guido; Dante's love for Florence, for his party and family, and for his friend Guido.

John Freccero notes that while appreciating the "theatricality" and "psychological depth" of Dante's dramatic encounter with Cavalcante, modern critics fail to discuss the importance of Guido.[5] In recent years, however, scholars have in effect studied the canto in relation to Guido Cavalcanti, Dante's former "first friend." Indeed, the entire conversation between Cavalcante and Dante centres on Guido. Hoping to see his son, Cavalcante rises up on his knees and weeping he asks *se per questo cieco / carcere vai per altezza d'ingegno, / mio figlio ov'è? e perché non è teco?* (if you pass through this dark / prison by virtue of your lofty genius, / where is my son and why is he not with you?).[6] Cavalcante does not understand that Dante's journey is a gift of grace. While pointing to Virgil as one who leads him, Dante explains that *Da me stesso non vegno: / colui ch'attende là per qui mi mena / forse cui Guido vostro ebbe a disdegno* (I come not on my own: / he who stands there waiting leads me through, / perhaps to one Your Guido held in scorn [*Inf.* 10, 61–3]). Dante does not descend by his own power. His journey is a gift of grace and not a result of his own *ingegno.*

Cavalcante mistakenly understands Dante's use of the past definite to mean that his son is dead ("*Come?/ dicesti 'elli ebbe'? Non viv' elli ancora? / non fiere li occhi suoi lo dolce lume*?" ("What? / Did you say 'he held'? Lives he not still? / Does not the sweet light strike upon his eyes?" [*Inf.* 10, 67–9]).[7] Overcome by grief, he falls back, supine in his tomb (*Inf.* 10, 70–2). The sole force and power behind Cavalcante's movement is paternal love. His love for his son Guido comes forth through his sudden appearance (full of desire to see his son) and disappearance (full of grief at hearing the definitive preterite "*ebbe*"). Dante's *forse cui Guido ebbe a disdegno* has been one of the most debated and disputed passages in the entire poem. Why does he use the *passato remoto*, the past definitive, *elli ebbe* (he had)?[8] The ambiguity created by the use of the simple past leaves the reader wondering if Dante is, as Freccero suggests, passing his "final judgment" on Guido, thereby condemning his former friend to damnation. It is implausible that the poet made use of the past definite without being fully cognizant of its implications. As Freccero notes, we can only conclude that he meant to use it.[9] It may very well be the case, as Freccero argues, that Dante's use of the past definite is his subtle way of sealing Guido's fate once and for all. Nonetheless, the very subtlety and "ambiguity" with which Dante makes his accusation against Guido is a sign of his unending loyalty to the memory of his former "first friend." If it is true that "the poet has expressed his personal ambivalence toward Guido with calculated ambiguity,"[10] it is equally true that the "calculated ambiguity" veils a sense of guilt towards Guido or, at the very least, an unwillingness to explicitly denounce and condemn his former first friend. As a Christian poet, Dante is forced to take a stance regarding heresy, although his loyalty to the memory of his friendship with Guido makes him stop short of clearly and explicitly passing judgment. If indeed "the warning of the pilgrim is 'an uncertain trumpet' sounded for his former friend,"[11] the very "uncertainty" with which Dante plays his trumpet mirrors the uneasiness he feels in openly condemning Guido, a friend whom he had deeply loved and respected. The sounding of the "uncertain trumpet," is a reminder that Guido forever lives in Dante's memory.

As Freccero notes, when considering the verse in light of the fiction that Guido is still alive, Dante's mention of his name may be understood as a warning to his friend that unless he mends his ways he might incur the same punishment as his father. When considering the verse in light of the fact that Guido had been dead for a decade when Dante wrote this passage, Dante's warning may in fact be his final decree on his first friend. For Freccero, "Guido's 'disdain' represents the abyss that divided the two friends."[12] Whatever one takes Guido's "disdain" to mean, one thing seems certain: while their earlier disagreements revolved around topics of love and poetry, the "abyss" that ultimately divided the two friends revolved around matters of faith and happiness. Since Virgil leads to Beatrice, Beatrice leads to God, and both lead the pilgrim on the path towards heavenly bliss, Guido's "disdain," whether directed at Virgil or Beatrice, ultimately is for spiritual truth and happiness. In his adherence to philosophical truth, obtained by means of his human intellect, Guido repudiated Christian faith. For Aquinas, heresy is a sin against the intellect, for although its primary cause is pride, it stems from one's refusal to accept the truth of faith. In *Paradiso* 17, Dante notes that he will not be a "timid friend to the truth."[13] Both friends sought truth and happiness, but in different places. While Guido sought them in secular knowledge and philosophy, Dante sought them in Revelation and Christian faith. Guido's pride would prevent him from accepting the fallibility of human knowledge and intellect. Dante, on the other hand, arrives at the realization that ultimate knowledge and happiness reside in God. In the end, the disjunction between the two friends acquires significance in light of a disparity concerning faith and happiness. Let us now turn our attention to Dante's *Vita Nuova*, to his friendship with Guido Cavalcanti in that work, and to his encounters with other friends in the *Commedia*.

Love and friendship are at the heart of the *Vita Nuova*.[14] In effect, and as Mazzotta points out, Dante's *Vita Nuova* is a text which contemplates, among other topics, the duality between love and friendship, between Cavalcanti, the friend, and Beatrice, the beloved.[15] Who takes precedence: Guido, the benevolent friend, with whom Dante will communicate ideas and share discourse, or Beatrice, the beloved, who will deny him her "sweet greeting" (*dolcissimo salutare*) in 10, 2? Which is primary, love or friendship? As seen earlier in this study, in *De Amicitia*, Cicero notes that *amor enim, ex quo amicitia nominata est ad benevolentiam coniungendam* (For it is love, from which the word "friendship" is derived, that leads to the establishing of goodwill [*DA* viii, 26]). For Cicero, love is primary and friendship entails it. In the *Vita Nuova*, Dante seems to acknowledge that love, even the most misguided of loves, is better than friendship.[16] Love is a passion, a dynamic force that thrusts forth, setting all things in motion, in contrast to the more constant comfort and consolation that friendship renders. As Aristotle notes, love "implies intensity and desire" (*NE* 9.5 1167a 34). Notwithstanding the primacy of love in the *Vita Nuova*, I shall here argue that in proposing a new type of love – one that leads away from death towards new life and away from misery towards ultimate happiness – the *Vita Nuova* prepares the way for Christian friendship. This life-affirming love that leads the lover on a journey towards God is none other than *caritas* (charity). And as Aquinas asserts, charity is friendship between mortals and God.[17] More cogently, in its reconceptualization of the nature of love as *amor benevolentiae*, the *Vita Nuova* moves away from secular friendship towards Aquinas's understanding of friendship as *caritas*. In its celebration of Christian love, the *Vita Nuova* celebrates Christian friendship, a union grounded in the love of God, who is the origin and inspiration. Dante distances himself from Guido, his "first friend," and moves towards Beatrice, who will become a true friend in Christ.

To be sure, Dante's friendship with Guido plays an important role in the *Vita Nuova*. It is Guido, Dante's first friend (*primo amico*) (III, 14), to whom the *Vita Nuova* is dedicated. Guido Cavalcanti, the son of Cavalcante de' Cavalcanti, was about ten years older than Dante. Despite the discrepancy in age, their friendship flourished through discourse, common interest, and through their mutual love of poetry.[18] In a spirit of benevolence and goodwill, the two friends "turn together," to partake in intellectual discourse and share ideas about their poetic craft.[19] Dante's friendship with Guido can be traced back to Guido's poem *Vedeste, al mio parere, enne valore* (You saw, in my opinion, every power).[20] Guido's poem is a response to Dante's sonnet, *A ciascun'alma presa e gentil core* (To every love-taken soul and noble heart), a poem that dramatizes Dante's *maravigliosa visione* (marvelous vision) in chapter 3.[21] The God of Love holds the poet's heart in his hand and then feeds it to the lady.

As Mazzotta notes, Guido's interpretation of Dante's vision, like the interpretation of other poets, is incorrect.[22] Guido erroneously concluded that in his dream vision, Dante had seen Love, which will live in the realm of philosophical and objective ideas.[23] By transporting love to the realm of philosophical ideas, Guido distorts and diminishes the significance of Dante's particular and subjective experience, translating it into an abstraction and philosophical generality.[24] In retrospect Dante, the narrator, recognizes that Guido's transportation of love to a realm of abstractions is a blunder, or to use Mazzotta's words, "a philosophical illusion,"[25] which reflects a significant incomprehension regarding the vitality and poignancy of Dante's subjective experience.

While formulating his own ideas on love, Dante moves away from his friend Guido. His first friend to whom Dante dedicated the *Vita Nuova* is superseded by Beatrice who, as the god of love in chapter XXIV notes, is love itself. To be sure, Dante's understanding of love grew out of Cavalcanti's and Guinizelli's ideas on love. Dante's literary career began under the tutelage of Guido, whose lyric genius, philosophical knowledge, and aristocratic lineage distinguished him as a great Italian poet. Indeed, the first part of the *Vita Nuova,* where the lover recounts the pains of love, is Cavalcantian in nature. In chapter II, Dante describes the disruptive effects of love on his "spirits" during his first vision of Beatrice. Guido's influence is also present in the "marvelous vision" in Chapter III, when the lord of love holds and feeds Dante's flaming heart to Beatrice against her will. Guido himself had used this image of a flaming heart in his poem "Perche' non fuoro a me gli occhi dispenti."[26] Despite Guido's influences in the first part of the *libello* (little book), in the later poems and in the prose, Dante presents a rupture between himself and his first friend.

Towards the middle of the *Vita Nuova,* Dante is moving away from Guido's conception of love and leading more towards Guinizelli's notion of love and his style of praise, a style that seems more fitting for a new theologized conception of love.[27] In the *Vita Nuova*, we see Dante's conception of love undergoing a transformation. As Hollander notes, Dante's pains of love expressed in the first part of the *Vita Nuova* (II–XVII) is Cavalcantian in nature, his praise of his beloved in the second part (XVIII–XXVII) is under Guinizelli's authority, and his understanding of the beloved's divine nature and a higher love found in the final part (XXVIII–XLII), from the time of Beatrice's death (XXVIII) till the end, is under the jurisdiction of Dante himself.[28] By the end of the *libello*, Dante has distanced himself from Guido's tragic love. He has arrived at a higher love, one that leads to transcendence and spiritual salvation.

It seems that at some point between 1290 and 1300, Dante and Guido had a disagreement regarding the purpose of love poetry.[29] For some critics this falling out is illustrated in Guido's sonnet to Dante, *I'vegno 'l giorno a te 'nfinite volte* (I come to you during the day countless times). Guido might here be referencing Dante's moral lapse, or his supposed betrayal of the memory of Beatrice. Paget Toynbee suggests that what Guido had in mind in this sonnet was "Dante's degrading intercourse with such company as Forese Donati."[30] Giorgio Padoan, following Contini's lead, finds that the sonnet's hostile attitude towards Dante accounts for Guido's *disdegno* (scorn) in *Inferno* 10.[31] Whether or not one subscribes to Padoan's theory, it is likely that at some point in time Guido and Dante had a disagreement and, among other topics, the point of contention was love, a theme of primary interest to both poets. Dante's falling out with Guido becomes quite evident at certain points in the prose of the *Vita Nuova.*

If Dante's friendship with Guido can be traced back to *Vedeste al mio parere, enne valore* (You saw, in my opinion, every power), his disjunction with Guido can be traced to *Donne ch'avete intelletto d'amore* (Ladies who have understanding of love), a song of praise in the manner of Guinizelli. The *canzone* marks a definitive moment in Dante's praise of Beatrice. It marks a movement away from Guido and in its celebration of his beloved, a movement towards *il dolce stil nuovo* (sweet new style [*Purg.* 24, 57]) of Guinizelli. The *canzone* marks a shift from self, Dante's preoccupation with his own pains, to other, his appreciation of Beatrice and her praises. It marks a shift from a limiting type of love (sensual love) to a more complete and encompassing love. This higher type of love leads the lover outside of himself and his personal misery, towards the beloved and her praises. In this second stage, Dante learns that his *beatitudine* (happiness [XVIII, 6]) is derived from loving, appreciating, and praising Beatrice for her own sake, or for what she is, rather than for what she can offer him (her acknowledgment). The next sonnet (XX, 1–2), *Amore e 'l cor gentile sono una cosa, / sì come il saggio in suo dittare pone* (Love and the noble heart are but one thing / so says the wise man in his poem) and his reference to Guinizelli in *Purgatorio* 26, 97–9, and 112–14, make it clear that towards the middle part of the *Vita Nuova*, Dante is moving towards Guinizelli's poetic style and away from Guido's style.[32] His praise of his beloved is most evident in the sonnet *Tanto gentile e tanto onesta pare* (So gentle and so full of dignity appears). In chapters XXV and XXVI, Dante describes the bliss or happiness Beatrice inspires in those who witness her person. In his reconceptualization of love as a disinterested affection, Dante is also moving towards the classical and Christian conception of friendship as a disinterested love valued and sought after because of the love itself.

Dante's disjunction with his first friend becomes even more pronounced in chapter XXIV, where the god of love announces his exit from the work, relinquishing his position to Beatrice, and Dante sees Beatrice preceded by Cavalcanti's Giovanna, as Christ was preceded by John the Baptist. Immediately following this analogy, the god of love identifies Beatrice with love itself (*E chi voleste sottilmente considerare, quella Beatrice chiamerebbe Amore per molta simigliana che ha meco* – And whoever should consider subtly would call that Beatrice *Love* because of the great resemblance which she has to me).[33] As Beatrice replaces the god of love, Dante's conception of love undergoes a transformation. He promotes a new type of love, one that brings light where there is darkness, new life where there is death. In chapter XXV, while expressing his thoughts about the craft of poetry, Dante explains that Love is not a substance, but rather that it is "an accident in a substance," or a passion present in a person. At first glance, this explanation seems to concur with Guido's philosophical conception of love, as expressed in his *Donna me prega* (A lady bids me). In effect, chapter XXIV (with the god of love taking leave from the prose narrative) with chapter XXV (where the reality of love as a person is questioned) work together to discredit Guido's position on love. Dante is here moving in a new direction. While the god of love represents the old conception of love (the lyric tradition of Provence having roots in the Troubadours), Beatrice signals a new tradition, a conception of love that is grounded in charity and in the mutual love of God and mortals. The disappearance of the god of love halfway through *Vita Nuova* is indicative of this change from old to new, from *amor* to *caritas*.[34] While the god of love is not a person and love cannot be a substance on earth, an individual can participate in substantial love by means of charity. Unlike the god of love, Beatrice is no mere representation of love, she partakes in substantial love.[35] Dante's distance from his first friend will acquire new clarity once we revisit Guido's conception of love and then return to Dante's new position.

Guido understands love as a negative force that is primarily disruptive in nature. Accordingly, love leads the lover to disorder, to an imbalance, to self-destruction, and ultimately to the very threshold of death. In his love song *Donna me prega*, Guido presents love as a passion, or appetite. As an uncontrollable appetite, love disrupts the lover's rational equilibrium, one's very essence, thus leading the lover to a state of confusion and *tristitia* (melancholy), rather than to enlightenment and bliss. The lover's *tristitia* is manifested through visible signs: pallor, sighs, and a disheveled physical appearance. For Guido the lover's suffering is due to an error in judgment. Driven by his blind passion, the lover erroneously confuses the beloved with the true object of love.[36] Taking a rather philosophical stance, Guido views the beloved as a mere representation of the true object of love; hence, she is less perfect and less complete than the ideal. Accordingly, the beauty of the beloved is a mere image of the ideal or universal beauty that the lover desires. Thus, in loving the beloved, the lover can never be fully satisfied, for what he ultimately seeks to reach is universal beauty, truth, virtue, and love. While weakening his reasoning capacity and heightening his senses, the lover's passion misdirects his yearning towards the woman, rather than towards the universal ideals. Guido's philosophical musings on love may bring to mind Plato's World of Ideas. In Guido, however, this type of philosophical inquiry acquires significance in relation to poetry. And so, important questions remain to be answered. What precisely is Dante's new position on love by the end of the *Vita Nuova*? And to what degree did he distance himself from his first friend, Guido?

Singleton argues that just as Dante's old conception of love had "an established and public existence" grounded in the lyric tradition of Provence and the troubadours, his new view has an established position grounded in theology.[37] In this manner, Dante's new conception of love is placed within and understood in relation to the theological tradition, or the Christian conception of love. As the Fourth Gospel reveals, God is love. Love is God, and it is substantial. As a substance, love is to be found only in God. The love that is God moves all of creation in an upward motion towards Him. For Guido, the experience of love was tragic, for it led the lover to suffering and even death. In response to Guido Orlandi's question of whether love was life or death, Guido replied, "From Love's power death often comes," in his song beginning *Donna me prega*.[38] In contrast, in the *Vita Nuova*, the beloved is a messenger from God who leads the lover to new life and to God. As charity, Beatrice is no mere representation of substantial love but an active participant in the substantial love that is God. As such, she becomes the bridge between the human and the divine.

While embracing a Christian conception of love, Dante resolves Guido's conflict between the image of love, which is found in the beloved, and the ideal, substantial love itself. In this manner, Dante resolves the conflict between troubadour love and Christian love; between the love of woman and the love of God. For Guido, love is a force that has a descending order: it leads the lover on a downward spiral movement away from ideal love and beauty towards self-destruction and even death. But for Dante, love is a force that has an ascending order: it leads the lover on an upward journey towards salvation and transcendence, towards substantial love, or God. The beloved is a necessary component in this upward movement; she becomes the medium through which the lover reaches God. The beloved, a gift from God, is primary in the circular motion of love; she descends from Heaven so that she and her beloved may ascend back to Heaven. As a gift from God and in her miraculous nature, Beatrice brings those who look at her towards salvation.

The death of Beatrice (XXVIII) marks love's final movement towards Heaven. As Hollander notes, the last part of the *Vita Nuova* concerns itself with "*la nova materia*" (the new subject [XXX, i]), or with Beatrice "in death."[39] Through his *meravigliosa visione* Dante learns to understand Beatrice in relation to heavenly bliss. After her death, the references to Jeremiah (XXVIII, i; XXX, i), the Trinity (XXIX, iii), Jesus Christ (XL, i), and God Almighty (XL, vii) all lend credence to her divine significance. In the final stage of love, the beloved is loved not merely in her essence, or for herself, but in God. The *Vita Nuova* ends with the hope that one day Dante may once again see Beatrice, who in turn sees God. He promises to write about her heavenly significance at a later time – a promise that is ultimately fulfilled in his *Commedia*. In effect, the *Vita Nuova* ends where it began – in Heaven. The book begins by referencing Beatrice's blessedness and heavenly origin (*la gloriosa donna della mia mente, la quale fu chiamata da molti Beatrice* – the heavenly lady of my mind, who was called by many Beatrice [*Vita Nuova* II, i]), and it ends with a vision of Beatrice in heaven. The cyclical journey of love has been completed, and Dante hopes that one day he will be able to rejoin Beatrice in that heavenly sphere from which she originated and to which she has returned.

Guido may have subscribed to the idea that love had a supernatural origin, but he rejected the possibility that the lover could reach bliss in the natural realm by means of loving the beloved. Accordingly, the beloved had a supernatural origin, but was less perfect than the ideal. In offering a life-affirming and less tragic conception of love, Dante's *Vita Nuova* offers a solution to Guido's conflict. For this reason, the *Vita Nuova* may be seen as a gift of friendship, perhaps, as Singleton notes, primarily for his first friend.[40] Dante's journey away from Guido and towards Beatrice continues well into the *Commedia*, where she returns in her blessedness to lead Dante towards divine bliss.

In addition to Guido Cavalcanti, friends in Dante's circle included Brunetto Latini, Forese Donati, Giovanni Villani, Cino da Pistoia, Lapo Gianni, and

Casella. Some of these relationships were quite complex. A good case in point is Dante's friendship with Cino da Pistoia.[41] While he is given great homage in *De vulgari Eloquentia*,[42] Cino is absent from the *Commedia*.[43] While most of the studies of the friendship between the two poets focus on Dante's poetic influence upon Cino,[44] some point to Cino as a source of poetic inspiration for Dante.[45] As was the custom, friends among the literary circles conversed by means of letters, poems, sonnets, songs (*canzoni*), and *tenzoni* written on parchment paper known as *brevi* or *cedole*.[46] Their exchanges revolved around topics such as love, friendship, and poetry. Often these literary compositions were passed on from one reader to another, thus shared among readers as a form of communication. Dante lived in a world where friendship and poetry were interlocked. As Teodolinda Barolini notes, in Dante there is a close link between "making poetry and making friends."[47] Conversing is a favourite activity among poets and among friends.[48] Friendship is a common theme in Dante's lyric poetry; indeed, it is one of his most important themes and can be traced back to his earliest *rime* (sonnets): *Guido, I' vorrei che tu e Lapo Ed Io, Deh Ragioniamo, Sonar bracchetti* (Guido, I wish that Lapo, thou, and I, Could be by spells conveyed, as it were now, Upon a barque), and *Volgete gli occhi* (Turn your eyes).[49] The interplay between poetry and friendship is also evident in *I' vegno 'l giorno a te 'nfinite volte* (I come to thee by daytime endless times [Cavalcanti, Sonnet XLI]). In this sonnet Guido addresses his friend's "abasement." Whether this abasement refers to the loss of Beatrice, as believed by Michele Barbi and others, or to Dante's distancing himself from the courtly love tradition, as believed by Francesco D'Ovidio and others, it is clear that Guido's sonnet expresses sincere concern: it is a poem written by a friend for the sake of a friend (very likely Dante) who is suffering.[50] The close link between poetry and friendship is further emphasized in the *Vita Nuova*, where Dante refers to writing as "speaking" (*parlare*), "saying words" (*dire parole*), and reading as "hearing" (*udire*).[51] The importance of speaking is also highlighted in *Inferno* 2, where *parola* (word) is used more often than in any other canto (in lines 43, 67, 111, 135, 137), and *parlare* (speaking) appears in lines 72, 113, and 126. As we shall see later in this study, it is by means of speaking and discourse that movement in *Inferno* 2 is initiated and changes occur. In the *Commedia,* the primacy of poetic discourse in friendship is most evident in Dante's encounter with Casella, Brunetto Latini, Forese Donati, and Statius.

Brunetto Latini was Dante's friend and teacher. What did Dante and Brunetto have in common? Brunetto was an intellectual, a Florentine poet in exile, very much involved in the political life of his city. He was a leading literary and political figure from about 1266–94.[52] Whether it was Brunetto's *Tesoretto* that served as a model for the idea of an allegorical spiritual journey, or his *Tresor* that taught Dante how to achieve immortality through scholarly endeavors,[53] one thing is certain: Dante held Brunetto in high regards, as a loving father figure (*che' 'n la mente m'è fitta, e or m'accora, / la cara e buona imagine paterna / di voi quando nel mondo ad ora ad ora / m'insegnavate come l'uom s'etterna: / e quant'io l'abbia in grado,mentr'io vivo / convien che ne la mia lingua si scerna* – For I remember well and now lament / the cherished, kind, paternal image of You / when, there in the world, from time to time, / You taught me how man makes himself immortal. / And how much gratitude I owe for that / my tongue, while I still live, must give report [*Inf.* 15, 82–7]). Brunetto, in turn, addresses Dante with the type of tender affection that a father addresses his son when he says "O figliuol mio" (O my son [*Inf.* 15, 31]). The adjectives "*cara*" "*buona*" and "*paterna*," coupled with the noun "figliuol" and the possessive "mio" certainly are meant to recall the intimate and affectionate bond between a father and his son. Here, as in *Convivio* I, xii, 4–6, Dante's relationship with Brunetto reflects Aquinas's view of the union of father and son as being a union between two who are most like each other.[54]

Dante's encounter with Brunetto in *Inferno* 15 is a tender and touching moment, one that evokes paternal affection (v. 31; v. 83), reverence (v. 45), comfort (v. 60), honour (v. 70), kindness (v. 83), and gratitude (v. 86). As he recognizes Dante, Brunetto outstretches his arm to touch his hem, and unable to contain his joy he cries out: "*Qual maraviglia!*" ("What a wonder!" [*Inf.* 15, 24]). Similar to the encounter with Forese, Dante recognizes Brunetto despite his changed appearance (*ficcai li occhi per lo cotto aspetto, / sì che 'l viso abbrusciato non difese / la conoscenza sua al mio 'ntelletto* – I fixed my eyes on his scorched face / until beneath the charred disfigurement / I could discern the features that I knew [*Inf.* 15, 26–8]). Extending his hand towards Brunetto's face, Dante cries out "*Siete voi qui, ser Brunetto?*" ("Are You here, Ser Brunetto?" [*Inf.* 15, 30]). Brunetto and Dante walk and talk together, Brunetto walking on the lower path, following at Dante's hem, and Dante walking on the higher path, just away from the flames, with his head bowed *com'uom che reverente vada* (like one who walks in reverence [*Inf.* 15, 45]). In response to Brunetto's inquiry (*Inf.* 15, 46–8), Dante explains that his sinful state has brought him to Hell and points to his guide, as one who leads him (*Inf.* 15, 49–54). Brunetto then foretells Dante's promising career and exile, pointing to the "malignant, avaricious, envious and proud" Fiesolani as his political enemies (*Inf.* 15, 55–78). His final wish is for Dante to remember him through his work, the *Tesoretto* (*Inf.* 15, 119–20).

While Brunetto Latini was his teacher and friend, Forese Donati was a friend with whom Dante exchanged compositions written in a "low style."[55] Dante's encounter with Forese in *Purgatorio* 23 is one of the most touching scenes in the entire poem. It is a tender and intimate moment between two friends who, though separated by death, meet again in the realm of the dead. It is a scene that sheds light on the power and constancy of friendship – true friendship survives even death. Dante recognizes his friend by the mere sound of his voice, for Forese's visage and features had been disfigured. The sound of Forese's voice is "that spark" that "relit the memory / of his changed features / and I knew Forese's face" (*Purg.* 23, 46–8). That Dante recognizes his friend by the mere sound of his voice, the necessary tool for conversing, is significant, for it emphasizes the depth of their bond, but also the importance of speaking (*parlare*) in friendship. Forese implores Dante not to pay attention to his physical disfiguration (*Purg.* 49–51). In a spirit of true friendship, Forese shifts attention from himself and his own physical disfiguration, misery, and suffering to his friend's well-being when he says *ma dimmi il ver di te, dì chi son quelle / due anime che là ti fanno scrota; / non rimaner che tu non mi favelle*! (but give me news about yourself / and tell me of those two souls over there, / escorting you. Do not hold back your answer [*Purg.* 23, 52–4]). As is customary in friendship, Forese asks Dante to speak the truth and not to hold back. In true humility and still intent on Forese's disfigured face, Dante delays speaking about himself ("*La faccia tua, ch'io lagrimai già morta, / mi dà pianger mo non minor doglia,*" / *rispuos'io lui,* "*veggendola sì torta* ... – 'Your face, over which I wept when you were dead, / now gives me no less cause for tears, / seeing it so disfigured,' I responded [*Purg.* 23, 55–7]). Like Forese, Dante's primary concern is for his friend's well-being rather than his own, and he asks what "withers away" his friend (*Però mi dì per Dio, che sì vi sfoglia; / non mi far dir mentr'io mi maraviglio, / ché mal può dir chi è pien d'altra voglia* – In God's name, tell me what so withers you away. / Don't make me speak while I am so astounded, / for a man intent on other things speaks ill [*Purg.* 23, 58–60]). Dante fears that his astonishment at Forese's disfigurement might get in the way of his speech.

Dante's recognition of Forese's voice brings to mind a similar episode with Casella. It is only after Dante hears Casella's voice that he recognizes his old friend: *Soavemente disse ch'io posasse; / allor conobbi chi era e pregai / che, per parlarmi, un poco s'arrestasse* (Gently he requested that I stop. / Then I knew him. And I asked him / to stay a while and speak with me [*Purg.* 2, 85–7]). The episode with Casella, recalling the equally affectionate encounter with Forese, serves to remind the reader of the primacy of *parlare* in friendship, and that true friendship survives even death (*Così com'io t'amai / nel mortal corpo, così t'amo sciolta* ... – "Even as I loved you in my mortal flesh," he said, / "so do I love you freed from it" [*Purg.* 2, 88–9]). After recognizing Casella, Dante asks his old friend to stay a bit and speak to him. Casella consents, and while professing his unwavering love for Dante, he questions his friend as to why he is in Hell (*Purg.* 2, 89–90). Dante explains that his journey is a prelude to a second and final journey, and in turn wants to know why Casella had to wait so long to get there ("*Casella mio, per tornar altra volta / là dov'io son, fo io questo viaggio" / diss'io; "ma a te com'è tanta ora tolta?"* – "O Casella, I make this voyage to return / another time," I said, "here where I've come. / But why did it take you so much time to get here?" [*Purg*. 2, 91–3]).[56] Casella explains that he was denied a seat in the ship many times. Perhaps Casella was not ready to begin his journey towards God. As Hollander suggests, he may have lacked the necessary fervour for such a journey.[57] Whatever the case may be, the episode with Casella highlights the constancy of friendship. The exchange of embraces, smiles, gentle gestures, and affectionate words all serve to remind the reader that this is a tender and loving moment between two friends. One can only imagine the overwhelming joy Dante must have felt in hearing the voice of his beloved lost friend as he affectionately smiles and embraces Dante.

Dante asks Casella to sing him a love song to soothe his soul, if no new law forbids it (*Purg*. 2, 106–11). The song that Casella sings is one of Dante's own songs, the second *canzone* in the *Convivio* composed in praise of Philosophy: *Amor che ne la mente mi ragiona* (Love that converses with me in my mind [*Purg*. 2, 112]).[58] To be sure, friends turn to each other in times of need, as friendship brings comfort and consolation. Traditionally, the willingness to provide assistance and consolation has been interpreted as a sign of friendship. That Dante courteously asks to be consoled and that Casella happily obliges to Dante's request does not surprise. What is surprising is the song that Casella sings. It is a song of praise for the *donna gentile*, a lady who in the *Convivio* managed to replace Beatrice. Dante here seems to regress to his old ways of loving. Both friends are slipping away from the "new law" towards secular matters, songs of praise for Philosophy. In the *Divine Comedy* it is Beatrice, rather than philosophy, who guides the soul towards salvation. While bringing consolation, the old song initiates Dante's regression into an old way of loving, thus it is dangerous. The song is so enticing that all present are spellbound (*Noi eravam tutti fissi e attenti / a le sue note* – We were spellbound, listening to his notes [*Purg*. 2, 118]). The listeners are fixated on the song and linger behind instead of climbing the slope towards salvation.[59] It is Cato's rebuke that drives the "laggard spirits" to climb up the Mountain of Purgatory (*Purg*. 2, 118–21).[60] Implicit in the Casella episode is the power of discourse and, more specifically, the power of poetic discourse. Also implicit in the Casella episode is the interplay between poetry and friendship and between philosophy and friendship.

The word "*consolare*" (to console) in verse 109 brings to mind the *Donna Gentile* in the *Convivio* and Lady Philosophy in Boethius's *Consolation of Philosophy*.[61] *Consolare* acquires significance within the interplay between friendship and philosophy. Through his celebration of philosophy, Casella consoles his friend as the *Donna Gentile* and as Lady Philosophy had done in the earlier works. In chapter two of this study, it was noted how in the third book of the *Convivio* Dante draws an analogy between friendship and philosophy.[62] In that passage, while referencing Book 9 of the *Nicomachean Ethics*, Dante argues that just as the efficient cause of true friendship is virtue, the efficient cause of philosophy is truth. And while the end of friendship is the happiness experienced in living the rational life in proximity to friends, the end of philosophy is the happiness attained in the perception of truth. Dante, like Aristotle, understood the importance of both philosophy and friendship in relation to moral perfection and happiness. Unlike Aristotle, however, Dante's journey towards ultimate perfection and happiness is an ascent towards divinity. The opening lines of the *Convivio* support Boethius's claim in Book III of the *Consolation* that philosophy is the means by which to satisfy one's natural hunger for happiness. In *Purgatorio*, however, the goal is supernatural bliss.[63] In moving the soul towards truth and goodness, philosophy lifts the soul up towards the moral goodness and happiness. And yet, philosophy cannot lead to ultimate bliss, since that is under the jurisdiction of theology, an activity grounded in divine wisdom. Casella's song is an inappropriate choice to sing in *Purgatorio*, since it is a place where only those songs that give praise to God are permissible.[64] The intellectual "*pane*" (bread) shared in the *Convivio*[65] can no longer satiate in the *Commedia*. While transcending passionate love, the song fails to celebrate divine love. And while providing comfort and enchantment, the words obscure ultimate truth, rather than revealing it. Let us return to the episode of Forese, where the primacy of conversation in friendship is even more marked.

Close to the end of *Purgatorio* 23, Dante tells Forese *se tu riduci a mente / qual fosti meco, e qual io teco fui, / ancor fia grave il memorar presente* (If you recall / what you were with me and I was with you, / that memory now would be painful [*Purg.* 23, 115–17]). Even those commentators who understand "what you were with me and I was with you" (*Purg.* 23, 116) to mean the actual relationship that Dante had with Forese fail to understand the full implication of the line. They conclude that what brings pain is the memory of, to use Benvenuto's words, *delectabilia non honesta* (improper pleasures) that the two shared during their relationship.[66] I would add that the memory of the friendship, and of the happiness they derived from it, brings pain because both were incomplete and imperfect in their exclusion of God. Their earthly friendship was formed on a misguided type of love. Each friend loved the other in and for himself, rather than in and for the love of God. In Purgatory, a place where both friends have good reason to hope for better and for a more complete happiness, the memory of an earlier incomplete friendship is cause for pain. Dante's conversation with

Forese continues well into *Purgatorio* 24, where we meet the two friends walking and talking.

The interplay between "walking" (*l'andar*) and "talking" (*dir*), between "motion" (*l'andar*) and "conversing" (*ragionamento*) in *Purgatorio* 24, 1–3 highlights the primacy of discourse in friendship. Neither did walking slow their talking, nor did talking slow their walking. In fact, the act of conversing seems to speed both along the way. The focus here is on the two friends, Dante and Forese, who are walking while talking – we have not heard from Virgil since the fifteenth line of the previous canto. But while Virgil is here silent, we still hear about him through Dante's indirect reference to him in relation to Statius, who is moving along more slowly than he normally would, out of respect and admiration for Virgil (*Purg.* 24, 8–9). While the immediate focus is on Dante and Forese, and on their dialogue, we get a glimpse of the other pair, Virgil and Statius, who are also moving along together. Here are four poets (two of which are classical), grouped in pairs, whose affinity and affection for each other is shared and mirrored through their conversation and proximity as they converse and move along together. In a primary way, conversation is the means by which both poets and friends interact and arrive at truth.

The centrality of conversation witnessed in *Purgatorio* 23 and 24 can be traced back to *Purgatorio* 22, where Dante follows Virgil and Statius while listening to their conversation (*Elli givan divanzi, e io soletto / di* retro, e *ascoltava i lor sermoni, / ch' a poetar mi davano intelletto* – They went along in front and I, alone, / came on behind, listening to their discourse, / which gave me understanding of the art of verse [*Purg.* 22, 127–9]).[67] As Virgil himself explains, his love for Statius predates their encounter and dates back to the time when Juvenal descended into Limbo and informed Virgil of Statius's affection for him. Virgil's goodwill towards Statius was grounded in the knowledge that Statius had affectionate feelings for him (*mia benvoglienza inverso te fu quale / più strinse mai di non vista persona* – was as great / as anyone has ever felt for someone never seen [*Purg.* 22, 16–17]). Statius's virtuous character and the knowledge of his affection for him were the source of Virgil's amicable feelings towards Statius. In turn, Virgil's poetic skill was the source of Statius's affection for him.

While inquiring about the sin of avarice, Virgil requests that Statius speak to him as a friend (*Ma dimmi, e come amico mi perdona /se troppo sicurtà m' allarga il freno, / e come amico omai meco ragiona* – But tell me – and as a friend forgive me / if with too much assurance I relax the reins, and as a friend speak with me now [*Purg.* 22, 19–21]). Fearing that his questioning may be interpreted as a form of intrusiveness, Virgil asks to speak with Statius *come amico* (as a friend [*Purg.* 22, 19]).[68] In prefacing his question with the words *come amico*, Virgil hopes to gain Statius's trust and alleviate his fears. Virgil and Statius both know that when one converses with friends, even about the most unpleasant matters, one is looking neither to offend nor to find fault, but to simply find truth. Virgil's question is asked in a spirit of friendship and, as such, it has roots in benevolence. Statius well understands this point. Rather than taking offence at the question, Statius smiles and welcomes Virgil's words as a sign of affection (*Queste parole Stazio mover fenno / un poco a riso pria; poscia rispuose: 'Ogne tuo dir d'amor m'è caro cenno* – These words made Statius smile a little / before he answered: 'Every word of yours / is to me a welcome token of your love' [*Purg.* 22, 25–7]). Friends welcome each other's questions, for they know that it is in questioning and in answering that they will arrive at a common understanding of truth.[69] To borrow Fabrizio's words to Ruccelai in Macchiavelli's *Art of War,* "when one converses with friends one simply discusses, one is not finding fault."[70] Friendship is grounded in honesty and truth, rather than in secrecy and deception.

Virgil continues his questioning. Given the lack of evidence in Statius's works, he wonders when and how Statius was converted to Christianity (*Purg.* 22, 55–63). Statius's answer is clear enough: it was Virgil who led him to his love of poetry and to his love of God (*Tu prima m'inviasti / verso Pernasso a ber ne le sue grotte, / e prima appresso Dio m'alluminasti* – It was you who first / set me towards Pernassus to drink in its grottoes, / and you who first lit my way towards God [*Purg.* 22, 64–6]). According to Statius, Virgil served as a source of moral inspiration for others who came after him, though he himself did not see the light (*Facesti come quei che va di notte, / che porta il lume dietro e sé non giova, / ma dopo sé fa le persone dotte* – As one who goes by night, carrying / the light behind him – it is no help to him, / but instructs all those who follow [*Purg.* 22, 67–9]). It was Virgil who inspired Statius to intellectual and moral excellence (*Per te poeta fui, per te cristiano* – Through you I was a poet, through you a Christian [*Purg.* 22, 73]).[71]

With its emphasis on virtue, knowledge, reciprocal benevolence, and a desire for truth, the relationship between Virgil and Statius resembles classical friendship. Upon a closer look, however, one realizes that in its ability to set Statius on the right path towards God and spiritual salvation, the relationship between the two poets transcends classical friendship. That Statius's conversion occurred through Virgil, a pagan, is a fact that continues to puzzle readers and scholars alike. Perhaps Statius's conversion might seem less puzzling once understood in light of the needed interaction between moral excellence and spiritual salvation. To fully grasp the importance of Virgil in relation to Statius's salvation, one must return to Virgil's discourse on love in *Purgatorio* 18.

In *Purgatorio* 18, Virgil gives a philosophical explanation of the process of love and explains how the image of the beautiful object arouses in the sensitive soul a desire for the beautiful. When Dante asks how we choose between good and bad, Virgil replies that the explanation to his question exceeds his own capacity to delve into the realm of faith. Hence, Virgil instructs Dante to ask Beatrice, who is well versed in faith. While admitting to his own shortcomings regarding the recognition of ultimate good, Virgil asserts the importance of reason in love. He explains that while all love is natural, only love that is ruled by reason is morally good (*Purg.* 18, 40–75). The type of love Virgil here has in mind stands in direct opposition to that experienced by Dido. The moral life promoted by the virtuous pagan is a necessary precondition for spiritual perfection. While inadequate in matters of faith, Virgil's virtue – his moral excellence – is a necessary precondition to spiritual salvation. It is Virgil who leads Dante to Beatrice, and it is Virgil who leads Statius to God. Lacking in faith, Virgil is unable to speak the Word directly, and yet, as the prime example of moral excellence, he becomes a messenger of the Word. As such, Virgil plays a primary role in Statius's conversion. Furthermore, he plays a primary role in the perfection of Statius's poetic skills.

In *Purgatorio* 21, during their initial meeting, Statius traces his own poetic abilities to Virgil and to the *Aeneid*, as the divine torch from which he derived his own poetic inspiration (*Al mio ardor fuor seme le faville, / che mi scaldar, de la divina fiamma / onde sono allumati più di mille* – The spark that kindles the fire in me / came from the holy flame / from which more than a thousand have been lit [*Purg.* 21, 94–6]), and finally refers to Virgil's *Aeneid* as his *mamma* and nurse (*de l'Eneïda dico, la qual mamma / fummi, e fummi nutrice, poetando:* – I mean the *Aeneid.* When I wrote my poems / it was my *mamma* and my nurse [*Purg.* 21, 97–8]). Once again, poetic discourse serves as a source of inspiration, comfort, and consolation. Dante himself confirms Statius's poetic debt to Virgil as he introduces him as *quel Virgilio dal qual tu togliesti / forte a cantar de li uomini e d'i dèi* (the very Virgil from whom you took the power to sing of men and of gods [*Purg.* 21, 125–6). In confirming Statius's poetic debt to Virgil in his own poetic composition, Dante is admitting his own debt to Virgil.[72] By means of discourse and, more particularly, by means of poetic discourse, friends and poets are moved to action, to artitstic creation, and even to spiritual salvation.

Following our discussion of the *Vita Nuova*, we may now proceed to a study of *Inferno* 2, a canto that celebrates the interplay between *amor* (love) and *amicizia* (friendship), discourse and friendship, movement and friendship.

Chapter Six

Amor and *Amicizia* in *Inferno* 2

The changes that occur in *Inferno* 2 are studied here in relation to discourse and friendship, and in relation to the interplay between love (*amor*) and friendship (*amicizia*). The salvific power of friendship is reflected in the changes, movement, and discourse that transpire in the course of the canto, and it is by means of discourse that friends are moved both to compassion and to action. By exploring this theme, *Inferno* 2 brings to the foreground the importance of friendship in the wayfarer's journey towards happiness.[1] It is an act of friendship that draws Dante out of his *stasis* and spiritual misery to experience eternal happiness.[2] Along these lines, friendship will be viewed as a handmaiden to spiritual happiness and perfection.

Dante's journey towards perfection and happiness occurs by means of a hierarchy of friends – Virgil and Beatrice – who initiate and facilitate this movement towards higher degrees of vision and truth by means of compassion, active benevolence, and guidance. Virgil and Beatrice do not merely wish Dante good: they become integral parts of his goodness. Notwithstanding their lengthy speeches, Virgil and Beatrice are not passive observers so much as they are active participants who help Dante in words and in deed. Beatrice descends from Heaven and reaches Limbo to enlist Virgil's assistance so that Dante may be saved.[3] Compassion moves her to act on Dante's behalf (*Oh pietosa colei che mi soccorse!* – O how compassionate was she to help me [*Inf.* 2, 133]). She in turn moves Virgil, first to compassion, (*nel primo punto che di te mi dolve* – when first I felt compassion for you),[4] and then physically to action. He leaves Limbo to arrive at the *selva oscura* (dark wood [*Inf.* 1, 2]) to lead Dante to safety (*E venni a te così com'ella volse: / d'innanzi a quella fiera ti levai / che del bel monte il corto andar ti tolse* – And so I came to you just as she wished. / I saved you from the beast denying you / the short way to the mountain of delight [*Inf.* 2, 118–20]). Both friends travel great distances to ensure Dante's safety and well-being. Distance makes their friendship more palpable and real. By means of his union with each, Dante's will and intellect are corrected and perfected. *Amor*, the ultimate moving force, is mediated through the intercession of benevolent friends.

In a primary sense, Dante's journey begins with Inferno 2.[5] It is here that both Dante and the reader learn about the heavenly story. It is here also that the journey is placed under auspices of *amor* and *amicizia*, and that the interplay between Virgil and Beatrice is established in relation to Dante's salvation. My discussion of *Inferno* 2 centres on three key moments in the canto. The first is found at the beginning, when despite Virgil's presence, Dante feels alone and refers to himself (*e io sol uno* – and I, alone [*Inf.* 2, 3]). The second passage is located at the point when Beatrice speaks to Virgil in Limbo and refers to Dante as *l'amico mio e non de la ventura* (my friend, who is no friend of Fortune [*Inf.* 2, 61]). The third passage appears as Beatrice terms love the force behind her descent to Limbo, as with her speech, *Amor mi mosse che mi fa parlare* (The love that moved me makes me speak [*Inf.* 2, 72]). Each of these pivotal passages places Dante's journey within a context of friendship, as a progression away from isolation and misery towards inclusion and happiness, stressing the importance of both Beatrice and Virgil in relation to Dante's salvation. As will be shown, the first passage stresses Dante's alienated self, through a preoccupation with his subjective "I." In the second passage, Beatrice identifies herself as a true friend to Dante. And in the third passage, the necessary link between *amor* (love) and *amicizia* (friendship) is implicitly established.

Traditionally, *Inferno* 2 has been viewed as a prologue to the first canticle,[6] and *Inferno* 1 as the preface to the entire *Commedia*. This distinction is emphasized by the invocation's position in the second canto rather than in the first, as is the case with the other two canticles.[7] Notwithstanding this categorization, as many commentators have noted, structural similarities between the first two cantos create a sense of continuity and unity. Some of the events in *Inferno* 2 echo those in *Inferno* 1. For instance, the last verse of the second canto, *intrai per lo cammino alto e silvestro*, echoes the beginning of the first canto, *cammin* (v. 1), *selva* (v. 2), *intrai* (v. 10) and *alto* (v. 16).[8] Richard Lansing notes the parallel movement from fear to hope and from hope to fear.[9] While at the beginning of *Inferno* 1, Dante is impeded by external obstacles (the three beasts), at the beginning of the second canto, his own fears and doubts stand in his way. In both cantos, it is Virgil who by means of *parlare* (speaking) serves as a source of comfort, courage, hope, and strength.

Parlare holds a primary role in *Inferno* 2. As will be shown, by means of speaking, characters are moved, first emotionally (to compassion) and then physically (to action). *Parola* (word) is in fact used more often here than in any other canto (at lines 43, 67, 111, 135, 137), while *parlare* (used at lines 72, 113, 126) parallels *paura* (fear) in *Inferno* 1, which comes up five times.[10] The extensive use of dialogue in the canto has led some scholars to view *Inferno* 2 as "the canto of the word."[11] The use of dialogue and the lack of explicit action have led others to erroneously label *Inferno* 2 as the "canto of *stasis*."[12] It is a label that fails in light of the major emotional changes and physical movement that take place in the canto. Rachel Jacoff and William Stephany take into account the important inward changes that occur in Dante in his interaction with others and the world around him and characterize *Inferno* 2 as "a canto of motion."[13] While their characterization is indeed true, as we shall see shortly, the authors fail to note the primacy of friendship in relation to movement. In contrast to those who interpret the extensive use of dialogue as a sign of *stasis*, one must here argue that in effect it is by means of dialogue, of *parlare*, and, more particularly, by means of the language of friendship that movement is initiated and changes occur.[14] In short, *Inferno* 2 highlights the power of *parlare* in relation to friendship and truth.

While commentators note the relationship of discourse and motion, discourse and compassion, and love and motion,[15] they fail to appraise the relationship of discourse and friendship, *amor* (love) and *amicizia* (friendship), and friendship and poetry. For Jacoff and Stephany, the relationship between language and motion in *Inferno* 2 establishes the potential role of poetry in the poem.[16] While their observation is indeed a valid one, the authors fail to note the potential role of poetry in relation to friendship; ultimately, they fail to grasp the power of friendship in the poem. As seen earlier in this study, conversation is primary in friendship; through conversation, friends arrive at a common understanding of truth. Conversation strengthens the bond of friendship, and, as Aristotle notes, friendship is an activity that leads to perfection and happiness. While establishing the potential role of poetry through the relationship between language and motion, *Inferno* 2 also establishes the potential role of friendship through its relationship with conversation and with poetry. As will be shown, the changes that occur in *Inferno* 2 must be understood within the context of friendship, as an active relationship.

At the opening of *Inferno* 2 friendship is indirectly evoked through the theme of alienation. Despite Virgil's presence, Dante describes himself as being alone (*e io sol uno* – and I, alone [*Inf.* 2, 3]), a phrase that accurately renders the depth of his isolation. Alienation is portrayed through Dante's preoccupation and obsessive concern with his personal I (*io*), a pronoun used five times in the span of four lines.[17] The somber atmosphere and heavy tone established by the nocturnal setting further intensifies his sense of estrangement. As Siro A. Chimenz notes, the nocturnal setting mirrors Dante's loss of hope and faith.[18]

Night signals the abyss that assails Dante's spirit, or as Mazzoni notes, it signals his distance from God.[19] In distancing himself from God, Dante distances himself from the community of God. At this point in the journey, Dante feels alone because he loves and knows himself in a limited way. He does not yet comprehend the power of *caritas*. As Augustine notes, *caritas* universalizes love, directing it to a community of individuals united in faith (*Conf.* IV, IV). As Dante is about to delve into the abyss of Hell, an act of friendship alone can save him.

Commentators have read the verse *e io sol uno* in various ways. Some find in it an affirmation of an allegorical interpretation of Virgil as Reason,[20] while others hear echoes of classical literature.[21] Against Buti's allegorical interpretation and by calling attention to Virgil's historical identity, Hollander presents a moral interpretation of the line: despite Virgil's presence, Dante is morally alone.[22] The notion that Dante is morally alone, since he alone can change, may amount to a valid excursus, though it diminishes the primacy of Virgil and his friendship. While it may well be the case that change ultimately lies with Dante himself, it is also true that by means of Virgil's compassion, discourse, and active benevolence Dante's spirit is awakened to the light of hope. It is Virgil who, through his discourse, draws Dante out of his *stasis*. In contrast to Buti's allegorical reading and Hollander's moral reading of the line, it must here be argued that at the beginning of *Inferno* 2, Dante stands alone because in his limited vision he does not understand his journey as a gift of divine grace and *caritas*.

The claim that Dante is alone at the beginning of *Inferno* 2 because Virgil's lack of faith means he cannot provide moral support seems to overlook a few important points. First, it does not take into consideration that in choosing Virgil as his guide, Dante confirms, to a certain extent, Virgil's moral authority. It also ignores the fact that while fallible in spiritual matters, Virgil is the epitome of moral excellence and earthly perfection. While it is true that Virgil can rise no further than the Earthly Paradise, it is equally true that he sets Dante on the path to Beatrice, thus taking him closer to spiritual perfection. As Auerbach observes, Virgil is chosen both for his poetic mastery and his moral excellence, his *iustitia* and *pietas*.[23] As the embodiment of *iustitia* and *pietas*, therefore, Virgil is more than qualified to lend moral support. He is more than qualified to lead Dante to the very threshold of a new vision into a new world of eternal happiness. Having lived before the advent of Christ, Virgil is also free of moral blame, although he seems at times not to think so. As one of the honourable and virtuous pagans in Limbo, he is free of sin. As Virgil himself notes, the virtuous pagans are those who did not sin (*Inferno* 4, 34). Later, while discussing the moral virtues, he again refers to the pagans as those without sin (*sanza vizio /*

connober l'altre e seguir tutte quante – yet blameless, / knew the others and followed every one [*Purg.* 7, 35–6]). While lacking in faith, as one of the virtuous pagans, Virgil is more than capable of serving as moral guide.

Feeling alone and assailed by fears, Dante hesitates and questions his own abilities and merit in the light of his challenge (*Poeta che mi guidi, / guarda la mia virtù s'ell' è possente, / prima ch' a l'alto passo tu mi fidi* – Poet, you who guide me, / consider if my powers will suffice / before you trust me to this arduous passage [*Inf.* 2, 10–12]). While at the end of the first canto he had confidently accepted the challenge set before him (*Allor si mosse, e io li tenni dietro* – Then he set out and I came on behind him [*Inf.* 1, 136]), he regresses at the beginning of the second, fearing that his journey might lead to madness (*temo che la venuta non sia folle* – I fear it may be madness [*Inf.* 2, 35]). In comparison to both Aeneas and St Paul he does not deem himself worthy of so great a journey (*Ma io, perché venirvi? O chi 'l concede? / Io non Enëa, io non Paulo sono; / me degno a ciò né io né altri 'l crede* – But why should I go there? Who allows it? I am not Aeneas, nor am I Paul. / Neither I nor any think me fit for this [*Inf.* 2, 31–2]). Considering the political importance of Aeneas's voyage and the spiritual significance of Paul's journey, it is not surprising that their voyages should receive divine sanction.[24] Why should Dante be granted the same privilege? While in the first canto he had accepted the challenge, now, upon closer considerationon, he begins to doubt his own abilities and is assailed by fears.[25] He does not understand that like Aeneas's journey, his own has received divine sanction, but that unlike Aeneas's journey, his will lead to ultimate happiness, the beatific vision of God. In a state of moral confusion, Dante cannot comprehend the sense of his own words. Trusting in Virgil's wisdom, he asks the Roman poet to interpret the true meaning of his words (*Se' savio; intendi me' ch'i' non ragiono* – You are wise, / you understand what I cannot express [*Inf.* 2, 36]). Virgil interprets Dante's words as a sign of cowardice rather than humility.[26] He interprets Dante's *non essere degno* (not fit [*Inf.* 2, 33]) as cowardice and remarks *s'i' ho ben la parola tua intesa, / ... l'anima tua è da viltade offesa* (if I have rightly understood your words, / ... your spirit is assailed by cowardice [*Inf.* 2, 43–5]). By exposing the cowardice behind the apparent humility, Virgil effectively teaches Dante that *caritas* is, as a gratuitous gift of grace, less grounded in merit than on grace. Ironically, Virgil, the pagan poet who has seen Christ,[27] teaches Dante important lessons about *caritas*.

In an attempt to explain Dante's change of heart at the opening of *Inferno* 2, Jacoff and Stephany look to Virgil for answers. The authors argue that at the end of the first canto, Virgil had responded to Dante's individual crisis inappropriately, by providing a universal solution in the prophecy of the Veltro.[28] They argue that Virgil implies but never makes clear the connection between the prophecy of the Veltro and Dante's individual journey. However, towards the end of *Inferno* 1, Virgil tells Dante that for his own sake it is best that he follow him (*Inf.* 1, 112–13). Dante's response to Virgil would seem to indicate that he understood the particular and personal significance of the journey (*a ciò ch'io fugga questo male e peggio, / che tu mi meni là dov'or dicesti, / sì ch'io veggia la porta di san Pietro / e color cui tu fai cotanto mesti. / Allor si mosse, e io li tenni dietro* – So that I may escape this harm and worse, / lead me to the realms you've just described / that I may see St. Peter's gate / and those you tell me are so sorrowful. / Then he set out and I came on behind him [*Inf.* 1, 132–6]). Dante seemed to have understood the purpose of his personal journey: to escape his present precarious situation and his eternal damnation. Even if, as Jacoff and Stephany argue, in *Inferno* 1, Virgil had failed to make a clear connection between the prophecy of the Veltro and Dante's personal journey, in *Inferno* 2 he clarifies matters by recounting the heavenly story he had heard from Beatrice, which establishes a direct link between Dante's personal journey and *amor*, the love that moves all things in the universe.

In effect, Dante's change of heart at the beginning of *Inferno* 2 mirrors his own limited vision. What is his journey if not a movement towards a better vision? This higher vision requires a shift in focus, from self to the other, from a subjective and limited understanding of truth to a more encompassing understanding of universal truth. It requires Dante's perspective to shift from a limited awareness of self to an awareness of self in relation to others, and ultimately, in relation to God through the transfiguring power of *caritas*. The use of *nostra vita* (our life [*Inf.* 1, 1]) and *mi ritrovai* (I came to myself [*Inf.* 1, 2]) in the first two verses of the first canto highlights the interlocking of particular truth (subjective "I") and universal truth (Other). While Dante the author seems cognizant of the close link between the two types of truths, Dante the pilgrim, still lacking in self awareness, struggles to comprehend the connection. In the second canto, the phrase *io sol uno* (I alone [Inf. 2, 3]) marks a radical shift from universal truth to particular truth, from an objective reality to a subjective reality, from outer world to Dante's inner world of fears and alienation. Despite Virgil's presence, Dante is vulnerable and overwhelmed by the challenges and struggles set before him and feels estranged from himself and his environment. The increasing agony of his estrangement prevents him from seeing that there is indeed cause to hope for better. His estrangement is debilitating; it simultaneously prevents him from knowing himself in relation to a higher truth and drags him deeper into *stasis*.

At this point in the journey, Dante understands himself as an isolated entity. He does not comprehend that, ultimately, one does not know oneself in isolation; to truly know oneself one must know the Other, or to borrow Giuseppe Mazzotta's words, "… to know oneself one has to know the whole … one knows oneself only in the light of the whole."[29] In *Inferno* 2, Dante is on the verge of a new way of seeing. He is on the verge of seeing his personal journey in relation to a higher and more encompassing truth, or in relation to *amor*, the force by means of which all things are moved towards transcendence and perfection. Through the heavenly story he narrates, Virgil dispels the shadows of fears and doubts that assail Dante's spirit, drawing Dante outside of himself and his subjective "I," towards an appreciation of *caritas*, as a force that universalizes love, directing it towards a community of individuals united in faith.[30] While it is true that Virgil and Dante have not yet "shared the traditional peck of salt"[31] that is neeeded in friendship, through Virgil's discourse, assistance, and guidance Dante is brought to new clarity and elucidation.

In the first canto (*Inf.* 1, 130) and again at the beginning of the second (*Inf.* 2, 10), Dante is still thinking of Virgil primarily as a poet, and in particular, as the poet from whom he learned his own poetic style. Dante errs in believing that the love of poetry he shares with Virgil will get him out of this spiritual predicament and that secular knowledge is the path to redemption.[32] He erroneously believes that salvation can be reached by means of poetic perfection and human wisdom,[33] although Virgil himself makes it clear that the literary path is no longer sufficient. In *Inferno* 1, in response to Dante's fears, Virgil explains that to escape the imminent danger, a different path must be taken (*Inf.* 1, 91–3). He implicitly evokes Beatrice as one whose authority is above his own when he says *anima fia a ciò più di me degna* (you'll find a soul more fit to lead than I [*Inf.* 1, 122]). In the *Commedia*, while Virgil is the master of verse from whom Dante has taken his poetic style, he is also a messenger of divine truth. That Virgil is a messenger of divine truth becomes ever so clear in the Statius episode.[34] It was Virgil, who through his example and by means of the fourth Eclogue, taught Statius how to be a poet and a Christian (*Purg.* 22, 73). While Statius's conversion is Dante's fictional creation, the episode serves to underscore the importance of Virgil in the light of spiritual salvation,[35] as his fictional conversion is a parallel for Dante's real conversion.[36] In *Inferno* 2, Dante begins to learn about the limits of poetry.[37] He learns that spiritual perfection is ultimately obtained by means of divine grace.

By describing his encounter with Beatrice in Limbo, Virgil moves Dante both emotionally – *Tu m'hai con disiderio il cor disposto / sì al venir con le parole tue, / ch'i' son tornato nel primo proposto* (Your words have made my heart / so eager for the journey / that I've returned to my first intent [*Inf.* 2, 136–8]) – and physically – *e poi che mosso fue, / intrai per lo cammino alto e silvestro* (and when he moved ahead / I entered on the deep and savage way [*Inf.* 2, 141–2]). Ultimately it is through Virgil's discourse that Dante's spirit is awakened (*Inf.* 2, 37–42) to resolution and hope, and he is physically moved to action (*Inf.* 2, 136–8). While discourse is indeed an expression, or articulation of movement, it is also the basis of friendship. By means of discourse, friends arrive at a common understanding of truth. Indeed, Virgil draws Dante out of his paralysis to embrace the challenge set before him by relaying the story of compassion and *caritas* that Beatrice told him in Limbo (*Inf.* 2, 49–126). Mary, who is *donna gentile* (a gracious lady [*Inf.* 2, 94]), feels compassion for Dante and moves Lucy to compassion and action. In her compassion for Dante and by means of her discourse, Lucy in turn moves Beatrice to compassion, who then descends to Limbo and by means of her own discourse moves Virgil to compassion and action (*nel primo punto che di te mi dolve* – when first I felt compassion for you [*Inf.* 2, 51]). Lucy is dismayed by Beatrice's seeming lack of compassion for Dante (*loda di Dio vera, / chè non soccorri quei che t'amò tanto, / ch'uscì per te de la volgare schiera?* – Beatrice, true praise of God, / why do you not help the one who loved you so / that for your sake he left the vulgar herd? [*Inf.* 2, 103–5]). Lucy's appeal to Beatrice's dual nature –her divinity and her humanity – moves Beatrice to compassion and action (*Inf.* 2, 103–5). While reminding Beatrice that it was for her sake that Dante left *la volgare schiera*, Lucy recalls the *Vita Nuova*.[38] This was a time when Dante turned away from a more conventional love of poetry to what he names the *dolce stil novo*,[39] a poetry that celebrates Beatrice in her higher and Christological significance.[40] In retrospect, Lucy's harsh tone is justified. Why is Beatrice seemingly indifferent to the suffering of her friend? Why is she not rushing to his rescue at a time when he most needs her help? Does she not hear his anguished cry and does she not see the imminent danger facing him (*Inf.* 2, 106–8)? Eager to deliver Dante from danger and lead her friend towards his good, Beatrice descends from her heavenly seat to seek Virgil's assistance in Limbo (*Inf.* 2, 109–14).

The story of compassion that begins with Mary and ends with Virgil, as told in *Inferno* 2, highlights the harmonious balance between *amor* (love) and *amicizia* (friendship), discourse and friendship, and action and friendship. Mary, a gracious heavenly lady (*Inf.* 2, 94), initiates the process of compassion that begins in the heavens and ends on earth. She moves Lucy, who in turn moves Beatrice, who then moves Virgil. Beatrice descends to Limbo and appeals to Virgil's secular nature, to his wisdom and moral excellence, to his courteous character (*cortese* [*Inf.* 2, 59]), and to his poetic speech (*Inf.* 2, 67). She trusts that through the power of his poetic discourse, Virgil will bring Dante to safety, telling him *or movi, e con la tua parola ornata / e con ciò c'ha mestieri al suo campare, / l'aiuta sì ch'i' ne sia consolata* (set out, and with your polished words / and whatever else is needed for his safety, / go to his aid, that I may be consoled [*Inf.* 2, 67–9]). The rhetorical emptiness in the line has not gone unnoticed. As one of the blessed Beatrice has no need for consolation. Chimenz reads the line as a testament of her dual nature; she is divine, yet capable of the most refined human emotion.[41] I would add that the line is also memorable for the importance it places on compassion and benevolence as essential elements in friendship. Beatrice, a true friend, will find consolation in the knowledge that Dante is safe and out of danger. She begins her speech with a sort of *captatio benevolentiae* in the hope that Virgil in turn will show benevolence to Dante. She then promises to praise Virgil to God once she returns to heaven. She ends her speech in the same way she had begun, by complimenting Virgil, and finally she weeps.[42] In turn, Virgil responds to Beatrice's tears by eagerly coming to Dante's rescue, saying *tanto m'aggrada il tuo comandamento, / che l'ubidir, se già fosse, m'è tardi; / più non t'è uo' ch'aprirmi il tuo talento* (so pleased am I at your command that my consent, / were it already given, would be given late. You have but to make your desire known [*Inf.* 2, 79–81]). Beatrice's tears and Virgil's response to them are signs of goodwill and thus of friendship. For as Cicero notes, "friendship cannot exist in the absence of goodwill."[43]

That Beatrice is a friend to Dante is a fact that she herself makes clear. In her plea to Virgil, she describes Dante as her friend rather than a friend of Fortune: *l'amico mio, e non de la ventura, / ne la diserta piaggia è impedito* (my friend, who is no friend of Fortune, / is so hindered on his way upon the desert slope [*Inf.* 2, 61–2]). Beatrice's famous declaration of friendship in *Inferno* 2 has stirred several interpretations.[44] In an enlightening study of *Inferno* 2, Jacoff and Stephany provide a rather thorough overview of the interpretive history of the line.[45] While studying the line in relation to friendship and in an effort to place it within a history of literary interpretation, a summary of the authors' overview is here provided. The more obvious and literal interpretation of the line is that Dante is a friend of Beatrice although he is a victim or an enemy of fortune. This interpretation, as noted by Jacoff and Stephany, dates back to Jacopo della Lana, Boccaccio, and l'Anonimo Fiorentino.[46] As the authors note, a common argument against this interpretation is that in 1300, the fictive time of the *Commedia,* Dante was in fact blessed with good fortune. Jacoff and Stephany contribute significantly to the interpretation of *Inferno* 2 when they expose the faultiness of this argument by pointing out the Boethian resonance in Dante's line. The authors call attention to the similarity between Beatrice's words and those of lady Philosophy in her discussion of fortune and friendship in the *Consolation of Philosophy*.[47] In the beginning of Book II of the *Consolation*, lady Philosophy warns Boethius against the deceptions of Fortune and of her friendship, saying *Intellego multiformes illius prodigii fucos et eo usque cum his quos eludere nititur blandissimam familiaritatem, dum intolerabili dolore confundat quos insperata reliquerit* (I know the many disguses of that monster, Fortune, and the extent to which she seduces with friendship the very people she is striving to cheat, until she overwhelms them with unbearable grief at the suddenness of her desertion).[48] Philosophy teaches Boethius a lesson about the paradoxical nature of good and bad fortune: good fortune deceives while bad fortune, through the constancy of her fickleness, instructs about the fragility of happiness. Philosophy concludes *nunc et amissas opes querere; quod pretiosissimum diuitiarum genus est amicos inuenisti*" (So you are weeping over lost riches when you have really found the most precious of all riches – friends who are true friends).[49] In losing what appeared to be his good fortune, wealth, power, and riches, Boethius found the most valuable asset – true friendship. The love of friends is a constant through fortunate times and unfortunate times. During unfortunate times, false friends disappear while true friends remain faithful in their love. While emphasizing the Boethian resonance in Dante's line, Jacoff and Stephany argue that in 1300, what then appeared to be Dante's good fortune in reality was his bad fortune.[50] Deceived by false goods, Dante had turned away from Beatrice. She, on the other hand, a true and committed friend, remained loyal in her love for Dante.

The depth of her love and devotion is asserted by Beatrice herself in *Purgatorio* 30, as part of her explanation to the angels for her harshness towards Dante (*Purg.* 30, 126–39). She explains that notwithstanding Dante's transgressions, after her death she continued to guide and inspire him (*questi si tolse a me, e diessi altrui / ... e volse i passi suoi per via non vera, / imagini di ben seguendo false – Né l'impetrare ispirazion mi valse, / con le quali e in sogno e altrimenti / lo rivocai: sì poco a lui ne calse! ... / Per questo visitai l'uscio d'i morti* – he took himself from me / and gave himself to others ... He set his steps upon an untrue way, / pursuing those false images of good ... useless the inspiration I sought and won for him, / as both with dreams and other means/ I called him back, so little did he heed them ... /And so I visited the threshold of the dead [*Purg.* 30, 126–39]). Beatrice had good reason to turn her back on Dante, yet she remained steadfast in her love for him.

Beatrice's friendship is as constant as is her love, it has survived death. As Cicero makes clear, the bond of friendship cannot be destroyed by death, so "a friend though absent or deceased lives in the memory of his friend."[51]

A second interpretation of this passage, one adopted by l'Ottimo, Guido da Pisa, Buti, and most sixteenth-century commentators, understands Dante's line as a reference to his love of Beatrice in her role as Theology or Revelation.[52] Still a third reading, one promoted by Benvenuto, understands the line to mean that Dante is the true friend of Beatrice, whose love is not subject to the whims of fortune.[53] In 1943, Mario Casella understood the line as a sign of Dante's disinterested love of Beatrice, not dissimilar to his love of the Beatrice in the *Vita Nuova*.[54] Sharing in Benedetto Croce's hostility towards any allegorical interpretation of poetry[55] and favoring Casella's reading, Mazzoni argues that all allegory is *forzatura interpretativa che nuoce alla poesia* (forced interpretation that harms poetry).[56] Accordingly, he rejects all allegorical interpretations of Beatrice.[57] Favouring the literal sense, Mazzoni understands the line to mean that, as a friend to Beatrice, Dante is not a friend to Fortune, not that he is a victim of Fortune.[58] Both Casella and Mazzoni note that Dante loves Beatrice with a kind of selfless love that bespeaks complete friendship. Mazzotta interprets *l'amico mio, e non de la ventura* (my friend, who is no friend of Fortune [*Inf.* 2, 61]) as preparation and prefiguration for their union in the Garden of Eden.[59] Whatever interpretation one may favor, it seems sensible not to ignore the Boethian echo. Reminiscent of Lady Philosophy's words in Book II of the *Consolation*, the contrast between friendship and Fortune in Beatrice's line parallels the contrast between true and false friendship. A union grounded in selfless love, character, and virtue, true friendship is constant through good times and bad. In contrast, false friendship, grounded in extrinsic and mutable attributes, alters in times of bad fortune. Beatrice served as a constant guide to Dante, even after her death: as she herself confirms, she came to him even in dreams.

The meaning of *amico mio e non de la ventura* (my friend, who is no friend of Fortune [*Inf.* 2, 61]) has been closely associated with another much-disputed tercet: *O donna di virtù, sola per cui / l'umana spezie eccede ogne contento / di quell ciel c'ha minor li cerchi sui* (O lady of such virtue that by it alone / the human race surpasses all that lies / within the smallest compass of the heavens [*Inf.* 2, 76–8]). Moore, Singleton, Jacoff, and Stephany all note the Boethian resonance in Beatrice's verse and in Virgil's response: Beatrice's line echoes Book II and Virgil's line echoes Book I of the *Consolation*.[60] According to Michele Barbi, Virgil was addressing *virtù* rather than Beatrice. For Barbi, Beatrice is Dante's beloved of the *Vita Nuova* and thus cannot also be allegory.[61] In favoring Barbi's interpretation, Giorgio Petrocchi removed the comma after *virtù* so that the focus is on *virtù* rather than on Beatrice.[62] Anxious to defend Beatrice's historical identity, Mazzoni favors Barbi's reading of the verse.[63] In contrast, Singleton firmly rejects Barbi's understanding of the line, viewing the literal reading of Beatrice as too limiting.[64] Establishing a close link between Beatrice's words and Virgil's response to them, Singleton reads the line from Virgil's perspective. In referring to Dante as "amico mio e non de la ventura," Singleton argues, Beatrice is speaking a language that Virgil is capable of understanding.[65] Accordingly, Virgil understands Beatrice in the only way he can, as an allegory in relation to the *donna gentile* in the *Convivio*.[66] This is not the case for Mazzoni. Intent on upholding the historical interpretation, Mazzoni overlooks the Boethian resonance in both lines, claiming that *il riscontro boeziano addotto da E. Moore non vincola quanto all'interpretazione* (the Boethian comparison alleged by E. Moore is not bound to the interpretation).[67] According to Mazzoni, Dante is not a friend to Fortune, but he is not a victim of Fortune.[68] The sense is that Beatrice establishes Dante as her friend in the true spiritual sense, though he is not friendly to Fortune. For Siro Chimenz, *O donna di virtù* echoes the *regina delle virtudi* of the *Vita Nuova*, a reference to Beatrice's human virtues. Accordingly, as a virtuous pagan, Virgil is here bestowing upon Beatrice the highest compliment he is capable of giving.[69] Commentators who hear the Boethian resonance in Beatrice's line go on to read it in relation to Virgil's response.[70] In noting the close link between Beatrice's words and Virgil's response, Singleton, More, Jacoff, and Stephany all seem to take into account the implied relation between Philosophy and Revelation, poetics and Theology. In defending Beatrice's dual nature, Singleton exposes the limitations of Barbi's literal reading and interprets it as a type of "heresy."[71]

While recognizing the Boethian resonance in both lines, hardly anyone today would see Beatrice as mere allegory. Of the various interpretations offered, the most encompassing seems to be that which recognizes Beatrice in her dual nature as both a historical and an allegorical figure.[72] In the *Commedia*, Beatrice exists simultaneously in her dual nature: she is both historical and Christological,[73] and scholars are quick to point out her resemblance to Christ. For Almicare Iannucci, Beatrice's descent in Limbo echoes Christ's harrowing of Hell, and in this manner she becomes a *figura Christi*.[74] Indeed, Beatrice is *loda di Dio vera* (true praise of God [*Inf.* 2, 103]) and *donna beata e bella* (So blessed and so fair [*Inf.* 2, 53]). However, she is also the beloved in the *Vita Nuova*, who has travelled great distances for the sake of her friend's well-being. Beatrice's human compassion is explicitly evoked through her tears for Dante (*Poscia che m'ebbe ragionato questo, / li occhi lucenti lagrimando volse* – After she had said these things to me, / she turned away her eyes, now bright with tears [*Inf.* 2, 115–16]). From Boccaccio's day to the present, commentators have recognized in Beatrice's tears a distinct sign of her humanity.[75] Her tears have been interpreted as another affirmation of her dual nature, but commentators have failed to interpret her tears as a sign of friendship. These are the tears of a friend who suffers because her friend is suffering. She shares in Dante's misfortune as if it were her own. Sharing in a friend's misfortune is a true mark of friendship, for as Cicero notes, "a friend places the well-being and interest of his friend before and above his own. He shares in the friend's success and his misfortunes as if it were his own."[76]

Virgil himself is amazed at the degree of Beatrice's selflessness. She is not concerned with her personal safety (*Inf.* 2, 82–4) and does not fear Hell. Virgil's surprise signals his own limitations in matters of religion.[77] He does not know that the blessed neither fear evil nor can they be harmed by it.[78] As a blessed soul, Beatrice is untouchable by the sufferings of Hell.[79] As she herself makes clear, she does not fear Hell since she cannot be harmed by its evil: "*Da che tu vuo' saver cotanto a dentro, / dirotti brievemente," mi rispuose, / "perch' i' non temo di venir qua entro / Temer si dee di sole quelle cose / c'hanno potenza di fare altrui male; / de l'altre no, ché non son paurose*" ("Since you are so eager to know more," / she answered, "I shall be brief in telling you / why I am not afraid to enter here. / We should fear those things alone / that have the power to harm. / Nothing else is frightening" [*Inf.* 2, 85–90]). Beatrice's only fear is for Dante, that he is so lost in self-deception that it might be too late for his salvation. As she says, *e temo che non sia già sì smarrito, / ch'io mi sia tardi al soccorso levata* (I fear he has gone so far astray / that I arose too late to help him [*Inf.* 2, 64–5]). Given the fact that the blessed have the ability to see things through divine knowledge of all time, Beatrice's fear for Dante would seem unfounded: she knows that he will be saved.[80] While Beatrice may know that her friend will be saved, Dante never says this; rather, the critics deduce it. While the narrative may betray a certain rhetorical emptiness behind both her fear for Dante (*Inf.* 2, 64–6) and her promise of praise to Virgil (*Inf.* 73–4), her friendship (*Inf.* 2, 61) and compassion for Dante (*Inf.* 2, 65–6) are rich with significance. Her fear for Dante is grounded in goodwill. She fears for his safety because she loves him. In contrast, Dante's fears at the beginning of the canto (*Inf.* 2, 35) are grounded in a misguided love of self: they are limiting and destructive; they immobilize him, preventing him from overcoming his limited self.[81] Assailed by self-doubts and fears, Dante does not understand that true freedom lies in transcendence, in the union of one individual with another.[82]

While being compassionate towards Dante, Beatrice is unmoved by Virgil's suffering (*I' son fatta da Dio, sua mercé, tale, / che la vostra miseria non mi tange, / né fiamma d'esto 'ncendio non m'assale* – I am made such by God's grace / that your affliction does not touch, / nor can these fires assail me [*Inf.* 2, 91–3]). The blessed reserve concern only for the living, those for whom there is still hope of salvation.[83] It is willed in the heavens, *duro giudicio*, (*Inf.* 2, 96) that the damned not be offered compassion. Virgil was *ribellante a la sua legge* (A rebel to His law [*Inf.* 1, 125]), and for that reason he is forever denied the gift of *caritas*. Beatrice is compassionate towards Dante, because there is still hope for his salvation. There is no hope for Virgil. Notwithstanding his *pietas* and *iustitia*, and through no fault of his own, Virgil resides among the souls who are damned. Beatrice's compassion for Virgil's suffering would be pointless. While serving as a messenger of divine truth, our magnanimous and virtuous poet is forever denied the light of perfect wisdom.

Dante does not seem to recognize nor appreciate his own good fortune. Why does he hesitate and think himself alone when in fact he has the loving support and devotion of three blessed ladies? Through a series of interrogatives Virgil voices his frustration:[84] *Dunque: che è? perché, perché restai, / perché tanta viltà nel cor allette, / perché ardire e franchezza non hai, / poscia che tai tre donne benedette / curan di te ne la corte di cielo, / e 'l mio parlar tanto ben ti promette* (What then? Why, why do you delay? / Why do you let such cowardice rule your heart? / Why are you not more spirited and sure, / when three such blessed ladies / care for you in Heaven's court / and my words promise so much good? [*Inf.* 2, 121–6]). Finally, by means of *vere parole* (the truthful words [*Inf.* 2, 135]), Virgil moves Dante to his *primo proposto* (that I've returned to my first intent [*Inf.* 2, 138) and Dante's failing spirit is rejuvenated and strengthened by Virgil's discourse: *Quali fioretti dal notturno gelo/ chinati e chiusi, poi che 'l sol li 'mbianca,/ si drizzan tutti aperti in loro stelo,/ tal mi fec'io di mia virtude stanca,/ e tanto buono ardire al cor mi corse,/ ch'i' cominciai come persona franca* (As little flowers, bent and closed / with chill of night, when the sun / lights them, stand all open on their stems, / such, in my failing strength, did I become. / And so much courage poured into my heart / that I began, as one made resolute [*Inf.* 2, 127–32]). The two poets proceed as one, both committed in one mission (*Or va, ch'un sol voler è d'ambedue: / tu duca, tu segnore e tu maestro* – Set out then, for one will prompt us both. / You are my leader, you my lord and master [*Inf.* 2, 139–40]).

The ending of Canto 2 (*Inf.* 2, 141–2) echoes the end of Canto 1 with Virgil leading the way and Dante following (*Inf.* 1, 136). Scholars note that while at the end of the first canto, Dante's lack of initiative and enthusiasm is implied in the verse *allor si mosse, e io li tenni dietro* (then he set out and I came on behind him [*Inf.* 1, 136]), at the end of *Inferno* 2 his own will is affirmed with the word *intrai*.[85] They argue that while at the end of Canto 1 Dante has become a follower of Virgil, at the end of Canto 2 his own will is re-emphasized. While it is true that, by means of Virgil's reassuring words, Dante's will is reawakened to resolution, strength, and courage, it is equally true that at the end of the second canto, Dante's will is united and becomes one with the will of Virgil (*Inf.* 2, 139).

As Guy Raffa notes, Dante's affectionate and tender union with Virgil comes forth at defining moments through the physical representation of the two poets united as one.[86] We have seen how at the end of *Inferno* 2, Dante and Virgil proceed together as one, and the individual will of each is united and becomes one with the will of the other ("*Or va, ch'un sol volerre è d'ambedue*" – "Set out then, for one will prompts us both" [*Inf.* 2, 139]). Later, after Dante's harangue against Pope Nicholas III, Virgil embraces Dante, and holding him close to his chest he carries him out of the *bolgia* (*Inf.* 19, 124–6), placing him *soavemente* (gently [*Inf.* 19, 130]) upon the bridge that overlooks the fourth *bolgia* (*Inf.* 19, 130). Never does Virgil tire of holding Dante "*a sé distretto*" ("so close" [*Inf.* 19, 127]). In *Inferno* 23, Dante alludes to a father and son relationship with Virgil, as he describes being tenderly and affectionately carried on Virgil's breast "*come suo figlio, non come compagno*" ("as if I were his child, not his companion" [*Inf.* 23, 51]). In *Inferno* 31, Antaeus holds Virgil, who in turn holds Dante (*Fatti qua, sì ch'io ti prenda* – Here, let me take hold of you! [*Inf.* 31, 134]). As Virgil and Dante embrace each other their bodies form one bundle (*poi fece sì ch'un fascio era elli e io* – then he made a single bundle of himself and me [*Inf.* 31, 135]). The representation of the two bodies interlocked into a harmonious whole, as in "*un fascio*" (a bundle), forcefully captures the strength of their union: one is undistinguishable from the other. And in *Inferno* 34, as the two poets are getting ready to leave Hell, Virgil grasps on Satan's opened wings while Dante, at Virgil's request, attaches himself to Virgil's neck (*Inf.* 34, 70–5). With vitality and force these images serve to highlight the deep affection, trust, solidarity, and friendship between the two poets. During these crucial moments, there is no conflict between Dante's subjective will and the will of the Other – each extends and becomes one with the other, the truth of one comprises the truth of the other, and the conflict of opposed wills is resolved through a semiosis.

Dante follows in the tradition of both the classical and Christian model of friendship, with its understanding of a friend as *allos autos* ("another self.") As seen earlier in this study, Aristotle, Cicero, Augustine, and Aquinas all understood a friend to be another self. Aristotle argues that "the excellent person is related to his friend in the same way that he is related to himself, since a friend is another himself."[87] In *De Amicitia*, Cicero notes that through a close union, shared experiences, proximity, and discourse, friends become one out of two, "*unum ex duobus*" (*DA* XXI, 81). Cicero concludes *verum etiam amicum qui intuetur, tamquam exemplar aliquod intuetur sui* (again, he who looks upon a true friend, looks as it were, upon a sort of image of himself [*DA* VII, 23]). Accordingly, a friend is *alter idem* "another self" (*DA* XXI, 80). Earlier, in chapter four, we saw how in the *Confessions* Augustine refers to his childhood friend as his "second self" (*ille alter eram*).[88] And Aquinas understands a friend as *alter ipse* (another self).[89]

The point needs to be made that while his union with Virgil resembles classical friendship, in the *Commedia,* Dante quotes neither Aristotle nor Cicero in describing his relationship with the pagan poet. With its emphasis on reciprocity, active benevolence, reason, and virtue, the union between Dante and Virgil indeed resembles classical friendship. It is a union that looks to moral rectitude. Virgil is described as *magnanimo* (great soul [*Inf.* 2, 44]),[90] an essential attribute of classical friendship. Along with Socrates, Plato, Aristotle, Cicero, and the other inhabitants of Limbo, Virgil is one of the *spiriti magni* (great spirits [*Inf.* 4, 119]). Their friendship is grounded in common interests – the love of poetry, of intellectual pursuits, and of the Good – and from their first encounter in *Inferno* 1, one senses great solidarity grounded in them (*O de li altri poeti onore e lume ... Tu se' lo mio maestro e 'l mio autore* – O glory and light of all other poets ... You are my teacher and my author [*Inf.* 1, 82–5]). Dante holds Virgil in the highest regard as the poet who more than any other influenced his poetic style, telling him *tu se' solo colui da cui io tolsi / lo bello stilo che m'ha fatto onore* (you are the one from whom alone I took / the noble style that has brought me honor [*Inf.* 1, 86–7]). It was his deep love and admiration for Virgil that pushed him to seek out the *Aeneid* (*che m'ha fatto cercar lo tuo volume* – that made me delve so deep into your volume [*Inf.* 1, 84]).

While Dante and Virgil may in fact find pleasure and benefit in each other's company, the primary motivation for their union is a reciprocal love of the *bene* (Good [*Inf.* 2, 126]) that Virgil promises and Beatrice delivers. As Aristotle notes, "complete friendship" exists only among "good people similar in virtue" (*NE* 8.3 1157a 20). If it is true that at his first introduction in the poem Virgil is presented as one who failed to speak the Word,[91] it is equally true that it is Virgil who, through his compassion, active benevolence, and discourse takes Dante a step closer to the Word. While Virgil's initial silence (*chi per lungo silenzio parea fioco* – faint in the wide silence [*Inf.* 1, 63]), may point to his inability to speak the Word directly, as Hollander suggests, his subsequent discourse paradoxically emphasizes his role as messenger of the Word. Virgil's initial silence is superseded by a discourse that acquires significance in relation to divine truth. Notwithstanding the numerous Virgilian echoes,[92] in the *Commedia* Virgil is much more than a source of poetic inspiration: he is an active participant in search of Dante's good. He guides Dante through the abyss of Hell up to the summit of Mount Purgatory. As Mazzotta observes, "Virgil gratuitously shows himself forth to rescue the wayfarer from his despair."[93] While it is true that Virgil is sent by Beatrice, it is equally true that he willingly and graciously accepts the challenge. He gives of himself selflessly for the sake of Dante's salvation.

Dante's first spoken words to Virgil are a call to friendship, a supplicating plea for help: "*Miserere di me*" (Have mercy on me [*Inf.* 1, 65]). Traditionally, unhesitating assistance has been considered a sign of friendship. It is natural for friends to turn to each other and provide assistance in times of adversity. Failure to provide help in times of need may be interpreted as a sign of animosity and even enmity. In a primary sense, adversity is the true test of friendship. As Menandes notes, "a worthy friend is a physician to your pain." While friends can count on each other for assistance, foes cannot. Indeed, the failure to rush to a friend's side, particularly in times of need, is interpreted by both Aristotle and Cicero as the absence of goodwill. Cicero notes that "friendship alleviates the greatest calamity ... A friend shares in his friend's success and in his misfortunes as if it were his own," and that friendship cannot exist in the absence of goodwill.[94] For all of these reasons, Dante's first spoken words to Virgil are to be understood as a cry for help and, indirectly, a cry for friendship. Lost and full of fear, with the way up the slope impeded by the three beasts, Dante turns to Virgil for help. He wants to be saved from the she-wolf that has driven him back to the dark wood. Weeping and trembling with fear, Dante seeks protection and assistance ("*aiutami da lei, famoso saggio, / ch'ella mi fa tremar le vene e i polsi*" – "save me from her, famous sage / she makes my veins and pulses tremble" [*Inf.* 1, 89–90]). Virgil responds as a friend should respond – with unhesitating assistance and support, or with active goodwill. Friendship leads to goodwill: *amor enim, ex quo amicitia nominate est, princeps est ad benevolentiam coniungendam* (for it is love, from which the word friendship is derived, that leads to the establishing of goodwill [*DA* VIII, 26–7]). Virgil advises Dante to take another path (*Inf.* 1, 91), offers guidance (*Inf.* 1, 112–14), leads Dante out of the dark wood, guides Dante through Hell and most of Purgatory, and finally leaves him in the care of Beatrice in the Earthly Paradise. The readiness with which Virgil comes to Dante's assistance makes his friendship all the more transparent. Virgil's unhesitating helpfulness is a sure sign of his friendship.

Miserere also underscores the interplay between classical and Christian thought: the biblical reference points to the first word of Psalm 50, and the classical reference points to Aeneas's words to his mother, Venus: *sis felix nostrumque leves, quaecumque, laborem* (be though gracious, whoe'er though art, and lighten this our burden).[95] Virgil, the author of the *Aeneid*, responds to *Miserere* with unhesitating assistance. In *Inferno* 2, through the heavenly story Virgil retells, Dante learns to understand Virgil's *misericordia* [*Inf.* 2, 51] in relation to Beatrice's *misericordia*, and ultimately in relation to the *misericordia* of Mary. E.R. Curtius describes the union of Dante and Virgil as an awakening.[96] Along these lines, Virgil is awakened by means of the explicit references of the

Aeneid in the Christian poem. In effect, though, the awakening is reciprocal. Dante is as much awakened by Virgil's friendship, goodwill, guidance, and discourse as Virgil is awakened by Dante's references to the *Aeneid*. Following the classical tradition, Dante's friendship with Virgil is grounded in reciprocity, common interest (a mutual love of poetry), and a mutual love of the moral good.

Dante's choice of Virgil as guide in a Christian poem has perplexed scholars. Most Dantisti, uncomfortable with Dante's choice, have attempted to escape the dilemma by explaining Virgil as a general symbol of human reason or as the reason that each person possesses. Since the time of Emperor Constantine, a strictly Christian interpretation has been offered, making reference to Virgil's fourth eclogue as a prophetic foretelling of the coming of Christ. While Dante would allow that one interpretation of Virgil could be allegorical, it would be unwise to follow early commentators who evaded the so-called "scandal"[97] of having a pagan guide in a Christian poem by personifying him as reason. To be sure, there are scholars who dissent from the traditional allegorical interpretation of Virgil as a prophetic Christian figure.[98] In favour of a historical interpretation, Hollander reminds the reader that it is precisely Virgil's historical reputation as master of the tragic style and author of the Roman epic poem that earns him the imminent role as guide, mentor, and teacher in Dante's poem.[99] In fact, Virgil identifies himself as the pagan Roman poet of the *Aeneid* (*Inf.* 1, 67–75), and Dante recognizes him as the great poet from whom he learned his own poetic style (*Inf.* 1, 82–7). Virgil's friendship with Dante is grounded in a mutual love of poetry, but also in a love of virtue and wisdom. As he himself makes clear while speaking with Sordello, he upheld the four moral virtues of prudence, temperance, justice, and fortitude. Dante loves Virgil for his magnanimous soul (*Inf.* 2, 44) and for his poetic mastery (*Inf.* 1, 83–4). Notwithstanding Virgil's poetic and moral excellence, it is Beatrice who teaches Dante how to love another in God. Having lived prior to the Advent of Christ, Virgil is privy to neither faith nor *caritas*.

Perhaps the most important passage in *Inferno* 2 occurs in the exact centre, the twenty-fourth of the forty-seven *terzine*.[100] With its insistence on love as the primary force of movement, this *terzina* establishes the relation between love and motion, and also the close link between *amor* (love) and *amicitia* (friendship). While noticing the relationship between love and motion[101] and between compassion and motion,[102] commentators overlook the relationship between *amor* and *amicitia*. Love moved Beatrice to compassion, love moved her to action, and love makes her speak (*Inf.* 2, 72). By referencing love as the ultimate force of her compassion, movement and speech, Beatrice is indirectly referencing the relationship between *amor* and *amicitia*. In *De Amicitia*, Cicero notes that love is primary and friendship derives from it: *Amor enim, ex quo amicitia nominate est* (For it is love, from which the word friendship is derived, that leads to the establishing of goodwill [*DA* VIII, 26–7]). *Amor* leads Beatrice to *amicizia*, or to active goodwill. The full significance of the line *amor mi mosse, che mi fa parlare* (The love that moved me and makes me speak [*Inf.* 2, 72]) is grasped once it is understood in relation to *l'amico mio, e non de la ventura* (my friend, who is no friend of fortune [*Inf.* 2, 61]). This reference to *amor* in this *terzina*, thus, is an indirect reference to *amicizia*. Beatrice's *amicizia* acquires significance in relation to *amor*, the force that moves all things in the universe. She is a friend to Dante because she loves him truly, and she loves him in her love of God. *Amor* moves her to act and speak on his behalf. *Amor* moves her first to compassion and then to action (physically from Heaven to Limbo) to promote Dante's good. Her love originates in divinity (*Donna è gentil nel ciel che si compiange / di questo ' mpendimento ov'io ti mando, / si che duro giudicio là sù frange* – There is a gracious lady in Heaven so moved / by pity at his peril, she breaks stern judgment / there above and lets me send you to him [*Inf.* 2, 94–6]), and it returns to divinity (*vegno de lo loco ove tornar disio; / amor mi mosse, che mi fa parlare* – I come from where I most desire to return. / The love that moved me and makes me speak [*Inf.* 2, 71]). That *amor* acquires significance in relation to *amicitia* becomes ever more clear in the sphere of Venus. Charles Martel also serves as a good case in point as, in *Paradiso* 8, 55–7, he recognizes Dante's love for him while still on earth (*Assai m'amasti, e avesti ben onde; / che s'io fossi giù stato, io ti mostrava / di mio amor più oltre che le fronde* – You loved me well, and with good reason. / Had I remained below, to you I would have shown / much more than the mere fronds of my affection [*Par.* 8, 55–7]). The repeated use of *amore* and *amare* in the sphere of Venus at first makes us think of Venereal love (of Dido at the very beginning of the canto), but once we reflect, we may see it as equal to Christian friendship.[103]

The twenty-fourth *terzina* of *Inferno* 2 further establishes the role of Virgil and Beatrice in a hierarchical order and clearly establishes Beatrice's authority over Virgil. It is Beatrice that descends from on high and moves Virgil. Without Beatrice's intervention, Virgil would not have been drawn into the action of the poem in the first place, nor would he have known about Dante's perilous state. In *Inferno* 10 (100–8), the reader is informed that the damned are not privy to events that transpire on earth. It is Beatrice and not Virgil who initiates movement and change in the poem (*Inf.* 2, 40–51). *Amor* moves Beatrice to compassion and action, and she in turn moves Virgil (*I' son Beatrice che ti faccio andare* – I who bid you go am Beatrice [*Inf.* 2, 70]), who willingly obeys her request (*Inf.* 2, 79–81). In witnessing Beatrice's compassion for Dante, Virgil himself is moved first to compassion and then to action, and moves physically towards Dante: *Poscia che m'ebbe ragionato questo, / li occhi lucenti lagrimando volse, / per che mi fece del venir più presto. E venni a te così com'ella volse: / d'innanzi a quella fiera ti levai / che del bel monte il corto andar ti tolse* (After she had said these things to me, / she turned away her eyes, now bright with tears, / making me more eager to set out. / And so I came to you just as she wished. / I saved you from the beast denying you / the short way to the mountain of delight [*Inf.* 2, 115–20]). The immediacy with which Virgil responds to Beatrice's request bespeaks of deep respect and admiration (*Inf.* 2, 79–81]).

If, as Hollander argues, in *Inferno* 2 Dante begins the unpleasant but necessary process of downgrading Virgil's authority for the sake of affirming a higher truth,[104] the canto likewise begins the process of reasserting the authority of Beatrice, which was previously undermined in the *Convivio* by the *donna gentile*.[105] Virgil himself admits to his own unworthiness as he affirms Beatrice's authority as *anima fia ciò più di me degna* (a soul more fit to lead than I [*Inf.* 1, 122]).[106] This discrepancy in authority and worth parallels the discrepancy between philosophy and theology, human reason and revelation.[107] Vested in Christian truth, Beatrice is a worthier, more perfect friend: she loves Dante through God. Lacking in faith, Virgil is a virtuous but fallible friend. Notwithstanding the importance of his role as mediator and messenger of grace, Virgil cannot speak the Word directly. Virgil's discourse is limited and imperfect: it conveys a limited and imperfect truth. His subordinate role is to be understood in relation to Beatrice's authority. As Beatrice gains more authority, Virgil begins to lose his. Virgil is *savio* (wise [*Inf.* 2, 36]), yet he is forever condemned to Hell. In contrast, Beatrice is *loda di Dio vera* (true praise of God [*Inf.* 2, 103]), and resides among the blessed in Heaven.

The distinction between Beatrice and Virgil as friends is further reflected in their linguistic style. For the most part, Beatrice's language is immersed in divinity and mirrors religious truth, while Virgil's language is immersed in poetic rhetoric and mirrors secular truth. Beatrice's speech is *soave e piana* (gentle and clear [*Inf.* 2, 56]) and she speaks *con angelica voce* (with an angel's voice [*Inf.* 2, 57]). Her humble and sweet speech is the language of God; she is *pietosa* (compassionate [*Inf.* 2, 133]) and speaks with *vere parole* (truthful words [*Inf.* 2, 135]). In contrast, Virgil speaks with *parola ornata* (polished words [*Inf.* 2, 67]).[108] The distinction between *piana* and *ornata* is to be placed and understood within the medieval distinction of rhetorical styles, between the plain (*umile*) and the ornate or high *(alto)*.[109] Benvenuto da Imola (1373) was the first to place the stylistic distinction between Virgil and Beatrice within a religious context: "divine speech is sweet and humble, not elevated and proud, as is that of Virgil and the poets."[110] As Benvenuto argues, the stylistic distinction between *soave e piana* and *parola ornata* establishes the distances between divine and human language.[111] Beatrice's speech reflects the humble style adopted in the *Commedia*, while Virgil's speech reflects the high style adopted in the *Aeneid*.[112] Virgil's human speech stands in opposition to Beatrice's divine speech. By means of a distinct speaking style, a particular type of speech, each friend leads Dante to a different level of truth.[113] Virgil's elevated speech is the language of humans, which may be prone to human pride and, as Mazzotta observes, to duplicity.[114] As precise as Mazzotta's observation is, it is important to keep in mind that it is to human language that Beatrice appeals when she enlists Virgil's assistance. Virgil does not intend to deceive, yet his speech is as fallible as his understanding of the truth.[115] Notwithstanding its fallibility, the value of Virgil's discourse is inestimable. As seen earlier, it is precisely by means of discourse (the Heavenly story he retells) that Virgil draws Dante outside of himself in *Inferno* 2, moving him, both emotionally and physically, to action. It is by means of discourse that Virgil brings Dante to moral rectitude. The interplay between Beatrice's humble (*umile*) speech and Virgil's ornate (*alto*) speech parallels the interplay between classical and Christian thought, poetry and friendship.

If Beatrice's speech and friendship acquire significance in relation to divine truth and *caritas*, Virgil's speech and friendship acquire significance in relation to moral excellence. Virgil is an *anima cortese* (courteous spirit [*Inf.* 2, 58]), who moves Dante by means of his *parlare onesto* (noble speech [*Inf.* 2, 113]), a discourse that is grounded in moral excellence and decorum.[116] In effect, Virgil's *parlare onesto* is the language of friendship. As seen earlier, moral excellence is a primary attribute of friendship. Both Aristotle and Cicero understand friendship as a union grounded in virtue, or moral excellence.[117] Virgil's moral excellence is juxtaposed against Beatrice's *virtù* (O lady of such virtue [*Inf.* 2, 76]), spiritual excellence, faith, charity, and temperance. The contrast between Virgil and Beatrice as friends is to be understood within the context of the interrelationship between *humanitas* and *caritas*. It is by means of both friends, and the specific vision that each lends, that Dante achieves happiness and perfection. As seen earlier, in all her blessedness and Christological significance, Beatrice needs Virgil's assistance. For all of her *virtù* and *vere parole*, Beatrice is unable to reach Dante directly and relies on Virgil's *parlare onesto* (noble speech [*Inf.* 2, 113]). That Beatrice reaches Dante through Virgil further confirms his role as a messenger of the Word.

Precisely because "ethics is the very foundation of a life with God,"[118] Virgil's virtue and wisdom are the foundation for the spiritual perfection that Beatrice brings. The moral life promoted by the virtuous pagan is a necessary precondition for spiritual perfection and heavenly bliss.[119] While not privy to faith, Virgil recognizes the necessity of faith. Rather than standing antagonistic to each other, in the *Commedia*, Virgil and Beatrice complement each other. From this standpoint, Dante's gradual ascent towards perfection and happiness acquires significance in relation to the particular vision and truth that each friend lends. Each fulfils a specific function, and both work in unison for the sake of Dante's spiritual salvation.

The changes and movement that transpire in *Inferno* 2 have been studied in relation to the interplay between *amor* (love) and *amicizia* (friendship), and between Virgil and Beatrice, who are understood to be two benevolent and distinct friends. More generally, an attempt has been made to show that *Inferno* 2 begins the process of unlearning how to be "bound fast in the friendship of mortal things."[120] Dante's friendship with Virgil has been seen as a preparation and prefiguration for his union with Beatrice in the Garden of Eden (*Purg.* 30, 11–19). It has in fact been argued that as a pagan friend Virgil leads Dante to the experience of earthly happiness, but cannot lead him to transcendence. It remains to be shown in the next chapter that the harmonious balance between humanity and divinity introduced in *Inferno* 2 reaches an exaltation in *Purgatorio* 30, with the disappearance of Virgil and appearance of Beatrice. It may then become clear how the transition from Virgil to Beatrice in *Purgatorio* 30 marks Dante's transmutation of classical friendship.

Chapter Seven

Friendship in *Purgatorio* 30 and *Purgatorio* 31

> Trasumanar significar *per verba*
> non si poria; però l'essemplo basti
> a cui esperïenza grazia serba.
>
> To soar beyond the human cannot be described
> in words. Let the example be enough to one
> for whom grace holds this experience in store
> (*Paradiso* 1, 70–2)

Friendship in relation to Dante's "spiritual movement"[1] towards God and the idea of friendship in relation to knowing and loving remain to be considered, particularly in relation to the happiness found at the summit of the Earthly Paradise. It will be shown how the interplay between humanity and divinity introduced in *Inferno* 2 reaches exaltation in *Purgatorio* 30.[2] Dante's transmutation of classical friendship is understood parallel to his experience of *trasumanar* (to soar beyond the human [*Par.* 1, 70]), the movement away from humanity and towards divinity. *Trasumanar* is a verb devised by Dante to signify a crossing over from the human into the divine, the passing beyond humanity to join divinity.[3] The term implies a process of change and transformation, an upward movement towards illumination and perfection. At the same time that it signifies movement from one state to another, *trasumanar* presumes the existence of both states. It will be seen how, at the summit of Purgatory, both the human and the divine are represented in the figures of Virgil and Beatrice. In the end, therefore, what needs to be addressed here is Dante's transmutation of classical friendship in relation to the shift in focus from Virgil to Beatrice, from philosophy to revelation, in *Purgatorio* 30. Dante's friendship with Virgil, a union resembling classical friendship, is understood as a preparation for and prefiguration of his friendship with Beatrice. Beatrice's return at the summit of Purgatory can be interpreted as a completion and a fulfilment of Dante's union with Virgil. Similarly, Beatrice's return in the *Commedia* will be seen as a completion and fulfilment of the role of the "*donna* gentile" (gentle *Lady*) in the *Convivio.*

Purgatorio 30 serves as a bridge between the first sixty-three cantos of the *Commedia* and the remaining thirty-six.[4] As Bruno Panvini notes, all that has transpired thus far has been a preparation for the triumphant return of Beatrice.[5] The canto acquires significance in relation to the transition from Beatrice to Virgil,[6] and Dante's instruction under the guidance of Virgil ends and his instruction under the tutelage of Beatrice begins.[7] At the summit at the Earthly Paradise, Dante loses a good friend but regains a better one. Dante's union with Beatrice is here understood as Christian friendship, since it is vested in spiritual significance.[8] At the summit of the Earthly Paradise, Dante begins to understand his own salvation as a gift of grace.[9]

For Giuseppe Mazzotta, the transition from Virgil to Beatrice at the summit of Purgatory is to be interpreted as a "Pauline rite de passage."[10] Accordingly, the Garden of Eden signals Dante's transition from his old sinful self to his purged and more perfect self. To be sure, Beatrice acquires significance in relation to theology, faith, Christ, Sapientia, and grace.[11] Since revelation is an act of grace, Beatrice is to be understood as a symbol of both grace and revelation.[12] As a gratuitous gift of grace, Dante's union with Beatrice is the highest form of Christian friendship, or *caritas.*[13] It is the means by which he is made to participate in divinity.[14] Through his union with Beatrice, Dante is introduced to a higher way of knowing and loving. She teaches him how to know and love all of creation in relation to God. Mazzotta interprets Dante's movement through Purgatory as a dual baptism: first as preparation to grace, and then in the Garden with the descent of Beatrice as the direct experience of grace.[15] If one is to follow Hollander's suggested schema, then it follows that through Virgil, Dante's will is first corrected (*Inf.* 1–34) and then perfected (*Purg.* 1–29); through Beatrice, his intellect is corrected (*Purg.* 30–*Par.* 30); through Bernard, his intellect is perfected (*Par.* 30–end).[16] Virgil restores Dante's will to newfound health, but he cannot do any more than this.[17] He prepares Dante for divine grace, but it is Beatrice who takes him to a direct experience of it (*E se la mia ragione non ti disfama, / vedrai Beatrice, ed ella pienamente / ti torrà questa e ciascun' altra brama* – And if my words do not requite your hunger, / you shall see Beatrice. She will deliver you / entirely from this and every other craving [*Purg.* 15, 76–8]). And while Virgil leads Dante to moral rectitude and earthly wisdom, Beatrice leads him to divine wisdom and eternal bliss.[18]

Against Sanguineti's claim that the transition from Virgil to Beatrice in *Purgatorio* 30 signifies the succumbing of morality to faith and of the moral life to the religious life,[19] one must argue here that in Dante there is no perceivable conflict between ethics and theology; rather, the second is a fulfilment and a completion of the first. In effect, there is no conflict between Virgil and Beatrice as friends. As Sanguineti himself observes, the moral life is in some way comprised in the religious life.[20] Dante's spiritual process is also an ethical process as absolute wisdom does not exclude ethics, but encompasses it.[21] Virgil, to whom Dante has entrusted the health of his soul, prepares and leads Dante to revealed truth.[22] In the *Commedia*, Virgil is simultaneously the ancient Roman poet who guides and leads through natural reason,[23] and the messenger of Christ who guides and leads through natural reason.[24]

While rejecting a strictly allegorical interpretation of Virgil as reason, it is undeniable that the pagan poet leads Dante up to the summit of Mount Purgatory by means of his *ingeno and arte* (intellect and skill [*Purg.* 27, 130]). Notwithstanding the primacy of Virgil's role, Dante's friendship with the pagan poet is imperfect and limited. Even the best of classical friendship is, from the vantage point of a Christian, misguided and lost. The authority of Virgil in the *Commedia* is fallible and on various occasions, undermined. For Hollander, Virgil's fallibility signals the distance between the two poets.[25] Virgil himself is aware of his own limitations. In the first canto of the *Inferno*, for instance, Virgil places Beatrice's authority above his own, viewing her as a worthier guide, as *anima ... più di me degna* (a soul more fit to lead than I [*Inf.* 1, 122]).[26] Both in the *Inferno* and in the *Purgatorio*, the reader is periodically reminded of Virgil's fallibility.[27] In *Purgatorio* 18, after having presented a philosophical analysis of love and while promoting the primacy of reason in love, Virgil confesses his own limitations concerning good and bad choices in matters of love. He instructs Dante to look to Beatrice for issues of faith, as he himself lacks such knowledge. In *Purgatorio* 6, while discussing the value of prayers, Virgil directs Dante's attention to Beatrice (*Veramente a così alto sospetto / non ti fermar, se quella nol ti dice / che lume fia tra 'l vero e lo 'ntelletto / Non so se 'ntendi: io dico di Beatrice; / tu la vedrai di sopra, in su la vetta / di questo monte, ridere e felice* – But do not let these doubts beset you / with high questions before you hear from her / who shall be light between the truth and the intellect / I don't know if you understand: I speak of Beatrice. / You shall see her above, upon the summit / of this mountain, smiling and in bliss).[28] In such instances, when Virgil's limitations are most evident, it is Beatrice's authority and power that become most transparent.

We have seen that while functioning as messenger of the Word, Virgil cannot speak the Word directly. His discourse is as fallible as the truth it conveys.

Beatrice alone speaks the Word directly, for as Gentile notes, she is the light by means of which Dante is led to ultimate truth.[29] Virgil himself is cognizant of this fact, and tells Dante *quanto ragion qui vede, / dir ti poss'io; da indi in là t'aspetta / pur a Beatrice, ch'è opra di fede* (as far as reason may see in this. / I can tell you to go further you must look / to Beatrice, for it depends on faith alone [*Purg.* 18, 46–8]).[30] While pointing out his own limitations, Virgil calls attention to the authority of Beatrice (*Purg.* 15, 76–8). Beatrice, rather than Virgil, will lead Dante to perfect vision and complete happiness.[31] The fallibility of Virgil's authority in matters of faith underscores his limitations both as guide and teacher.[32]

While Virgil's intellective power may be imperfect, his deep affection for Dante is not. And, Dante loves Virgil in spite of his imperfection. Teodolinda Barolini argues that it is precisely at those moments of Virgil's greatest fallibility as guide and teacher that Dante "tightens the affective screws."[33] Barolini notes that such affective language makes its first appearance preceding Virgil's defeat by the devils in *Inferno* 9. In *Inferno* 8, as Virgil leaves Dante alone for the first time, we find the first reference to Virgil as *padre* together with *dolce*: *Così sen van, e quivi m'abbandona / lo dolce padre* ("He goes away and leaves me there, / my gentle father" [*Inf.* 8, 109–10]). The adjectives *dolce* (sweet) and *caro* (dear) then appear in *Inferno* 23 and *Inferno* 24, after Virgil is duped by Malacoda (*care piante* [*Inf.* 23, 148], *piglio / dolce* [*Inf.* 24, 20–1]).[34] While it is true that Virgil functions as guide, master, and teacher, it is equally true that at the beginning of *Inferno* 24, his authority has been seriously undermined: he has been duped by Malacoda. As Virgil's authority is progressively undermined, his affective bond with Dante is strengthened and gains transparency. Their relationship evolves from a union between teacher and student, between one who knows and leads and one who learns and follows, into a tender and loving bond between two loyal friends. Virgil is loved and admired in spite of his fallibility. Through Virgil, Dante learns a valuable lesson about the importance of poetry in relation to friendship and about the power and the limits of the "word." His friendship with Virgil must be understood in relation to this ambiguity.

On the one hand, Virgil's intellective fallibility reveals him as a less perfect guide and master. On the other hand, this fallibility together with his growing display of physical affection reveals Virgil as a benevolent friend. The frequency of the adjective *dolce* and noun *padre* increases as Virgil's intellective power decreases.[35] The progression of affective language escalates, reaching its peak with the use of the superlative, "issimo" in *Purgatorio* 30. It is at the very moment of Virgil's departure that we hear Dante refer to him as *dolcissimo patre* ("sweetest of fathers" [*Purg.* 30, 50]). The use of the superlative at the very moment of Virgil's disappearance is significant, for it forces the reader to feel not only the depth of Dante's affection for Virgil but also the degree of his grief. As Barolini observes, Dante mourns the loss of his sweet father in the same manner that one would mourn the death of a beloved parent.[36] Virgil's disappearance does not diminish Dante's love for him but actually intensifies it. Distance makes love and friendship all the more real. As Scipio, although dead "still lives and will always live"[37] in Laelius's memory, Virgil, although absent, will forever live in Dante's mind and heart. For as Laelius notes, "friends though absent, are at hand ... so great is the esteem on the part of their friends, the tender recollection and the deep longing that still attends them."[38]

Virgil's tender affection for Dante is similar to that of a "sweet father," but also similar to that of a mother who flees with her son and is *avendo più di lui che di sé cura* (more concerned for him than for herself [*Inf.* 23, 41]). Virgil's diplay of affection grows as he carries the pilgrim on his breast *come suo figlio* (as if [Dante] were his child [*Inf.* 23, 51]). For Barolini, "this line serves notice that a new affective tie has in fact been created, and that its existence is not confined to figures of speech."[39] A mother's love for her child may not be grounded in reciprocity, and yet it resembles *philia* because of the element of selflessness. For Aristotle, "friendship consists more in loving than being loved," so a mother's love for her child is understood as "a sign" of friendship.[40] Following in Aristotle's footsteps, Aspasius, who commented on Aristotle in the second-century AD, argues that the love between parents and their children "strongly resembles philia because parents wish good things for their sons for their own sakes."[41] Ultimately, it is Virgil's active benevolence, his compassion, goodwill, and selflessness (necessary attributes of friendship) that supercede his intellective powers as guide, teacher, master, and poet.[42] If Cicero is correct in defining friendship as a variation of love,[43] Virgil's love for Dante is none other than friendship.

Virgil's friendship with Dante gains significance in relation to truth. Like Aquinas, Dante recognizes the importance of secular truth in relation to ultimate truth, or to the knowledge of God.[44] Philosophy and reason precede, but they do contradict theology and divine wisdom; similarly, as Panvini notes, the human virtues precede grace and the theological virtues without contradiction.[45] This fact is confirmed by the cardinal virtues themselves (*Noi siam qui ninfe e nel ciel siamo stelle: / pria che Beatrice discendesse al mondo, / fummo ordinate a lei per sue ancelle* – Here we are nymphs and in Heaven we are stars. / Before Beatrice descended to the world / we were ordained to serve her as her handmaids [*Purg.* 31, 106–8]). The cardinal virtues on earth lead man to moral rectitude, which precedes celestial perfection. By means of his own powers, through human reason and virtue, the virtuous and magnanimous pagan leads Dante to moral rectitude, making him better disposed to choose right over wrong, good over evil.[46] Virgil leads Dante to the perfection of his secular nature and to the experience of the happiness that man is capable of attaining by means of his human virtue.[47] More than this Virgil cannot do, further than than this point he cannot go: e *se' venuto in parte / dov'io per me più oltre non discerno* (and now come to a place / in which, unaided, I can see no farther [*Purg.* 27, 128–9). One's salvation is an act both of humanity and divinity.

As Panvini notes, Dante completes and fulfils Aquinas's doctrine in positing one's salvation as the work of both grace and human reason.[48] While recognizing the importance of grace, Dante also recognizes the importance of human reason in relation to salvation. In Dante there is no conflict between pagan thought versus Christian thought, earthly life versus the Hereafter. The first is completed and fulfilled in the latter. The return of Beatrice in the *Commedia* is a completion and fulfilment of Dante's friendship with Virgil. That Dante held classical friendship in the utmost regard as a union grounded in the highest part of an individual – his reason – is evidenced by his choice of Virgil as both guide and friend. The importance of Virgil parallels the importance of philosophy and morality in relation to spiritual salvation.[49] To the extent that it leads Dante to moral rectitude and earthly perfection, friendship with Virgil is preparation and prefiguration for the more perfect type friendship with Beatrice. To borrow the words of St Ambrose, Dante's union with Virgil is "a foretaste of the harmony of Heaven."[50]

Virgil bridges the distance between classical and Christian thought.[51] While taking Dante to moral rectitude, Virgil also takes him to Beatrice, to the very threshold of his *trasumanar*. Once his will is *libero, dritto e sano* (free, upright, and sound [*Purg.* 27, 140]), Dante has no need for Virgil's guidance and discourse (*Non aspettar mio dir più né mio cenno* – No longer wait for word or sign from me [*Purg.* 27, 139–40]). Dante is now ready to cross over from humanity to divinity.[52] Virgil has vested Dante with of the highest form of authority, (*per ch'io sovra te corono e mitrio* – over yourself I crown and miter you),[53] and once Dante is in complete control of his will and can rule himself morally, he is ready to transcend the natural world and reach the supernatural. It is at this very point that Virgil disappears to make room for Beatrice who will lead Dante to divinity.[54]

Beatrice's constant love and devotion is a sign of friendship. On Earth, despite Dante's transgressions, she continued to guide him to God and sustained him for a period of about sixteen years (1274–90): *Alcun tempo il sostenni col mio volto: / mostrando li occhi giovanetti a lui, / meco il menava in dritta parte vòlto* (For a time I let my countenance sustain him. / Guiding him with my youthful eyes, / I drew him with me in the right direction [*Purg.* 30, 121–3]). In the afterlife, she continued to inspire and guide him through dreams and other means (*Né l'impetrare ispirazion mi valse, / con le quali e in sogno e altrimenti / lo rivocai: sì poco a lui ne calse!* – Useless the inspiration I sought and won for him, / as both with dreams and other means / I called him back, so little did he heed them [*Purg.* 30, 133–5]).[55] Notwithstanding her transfiguration and her association with Sapienza and Grace, Beatrice never ceases to be the particular friend and the beautiful lady with whom Dante fell in love in Florence. She looks exactly the same and wears the same colors she wore the first time Dante set eyes on her.[56] Their friendship was and still is extremely personal.[57] Similarly, notwithstanding his association with reason and philosophy, Virgil is still the particular and historical ancient Roman poet from whom Dante took his own poetic style.[58] As Auerbach notes, what distinguishes the *Commedia* from other journeys in the Hereafter is the preservation and continuation of the totality of the human figure with all of its particular and historical attributes.[59] It would seem that in the *Commedia*, Dante's personal affections are transmuted to a universal level[60] without ever losing their human pathos.

The transition from Beatrice to Virgil at the summit of Purgatory signifies the fulfilment and completion of Dante's moral perfection. It also signifies the transmutation of classical friendship into a relationship that encompasses God. Following in the footsteps of Aquinas, Dante recognizes the importance and the limitations of philosophy and natural reason in relation to a person's ultimate perfection and happiness. In the absence of grace, an individual's natural powers are insufficient for a direct experience of perfect good and perfect truth.[61] For Dante as for Aquinas, divine grace is the means by which an individual returns to God.[62] By the same token, grace operates through reason. Beatrice cannot reach Dante directly in his corruptible nature and needs the assistance of Virgil.[63] Gentile interprets Beatrice's reliance on Virgil as a subjugation of theology to reason.[64] However, this is less a subjugation than the synthesis and collaboration between the two.

The seriousness with which Dante treats philosophy in both the *Convivio* and in the *Commedia*[65] is equal to the seriousness with which he treats Virgil in relation to his own salvation. Even in the *Commedia*, where philosophy is not assigned a specific part, it is represented by the ancient philosophers in Limbo and by the philosophical discourse of Virgil, Marco Lombardo, and Aquinas.[66] The privileged position assigned to the ancient philosophers in the *Commedia* is an indication that the importance of philosophy is never forgotten.[67] Notwithstanding the primacy of philosophy in relation to truth, the *Commedia* presents its limitations in relation to divine wisdom and celestial happiness. Ultimately, philosophy cannot by its own powers lead man directly to divine truth: this lies under the jurisdiction of perfect vision. And perfect vision is under the jurisdiction of Beatrice as divine grace. According to Barbi, it is precisely because

Dante feels so confident about his faith and is willing to recognize the limits of reason that he feels an urgency to reach for truths that are inaccessible to the human mind.[68] It is Beatrice and not Virgil who takes Dante to those truths.

The top of the mountain may in fact be Eden itself, a place where Dante experiences the happiness that was first enjoyed by Adam and Eve before the fall.[69] It may also be an idyllic world reminiscent of the golden age, a place where one can live in peace while enjoying the pleasures of friendship.[70] Mount Purgatory is a place where Dante's soul becomes free of sin and of the weight of the flesh; it is a return to innocence.[71] And it is a place where, through the guidance of friends, Dante finds happiness and the Good. If, as Aristotle asserts, friendship is an activity that promotes happiness,[72] the happiness found at the top of the mountain is to be understood in relation to Dante's unions with Virgil and Beatrice, understood as distinct types of friendship. Virgil himself is cognizant of the fact that the goal at the top of the mountain is happiness. In *Purgatorio* 27, while encouraging Dante to continue the struggle up the hill, Virgil represents the goal as a tree of many branches: *Quel dolce pome che per tanti rami / cercando va la cura de' mortali, / oggi porrà in pace le tue fami* (That sweet fruit which mortals, with great effort, / seek on many different boughs / shall today give peace to all our cravings [*Purg.* 27, 115–17]).[73] The branches symbolize the various meanings attached to happiness. While happiness may be attained through different paths, and while the life of reason is the happiest in this life, perfect happiness is not to be found in this life.[74] It would seem that at the summit of the mountain, Dante regains that happiness enjoyed by Adam and Eve before the fall.[75]

That the goal at the top of the mountain is happiness is first affirmed by Virgil [*Purg.* 27, 115–17]), and then reaffirmed by Beatrice as she demands that Dante recognize her for the true good that she is: *Guardaci ben! Ben son, ben son Beatrice. / Come degnasti d'accedere al monte? / Non sapei tu che qui è l'uom felice?* (Look over here! I am, I truly am Beatrice. / How did you dare approach the mountain? / Do you not know that man here lives in joy? [*Purg.* 30, 73–5]). As Beatrice makes clear, the happiness that Dante finds at the summit of Purgatory is to be understood in relation to her as true good. The triple use of the word *ben* echoes the triple use of "Virgil"[76] uttered by Dante and the triple use of the word "weep" uttered by Beatrice.[77] This echo reinforces Beatrice's earlier point that Dante should not weep over Virgil's disappearance, for in losing Virgil he has gained a greater good, and one might add, a better friend. While the Italian word *ben* means "really," it also implies the sense of its root, "good."[78] Beatrice's very name signifies happiness, and the gift she bears is beatitude.[79] Since friendship is a union grounded in the Good, the good Beatrice bears is a sign of complete friendship. In her love of Christ, Beatrice leads Dante towards complete happiness. At the summit of Purgatory, Dante is made happy when he finally reaches Beatrice. Having delivered the "promise of good" he had made back in *Inferno* 2, 126 (taking Dante directly to Beatrice), at the top of Mount Purgatory Virgil takes his leave, entrusting Dante to the care of a worthier guide, a greater good, and a better friend.

The distinction between Virgil and Beatrice as friends is fully grasped once placed within the context of a person's two ends, natural and supernatural:[80] earthly happiness and heavenly bliss.[81] Beatrice is the grace by means of which Dante, through the intervention of Virgil, is called back home to God.[82] Dante's friendship with Virgil and Beatrice must be understood within the context of those things that belong to reason and those that belong to faith,[83] things that are seen and things that are unseen. In the *Monarchia*, a person's first goal is presented as earthly happiness (*beatitudo hujus vitae*) attained in Eden by means of philosophy (*per philosophica documenta*). This first goal entails proper operation according to the moral and intellectual virtues. A person's second goal is presented as spiritual happiness (*beatitudo vitae aeternae*) and it is located in the heavenly paradise. The second goal is attained by means of revelation and the scripture (*per documenta spiritualia*), and it entails the proper operation according to the theological truths.[84] The *Monarchia* argues for a complete independence of the two goals. The first goal is not subjugated to the second, and the attainment of the first is not a precondition for the fulfilment of the second.[85] Friendship with Virgil leads to the fulfilment of the first goal, while friendship with Beatrice leads to a fulfilment of the second. As it is grounded in natural reason, Dante's union with Virgil leads to moral rectitude, and to the correction and perfection of his will.[86] Independently of Beatrice, the pagan poet guides and leads Dante to earthly perfection and happiness. As Michele Barbi observes, while seeking Virgil's assistance, Beatrice leaves him free to choose the means by which he will guide Dante out of danger.[87]

Applying Aquinas's formulation of the three types of vision, Singleton interprets the transition from Virgil to Beatrice at the summit of Purgatory and the transition from Beatrice to St Bernard at the summit of *Paradiso* as a transition of lights in a hiearchical order from lowest to highest.[88] As *lumen gratiae*, Beatrice is the path to perfect vision and truth; as *lumen naturale*, Virgil is the path to finite vision and truth.[89] As a union grounded in contemplation according to natural reason and perfect virtue, Dante's union with Virgil resembles virtue friendship, as defined by Aristotle in the *Nicomachean Ethics*.[90] Dante's union with the Roman poet is an activity that leads to operation according to perfect virtue. It leads to the virtuous life, lived in accordance with reason. As the light of grace, Beatrice leads Dante to perfect vision and divine love.[91] Friendship with Beatrice is an activity that leads to operation according to divine wisdom and grace. It is the means by which Dante is raised to the light of God while still in this life, *in via*. Friendship with Beatrice is the epitome of Christian friendship, it is *caritas*.

As Singleton notes, to move with Virgil is an *umanar* – to move within the confines of human nature – while to move with Beatrice is is a *trasumanar* – to move beyond the human.[92] Dante's friendship with Virgil is to be placed within the limitations and powers of human nature. Beatrice leads away from *gravitas* and *visio corporalia* (earthly vision) towards *visio spiritualia* (spiritual vision).[93] As Newman notes, "purgatory mediates between the shadowed corporeality of Hell and the lucid incorporeality of Heaven."[94] In Purgatory, Dante begins to see celestial light, but his moral confusion does not yet permit him to see clearly: his vision must first be perfected before he can look upon it directly and he still requires a medium or mirror through which the brilliance of that light may be reflected;[95] Beatrice's eyes become that medium. By gazing into her eyes, Dante is transformed as Glaucus was metamorphosed into a god of the sea.[96] Beatrice is the medium through which Dante experiences divinity. In her dual nature, both human and divine, Beatrice mirrors Christ.[97] In Hell, her eyes moved Virgil to compassion;[98] in Purgatory (*Purg.* 31, 119–23) and then again in Paradise (*Par.* I, 64–6) those very same eyes moved Dante towards divinity. After looking at Beatrice, Dante proceeds to turn his eyes to Heavenly beauty (*fissa con li occhi stava; / e io in lei / le luci fissi, di là sù rimote* – her eyes all fixed upon the eternal wheels; / and I fixed mine on her).[99] In *Paradiso*, Dante has finally learned not to be "too fixed" on Beatrice herself, but to see her as the medium through which he experiences *trasumanar*. Before he can undergo such a transformation, however, he must first admit to wrongdoing, he must confess: (*Alto fato di Dio sarebbe rotto, / se Letè si passasse e tal vivanda / fosse gustata sanza alcuno scotto / di pentimento che lagrime spanda* – Broken would be the high decree of God / should Lethe be crossed and its sustenance / be tasted without payment of some fee: / his penitence that shows itself in tears).[100]

Beatrice forces Dante to admit to wrongdoing and to see himself without self-deception. She demands a confession ("*dì, dì se questo è vero; a tanta accusa / tua confession conviene esser congiunta*"– 'say if this is true. To such an accusation / your confession must be joined').[101] Frozen by fear and overwhelmed with confusion, Dante sheepishly utters "yes" (*Confusione e paura miste / mi spinsero un tal "sì" fuor de la bocca,* – Confusion and fear, mixed together, / drove from my mouth a yes [*Purg*, 31, 13–14]). Under the heavy burden of moral guilt, he weeps and sighs.[102] Shortly thereafter, while still weeping, he gives a full confession: *Piangendo dissi*: *"Le presenti cose / col falso lor piacere volser miei passi, / tosto che 'l vostro viso si nascoste"* (In tears, I said: "Things set in front of me, / with their false delights, turned back my eyes / the moment that

Your countenance was hidden").[103] Dante's transgressions would seem to consist in having loved earthly false goods. Confession forces Dante to recognize his own fallibility in relation to a higher truth. As Theophil Spoerri notes, confession lies at the very centre of Purgatory and the entire *Commedia*.[104] Before Dante can know and love himself in relation to God, he must first humble himself before Beatrice and admit to any wrongdoing.[105] Confession is a necessary first step to salvation, for it leads to self-awareness and self-knowledge.[106] Self-knowledge, in turn, leads to humility, a precondition for salvation.[107] To truly know oneself is to know others and to feel compassion for their misery.[108] As Etienne Gilson observes, "the end of humility is compassion,"[109] and compassion is the offspring of *caritas*. Through confession, Dante transcends his personal "I" and becomes a member of the community of Christ.[110] Humility permits Dante to unite his will with the will of God.[111]

In his interpretation of the term *trasumanar*, Jacopo della Lana notes the importance of Beatrice in relation to Dante's transcendence. Through Beatrice's vision, Dante is transmuted – he transcends his humanity and becomes better able and disposed to contemplate divinity.[112] According to Botterill, the role played by Beatrice in relation to Dante's transformation is even more significant than that which Jacopo envisions. Indeed, on fixing his gaze into Beatrice's eyes, Dante does not merely become more disposed to contemplate divinity, but through the divine splendor reflected in Beatrice's eyes,[113] he shares in divinity and becomes godlike.[114] In contrast to Jacopo, Francesco da Buti notes the importance of change and grace (*per grazia*) in relation to Dante's *trasumanar*.[115] To be sure, the experience of *trasumanar* presupposes *umanar*. The point of departure in Dante's journey towards divinity is humanity. Beatrice takes Dante to experience perfect vision and heavenly bliss, but it is Virgil whose natural reason leads him to the very threshold of revealed truth.[116] Without the assistance of Virgil, Dante would never have reached Beatrice:[117] Virgil instils and restores moral health (*Virgilio a cui per mia salute die' mi*. – Virgil, to whom I gave myself for my salvation [*Purg*. 30, 51]).[118]

Instead of consoling Dante for the loss of Virgil,[119] as one would expect, Beatrice calls Dante by name and then tells him to save his tears for a more serious cause: *Dante, perché Virgilio se ne vada, / non pianger anco, non piangere ancora; / ché pianger ti conven per altra spada* (Dante, because Virgil has departed, / do not weep, do not weep yet, / there is another sword to make you weep).[120] Dante's self-nomination in the poem coincides with his conversion.[121] This is the first and only time in the poem where Dante names himself and shortly thereafter deems it necessary to defend doing so: *quando mi volsi al suon del nome mio, / che di necessità qui si registra* (as I turned when I heard her call my name, / which of necessity is here recorded).[122] Why the necessity to name himself at this precise moment in the journey, the first and only time in the body of his poem?[123] The justification given in *Purgatorio* 30, 63 echoes that of the *Convivio*,[124] where Dante gives two reasons for an author's self-nomination: first, as in Boethius's *Consolation*, to defend oneself against infamy; second, as in Augustine's *Confessions*, for the purpose of instruction.[125] Robert Hollander understands "this verse is perhaps the climax of the poem,"[126] and he regards all prior action as a preparation leading up to this point. Dante's self-nomination is a sign that a new phase in the journey has commenced. In calling out his name, Beatrice appeals to the new Dante, who after his confession (*Purg.* 31, 31–6) will emerge from the waters of Lethe purified and reborn in Christ.

Beatrice next demands that Dante recognize her for the true good that she is (*Guardaci ben! Ben son, ben son Beatrice* – Look over here! I am, I truly am Beatrice [*Purg.* 30, 73]). She demands that he recognize her for who she truly is, or that he now see clearly the meaning of her name. The meaning of her name must be understood in relation to God, who is pure name, or *Logos*. After demanding that Dante see her for who she truly is – a blessed lady – Dante is forced to see himself with clear vision: *Come degnasti d'accedere al monte? / non sapei tu che qui è l'uom felice?* (How did you dare approach the mountain? / Do you not know that here man lives in joy? [*Purg.* 30, 74–5]). Without recognition of wrongdoing, there cannot be repentance; without repentance, there cannot be change. At the sight of his own reflection in the water of Lethe, Dante lowers his eyes in shame (*Li occhi mi cader giù nel chiaro fonte; / ma veggendomi in esso, i trassi a l'erba, / tanta vergogna mi gravò la fronte* – I lowered my eyes to the clear water. / But when I saw myself reflected, I drew them back / towards the grass, such shame weighed on my brow [*Purg.* 30, 76–8]). Beatrice's words force Dante to see himself with a new perception, as a man lost in sin.

That Beatrice scolds Dante for his tears (*Purg.* 30, 67–75) should not come as a surprise. For, as Cicero notes, friends openly give advice with frankness and, when necessary, with sterness.[127] While she may seem overbearing to Dante (*Così la madre al figlio par superba* – as a mother may seem overbearing to her child [*Purg.* 30, 79]), what is clearly conveyed is the depth of her love. And while her sternness has a bitter taste for Dante (*Purg.* 30, 80–1), Beatrice's rebuke is a sign of her love for him, similar to the love that a mother has for her child. Beatrice continues to judge and rebuke Dante for his transgressions. She laments that he did not fulfil his true potential (*Purg.* 30, 115–17). As a true friend, she had sustained and guided Dante on the right path (*Purg.* 30, 121–2), although, after her death he directed his attention to others (*di mia seconda etade e mutai vita, / questi si tolse a me, e diessi altrui* – when I changed lives, he took himself from me / and gave himself to others).[128] When she died, although her beauty and virtue increased, he set himself on the wrong path and followed false images of the good [*Purg.* 30, 130–2]). Even still, she did not abandon her friend. She sought to inspire him "with dreams and other means" (*Purg.* 30, 133–6). But he "sank so low" (*Purg.* 30, 136) in his abyss that she had no other recourse "except to make him see the souls in perdition" (*Purg.* 30, 138). And so she traveled to the very "threshold of the dead" (*Purg.* 30, 139) where weeping, she enlisted Virgil's assistance, imploring him to guide her friend towards a better vision and a greater good.

In the Garden of Eden, all details surrounding Beatrice's arrival confirm her Christological meaning. She arrives on a sacred chariot surrounded by one hundred ministers and messengers of God who welcome her arrival[129] by tossing flowers up into the air,[130] singing *Benedictus qui venis! ... Manibus,* oh, *date lilia plenis!*[131] That the meaning of Beatrice is involved in Christ is also made plain by her apparel. She is a crowned with an olive branch (*cinta d'uliva* [Purg. 30, 31]), associating her with wisdom. She wears a white veil (*candido vel*) and a green mantle (*verde manto*), and is otherwise dressed in red (*vestita di color fiamma viva*), associating her to the theological virtues of faith, hope, and charity (*Purg.* 30, 31–3).[132] In her dual nature, both human and divine, Beatrice's descent must be placed within the context of Christ's descent to Earth and Dante's ascent to God.[133] Mirrored in her eyes is the dual nature of the Word incarnate.[134]

Recognizing the old passion that had ignited his soul, Dante turns to Virgil, uttering a line that echoes Dido's words "agnosco veteris vestigial flammae" (*Aeneid,* IV, 23): *conosco i segni de l'antica fiamma* (I know the signs of the ancient flames [*Purg.* 30, 48]). Dido's love for Aeneas, however, was misguided, since it was grounded in passion. In declaring her love for Aeneas, Dido breaks her vows to her dead husband, Siccheaus. While Dante immediately recognizes Beatrice as the lady with whom he had fallen in love, he must soon learn to recognize her divinity. Beatrice's maidens, the four cardinal virtues of Prudence, Courage, Justice, and Temperance, encourage Dante to recognize Beatrice in her dual nature. They direct Dante's gaze into her mirroring eyes, saying *fa che le viste non risparmi; / posto t'avem dinanzi a li smeraldi / ond'Amor già ti trasse le sue armi* (do not withhold your gaze. / We have placed you here before the emeralds / from which, some time ago, Love shot his darts [*Purg.* 31, 115–17]).[135] The very eyes whose love had sustained him while on Earth continue to sustain him through the divine splendor mirrored in them (… *strinsemi li occhi a li occhi rilucenti, / che pur sopra 'l grifone stavan saldi. / Come in lo specchio il sol, non altrimenti / la doppia fiera dentro vi raggiava, or con altri, or con altri regimenti* – bound my eyes to those shining eyes, / which still stayed fixed upon the griffin. / Even as the sun in a mirror, not otherwise / the twofold beast shone forth in them, / now with the one, now with its other nature).[136] By gazing into her eyes, Dante learns a new way of seeing and knowing a higher truth.[137] He undergoes a transformation and becomes god-like, as Glaucus became after he tasted the grass.[138] If Virgil guides through the light of the intellect, Beatrice guides through the light of Grace.[139] Beatrice is eternal light and revealed Truth.[140]

That Beatrice is a friend in Christ is something that becomes ever so clear as the poem progresses. Through the intercession of the three theological virtues, faith, hope and charity, Dante is made to witness a sight miraculous in nature. These three bring Dante to witness Beatrice and the gryphon exchanging glances. Mirrored in the eyes of Beatrice is the dual nature of the gryphon, who represents Christ in his dual nature.[141] (*Purg.* 31, 79–81). Beatrice's eyes are manifestations of divine truth and of the dual nature of the Word incarnate.[142] Faced with such an extraordinary and miraculous vision, Dante concludes that his earlier intuition back in the *Vita Nuova* regarding Beatrice's divine nature (chapter 42) had indeed been correct. That Beatrice acquires significance in relation to divine beauty becomes evident: *Sotto' l suo velo e oltre la rivera / vincer pariemi più sé stessa antica, / vincer che l'altre qui, quand'ella c'era* (Even beneath her veil, even beyond the stream, / she seemed to surpass her former self in beauty / more than she had on earth surpassed all others [*Purg.* 31, 82–4]). The divine beauty mirrored in her eyes at once satiates Dante and leaves him craving for more.[143] The four cardinal virtues escort Dante to witness the beauty of her eyes, but it is the theological virtues who must sharpen Dante's vision for that miraculous sight (*Purg.* 31, 109–11).

If Virgil oversees the correction of Dante's will in *Inferno* and *Purgatorio*, it is Beatrice who oversees the correction of his intellect in the first nine heavenly spheres, after which Bernard oversees the perfection of Dante's intellect in the Empyrean.[144] Upon the restoration of Dante's soul's health (*Par.* 31, 89), Beatrice relinquishes her role to St Bernard and then resumes her place next to Rachel (32, 8–9). Beatrice has taken Dante up to divine vision and spiritual salvation, teaching him how to love her in God. That Dante's final address to her takes the form of a prayer (*Così orai* – This was my prayer [*Par.* 31, 91]) is a sign that he has learned the lesson she has come to teach: namely, to know and love her in Christ.[145] He prays that she will keep intact in him his new-found knowledge once he returns to Earth so he will not be drawn to earthly goods (*Par.* 31, 78–90). At the moment when Dante fully knows and loves Beatrice in Christ, their friendship is transmuted to a higher form. Only when Beatrice is with God in heaven does Dante stop addressing her with the more distant *voi* and begin to address her with the familiar *tu*,[146] an indication that Dante has learned to see Beatrice as a friend in Christ and has learned to recognize her in her dual nature. In learning how to know and love Beatrice in the right way, Dante learns how to know and love God. Through a clearer vision, Dante now sees and loves Beatrice in God.[147] Divine love is the universal force that unites all creation into the One.

According to Mazzotta, the return of Beatrice in *Purgatorio* 30 places Dante's poem within the grace of Augustinian theology.[148] In Book 13 of his *Confessions*, Augustine presents his doctrine of love as *pondus amoris* through the metaphorical use of stone and fire. Love is a fire that ignites the soul with its heat and carries it upward to its final resting place;[149] it is a force that uplifts man's soul to the heights of its own place.[150] Beatrice descends as sanctifying grace so that Dante's soul may ascend to God. Beatrice's love ignites and uplifts Dante's soul to eternal perfection and complete bliss. Echoing Dido's words, Dante himself refers to Beatrice's love as an ancient flame: *conosco i segni de l'antica fiamma* (I know the signs of the ancient flame [*Purg* 30, 48]). The difference is that Dido's love for Aeneas is misguided, for it is grounded in passion. With their dual reference, Virgilian and Augustinian, Dante's words reinforce the interplay between ancient and Christian thought. More particularly, the echo of Dido's words illuminates the contrast between sensual and spiritual love.

In the Earthly Paradise, when Dante gazes at Beatrice, the angels rebuke him for being *troppo fiso* (too fixed [*Purg*. 32, 9]). The angels sense that Dante still appreciates Beatrice as the young woman he loved in Florence, rather than the blessed lady who orchestrated his salvation. Dante's dilemma echoes Plato's *Phaedrus*.[151] How does one see and love physical beauty only as a reflection of a higher beauty? Joseph Mazzeo is of the opinion that while having no direct knowledge of the *Phaedrus*, Dante adopted the *Phaedrus*'s notion of salvation, love, and poetic inspiration in great detail,[152] with one difference being that for Plato, the goal is to reach truth, while for Dante it is to reach God.[153] For both Dante and Plato, the beauty of the beloved is a means by which the soul ascends to spiritual beauty. In Dante, however, the beloved is transformed and assumes a higher significance and even greater beauty in death.[154] Beatrice's love for Dante does not end with her death: it intensifies. Dante's friendship with Beatrice acquires importance in relation to distance and death. After her death, he is forced to understand her in relation to the life of the spirit, or in relation to divine truth and beauty. Friendship with Beatrice has withstood the test of time. While still alive she sustained Dante with her *volto* (countenance [*Purg*. 30, 121]), guiding him with *li occhi giovanelli* (youthful eyes [*Purg*. 30, 122]),[155] steering him *in diritta parte volto* (in the right direction [*Purg*. 30, 123]). After her death, she continued to guide and inspire him by means of dreams and other ways (*Purg.* 30, 134–5).[156] When Dante sank so deep in sin that all of Beatrice's attempts to save him fell short (*Purg.* 30, 136–7), she descended into Limbo to seek and pray for Virgil's assistance (*Purg.* 30, 139–41).[157] Even as Dante turned his back to her, in search of false goods (*Purg.* 30, 127–32), Beatrice remained constant in her love as a true friend. Friendship such as is seen in the *Purgatorio*, and then in its perfected form in *Paradiso*, is a union that overcomes distance, absence, and even death.

For Mazzeo, the return of Beatrice in the *Commedia* marks a sort of remaking of the *Phaedrus*'s doctrine of beauty and love.[158] Beatrice, a concrete and beautiful individual, initiates the upward flight towards universal love and beauty.[159] The dilemma facing Dante in the Earthly Paradise is how to appreciate and love Beatrice in God. To love her beauty truly is to know and love it in relation to God. Dante already knows how to love Beatrice in her humanity, but at the top of the mountain he must now learn to love her in her divinity. In *Purgatorio* 32, 9, Dante regresses to his old (sexual and personal) way of looking at Beatrice.[160] The old way is even more limiting than classical friendship, which, at its best, is at least not sinful, just misguided. Dante must learn to appreciate Beatrice's physical beauty as a manifestation of divine beauty. Love is a light that illuminates and pulls the soul upward towards perfect truth and perfect light, or God.[161] As Dante moves with Beatrice, beauty and light intensify until he is brought face to face with supreme beauty and eternal light, or God.[162] Friendship between Beatrice and Dante is therefore not a static union: it changes and is transmuted from the personal into the universal and spiritual.[163] Beatrice's beauty is the means by which Dante experiences pure light and beauty. For St Bernard, as for Dante, sensible beauty initiates a nostalgic desire for eternal beauty.[164] The beauty of Beatrice is a reminder of the beauty Dante had once seen and has now forgotten.[165] Beatrice is the *amanza del primo amante* (beloved of the first lover [*Par.* 4, 118]). Her love for Dante cannot be separated from her love for God. She loves Dante simultaneously in a personal sense and in a universal sense. Friendship with Beatrice is to be understood as *caritas*, the mutual love of humans and God. As Etienne Gilson notes, *caritas* "is the will common to man and God." By renouncing his personal will, Dante joins and becomes one with a community grounded in faith in Christ and attains universal truth.[166]

Friendship, as is seen in *Purgatorio* and then in its perfected form in *Paradiso*, is a union grounded in the love of God. It is a union that strives for eternity. God commands that we love our neighbour as ourselves for the love of Him. Through the incarnation of the Word, friendship acquires spiritual significance in relation to God. Christian friendship requires humility, it requires that one recognizes and loves oneself and others always in communion with God. Humility is a necessary component of compassion.[167] Firmly grounded in charity, Christian friendship comprises both the love of mortals and of God. One of the most striking aspects of Christian friendship is this sense of inclusiveness. While the object of love in classical friendship is human virtue,[168] the object of love in Christian friendship is God, who is ultimate good. Christian friendship is a union grounded in divine grace and charity, the highest form of love that was bestowed upon humans through the incarnation of Christ.[169] Charity alone directs the soul to God, for it alone renders the soul disinterested.[170] Dante's friendship with Beatrice converts and directs his soul from a limited love of self to a love of others in and for God. When all is said and done, Christian friendship is essentially the offspring of both *benevolentia* and *caritas*.[171] The close association between love and friendship takes this discussion to St Bernard[172] and his definition of love.

Although his presence in the *Commedia* is rather brief (*Par.* 31, 58 to *Par.* 33, 50), St Bernard (1091–1153) assumes a crucial position in the poem, perhaps the highest among Dante's guides.[173] Notwithstanding the primacy of his role in the *Commedia*, Bernard is rarely cited in Dante's other works. The only direct reference is found in the epistle to Cangrande (28), where Dante refers to Bernard by name: *legant Bernardum in libro De Consideratione* (let them read Bernard's book *Concerning Contemplation*). While as a Christian saint, Bernard's presence in a Christian poem might not seem all that odd,[174] given his absence in Dante's other works, the primacy of his role in the *Commedia* is somewhat puzzling. One must wonder why Dante chose St Bernard as his final guide. Why not choose Aquinas, Augustine, or St Francis as his final guide? Various possibilities have been suggested: perhaps it was because St Bernard was considered a leading figure in mystical theology; perhaps it was because of his devotion to Mary; or perhaps it was that Dante's indirect knowledge of St Bernard is to be traced to the Franciscans and other mystical thinkers.[175] Whatever the reason, one thing seems certain: Dante held St Bernard in the highest regard, as is evidenced by the primacy of his role in relation to Dante's own salvation.[176]

Some have argued that, in his representation of St Bernard as an old man, Dante contradicts the ground rule of *Paradiso* that all souls are, in their perfection, thirty-three – the age of Christ in his last year on Earth.[177] The representation of St Bernard as an old man might be better understood once placed within the context of a benevolent paternal figure. Dante in fact refers to St Bernard as a *tenero padre* [tender father [Par. 31, 63]), and St Bernard, in turn, addresses Dante as *figliuol* (son). The image of Bernard as a tender father brings to mind the image of Virgil in *Purgatorio* 30, 50. In the Earthly Paradise, at the precise moment when Beatrice appears, Dante turns back to speak to Virgil only to notice that his *dolcissimo patre* (sweetest of fathers) has in fact disappeared. Just as Virgil suddenly departs, entrusting Dante to the care of Beatrice (*Purg.* 30, 43–54), so does Beatrice now depart, leaving Dante under the care of St Bernard (*Par.* 31, 55–8).[178] The symmetry, the filial relationship evoked, and the use of affective language in both episodes highlight the affective ties. However, while Dante's affectionate union with Virgil acquires significance in relation to the moral good, Dante's union with St Bernard acquires significance in relation to *caritas*, love of God. St Bernard may very well be "Dante's last 'father' in the poem,"[179] as Hollander points out, but undeniably he is the most important. Under the guidance of St Bernard, Dante is led to experience universal truth: the universal order of things in God, then God in His essence, and the Trinity.[180] Through St Bernard, Dante attains perfect vision: he attains a vision of the glory of God, of eternal light. If Beatrice teaches Dante to love God for Himself, it is St Bernard who takes Dante into experiencing the final stage of loving God, or seeing himself in Him.[181] Of the three guides, it is St Bernard who takes Dante to the direct experience of the highest degree of love. While other reasons might very well have influenced Dante's choice, I shall argue here that it is Bernard's conception of love that ultimately drove Dante to choose St Bernard as his final guide. Dante's spiritual journey is an ascent towards perfect love, the ultimate mover of all creation. It is a journey back home to God, who is *caritas*.

For St Bernard, there are four levels or degrees of love: in the first, an individual loves himself for himself; in the second, an individual begins to love God out of need, because he realizes that he needs divine assistance to escape suffering and misery; in the third, an individual loves God for Himself; in the fourth, an individual loves himself only for God's sake.[182] As a way of explaining the fourth and final stage of loving God, when an individual sees himself in God, St Bernard quotes from Philippians 2:7.[183] In *Paradiso* 33, Dante also makes reference to Philippians 2:7: *mi parve pinta de la nostra effige* (to be painted with our likeness).[184] The fact that Dante resorts to the same Pauline passage confirms the supposition that Dante was acquainted with and inspired by St Bernard's thought.

In the same way that Dante's *trasumanar* takes into account *umanar*, the starting point of St Bernard's four degrees of love is the love of self.[185] Even in the fourth degree where one loves oneself for the sake of God, one's human nature and individual identity will remain but will be transfigured into a higher form.[186] Since a person is not pure spirit, it is natural that one would first love one's earthly self. In St Bernard's degrees of love an individual never stops loving himself; rather he learns how to love himself for God. The channelling of love in the proper direction occurs with the help of grace. Ultimately, love's fourth degree is a gift of divine grace and charity.[187] As John says, "God is charity" (1 Jn 4:8).[188] St Bernard himself notes, however, "charity is the mother of friendship ... it alone can render a soul disinterested."[189] Charity alone is powerful enough to direct the soul from a misguided love to the love of God.[190] In the end, therefore, Dante's salvation is essentially a gratuitous gift of Christian friendship, understood as *caritas*. His transmutation of classical friendship parallels his ascent from *umanar*, with Virgil, into *trasumanar*, with Beatrice.[191]

Notes

1. Introduction

1 Aristotle, *Nicomachean Ethics*, trans. Terence Irwin (Indianapolis: Hackett Publishing, 1985), 8.1 1155a1–2, p. 207: "After that the next topic to discuss is friendship; for it is a virtue, or it involves virtue, and besides it is most necessary for our lives."

2 Ibid., 8.1 1155a20–22, p. 208: "Members of the same race, and human beings most of all, have a natural friendship for each other; that is why we praise friends of humanity. And in our travels we can see how every human being is akin and beloved to a human being."

3 Ibid., 9.9 1169b17–19, p. 257: "For no one would choose to have all other goods and yet be alone, since a human being is political, tending by nature to live together with others."

4 David Armstrong, *Horace* (New Haven, CT: Yale University Press, 1989), p. 41.

5 H.H. Joachim, *The Nicomachean Ethics*, ed. D.A. Rees (Oxford: Clarendon Press, 1951), p. 250.

6 Michel de Montaigne, "On Friendship" in *Essays*, trans. J.M. Cohen (New York: Penguin Classics, 1983), p. 92. Following in Aristotle's footsteps, centuries later Montaigne hails friendship as the highest reward of a perfect society and contrasts it to the less noble and less perfect unions grounded in pleasure, power, or gain.

7 Cicero, *De Amicitia*, trans. William A. Falconer (Cambridge: Harvard University Press, 1992), VII, 24, p. 134: "Agrigentum quidem doctum quondam virum carminibus Graecis vaticinatum ferunt, quae in rerum natura totoque mundo constarent quaeque moverentur, ea contrahere amicitiam, dissipare discordiam."

8 David Konstan, *Friendship in the Classical World* (Cambridge: Cambridge University Press), p. 10.

9 Ibid., p. 11.

10 Aristotle, *NE* 8.2 1155b31–4, p. 210: "Love of a soulless thing is not called friendship, since there is no mutual loving ... For friendship is said to be reciprocated goodwill."

11 Ibid., 9.7 1168a20, p. 252: "Moreover, loving is like production, while being loved is like being acted on; and [the benefactor's] love and friendliness is the result of his greater activity." Cf. 9.9 1169b30–4, p. 258: "Being happy, then, is found in living and being active ... The activity of the good person is excellent, and [hence] pleasant in itself, as we said in the beginning." Cf. 8.9 1170a5–10, p. 259: "But the solitary person's life is hard, since it is not easy for him to be continuously active by himself; but in relation to others and in their company it is easier, and hence his activity will be more continuous."

12 Ibid., 8.3, 1156b6–9, p. 212: "But complete friendship is the friendship of good people similar in virtue; for they wish goods in the same way to each other in so far as they are good, and they are good in themselves." Cf. 8.8 1159b5, p. 223: "Equality and similarity, and above all the similarity of those who are similar in being virtuous, is friendship."

13 Ibid., 8.5 1158a30, p. 217: "For loving occurs no less towards soulless things, but reciprocal loving requires decision, and decision comes from a state; and what makes [good people] wish good to the beloved for his own sake is their state, not their feeling."

14 Konstan, *Friendship in the Classical World*, p. 1.

15 Aristotle, *NE* 8.1 1155a21–5, p. 208: "Moreover, friendship would seem to hold cities together, and legislators would seem to be more concerned about it than about justice. For concord would seem to be more similar to friendship and they aim at concord above all, while they try above all to expel civil conflict, which is enmity."

16 See Paul Oppenheimer, *Evil and the Demonic* (New York: New York University Press, 1996), p. 5: "One is aware, in other words, of dealing with a special world when dealing with evil. It is a world of pain in which the tyranny of passion and an obsession colours with fresh ghastly hues everything and everyone." Oppenheimer offers a comprehensive study of evil in all its possible forms and in association with criminality, pain, malevolence, desolation, confusion, chaos, and the irrational.

17 Aquinas, *Summa Theologiae* (New York: McGraw-Hill, 1975), Vol. 34, 2a2ae.23–33, p. 189: "It is always some evil that causes our neighbour's tears. Now evil always means some defect in the way a creature shares in the supreme good, and accordingly, charity makes us share our neighbour's sorrow to the degree that his sharing in the divine good is blocked."

18 Satan's pride made him an enemy to God. See Hollander's note to v. 35 and also his note to vv. 4–7. See also Oppenheimer, *Evil and the Demonic*, pp. 47, 151.

19 See Joan Ferrante, "The Relation of Speech to Sin in the *Inferno*," *Dante Studies* 87 (1969), pp. 33–46. Ferrante proposes an understanding of Satan as a parody of

the flame of the Holy Spirit: "Lucifer, who emits no sound but sends forth a silent and freezing wind of hate, a parody perhaps of the love inspiring tongues of flame brought to the Apostles by the Holy Spirit" (p. 38). Cf. Oppenheimer, *Evil and the Demonic*, p. 47. See also Dino S. Cervigni, "Dante's Lucifer: The Denial of the Word," *Lectura Dantis 3* (1988): 51–62.

20 Giuseppe Mazzotta, *Dante, Poet of the Desert* (Princeton: Princeton University Press, 1979), pp. 119–20: "But by referring to the enmity within the city, Dante also historicizes the concept of friendship and makes it the metaphor of unity and the means by which the pristine harmony of the city can be restored."

21 Ibid. p. 120.

22 See Jacques Derrida's *Politics of Friendship*, trans. George Collins (London and New York: Verso, 1997). Derrida's discussion of the topic acquires significance within an anti-genealogy that questions the conventional genealogy within which the concept of friendship developed and emerged. His vision of a new friendship may be understood in relation to the quote he takes from Nietzsche's *Human All Too Human*: "Perhaps to each of us there will come the more joyful hour when we exclaim: 'Friends, there are no friends!' thus said the dying sage; 'Foes, there are no foes! Say I, the living fool" (*Human All Too Human*, trans. R. Hollingdale [Cambridge: Cambridge University Press, 1986], p. 1, 149, 376).

23 For a thorough analysis of Aristotelian friendship, see Joachim's *Aristotle: The Nicomachean Ethics*. A valuable collection of essays on Aristotelian friendship is to be found in *Essays on Aristotle's Ethics* (Berkeley and Los Angeles: University of California Press, 1980), edited by Amelie O. Rorty – in particular, see John M. Cooper's "Aristotle on Friendship" in that collection – and Price's *Love and Friendship in Plato and Aristotle* (Oxford: Clarendon Press, 1989). For recent studies on Aristotelian friendship, see Michael Pakaluk's "Friendship and Comparison of Goods" in *Phronesis* 37.1 (1992) and Suzanne Stern-Gillet's *Aristotle's Philosophy of Friendship* (New York: State University of New York Press, 1995). Stern-Gillet observes that, while focusing on virtue, Aristotelian friendship is the loving and personal union between individuals rather than the love of an abstract quality. Aristide Tessitore's *Reading Aristotle's Ethics* (Albany: State University of New York Press, 1996) offers a clear and insightful interpretation of Aristotle's ideas on friendship in light of Aristotle's ethical system. For a study of the relationship between friendship and self-love in Aristotle see, W.F.P. Hardie's *Aristotle's Ethical Theory* (Oxford: Oxford University Press, 1968) and Anthony Kenny's *Aristotle on the Perfect Life* (Oxford: Clarendon Press, 1992). For a discussion on the *Virtuous Friends*, see C.D. Reeve's *Practices of Reason: Aristotle's Nichomachean Ethics* (Oxford: Clarendon Press, 1992). An insightful study of friendship in Plato and Aristotle is provided by *Love and Friendship in Plato and Aristotle* by A.W. Price (1989). Gregory Vlastos's "The Individual as an Object of Love in Plato" in *Platonic*

Studies (1973) is a classic study on the interplay between love and friendship in Plato and in Aristotle. A clear and concise study of Plato's *Lysis* is to be found in D. Bolotin's *Plato's Dialogue on Friendship: An Interpretation of the* Lysis (Ithaca: Cornell University Press 1979). For a comprehensive study of friendship in *De Amicitia*, see *Cicero: Laelius, on Friendship and the Dream of Scipio*, ed. J.G. Powell (Warminster: Aris & Phillips, 1990).

24 See Harry V. Jaffa, *Thomism and Aristotelianism* (Chicago: University of Chicago Press, 1952). Also worth reading is J. Bobik's "Aquinas on *communicatio*, the foundation of friendship and *caritas*," in *Modern Schoolman* 64 (1986): 1–18, and Eoin Cassidy's "The recovery of the classical ideal of friendship in Augustine's portrayal of *caritas*," in *The Relationship between Neoplatonism and Christianity*, ed. Thomas Finan and Vincent Twomey (Dublin: Four Courts Press, 1992): 127–40. For well written and clear interpretations of Dante's notion of love and of the difference between the pagan and the Christian notion of love, see A. Hilary Armstrong, "Platonic Eros and Christian *Agape*," *Downside Review* 79.255 (1961): 105–21; and Thomas Bergin, ed., "Dante's Idea of Love" in *From Time to Eternity* (New Haven, CT: Yale University Press, 1967). For the notion of beauty in relation to love, see Joseph Mazzeo, "Dante and the Phaedrus Tradition of Poetic Inspiration" in his *Structure and Thought in The Paradiso* (Ithaca: Cornell University Press, 1958). Mazzeo explores the relation between the Platonic notion of beauty and the Christian notions of ultimate beauty and love. The relationship between reason and Revelation is explored by Etienne Gilson in *Reason and Revelation in The Middle Ages* (New York: Charles Scribner, 1938). For general studies on Dante and philosophy, see Simon Gilson, "Dante and the Science of 'Perspective': A Reappraisal," *Dante Studies* 115 (1997); *Medieval Optics and Theories of Light in the World of Dante* (Lewiston, New York: Edwin Mellen Press, 2000); Simon Gilson, "Medieval Lore and Dante's *Commedia*," *Dante Studies* 119 (2001) [published 2003], 27–66; Simon Gilson, "Medieval Science in Dante's *Commedia*: Past Approaches and Future Directions," *Reading Medieval Studies* 27 (2001); Simon Gilson, "Rimaneggiamenti danteschi di Aristotelel: gravitas e levitas nella *Commedia*," in *Le culture di Dante. Atti del quarto Seminario internazionale*, ed. Michelangelo Picone et al. (2004); and Etienne Gilson's *Dante the Philosopher* (Florence: Cesati, 1948). For the Neoplatonic and Aristotelian influences on Dante, also see Joseph Mazzeo, "Light Metaphysics in the Works of Dante" in *Dante in America*, ed. A.B. Giamatti (Binghamton: Medieval and Renaissance Texts and Studies, 1983): pp. 293–324.

25 Konstan, *Friendship in the Classical World*, p. 5.

26 Ibid., p. 9. As Konstan notes, the different range of meanings of the terms *philos* and *philia* have added to the confusion over the meaning of the concrete noun, by misleading thinkers to assume that its use is as encompassing and broad as that of

philia. Scholars have erroneously assumed that there is no Greek word equivalent to the English word "friend." Nonetheless, Konstan is well aware of the wide range of meanings encompassed by the abstract noun *philia*, and that "there is no single Greek term quite equivalent to 'friendship.'"

27 Paul Millett, *Learning and Borrowing in Ancient Athens* (Cambridge: Cambridge University Press, 1991), p. 113: "It is true that from the viewpoint of comparative sociology, to say nothing of our own experience, the all inclusive quality of Greek friendship is anomalous."

28 Malcolm Heath, *The Poetics of Greek Tragedy* (Stanford, CA: Stanford University Press, 1987), pp. 73–4. According to Heath, friendship in classical Greece: "is not, at root, a subjective bond of affection and emotional warmth, but the entirely objective bond of reciprocal obligation; one's *philos* [friend] is the man one is obliged to help, and on whom one can or ought to be able to rely for help when oneself is in need"; Simon D. Goldhill, *Reading Greek Tragedy* (Cambridge: Cambridge University Press, 1986), p. 82: "The appellation or categorization of *philos* is used to mark not just affection but overridingly a series of complex obligations, duties and claims." (Heath and Goldhill quoted by Konstan, *Friendship in the Classical World*, p. 2)

29 Konstan, *Friendship in the Classical World*, p. 5: "It is now apparent that one strand of the argument developed in this book, according to which friendship in the classical world is understood centrally as a personal relationship predicated on affection and generosity rather than on obligatory reciprocity, challenges prevailing assumptions about the nature of social relations in antiquity. Rather than conceiving of Greek and Roman friendship as seamlessly embedded in economic and other functions, I am claiming for it a relative autonomy comparable to the status it presumably enjoys in modern life."

30 Ronald Syme, *The Roman Revolution* (Oxford: Oxford University Press, 1939), p. 157: "Roman political factions were welded together, less by unity of principle than by mutual interest and by mutual services (*officia*), either between social equals as an alliance, or from superior to inferior, in a traditional and almost feudal form of clientship: on a favourable estimate the bond was called *amicitia*, otherwise *factio*"; Peter Brunt, *The Fall of the Roman Republic and Related Essays* (Oxford: Oxford University Press, 1988), p. 352. Brunt cites Wilhelm Kroll for the notion that "*amicus* means in the everyday language of [Cicero's] time no more than a political follower." (Syme and Brunt quoted by Konstan, *Friendship in the Classical World*, p. 3; cf. Wilhem Kroll, 1933, p. 55; cf. Powell, 1995)

31 Konstan, *Friendship in the Classical World*, p. 13.

32 Ibid., p. 122.

33 Teodolinda Barolini, *Rime giovanili e della Vita Nuova*, p. 182.

34 Ibid.

35 Ibid., p. 183.

36 Dante Alighieri, *Letter to Can Grande della Scala*, quoted in Rachel Jacoff and William Stephany, *Lectura Dantis Americana: Inferno II*, eds. Robert Hollander, Anthony L. Pellegrini, Aldo D. Scaglione, and Joan M. Ferrante (Philadelphia: University of Pennsylvania Press, 1989), p. 1. While drawing a parallel between Augustine's *Confessions* and the *Commedia*, both products of conversion, the authors refer to Dante's intent in the Christian poem, as stated in the Letter to Cangrande, to relieve men from their misery and to lead them to happiness. Whether Dante wrote the whole *Epistle* is still much disputed. Mazzoni argues for the authenticity of the entire *Epistle*, an argument which Jacoff and Stephany seem to support. Robert Hollander also defends the authenticity of the *Epistle*; see his "The 'Canto of the Word' (*Inferno* 2)," *Lectura Dantis Newberryana* (Evanston: Northwestern University Press, 1990), p. 98. For a comprehensive discussion of the controversy see Manlio Pastore Stocchi's *voce* on "Epistole" in *Enciclopedia dantesca*, ed. Umberto Bosco (Rome: Istituto della Enciclopedia Italiana, 1970–8) and Padoan's discussion in "La 'mirabile visione' di Dante e l'Epistola a Cangrande," in *Il pio Enea, l'empio Ulisse: Tradizione classica e intendimento medievale in Dante* (Ravenna Longo, 1977), pp. 30–63. For more recent arguments against the authenticity of the *Epistle*, see Peter Dronke, *Dante and Medieval Latin Traditions* (Cambridge: Cambridge University Press, 1986), and Henry A. Kelly, "Dating the Accessus Section of the Pseudo-Dantean *Epistle to Cangrande*," *Lectura Dantis [Virginiana] 2* (1988): 93–102 cf. Jacoff and Stephany, note 75, pp. 122–3, *Lectura Dantis Americana: Inferno II*. For an attack on all these, see Robert Hollander, *Dante's Epistle to Cangrande* (Ann Arbor, MI: University of Michigan Press, 1993).

37 Simone de Beauvoir, *The Ethics of Ambiguity*, trans. Bernard Frechtman (New York: Citadel Press, 1948), p. 72.

38 Etienne Gilson, *Reason and Revelation in the Middle Ages* (New York: Charles Scribner, 1938), p. 78

39 See Giovanni Gentile, *Studi su Dante* (Florence: Sansoni Editore, 1965), p. 31: "La Teologia, dunque, non giunge all'uomo, non lo salva, se non per mezzo della ragione. Ma la ragione ha limiti invalicabili, oltre i quail occorre la fede, e quindi l'insegnamento teologico."

40 Ibid.: "Abbiamo ricordato quei versi fondamentali del c. VI del *Purgatorio*, in cui Virgilio esplicitamente rimanda le soluzioni definitive di certi problemi razionali a Beatrice. Altrove (*Purg*. XV, 76–78) dice pure apertamente, che *la* sua *ragion non disfama* e che solo Beatrice può togliere ogni *brama*. Altra volta accenna alla relazione che ... la filosofia ha con la teologia ... Il compimento dell'opera di Virgilio è all'entrata nel Paradiso terrestre dove egli si congeda da Dante in questi termini."

41 Ibid., p. 30: "Beatrice non può correre essa incontro a Dante sulla piaggia deserta; e fa capo a Virgilio, alla ragione. E questa non è più trascendenza, ma vero e proprio razionalismo: quell razionalismo tomistico che riesce in certo modo a sottomettere la teologia alla ragione.Questo accade, avvertiva Tommaso, propter defectum intellectus nostri; qui Beatrice direbbe che ha bisogno, essa, la Beatrice, di Virgilio, pel difetto di Dante; ma certo è, che senza Virgilio ella non sarebbe Beatrice, perché non beerebbe Dante, nè potrebbe beare nessuno."

42 Wallace, William A., "Aristotle in the Middle Ages," *Dictionary of the Middle Ages*, vol. 1, ed. Joseph R. Strayer (New York: Scribners, 1982), p. 462.

43 Quoted in Price, *Love and Friendship in Plato and Aristotle.*

44 See John Keats, "Ode on a Grecian Urn," in *The Bedford Introduction to Literature* (Boston: Bedford Books of St. Martin Press, 1996). Keats means something quite different by beauty. It is the sensuous ideal of beauty forever imprinted in the urn, untouched by the passage of time and the uncertainty of human passion, that Keats seems to admire and love. For an intelligent study on this ode, see Earl R. Wasserman, "Ode on a Grecian Urn," in *The Finer Tone: Keat's Major Poems* (Baltimore: Johns Hopkins UP, 1953, 1967), pp. 11–63. For a more contemporary study on the poem Wasserman himself refers to Brook Thomas's "A New Historical Approach to Keat's 'Ode on a Grecian Urn,'" (p. 2032).

45 Montaigne, "On Friendship," pp. 99–103. Montaigne speaks of the blending of two souls into one. In pondering the great loss of his dear friend Montaigne exclaims, "I had grown so accustomed to be his second self in everything that now I seem to be no more than half a man."

46 Cicero, *DA* VII, 23, p. 132: "Verum etiam amicum qui intuetur, tamquam exemplar aliquod intuetur sui."

47 Etienne Gilson, *The Mystical Theory of St. Bernard* (New York: Sheed and Ward, 1955), p. 8.

48 Aristotle, *NE* 8.1. 1155a1–4, p. 207: "After that the next topic to discuss is friendship; for it is a virtue, or involves virtue, and besides is most necessary to our life." Cf. Cicero, *DA* VI, 20–1, p. 130: "Sed haec ipsa virtus amicitiam et gignit et continet, nec sine virtute amicitia esse ullo pacto potest." Cf. Cicero, *DA* XXII, 83, p. 190: "Virtutum amicitia adiutrix a natura data est, non vitiourum comes, ut, quoniam solitaria non posset virtus ad ea quae summa sunt pervenire, coniuncta et consociata cum altera perveniret." Cf. Cicero, *DA* XXVII, 100, p. 206: "Virtus, inquam, C. Fanni, et tu, Q. Muci, et conciliat amicitias et conservat. In ea est enim convenientia rerumm, in ea stabilitas, in ea Constantia." Cf. Cicero, *DA* XXVII, 104, p. 210: "Vos autem hortor ut ita virtutem locetis (sine qua amicitia esse non potest) ut ea excepta nihil amicitia praestabilius putetis."

49 Aristotle, *NE* 9.8. 1169a20, p. 256: "Besides, it is true that, as they say, the excellent person labours for his friends and for his native country, and will die for them." Cf. Cicero, *DA* VI, 22–VII, 23.

50 Cicero, *DA* XXI, 80, p. 188: "Verus amicus numquam reperietur: est enim is qui est tamquam alter idem."

51 Konstan, *Friendship in the Classical World*, p. 167.

52 Aristotle, *NE* 8.7 1158b33–36, p. 221; cf. Konstan, *Friendship in the Classical World*, p. 168; cf. Erik Peterson, "Der Gottesfreund: Beiträge zur Geschichte eines religiösen Terminus," *Zeitschrift für Kirchengeschichte* 42 (1923): 161–202. Peterson argues that two contrasting views existed in classical antiquity, one of which accepted the possibility of friendship between the human and the divine, while the other, represented by Aristotle, rejected it. According to Peterson, these two divergent views find resolution in the works of the early Christian thinkers; cf. J.F. Dodek, "Friendship with God," in *the New Catholic Encyclopedia*, vol. 6 (1967): 207–8; cf. J. Moltmann, "Open Friendship: Aristotelian and Christian Concepts of Friendship," in *The Changing Face of Friendship*, ed. Leroy S. Rouner (1994), 20–42.

53 Dante, "*Epistle to Cangrande*," in *Critical Essays on Dante*, ed. Giuseppe Mazzotta (Boston: G.K. Hall & Co., 1991), pp. 3–4.

54 Ibid., p. 4.

55 Quoted in Konstan, *Friendship in the Classical World*, pp. 167–8.

56 Ibid., p. 149: "When the church fathers wrote about friendship, they were as often concerned with relations among monks, priests, or other devotees who lived together in religious communities as with forms of familiarity among lay people." Cf. B.P. McGuire, "Friendship and Community: The Monastic Experience," *Cistercian Studies* 95 (1988): 17–20, 38–40.

57 Ambrose, "On the Duties of Ministers" in *De Officiis* (391), ed. J. Davidson, vol. 10, (1963); quoted in Konstan, *Friendship in the Classical World*, p. 150: "Open your bosom to your friend, so that he may be faithful to you and that you may derive from him pleasure in your life. 'For a faithful friend is the medicine of life, and the blessing of immortality' (Eccl. 6:16)."

58 Konstan, *Friendship in the Classical World*, p. 153.

59 Ibid., p. 173.

60 See Paulinus of Nola, *Epistola* 13.2 in *Letters of St. Paulinus of Nola*, eds. Rev. Johannes Quasten, Rev. Walter J. Burghardt, and Rev. Thomas Comerford Lawler (New York: Paulist Press, 1966). While writing to Pammachius, Paulinus contrasts spiritual friendship, a union grounded in Christ, with secular friendship, a union grounded in the individual: "Therefore in the truth in which we stand in Christ, receive my spirit as it is expressed to you in this letter, and do not measure our friendship by time. For it is not as a secular friendship, which is often begotten more in hope than in faith, but rather that spiritual kind, which is produced by

God as its source and is joined in a brotherhood of souls. Consequently, it does not develop toward love by daily familiarity nor does it depend on anticipation of proof but, as is worthy of a daughter of truth, it is born at once stable and great, because it arises out of fullness through Christ" (quoted in Konstan, *Friendship in the Classical World*, p. 157); cf. Pierre Fabre, *Saint Paulin de Nole et l'amitie' chretienne* (Paris: Bibliotheque des Ecoles francaises d'Athenes et de Rome,1949), pp. 142–8; cf. Hélene Pétré, *Caritas: Ètude sur le vocabulaire latin de la charité chrétienne* (Spicilegium sacrum Lovaniense 22, Louvain, 1948), pp. 30–98; cf. C. White, *Christian Friendship in the Fourth Century* (Cambridge: Cambridge University, 1992), pp. 158–9. As Konstan notes, Fabre affirms that Paulinus never uses *amicitia* to refer to friendship grounded in Christ. White argues that despite the common association of Christian friendship with *caritas*, Paulinus "does occasionally use *amicus* without implying that he is talking to a non-Christian," and that in the eleventh epistle he uses *amicitia* as he discusses his friendship with Sulpicius Severus (quoted by Konstan, *Friendship in the Classical World*).

61 Konstan, *Friendship in the Classical World*, p. 161.

62 Ibid., p. 173; cf. B.J. Rogers, "The Poems of Venantius Fortunatus: A Translation and Commentary," dissertation (New Brunswick, NJ: Rutgers University, 1970), p. 43; J.W. George, *Venantius Fortunatus: A Latin Poet in Merovingian Gaul* (Oxford: Oxford University Press, 1992), pp. 144, 173–4.

63 Konstan, *Friendship in the Classical World*, p. 22.

64 Ibid.

65 Augustine, *City of God*, 19.25; cf. Konstan, *Friendship in the Classical World*, p. 160.

66 Augustine, *Sermons*, 361.1 (New York: New York City Press, 1995), cit. M.A. McNamara, *Friendship in Saint Augustine* (Staten Island, NY: Alba House, 1958), p. 206; cf. Augustine, *On the Trinity* 9.7.13., ed. Gareth B. Matthews, trans. Stephen McKenna (Cambridge: Cambridge University Press, 2002); Augustine, *On Christian Doctrine* 1.22.20, trans. James Shaw (Oxford: Benediction Classics, Oxford University Press, 2010); David Konstan, *Friendship in the Classical World*, p. 172 (Augustine quoted by Konstan).

67 See Konstan, *Friendship in the Classical World*, p. 165.

68 I am pleased to find that Guy P. Raffa independently (but after I wrote my dissertation, *Dante's Transmutation of Classical Friendship*, in 2009) offered a highly similar view of the matter in "A Beautiful Friendship: Dante and Vergil in the Commedia," *Modern Language Notes*, 127.1 (2012): S72–S80.

69 G. Heylbut, *Aspasii in Ethica nicomachea quae supersunt commentaria*, 179.28–180.5.

70 Charles Singleton, *Dante Studies 2: Journey to Beatrice* (Cambridge: Harvard University Press, 1958), p. 33.

71 Singleton, *Dante Studies 2: Journey to Beatrice*, p. 53.

72 Mazzotta, *Dante, Poet of the Desert*, p. 114.

73 Ibid.

2. Classical Friendship: Aristotle and Dante's *Convivio*

1 John A. Scott, "Aristotle," in *The Dante Encyclopedia*, ed. Richard Lansing (New York: Garland Publishing, 2000), p. 61.

2 Ibid., p. 61.

3 Wallace, "Aristotle in the Middle Ages," p. 460.

4 Ibid., p. 460.

5 Ibid., p. 461.

6 Ibid., pp. 456, 460–1: "The full influence of Aristotelian thought was not felt, however, until the remaining works were available in Latin. This eventuated in the mid twelfth century through the efforts of James of Venice (d. after 1142), who travels to Constantinople and translated the *Posterior Analytics, Physics, On the Soul, Metaphysics,* and minor works from the Greek ... A better translation of the *Nicomachean Ethics* was made about 1240 by Robert Grosseteste (ca. 1168–1253), along with *On the Heavens.* The entire Latin corpus was completed in the third quarter of the century by William of Moerbeke (ca. 1215–86)."

7 Scott, "Aristotle," *The Dante Encyclopedia*, p. 61. In Toledo, Michael Scoto (c. 1220–35) did a partial translation of the *Metaphysics* from an Arabic text.

8 Wallace, "Aristotle in the Middle Ages," p. 462.

9 Ibid.

10 Scott, "Aristotle," *The Dante Encyclopedia*, p. 62.

11 Maria C. De Matteis, "Aristotele," in *Enciclopedia dantesca*, vol. 1, ed. Umberto Bosco (Rome: Istituto Dell'Enciclopedia Italiana, 1970), p. 372.

12 Scott, "Aristotle," *The Dante Encyclopedia*, p. 62.

13 Etienne Gilson, *Reason and Revelation in the Middle Ages*, pp. 73–8.

14 Wallace, "Aristotle in the Middle Ages," p. 462.

15 Francesco De Sanctis, "The Subject of the Divine Comedy," in *Critical Essays on Dante*, pp. 77–8. De Sanctis focuses on the interplay between religion and philosophy in Dante. Both are necessary for the fulfilment of man's two ends, heavenly bliss and earthly happiness: "His mind submitted to the authority of the *Ethics* as to the Bible, to Aristotle as to St. Thomas; he believed implicitly that the great philosophers of antiquity agreed with the teaching of religion, and that they were wrong not because they saw wrongly, but because they did not see everything ... he maintained that spirit and matter were endowed each with its own life, without interference with the other; and from this he inferred in independence of the two powers, the spiritual and the temporal ... Both are organs of God on earth, 'two

suns'[*Purgatory*, 16, 106] who guide humanity, one in the ways of God, the other in the ways of the world, one to heavenly and the other to earthly happiness."

16 Karl Vossler, *Medieval Culture: An Introduction to Dante and His Times*, trans. William C. Lawton (New York: Harcourt, Brace and Company, 1929), vol. 1, p. 145.

17 Michele Barbi, *Life of Dante*, trans. Paul G. Ruggiers (Berkley: University of California Press, 1966), p. 45.

18 Ibid.: "He is, of course, a follower of Aristotelian philosophy, and he never tires of calling Aristotle the 'teacher and leader of human reason,' the philosopher 'most worthy of faith and obedience,' and of asserting that 'where the divine opinion of Aristotle opens its mouth, the opinion of all other men should be disregarded.'"

19 Scott, "Aristotle," *The Dante Encyclopedia*, p. 64.

20 Ibid.

21 Vossler, *Medieval Culture: An Introduction to Dante and His Times*, vol. 1, p. 185: "Plato, of whom he had only a second-hand knowledge, is much closer to him than Aristotle, whose *Nicomachean Ethics* he memorized almost as thoroughly as the *Aeneid* of his beloved Virgil." Contrary to Vossler's opinion, it must be affirmed that Dante was closer to Aristotle than to Plato.

22 Giovanni Gentile, *Studi su Dante* (Florence: Sansoni, 1965), p. 9: "Delle opere aristoteliche e psuedo-aristoteliche vi ricorrono a ogni passo citazioni che provano o vogliono provare come l'Autore le avesse studiate: l'Etica a Nicomaco, la Politica (che in realtà pare non conoscesse ancora direttamente), la Metafisica, la Fisica, il De coelo et mundo, il De generatione et corruptione, il De animalibus, il De anima, il De sensu et sensibili, la Rhetorica, il De juventute et senectute e il De causis. Di Platone, oltre la traduzione del Timeo, gia' ricordata, egli conosce, ma indirettamente, e rammenta talune dottrine, di cui attinge la notizia in S. Tommaso, in S. Agostino o in Cicerone; e altra volta dallo stesso Aristotele o da Alberto Magno."

23 Joachim, *Aristotle: The Nicomachean Ethics*, p. 246; cf. Aristotle, *NE* 8.2 1155b17.

24 Price, *Love and Friendship in Plato and Aristotle*, p. 1.

25 Ibid., p. 9: "On behalf of the theme that like loves like" (*Lysis* 214a6; *EE* 7.1. I235a7, cf. *NE* 8.1. 1155a34); on the attraction of opposite both again have natural philosophy in mind (*Lysis* 215e5–9; *NE* 8.1 1155b1–6, *EE* 7.1. 1235a13–16); the theme that only good men can be friends (*Lysis* 214b6–7, d5–e1, 215a4–5; *EE* 7.1 1234b26–7, *EE* 7.11235a31–3, cf. *NE* 8.1 1155b11–12). This is linked to the love of the like to the like by being supported by a claim that bad men not only wrong one another (*Lysis* 214b8–c3; *EE* 7.1 1235b24–5, *EE* 7.2.1236b13–14), but are not similar even to themselves (*Lysis* 214c7–d3; *NE* 9.4, *EE* 7.6); it is opposed by the thought that the good are self-sufficient (*Lysis* 215a6–c1; *NE* 9.9. 1169b3–8, *EE* 7.12. 1244b1–15). Plato's failure in the *Lysis* to define friendship in relation to the various uses of *philos* (212a8–213c9) inspires Aristotle's success: "A man becomes

a friend whenever being loved he loves in return" (*EE* 7.2. 1236a14–15, cf. *NE* 8.2. 1155b27–8). Plato assumes a close connection between *philos* in the senses of "friend"' and of "dear"; indeed, he fails to distinguish them, and so, to our eyes, rambles in and out of discussion of friendship in a way that threatens to dissolve the topic. Aristotle keeps the senses apart, but does not discard Plato's attention to things as well as persons that are dear. Indeed, he grounds and classifies kinds of friendship by reference to different categories of things that are loved: just as *inanimate* objects can be loved as being good, pleasant, or useful, so can men (*EE* 7.2. 1236a10–14); just as the good, pleasant, and useful differ in kind, so do lovings and friendships (*NE* 8.3. 1156a6–8). Hence both Plato and Aristotle view friendship against the general background of the structure of human desire. Aristotle's more developed analogue to Plato's "first dear" (219d1) came earlier (*NE* 1.2. 1094a18–22, *EE* 1.8. 1218b9–12); but for him the problem about how the good man can need friends reduces to the question of how friends can contribute to his own final good or *eudaimonia* (cf. *NE* 9.9. 1169b3–4, *EE* 7.12. 1244b5).

26 Price, *Love and Friendship in Plato and Aristotle*, p. 14.

27 Bolotin, *Plato's Dialogue on Friendship: An Interpretation of the* Lysis, p.11.

28 Ibid.

29 Ibid., p. 12.

30 Giovanni Gentile, *Studi su Dante*, p. 9: "L'Autore si mostra, infatti esperto conoscitore di quasi tutte le fonti del sapere filosofico e scientifico correnti sul finire del sec. XIII e al cominciare del XIV per l'Europa."

31 Erich Auerbach, *Dante Poet of the Secular World*, trans. Ralph Manheim (Chicago: University of Chicago Press, 1969), p. 71. According to the ideology of the *cor gentile*, love is intrinsically linked to the gentle heart, or to one possessing a noble character. Such a person is capable of both loving and of being loved.

32 Maria C. De Matteis, "Aristotele," in *Enciclopedia Dantesca*, pp. 372–3. See Dante's *Convivio* for a comprehensive list of Dante's references to Aristotle: "mio maestro" (*Conv.* I, ix 9; cf. *Epistle* XI, ii); "maestro de li filosofi" (*Conv.* IV, viii, 15); "maestro e duca de la ragione umana" (*Conv.* IV, vi 8; cf. *Conv.* IV, ii, 16); "maestro de la nostra vita" (*Conv.* IV, xxiii 8); "maestro di color che sanno" (*Inf.* 4, 131).

33 Ibid., IV, vi, 5–6, 8, p. 239: "Onde, quand'io provi che Aristotile è dignissimo di fede e d'obedienza, manifesto è che le sue parole sono somma e altissima autoritade. Che Aristotile sia dignissimo di fede e d'obedienza così provare si può ... Questi è Aristotile; dunque esso è dignissimo di fede e d'obedienza" (p. 239).

34 Ibid., IV, vi, 17, p. 242: "che l'autoritade del filosofo sommo, di cui s'intende, sia piena di tutto vigore."

35 Karl Vossler, *Medieval Culture: An Introduction to Dante and His Times*, vol. 1, p. 185: "From Aristotle he indeed took over the general plan, the terminology, the scholastic

division, the concepts of virtue and sins, but hardly one vital and fundamental thought. He never took seriously either the doctrine that makes of action the source of happiness and the condition of virtue, or the doctrine of the moral neutrality of the sensuous nature. If it were otherwise, how could he ever have insisted that moral purification comes through vision instead of through experience, through instruction and not through toil, through penance and not through discipline?"

36 Etienne Gilson, *Reason and Revelation in the Middle Ages*, p. 78.
37 Gentile, *Studi su Dante*, pp. 30–1.
38 Ibid., p. 31: "La teologia, dunque, non giunge all'uomo, non lo salva, se non per mezzo della ragione. Ma la ragione ha limiti invalicabili, oltre i quali occorre la fede, e quindi l'insegnamento teologico." In an effort to validate his claim Gentile refers to *Purgatorio* 6, where Virgil looks to Beatrice for solutions to particular problems that he himself is unable to resolve. Also, in *Purgatorio* 15, 76–8, Virgil openly admits that his reason "non disfama" and that Dante should look to Beatrice as one who can satisfy "ogni brama."
39 Ibid., pp. 13–14.
40 Ibid., p. 14.
41 Konstan, *Friendship in the Classical World*, p. 67.
42 Cooper, "Aristotle on Friendship," pp. 301–40.
43 Ibid., p. 203: "It should be clear why Aristotle's theory of friendship must be considered a cardinal element in his ethical theory as a whole. For it is only here that he directly expresses himself on the nature, and importance to a flourishing human life, of taking an interest in other persons, merely as such and for their own sake."
44 Ibid., p. 303.
45 Aristotle, *NE* 8.1 1155a1–4; 8.1 1155a22–8; 9.1 1169b17–19, p. 257: "For no one would choose to have [other] goods and yet be alone, since a human being is political, tending by nature to live together with others."
46 It is worth noting that in his understanding of on individual as a socio-political being, Aristotle does not take into consideration the figure of the misanthrope, whose antisocial behaviour would drive him to reject friendship.
47 Aristotle, *NE* 8.1 1155a20–3, p. 208: "Members of the same race, and human beings most of all, have a natural friendship for each other; that is why we praise friends of humanity. And in our travels we can see how every human being is akin and beloved to a human being"; ibid, 8.1 1155a23–6, p. 208: "Moreover, friendship would seem to hold cities together, and legislators would seem to be more concerned about it than about justice. For concord would seem to be similar to friendship and they aim at concord above all, while they try above all to expel civil conflict, which is enmity."

48 H.H. Joachim, *Aristotle: The Nicomachean Ethics*, p. 246.

49 Konstan, *Friendship in the Classical World*, p. 68: "Chief among the errors is the widespread supposition that Aristotle has no notion comparable to that of friendship in English, since for him *philia* covers so wide a range of relations as to be effectively a different concept. Indeed, it is. But one type of *philia* corresponds closely to friendship, namely, the affection that obtains between *philoi* or friends."

50 Ibid.

51 Ibid., p. 69.

52 Joachim, *Aristotle: The Nichomachean Ethics*, p. 246.

53 Ibid., p. 248.

54 Aristotle, *NE* 8.8 1159b13–15, p. 223: "The friendship that seems to arise most from contraries is friendship for utility ... for we aim at whatever we find we lack, and give something else in return."

55 Ibid., 8.3 1159b20–21, p. 224: "Presumably, however, contrary seeks contrary coincidentally, not in itself, and desire is for the intermediate."

56 Price, *Love and Friendship in Plato and Aristotle*, p. 119.

57 Stern-Gillet, *Aristotle's Philosophy of Friendship*, p. 73.

58 Konstan, *Friendship in the Classical World*, p. 76.

59 Ibid.

60 Stern-Gillet, *Aristotle's Philosophy of Friendship*, pp. 80, 84–5.

61 David Ross, *Aristotle* (London: Methuen and Co., 1968), pp. 231–2. cf. Aristotle, *NE* 8.11 1161b28; 9.4 1166a32; 9.9 1169b6; 9.10 1170b6; 8.12 1161b20.

62 Hardie, *Aristotle's Ethical Theory*, p. 328.

63 Kenny, *Aristotle on the Perfect Life*, p. 53. cf. Aristotle, *NE* 9.9 1169a18ff.

64 Price, *Love and Friendship in Plato and Aristotle*, p. 105.

65 Joachim, *Aristotle: The Nicomachean Ethics*, pp. 250–1.

66 Ibid.

67 Price, *Love and Friendship in Plato and Aristotle*, p. 123.

68 Cooper, "Aristotle on Friendship," p. 323.

69 Price, *Love and Friendship in Plato and Aristotle*, p. 122.

70 G.W.F. Hegel, *Phenomenology of Spirit*, trans. A.V. Miller (Oxford: Oxford University Press, 1977), p. 182

71 Aristotle, *NE* 9.12 1171b35–1172a14, pp. 265–6: "... what friends find most choiceworthy is living together. For friendship is a community, and we are related to our friend as we are related to ourselves ... But the friendship of decent people is decent, and increases the more often they meet. And they seem to become still better from their activities and their mutual correction. For each moulds the other in what they approve of, so that you will learn what is noble from noble people."

72 Price, *Love and Friendship in Plato and Aristotle*, p. 130.

73 Jaffa, *Thomism and Aristotelianism*, p. 126

74 Ibid., p. 133.

75 Foster, "The Mind in Love: Dante's Philosophy," in *Dante: A Collection of Critical Essays*, ed. John Freccero (New Jersey: Prentice Hall, 1965), p. 45.

76 Dronke, *Dante and Medieval Latin Traditions*, p. 91. See Dronke's note 19 where he points to Maria Corti's "L'amoroso uso di sapienza nel *Convivio*," in *La Felicità mentale* (Turin, 1983), pp. 110ff. According to Dronke, Corti "has given good reasons for believing that Dante also worked with one of Albert's two commentaries on the *Ethics*, the so-called *Super Ethica*" (p. 141).

77 Dante, *Convivio*, ed. Giorgio Inglese (Milan: Biblioteca Universale Rizzoli, 1999), II, xiv, 14, p. 134; cf. Thomas, *Ethic*. II I, 245, ed. R.M. Spiazzi, in *Decem Libros Ethicorum Aristotelis ad Nicomachum Expositio* (Turin: Marietti, 1964), p. 69; cf. Dronke, *Dante and Medieval Latin Traditions* (1986), p. 141. See Dronke's note 20.

78 Dante, *Conv.* IV, viii, 1 p. 247; cf. Thomas, *Ethic*. I I, I, p. 3. cf. Peter Dronke, *Dante and Medieval Latin Traditions* (1986), p. 141. See Dronke's note 21.

79 Dante, *Conv.* III, xi, 7–8, p. 190: "E ['n] la 'ntenzione d'Aristotile, ne l'ottavo de l'Etica, quelli si dice amico la cui amistà non è celata a la persona amata e a cui la persona amata è anche amica, sì che la benivolenza sia da ogni parte; e questo co[nvien]e essere o per utilitade, o per diletto, o per onestade" (p. 190). Cf., Aristotle, *NE* 8, 1156a3–1156b30, pp. 211–13. Aristotle classifies three types of friendship corresponding to three objects of love: friendship for utility, friendship for pleasure, and friendship for virtue. Of these three, only friendship grounded in the love of virtue is considered to be the most perfect and complete. Friendships grounded in the love of utility and on pleasure are incomplete since they are grounded in accidental attributes and extrinsic goods. Accordingly, the lesser types of friendship are "coincidental, since the beloved is loved not in so far as he is who he is, but in so far as he provides some good or pleasure" (p. 213).

80 Dante, *Conv.* III, xi, 9, p. 190: "E sì come l'amistà per diletto fatta, o per utilitade, non è vera amistà, ma per accidente – sì come l'Etica ne dimostra – così la filosofia per diletto o per utilitade non è vera filosofia, ma per accidente."

81 Dante, *Conv.* III, xi, 11–12, p. 191: "… per che, sì come l'amistà per onestade fatta è vera e perfetta e perpetua, così la filosofia è vera e perfetta, che è generata per onestade solamente, sanza altro rispetto, e per bontade de l'anima amica, che è per diritto appetito e per diritta ragione."

82 Ibid., III, xi, 13, pp. 191–2: "E sì come la vera amistade, astratta de l'animo, solo in sè considerata, ha per subietto la conoscenza de l'operazione buona, e per forma l'appetito di quella, così la filosofia, fuori d'anima, in sè considerata, ha per subietto lo'ntendere, e per forma uno quasi divino amore a lo 'ntelletto. E sì come de la vera amistade è cagione efficiente la vertude, così de la filosofia è cagione efficiente la veritade."

83 Ibid., III, xi, 14–15, p. 192: "e sì come fine de l'amistade vera è la buona dilezione, che procede dal convivere secondo l'umanitade propriamente, cioè secondo ragione (sì come pare sentire Aristotile nel nono de l'Etica), così il fine de la filosofia è quella eccellentissima dilezione che non pate alcuna intermissione o vero difetto, cioè vera felicitade, che per contemlazione de la veritade s'acquista."

84 Singleton, *Dante Studies 2: Journey to Beatrice*, p. 45.

85 Thomas Aquinas, opusc. 27, *De Principis Naturae ad Fratrem Silvestrum*: "Generatio est motus ad formam"; and *passim* in other works.

86 Dante, *Conv.* II, i, 10, p. 85.

87 Singleton, *Dante Studies 2: Journey to Beatrice*, pp. 101–5.

88 Aristotle, *NE* 9.9 1169b20, pp. 257–8: "Surely it is also absurd to make the blessed person solitary. For no one would choose to have all [other] goods and yet be alone ... This will also be true, then, of the happy person; for he has the natural goods, and clearly it is better to spend his days with decent friends than with strangers of just any character. Hence the happy person will need friends." And further, in 9.10 1170b15, p. 261: "Anyone who is to be happy, then, must have excellent friends."

89 Aristotle, *NE* 8.3 1156b5, p. 212. According to Aristotle, perfect friendship is grounded in the love of virtue. A true friend loves his friend for who he is essentially, for the good present in him: "But complete friendship is the friendship of good people similar virtue; for they wish goods in the same way to each other in so far as they are good, and they are good in themselves." Accordingly, only the friendship among good people is perfect friendship. See *NE* 8.6 1157b25, p. 217: "It is the friendship of good people that is friendship most of all, as we have often said." Friendship encourages virtue. See *NE* 9.9 1170a10, p. 259: "Further, good people's life together allows the cultivation of virtue, as Theognis says." In considering the relationship between friendship and happiness, Aristotle concludes that in the absence of friendship, happiness is impossible: "Surely it is also absurd to make the blessed person solitary. For no one would choose to have all [other] goods and yet be alone, since a human being is political, tending by nature to live together with others. This will also be true, then, of the happy person; for he has the natural goods, and clearly it is better to spend his days with decent friends than with strangers of just any character. Hence the happy person will need friends." Since happiness is an activity, and since it is easier to be active in the company of others, friendship promotes both activity and happiness. In *NE* 9.9 1169b30–1170a5, pp. 258–9, Aristotle concludes: "For we have said at the beginning that happiness is a kind of activity ... But the solitary person's life is hard, since it is not easy for him to be continuously active all by himself; but in relation to others and in their company it is easier, and hence his activity will be

more continuous. It is also pleasant in itself, as it must be in the blessedly happy person's case."

90 Dante, *Conv.* I, i, 1–2, p. 41: "Sì come dice lo Filosofo nel principio de la Prima Filosofia, tutti li uomini naturalmente desiderano di sapere. La ragione di che puote essere, ed è, che ciascuna cosa, da providenza di propria natura impinta, è inclinabile a la sua propria perfezione; onde, acciò che la scienza è ultima perfezione de la nostra anima, ne la quale sta la nostra ultima felicitade, tutti naturalmente al suo desiderio semo subietti." See also Thomas Aquinas, *Commentary on Aristotle's Metaphysics*, "Proem": "Omnes autem scientiae et artes ordinantur in unum, scilicet ad hominis perfectionem, quae est eius beatitudo" (Aquinas quoted by Singleton, "Goal at the Summit," in *Dante Studies 2: Journey to Beatrice*, p. 118, see note 5).

91 Dante, *Conv.* I, vi, 10–11, p. 59: "Ancora: sanza conversazione o familiaritade impossibile è a conoscere li uomini; e lo latino non ha conversazione con tanti in alcuna lingua con quanti ha lo volgare di quella, al quale tutti sono amici; e per consequente non può conoscere li amici del volgare. E non è contradizione ciò che dire si potrebbe, che lo latino pur conversa con alquanti amici de lo volgare: che però non è familiare di tutti, e così non è conoscente de li amici perfettamente; però che si richiede perfetta conoscenza, e non difettiva."

92 Aristotle, *NE* 1, 1098b30, p. 20: "First, our account agrees with those who say happiness is virtue [in general] or some [particular] virtue; for activity expressing virtue is proper to virtue." See also *NE* 1, 1099b25, p. 29: "... from our account [of happiness]. For we have said it is a certain sort of activity of the soul expressing virtue, [and hence not a product of fortune]." See also *NE* 1, 1102a5, p. 29: "Since happiness is an activity of the soul expressing complete virtue, we must examine virtue; for that will perhaps also be a way to study happiness better."

93 Singleton, *Dante Studies 2: Journey to Beatrice*, p. 23: "Evidently, happiness, on such a definition, is something which can fit very well into a pattern of moral allegory, since such allegory is always in terms of *agere*, of action or movement in the soul." See also Singleton's note 4 (p. 117). According to Singleton, the distinction in these two types of activity is crucial for an understanding of the moral allegory of the poem as *agere*. As Singleton notes, Aquinas often refers to this same distinction made by Aristotle. Cf. Aquinas, *ST* I–II, q. 3, a. I, ad 3: "Sicut dicitur in IX Metaph., duplex est action. Una quae procedit ab operante in exterioram materiam, sicut ucere et secare. Et talis operatio non potest esse beatitudo, nam talis operatio non est action et perfectio agentis sed magis patientis, ut ibidem dicitur. Alia est action manens in ipso agente, ut sentire, intelligere et velle, et huiusmodi action est perfectio et actus agentis. Et talis operatio potest esse beatitudo." (Aquinas quoted by Singleton, p. 117, note 4)

94 Aristotle, *NE* 1, 1095a20, p. 5: "most people virtually agree [about what the good is], since both the many and the cultivated call it happiness, and suppose that living well and doing well are the same as being happy. But they disagree about what happiness is, and the many do not give the same answer as the wise." See also *NE* 1, 1097b20: "Happiness, then, is apparently something complete and self-sufficient, since it is the end of the things pursued in action."

95 Singleton, *Dante Studies 2: Journey to Beatrice*, pp. 101–5.

96 Karl Vossler, *Medieval Culture: An Introduction to Dante and His Times*, p. 145.

97 Dante, *Conv.* III, xi, 13–15, pp. 191–2. Dante draws an analogy between true friendship and philosophy: "E sì come la vera amistade, astratta de l'animo, solo in sé cosiderata, ha per subietto la conoscenza de l'operazione buona, e per forma l'appetito di quella, così la filosofia, fuori d'anima, in sé considerate, ha per subietto lo 'ntendere, e per forma uno quasi divino amore a lo 'ntelletto. E sì come de la vera amistade è cagione efficiente la vertude, così la filosofia è cagione efficiente la veritade; e sì come fine de l'amistade vera è la buona dilezione, che procede dal convivere secondo l'umanitade propriamente, cioè secondo ragione (sì come pare sentire Aristotile nel nono de l'Etica), così fine de la filosofia è quella eccellentissima dilezione che non pate alcuna intermissione o vero difetto, cioè vera felicitade, che per contemplazione de la veritade s'acquista."

98 Ibid., I, i, 8–9, pp. 42–3: "Ma però che ciascuno uomo a ciascuno uomo naturalmente è amico, e ciascuno amico si duole del difetto di colui ch'elli ama, coloro che a così alta mensa sono cibati non sanza misericordia sono inver di quelli che in bestiale pastura veggiono erba e ghiande gire mangiando. E acciò che misericordia è madre di benificio, sempre liberalmente coloro che sanno porgono de la loro buona ricchezza a li veri poveri, e sono fonte vivo, de la cui acqua si rifrigera la naturale sete che di sopra è nominata."

99 Ibid., III, ii, 3–4, p. 149: "Amore, veramente pigliando e sottilmente considerando, non è altro che unimento spirituale de l'anima e de la cosa amata; nel quale unimento di propia sua natura l'anima corre tosto e tardi, secondo che è libera o impedita."

100 Dronke, *Dante and Medieval Latin Traditions*, p. 82: "The activities of knowing and loving become one together in contemplation. In medieval Aristotelian terms, the knower becomes one with what he knows, even as the lover becomes one with what he loves."

101 Dante, *Par.* 30, 1–6, p. 230. See Hollander's note to *Paradiso* 30, 1–6 (p. 240). Cf. Dronke, "The First Circle in the Solar Heaven," in *Dante and Medieval Latin Traditions*, p. 82: "The relations between knowledge and love are made manifest in *Paradiso* X: they are exemplified within the godhead, in the ordering of the

heavens, in Dante and Beatrice, in a host of images drawn from earthly phenomena, and – most comprehensively – in a circle of twelve lights: twelve radiant, fiery souls that show their power to know and love inseparably."

102 See Hollander's note to *Paradiso* 30, 64–9, p. 244. Cf. Dronke, "The First Circle in the Solar Heaven," in *Dante and Medieval Latin Traditions*, p. 82.

103 Dante, *Conv.* I, i, 7, p. 42: "the bread of the angels." Cf. Dronke, "The First Circle in the Solar Heaven," in *Dante and Medieval Latin Traditions*, p. 89. See Dronke's note 7, p. 144. Dronke draws attention to Bruno Nardi, *Nel Mondo di Dante* (Rome: Edizioni di "Storia e Letteratura," 1944), pp. 47–53. See also Dronke regarding Bruno's *Saggi e note di critica dantesca* (Milan-Naples: Ricciardi, 1966), pp. 386–90. Cf. Lange, 'Geistliche Speise,' *Zeitschrift fur deutsches Altertum* XCV (1966), 81–122.

104 Dante, *Conv.* I, i, 7, p. 42: "Oh beati quelli pochi che seggiono a quella mensa dove lo pane de li angeli si manuca! E miseri quelli che con le pecore hanno comune cibo!"

105 Dante, *Purg.* 2, 10–12: "Voi altri pochi che drizzaste il collo / per tempo al pan de li angeli, del quale / vivesi qui ma non sen vien satollo." I cite from Hollander's note to verse 12, p. 47: "Christians on earth will never be able to attain angelic understanding of the doctrine that nourishes them; for that they must await their afterlife in Paradise."

106 Dante, *Purg.* 31, 127–9: "Mentre che piena di stupore e lieta / l'anima mia gustava di quel cibo / che, saziando de sè, di sè asseta." See Hollander's note to verse 11.

107 Francesco De Sanctis, *Storia della letteratura italiana*, ed. Benedetto Croce (Bari: Laterza, 1965), vol. 1, p. 150: "Lo studio della filosofia è perciò un dovere: è via al bene, alla moralità."

108 On this see Erich Auerbach, *Studi su Dante*, trans. Maria Luisa De Pieri Bonino (Milan: Giacomo Feltrinelli, 1966), p. 64. According to Auerbach, Dante turns to philosophy out of need, a need that originates in the heart. In his philosophy, Dante synthesizes the doctrine of Aquinas with that of the *dolce stil novo.* I cite from Auerbach: "Il suo filosofare è nato da un bisogno del cuore, in esso trovò confermato ciò che presentava da tempo; la sua aspirazione all'unità universale vi trovò alimento, e subito egli cominciò a ricercare una completa concordanza fra ciò che portava in sè con le conoscenze ora acquisite ... e come Tommaso cercava di unire le dottrine peripatetiche con quelle cristiano-platonico-agostiniane, così Dante voleva unire il sistema tomistico con la mistica ideologica del 'cor gentile'" (p. 64).

109 Dante *Conv.* II, xii, 1–3, pp. 120–1: "io rimasi di tanta tristizia punto, che conforto non mi valeva alcuno. Tuttavia, dopo alquanto tempo, la mia mente, che si argomentava di sanare, provide, poi che né l mio né l'altrui consolare valea, ritornare al modo che alcuno sconsolato avea tenuto a consolarsi; e misimi a leggere quello non conosciuto da molti libro di Boezio, nel quale, cattivo e discacciato, consolato

s'avea. E udendo ancora che Tullio scritto avea un altro libro, nel quale, trattando de l'Amistade, avea toccate parole de la consolazione di Lelio, uomo eccellentissimo, ne la morte di Scipione amico suo, misimi a leggere quello."

110 Ibid., II, xii, 7, pp. 121–2: "E da questo imaginare cominciai ad andare là dov'ella si dimostrava veracemente, cioè ne le scuole de li religiosi e a le disputazioni de li filosofanti."

111 Ibid., II, xii, 5, p. 121: "E sì come essere suole che l'uomo va cercando argento e fuori de la 'ntenzione truova oro, lo quale occulta cagione presenta, non forse sanza divino imperio; io, che cercava di consolarme, trovai non solamente a le mie lagrie rimedio, ma vocabuli d'autori e di scienze e di libri; li quail considerando, giudica bene che la filosofia, che era donna di questi autori, di queste scienze e di questi libri, fosse soma cosa." Dante begins to love philosophy as a good in itself, rather than a source of consolation.

112 Ibid., II, xii, 7, p. 122: "Sì che in picciol tempo, forse di trenta mesi, cominciai tanto a sentire de la sua dolcezza, che lo suo amore cacciava e distruggeva ogni altro pensiero. Per che io, sentendomi levare dal pensiero del primo amore a la virtù di questo, quasi maravigliandomi apersi la bocca nel parlare de la proposta canzone."

113 For a discussion of the problem of the *donna gentile* and of the relation between the real lady and the symbol, see Francesco Mazzoni, "*Purgatorio* Canto XXXI," in *Lectura Dantis Scaligera* (Florence: Le Monnier, 1965), pp. 5–98. For a study of the same problem see: Gilson, Nardi, Barbi, Casella, Auerbach, Singleton, and Hollander, op. cit. and below.

114 Dante, *Conv.* II, xv, 12, p. 138: "E così, in fine di questo secondo trattato, dico e affermo che la donna, di cu'io innamorai appresso lo primo amore, fu la bellissima e onestissima figlia de lo Imperadore de lo universo, a la quale Pittagora pose nome Filosofia."

115 Dante, *Purg.* 30, 124–6: "Sì tosto come in su la soglia fui / di mia seconda etade e mutai vita, / questi si tolse a me, e diesi altrui." Beatrice rebukes Dante for having given himself to others shortly after her death.

116 Robert Hollander, *Dante: A Life in Works* (New Haven and London: Yale University Press, 2001), p. 113.

117 For an excellent study and a comprehensive source of the bibliographical material on this topic see Mazzoni, "*Purgatorio* Canto XXXI," in *Lectura Dantis Scaligera*, pp. 5–98.

118 Hollander, *Dante: A Life in Works*, p. 121.

119 Ibid., p. 122.

120 De Sanctis, *Storia Della Letteratura Italiana*, p. 151: "Mediante questo sacrificio, la ragione è stata avvalorata dalla fede, l'amore avvalorato dalla grazia, la filosofia è stata compiuta dalla teologia, la rivelazione."

121 Hollander, *Dante: A Life in Works*, p. 122: "This does not make philosophizing unnecessary but makes it relatively less valuable. In the *Comedy*, David and Aquinas both know more that is essential than Aristotle does, but Aristotle can aid us in the effort to know as they know."

122 Francesco De Sanctis, "The Subject the Divine Comedy," in *Critical Essays on Dante*, ed. Giuseppe Mazzotta (Boston: G.K. Hall, 1991), pp. 77–8. As De Sanctis notes, Dante emphasizes the cooperation of religion and philosophy and the independence of each. Both are necessary for the fulfilment of an individual's two end goals, which are heavenly happiness and earthly happiness: "His mind submitted to the authority of the *Ethics* as to the Bible, to Aristotle as to St. Thomas; he believed implicitly that the great philosophers of antiquity agreed with the teaching of religion, and that they were wrong not because they saw wrongly, but because they did not see everything ... he maintained that spirit and matter were endowed each with its own life, without interference with the other; and from this he inferred in independence of the two powers, the spiritual and the temporal ... Both are organs of God on earth, 'two suns' [*Purgatory* XVI, 106] who guide humanity, one in the ways of God, the other in the ways of the world, one to heavenly and the other to earthly happiness."

123 Dante, *Conv.* III, xv, 6–10; cf. *Conv.* III, iv, 9, and *Par.* 4, 40–2; cf. Foster, "The Mind in Love: Dante's Philosophy," p. 47.

124 Ibid., IV, xvii, 9–12; IV, xxii, 10–18; *Monarchia*, III, xvi, 7; *Purg.* 3, 34–9, *Par.* 2, 10–12, 4, 40–2. cf. Foster, "The Mind in Love: Dante's Philosophy," p. 47.

125 Foster, "The Mind in Love: Dante's Philosophy," p. 52: "In fact, she is the perfection of knowledge and love; she loves all she knows and knows all she loves."

126 Dante, *Conv.* II, xiii, 6, p. 124: "'l vero è lo bene de lo intelletto."

127 Hollander, *Dante: A Life in Works*, p. 122: "In the *Comedy*, David and Aquinas both know more that is essential than Aristotle does but Aristotle can aid us in the effort to know as they know."

128 Ibid.

129 Ibid. For Hollander, the fact that, in the *Commedia*, philosophy is presented as a handmaid of theology is a sign that "Dante corrects the central problem left by the *Conv.* which presents philosophy as his only lady."

130 Dante, *Conv.* III, vii, 16, p. 175: "Secondamente narro come ella è utile a tutte le genti, dicendo che l'aspetto suo aiuta la nostra fede, la quale più che tutte l'altre cose è utile a tutta l'umana generazione, sì come quella per la quale campiamo da etternale morte e acquistiamo etternale vita. E la nostra fede aiuta … manifesto è che questa donna, col suo mirabile aspetto, la nostra fede aiuta."

131 Ibid.: "E la nostra fede aiuta; però che, con ciò sia cosa che principalissimo fondamento de la fede nostra siano miracoli fatti per Colui che fu crucifisso—lo quale creò la nostra ragione, e volle che fosse minore del suo potere—e fatti poi

nel nome suo per li Santi suoi; e molti siano sì ostinati che di quelli miracoli per alcuna nebbia siano dubbiosi, e non possano credere miracolo alcuno sanza visibilmente avere di ciò esperienza; e questa donna sia una cosa visibilmente miraculosa, de la quale li occhi de li uomini cotidianamente possono esperienza avere, [e]d a noi faccia possibili li altri; manifesto è che questa donna, col suo mirabile aspetto, la nostra fede aiuta." cf. Hollander, *Dante: A Life in Works* (2001), p. 80.

132 Dante, *Conv.* III, viii, 10–11, pp. 177–8: "Dimostrasi ne li occhi tanto manifesta, che conoscer si può la sua presente passione, chi bene là mira ... Dimostrasi ne la bocca, quasi come colore dopo vetro. E che è ridere se non una corruscazione de la dilettazione de l'anima, cioè uno lume apparente di fuori secondo sta dentro?"

133 Hollander, *Dante: A Life in Works*, p. 81.

134 Dante, *Conv.* III, xv, 5, p. 205: "Dunque si vede come ne l'aspetto di costei de le cose di Paradiso appaiono. E però si legge nel libro allegato di Sapienza, di lei parlando: 'Essa è candore de la etterna luce e specchio sanza macula de la maestà di Dio.'"

135 Ibid., III, xv, 2–5, pp. 204–5: "E quisi conviene sapere che li occhi de la sapienza sono le due dimostrazioni, con le quail si vede la veritade certissimamente; e lo suo riso sono le sue persuasioni, ne le quail si dimostra la luce interiore de la sapienza sotto alcuno velamento; e in queste due cose si sente quell piacere altissimo de beatitudine, lo quale è Massimo bene in Paradiso ... E in questo sguardo solamente l'umana perfezione s'acquista, cioè la perfezione de la ragione, de la quale, sì come di principalissima parte, tutta la nostra essenza depende ... E però si dice nel libro di Sapienza: 'Chi gitta via la sapienza e la dottrina è infelice,' che è privazione de l'essere felice ... e felice è essere contendo, secondo la sentenza del Filosofo."

136 Ibid., III, xv, 11, p. 207: "Dove è da sapere che la moralitade è bellezza de la Filosofia ... così la bellezza de la sapienza, che è corpo di Filosofia, come detto è, resulta da l'ordine de le virtudi morali, che fanno quella piacere sensibilmente"; ibid., III, xv, 14, p. 208: "E però dico che, a fuggire questo, si guardi in costei, cioè colà dov'ella è essemplo d'umiltà, cioè in quella parte di sè [che] morale filosofia si chiama."

3. Cicero's *De Amicitia* and Dante's *Convivio*

1 Konstan, *Friendship in the Classical World*, p. 122.

2 C. Taylor, *Party Politics in the Age of Caesar* (Berkeley: Berkeley University Press, 1949), p. 8: "the good old word for party relationships." cf. David Konstan, *Friendship in the Classical World*, p. 123 (Taylor quoted by Konstan).

3 Konstan, *Friendship in the Classical World*, pp. 123, 135.

4 Cicero, *DA* IX, 31, p. 142: "sic amicitiam non spe mercedis adducti, sed quod omnis eius fructus in ipso amore inest, expetendam putamus."

5 Peter Brunt, *The Fall of the Roman Republic and Related Essays*, pp. 352, 367. cf. David Konstan, *Friendship in the Classical World*, p. 123 (Brunt quoted by Konstan).

6 Konstan, *Friendship in the Classical World*, p. 123.

7 Brunt, *The Fall of the Roman Republic and Related Essays*, pp. 354, 356. cf. Konstan, *Friendship in the Classical World*, p. 123–4. See Cicero's *DA* XXVI and *Partitiones oratoriae* 88 for the relation between *amor* and *amicitia*.

8 Brunt, *The Fall of the Roman Republic and Related Essays*, p. 381. cf. Konstan, *Friendship in the Classical World*, p. 124.

9 Cicero, *De Officiis*, trans. William A. Falconer (Cambridge: Harvard University Press, 1992) 3.43–6; Cicero, Letter to Cn. Pompeius Magnus in *Letters of Cicero*, vol. 1, trans. Evelyn S. Shuckburgh (London: George Bell and Sons, 1908); Konstan, *Friendship in the Classical World*, p. 131; Brunt, *The Fall of the Roman Republic and Related Essays*, p. 381.

10 Konstan, *Friendship in the Classical World*, p. 130.

11 Dante, *Conv.* II, xii, 3, p. 121: "e misimi a leggere quello non conosciuto libro di Boezio, nel quale, cattivo e discacciato, consolato s'avea. E udendo ancora che Tullio scritto avea un altro libro, nel quale, trattando de l'Amistade, avea toccate parole de la consolazione di Lelio, uomo eccellentissimo, ne la morte di Scipione amico suo, misimi a leggere quello."

12 Konstan, *Friendship in the Classical World*, p. 132.

13 Ibid., p. 131. Konstan notes that, for Fritz-Arthur Steinmetz, the inspiration for Cicero's discussion on violence against the state derives from contemporary circumstances and from his communication with Gaius Matius, a partisan of Cicero.

14 Konstan, *Friendship in the Classical World*, p. 131.

15 Cicero, Letter to Atticus 17.5–6 in *Letters to Atticus*, vol.1, ed. and trans. D.R. Shackleton Bailey (Cambridge: Harvard University Press, 1999): "In the true accomplishments of uprightness, integrity, conscientiousness, and scrupulousness, I put neither myself nor anyone else before you, while as for your love toward me, if I leave aside my brother's love and that at home, I award you first prize. For I have seen – seen and observed profoundly – your worries and your joys during my various vicissitudes. Your congratulations on my accomplishments have often been pleasurable to me and your solace of my anxiety welcome. Now, indeed, when you are absent I most miss not only the advice which is your forte but also our exchange of conversation, which is sweetest of all to me with you ... In short, neither my work nor rest, business or leisure, affairs at the forum or at home, public or private, can long do without your sweet and loving advice and conversation." Cf. Konstan, *Friendship in the Classical World*, pp. 124–5.

16 *On the Orator*, 1.32, cf. *Epistulae ad Familiares*, 9.24.3, ed. D.R. Shackleton Bailey, vol. 1 (Cambridge: Cambridge University Press, 1977). Quoted by Konstan, *Friendship in the Classical World*, p. 125.

17 Alfred Pretor, ed., *The Letters of Cicero to Atticus*, Book 1 (I.18). Cambridge: Deighton, Bell, And Co., 1873: "… nam illae ambitio sae nostrae fucosa eque amicitiae sunt in quodam splendore forensi, fructum domesticum non habent itaque, quum bene completa domus est tempore matutino, quum ad forum stipati gregibus amicorum des endimus, reperire ex magna turba neminem possumus quicum aut iocari libere aut suspirare familiariter possimus. Qua re te exspectamus, te desideramus, te iam etiam arcessimus."

18 Cicero, *DA* XIII, 50, p. 161: "Quid? Si illud etiam addimus, quod recte addi potest, nihil esse quod ad se rem ullam tam illiciat et tam trahat quam ad amicitiam similitudo, concedetur profecto verum esse, ut bonos boni diligant asciscantque sibi quasi propinquitate coniunctos atque natura. Nihil est enim appetentius similium sui nec rapacius quam natura."

19 Aristotle, *NE* 8.3 1156b25, p. 123: "These kinds of friendships are likely to be rare, since such people are few. Moreover, they need time to grow accustomed to each other; for, as the proverb says, they cannot know each other before they have shared the traditional peck of salt, and they cannot accept each other or be friends until each appears lovable to the other and gains the other's confidence." Aristotle here envisions friendship involving good people.

20 Ibid., 8.8, 1159b5, p. 223: "They neither request nor provide assistance that requires base actions, but, you might even say, prevent this."

21 Ibid., 9.3. 1165b13–22, p. 244.

22 Konstan, *Friendship in the Classical World*, p. 131. cf. Cicero, *DA* 21.77.

23 Konstan, *Friendship in the Classical World*, p. 131.

24 Cicero, *DA* XI, 37, p. 148. For Cicero there is no justification for sinning on behalf of a friend. Since one's virtue was the reason for the friendship, it is difficult to maintain the friendship once the virtue has been abandoned. cf. Konstan, *Friendship in the Classical World*, p. 131.

25 Konstan, *Friendship in the Classical World*, p. 132, cf. Cicero, *DA* 11.36.

26 Ibid., p. 133, cf. Cicero, *DA* XII, 40, p. 150: "Etenim eo loco, Fanni et Scaevola, locati sumus, ut nos longe prospicere oporteat futuros casus rei publicae. Deflexit iam aliquantulum de spatio curriculoque consuetudo maiorum."

27 Vossler, *Medieval Culture: An Introduction to Dante and His Times*, vol. 1, p. 203.

28 Ibid., pp. 203–4.

29 Cicero, *De Officiis*, I, xiii, 41. Quoted by Konstan, *Friendship in the Classical World*, 1997.

30 Vossler, *Medieval Culture: An Introduction to Dante and His Times*, p. 204.

31 Ibid., p. 203.

32 Cicero, *DA* XIX, 69, p. 178: "But it is of the utmost importance in friendship that superior and inferior should stand on equality. For oftentimes a certain pre-eminence does exist, as was that of Scipio in what I may call 'our set.' But he never affected any superiority over Philius, or Rupilius, or Mummius, or over his other friends of a lower rank." cf. Konstan, *Friendship in the Classical World*, p. 135.

33 Cicero, *DA* IX, 70. cf. Konstan, *Friendship in the Classical World*, p. 135.

34 Vossler, *Medieval Culture: An Introduction to Dante and His Times*, p. 200.

35 Boethius, *The Consolation of Philosophy*, trans. V.E. Watts (New York: Penguin Books, 1969), p. 23.

36 Vossler, *Medieval Culture: An Introduction to Dante and His Times*, p. 200. cf. Dante, *Conv.* IV, 12, 6–7; Cicero, *Stoic Paradoxa* I, 6 in *De Oratore De Fato, Paradoxa Stoicorum, Partitiones Oratoriae*, vol. 1, trans. E.W. Sutton and H. Rackham (Cambridge: Harvard University Press, 1942); Boethius, *De Cons.*, II, ii; Dante, *Inferno*, trans. Robert Hollander and Jean Hollander (New York: Anchor Books, 2002), 7, 64–6. Vossler refers to *Conv.* IV, 12. where Dante translates from Cicero's *Paradoxa* I, 6. Vossler points out that in the same passage Dante also appeals to the authority of Seneca and Boethius. The underlying message in all of the passages seems to be one and the same, namely, a person's thirst for happiness cannot be quenched through the possession of material wealth and political power.

37 Dante, *Conv.* IV, xii, 6, p. 264: "E però dice Tullio in quello De Paradoxo, abominando le richezze: 'Io in nullo tempo per fermo né le pecunie di costoro, né le magioni magnifiche, né le richezze, né le signorie, né l'allegrezze, de le quail massimamente sono astretti, tra cose buone o desiderabili esser dissi; con ciò sia cosa che certo io vedesse li uomini, né l'abondanza di queste cose, massimamente desiderare quelle di che abondano. Però che in nullo tempo si compie né si sazia la sete de la cupiditate; né solamente per desiderio d'accrescere quelle cose che hanno si tormentano, ma eziandio tormento hanno né la paura di perdere quelle.'"

38 Ibid., IV, i, "Le dolci rime d'amor," p. 216: "... riprovando `l giudicio falso e vile / di quei che voglion che di gentilezza / sia principio richezza. / ... Tale imperò che gentilezza voles, / secondo 'l suo parere, / che fosse antica possession d'avere / con reggimenti belli; / ... Di retro da costui van tutti quelli / che fan gentile per ischiatta altrui / che lungiamente in gran ricchezza è stata; / ed è tanto durata / la così falsa opinion tra noi, / che l'uom chiama colui / omo gentil che può dicere: 'io fui / nepote, o figlio, di cotal valente,' / benchè sia da niente ..."

39 Ibid., IV, i, "Le dolci rime d'amor," p. 218: "Dico ch'ogni vertù principalmente / vien da una radice: / vertute, dico, che fa l'uom felice / in sua operazione. / Questo è, secondo che l'Etica dice, / un abito eligente, / lo qual dimora in mezzo solamente, / e tai parole pone."

40 Ibid., IV, i, "Le dolci rime d'amor," p. 219: "È gentilezza dovunqu'è vertute, / ma non vertute ov'ella; / sì com'è 'l cielo dovunqu'è la stella, ma ciò non e converso."

41 Ibid., IV, i, "Le dolci rime d'amor," p. 218: "Dico che nobilitade in sua ragione / importa sempre ben del suo subietto, / come viltade importa sempre male; / e vertute cotale / dà sempre altrui di sè buono intelletto; / per che in medesmo ditto / convegnono ambedue, ch'en d'uno effetto."

42 Vossler, *Medieval Culture: An Introduction to* Dante and His Times, pp. 200–1: "He seems actually to have formed the conviction that a natural bridge united this antique virtue with Christian morality: 'Be not a miser nor a spendthrift; be the master of gold, and let not thyself be mastered by it'–these, he believes, are the principles on which the best men of antiquity nourished a Christian life."

43 Etienne Gilson, *The Mystical Theology of Saint Bernard,* trans. A.H.C. Downes (New York: Sheed and Ward, 1955), p. 10.

44 Scott, "Aristotle," *The Dante Encyclopedia*, p. 63.

45 Dante, *Conv.* II, xii, 1–2, pp. 120–1: "Come per me fu perduto lo primo diletto de la mia anima, de la quale fatta è menzione di sopra, io rimasi di tanta tristizia punto, che conforto non mi valea alcuno. Tuttavia, dopo alquanto tempo, la mia mente, che si argomentava di sanare, provide, poi che nè 'l mio nè l'altrui consolare valea, ritornare al modo che alcuno sconsolato avea tenuto a consolarsi."

46 Ibid., II, xii, 3–5, p. 121: "e misimi a leggere quello non conosciuto da molti libro di Boezio, nel quale, cattivo e discacciato, consolato s'avea. E udendo ancora che Tullio scritto avea un altro libro, nel quale, trattando de l'Amistade, avea toccate parole de la consolazione di Lelio, uomo eccellentissimo, ne la morte di Scipione amico suo, misimi a leggere quello ... E sì come essere suole che l'uomo va cercando argento e fuori de la 'ntenzione truova oro, lo quale occulta cagione presenta, non forse sanza divino imperio; io, che cercava di consolarme, trovai non solamente a le mie lagrime rimedio, ma vocabuli d'autori e di scienze e di libri; li quail considerando, giudicava bene che la filosofia, che era donna di questi autori, di queste scienze e di questi libri, fosse soma cosa." While seeking consolation, "argento" for the loss of his beloved, in the works of these two thinkers Dante finds a greater reward, philosophy, "oro."

47 Ibid., II, xii, 9, p. 122: "E perché, sì come detto è, questa donna fu figlia di Dio, regina di tutto, nobilissima e bellissima Filosofia."

48 Ibid., I, xii, 3, pp. 75–6: "Dico che, sì come vedere si può che scrive Tullio in quello De Amicitia, non discordano da la sentenza del Filosofo aperta ne l'ottavo e nel nono de l'Etica, naturalmente la prossimitade e la bontade sono cagioni d'amore generative; lo benificio, lo studio e la consuetudine sono cagioni d'amore accrescitive. E tutte queste cagioni ch'io porto al mio volgare, sì come brievemente io mostrerò."

49 Ibid., I, xii, 4–6, p. 76: "Tanto è la cosa più prossima quanto, di tutte le cose del suo genere, altrui è più unita: onde di tutti li uomini lo figlio è più prossimo al padre ... Per che, se la prossimitade è seme d'amistà, come detto è di sopra, manifesto è

ch'ella è de le cagioni stata de l'amore ch'io porto a la mia loquela, che è a me prossima più che l'altre."

50 Thomas Aquinas, *Sententia libri Ethicorum*, ed. R.A. Gauthier, in *Opera omnia* (Leonine ed.), vol. 47, bk. 2 (Rome: Sanctae Sabinae, 1969), VIII, lect. 12: "Filius est quodammodo pars patris ab eo separate. Unde haec amicitia propinquissima est dilectioni qua quis amat sipsum, a quo omnis amicitia derivatur.

51 Cicero, *DA* XIII, 50: "Quid? Si illud etiam addimus, quod recte addi potest, nihil esse quod ad se rem ullam tam illiciat et tam trahat quam ad amicitiam similitude ... Nihil est enim appetentius similium sui nee rapacious quam natura"; Aristotle, *EE* 7.1 1235a7. See also *NE* 8.1 1155a34.

52 Dante, *Conv.* IV, i, 1–3: "Amore ... è che congiunge e unisce l'amante con la persona amata; onde Pittagora dice: 'Ne l'amistà si fa uno di più.' E però che le cose congiunde comunicano naturalmente intra sè le loro qualita di...sì che l'amore de l'una si comunica ne l'altra, e così l'odio e lo desiderio e ogni altra passione. Per che li amici de l'uno sono da l'altro amati, e li nemici odiati; per che in Greco proverbio è ditto: 'De li amici essere deono tutte le cose comuni.'" Cf. Cicero, *DA* VI, 20: "Est enim amicitia nihil aliud nisi omnium divinarum humanarunque rerum cum benevolentia et caritate consensio, qua quidem haud scio an excepta sapientia nihil quicquam melius homini sit a dis immortalibus datum."

53 Cicero, *DA* XIV, 50: "... concedetur profecto verum esse, ut bonos boni diligent asciscantque sibi quasi propinquitate coniunctos atque natura. Nihil est enim appententius similium sui nec rapacious quam natura."

54 Dante, *Conv.* I, xii, 6–8, p. 76: "Per che, se la prossimitade è seme d'amistà, come ditto è di sopra, manifesto è ch'ella è de le cagioni stata de l'amore ch'io porto a la mia loquela, che è a me prossima più che l'altre. La sopra detta cagione, cioè d'essere più unito quello ch'è solo prima in tutta la mente, mosse la consuetudine de la gente, che fanno li primogeniti succedere solamente, sì come [più] propinqui, e, perchè più propinqui, più amati."

55 Ibid., I, xiii, 3–9, pp. 78–9: "Dico, prima, ch'io per me ho da lei ricevuto dono di grandissimi benifici ... questo mio volgare fu introduttore di me ne la via di scienza, che è ultima perfezione, in quanto con esso io entrai ne lo latino e con esso mi fu mostrato; lo quale latino poi mi fu via a più innanzi andare. E così è palese, e per me conosciuto, esso essere stato a me grandissimo benefattore. Anche: è stato meco d'uno medesimo studio, e ciò posso così mostrare ... Anche c'è stata la benivolenza de la consuetudine; ché dal principio de la mia vita ho avuta con esso benivolenza e conversazione, e usato quello diliberando, interpretando e questionando."

56 Ibid., I. xii, 1, p. 78: "Detto come ne la propria loquela sono quelle due cose per le quail io sono fatto a lei amico, cioè prossimitade a me e bontà propria, dirò come, per beneficio e Concordia di studio e per benivolenza di lunga consuetudine, l'amistà è confermata e fatta grande."

57 Ibid., I, iii, 3, p. 78: "Onde, con ciò sia cosa che due perfezioni abbia l'uomo, una prima e una seconda (la prima lo fa essere, la seconda lo fa essere buono), se la propria loquela m'è stata cagione e de l'una e de l'altra, grandissimo beneficio da lei ho ricevuto."

58 Cicero, *De Officiis* 1.13.41. Cf. John A. Scott, "Dante's Other World: Moral Order," in *Dante Alighieri*, ed. Harold Bloom (New York: Infobase Publishing, 2011). Cicero quoted by Scott (p. 151).

59 Dante, *Conv.* I, ix 4–5, pp. 66–7: "Tornando dunque al principale proposito, dico che manifestamente si può vedere come lo latino averebbe a pochi dato lo suo beneficio, ma lo volgare servirà veramente a molti. Ché la bontà de l'animo, la quale questo servigio attende, è in coloro che per malvagia disusanza del mondo hanno lasciata la litteratura a coloro che l'hanno fatta di donna meretrice; e questi nobili sono principi, baroni, cavalieri, e molt'altra nobile gente, non solamente maschi ma femmine, che sono molti e molte in questa lingua, volgari, e non literati."

60 Ibid., I, i, 1, p. 41: "Sì come dice lo Filosofo nel principio de la Prima Filosofia, tutti li uomini naturalmente desiderano di sapere. La ragione di che puote essere, ed è, che ciascuna cosa, da providenza propria natura impinta, è inclinabile a la sua propria perfezione; onde, acciò che la scienza è ultima perfezione de la nostra anima, ne la quale sta la nostra felicitade, tutti naturalmente al suo desiderio semo subietti." Cf. Aristotle, *Metaphysics*, I, l, 980a.

61 See Albert Russell Ascoli, "The Unfinished Author: Dante's Rhetoric of authority in *Convivio* and *De Vulgari Eloquentia*," *The Cambridge Companion to Dante* (Cambridge: Cambridge University Press, 2000), pp. 45–66. In a sonnet attributed to Frederick II, the emperor defines nobility in a way that is similar to the definition given by Dante: "Nor does great abundance of riches make a vile man worthy, but rather nobility comes down to the people through well-ordered behaviour." Ascoli argues that Dante was well acquainted with Frederick's sonnet and suggests that by attributing the "erroneous" idea to Frederick instead of Aristotle, Dante is able to "delineate his own intellectual authority over political authorities ... At the same time, he is able to have it both ways with Aristotelian philosophical authority" (pp. 55–6).

62 Dante, *Conv.* I, i, 2–6, pp. 41–2: "Veramente, da questa nobilissima perfezione molti sono private per diverse cagioni, che dentro a l'uomo e di fuori da esso, lui rimovono da l'abito di scienza ..."

63 Ibid., I, i, 7: "Oh beati quelli pochi che seggiono a quella mensa dove lo pane de li angeli si manuca! E miseri quelli che con le pecore hanno commune cibo!"

64 Ibid., I, i, 8–9, pp. 42–3: "Ma però che ciascuno uomo a ciascuno uomo naturalmente è amico, e ciascuno amico si duole del difetto di colui ch'elli ama, coloro che a così alta mensa sono cibati non sanza misericordia sono inver di quelli che in bestiale pastura veggiono erba e ghiande gire mangiando."

65 Cicero, *DA* XX, 72: "Quam ob rem, ut ei, qui superiors sunt, submittere se debent in amicitia, sic quodam modo inferiors extollere." See also *DA* XIX, 69.

66 Dante, *Conv.* I, i, 9, p. 43: "E acciò che misericordia è madre di benificio, sempre liberamente coloro che sanno porgono de la loro buona richezza a li veri poveri, e sono quasi fonte vivo, de la cui acqua si refrigera la naturale sete che di sopra è nominate."

67 Ibid., I, i, 11–13, pp. 43–4: "... ma vegan qua qualunque è [per cura] familiare o civile ne la umana fame rimasto ..."; "... e a li loro piedi si pongano tutti quelli che per pigrizia si sono stati, che non sono degni di più alto sedere ..."

4. Christian Friendship

1 Vossler, *Medieval Culture: An Introduction to Dante and His Times*, vol. 1, p. 204.

2 Boethius, *De Consol.*, Introduction, p. 30.

3 Ibid., Introduction, p. 13.

4 C.S. Lewis, *The Allegory of Love: A Study in Medieval Tradition* (Oxford: Oxford University Press, 1936), p. 46.

5 Boethius, *De Consol.*, Introduction, p. 7.

6 Morris, *Chaucer's Translation of Boethius de Consolatione Philosophiae* (London: N. Trubner & Co., published for the Early English Text Society, 1868), p. 2.

7 W.P. Ker, *The Dark Ages* (London: Heinemann, 1923), pp. 107 ff.

8 Boethius, *De Consol.*, Introduction, p. 8.

9 Boethius, *The Consolation of Philosophy*, trans. P.G. Walsh (Oxford: Oxford University Press, 1999), Introduction, 31: "Thus the *Consolation* is consolation in the wider sense of philosophical protreptic or exhortation – not in the Aristotelian sense of a protreptic to philosophy to satisfy that intellectual curiosity by which 'all men by nature desire to know', but 'a protrepic towards God', a philosophical exhortation with a specifically religious message." For the Aristotelian idea that all individuals by nature desire knowledge, see the initial remark of the *Metaphysics*. For an understanding of the *Consolation* as a "Protreptic towards God," see E.K. Rand, "On the composition of Boethius' *Consolatio philosophiae*," *Harvard Studies in Classical Philology* 15 (1904), 8. For this section of his Introduction P.G. Walsh gives homage to Anna Crabbe's essay, "Literary Design in the *De consolatione Philosophiae*," in *Boethius: His Life, Thought and Influence*, ed. Margaret Gibson (Oxford: Basil Blackwell, 1981), pp. 237–74.

10 Boethius, *De Consol.*, Introduction, p. 22.

11 Ibid., III, 2, p. 79: "For the desire for true good is planted by nature in the minds of men, only error leads them astray toward false goods."

12 For Dante's ideas on Fortune, see Vincenzo Cioffari, *The Conception of Fortune and Fate in the Works of Dante* (Cambridge: Dante Society of Cambridge, 1940), and Gianluigi Toja, "La Fortuna," *Studi Danteschi* 42 (1965), pp. 247–60.

13 Dante, *Inf.* 7, 86: "questa provede, giudica, e persegue." See Hollander's note to vv. 62–96.

14 Ibid., 7, 96: "volve sua spera e beata si gode." See Hollander's note to vv. 62–96.

15 Dante, *Par.* 10, 125, p. 238.

16 Boethius, *De Consol.*, Introduction, p. 8.

17 Ibid., III, 2, p. 80: "In spite of a clouded memory, the mind seeks its own good, though like a drunkard it cannot find the path home" cf. Dante, *Inf.* 1, 1–3 "Midway in the journey of our life / I came to myself in a dark wood, / for the straight way was lost."

18 Boethius, *De Consol.*, II, 8, p. 77: "If Love relaxed the reins / All things that now keep peace / Would wage continual war / The fabric to destroy / which motions beautiful. / Love, too, holds peoples joined / By sacred bond of treaty, / And weaves the holy knot / Of marriage's pure love. / Love promulgates the laws / For friendship's faithful bond. / O happy race of men / If Love who rules the sky / Could rule your hearts as well!"

19 Ibid., IV, 6, p. 142: "This is the love of which all things partake, / The end of good their chosen goal and close: / No other way can they expect to last, / Unless with love for love repaid they turn / And seek again the cause that gave them birth."

20 Ibid., I, 2, p. 38: "But it is time for healing, not lamenting."

21 Ibid., I, 2, p. 38: "It is nothing serious only a touch of amnesia that he is suffering, the common disease of deluded minds. He has forgotten for a while who he is, but he will soon remember once he has recognized me. To make it easier for him I will wipe a little of the blinding cloud of worldly concern from his eyes."

22 Ibid., I, 3, p. 39: "Why, my child, should I desert you? Why should I not share your labour and the burden you have saddled with because of the hatred of my name?" cf. Dante, *Inf.* 2. 61–6, p. 28: "l'amico mio, e non de la ventura, / ne la diserta piaggia è impedito / sì nel cammin, che volt'è per paura; / e temo che non sia già sì smarrito, / ch'io mi sia tardi al soccorso levata, / per quell ch'ì ho di lui nel cielo udito." (Dante translated by G. Petrocchi)

23 Ibid., I, 2, p. 38: "You are the man, are you not, who was brought up on the milk of my learning and fed on my own food until you reached maturity? I gave you arms to protect you and keep your strength unimpaired, but you threw them away." Cf. Dante, *Purgatorio*, transl. Robert Hollander and Jean Hollander (New York: Anchor Books, 2002), 30, 125–37, p. 674: "di mia seconda etade e mutai vita, / questi si tolse a me, e diesi altrui. / Quando di carne a spirto era salita, / e bellezza e virtù cresciuta m'era, / fu' io a lui men cara e men gradita; / e volse i passi suoi per via non vera, / imagini di ben seguendo false, / che nulla promession rendono intera. / Né l'impetrare ispirazion mi valse, /con le quali e in sogno e altrimenti / lo rivocai: sì poco a lui ne calse! / Tanto giù cadde, che tutti argomenti / a la salute sua eran già corti, / fuor che mostrarli le perdute genti" (Dante translated by G. Petrocchi).

24 Boethius, *De Consol.*, Introduction, p. 30.
25 Ibid., III, 9, p. 96: "So that it is impossible to find happiness among these things which are thought to confer each of the desired states individually ... Clearly, therefore, these things offer man only shadows of the true good, or imperfect blessings, and cannot confer true and perfect good."
26 Ibid., III, 2, p. 80: "And as for friendship, the purest kind is counted as a mark not of good fortune, but of moral worth, but all other friendship is cultivated for the sake of power or pleasure."
27 Ibid., III, 10, p. 102: "While only God is so by nature, as many as you like may become so by participation."
28 Ibid., Introduction, p. 8
29 Ibid., III, 10, pp. 99–101: "It is the universal understanding of the human mind that God, the author of all things, is good ... Reason shows that God is so good that we are convinced that His goodness is perfect. Otherwise he couldn't be the author of creation ... it must be admitted that the supreme God is to the highest degree filled with supreme and perfect goodness. But we have agreed that perfect good is true happiness; so that it follows that true happiness is to be found in the supreme God ... So that we have to agree that God is the essence of happiness."
30 Ibid., III, 10, p. 102: "Since it is through the possession of happiness that people become happy, and since happiness is in fact divinity, it is clear that it is through the possession of divinity that they become happy."
31 Ibid.: "Each happy individual is therefore divine. While only God is so by nature, as many as you like may become so by participation."
32 Steven Botterill, *Dante and the Mystical Tradition Bernard of Clairvaux in the "Commedia"* (Cambridge: Cambridge University Press, 1994), p. 231.
33 Dante, *Conv.* IV, xvii, 8, p. 287: "E queste sono quelle che fanno l'uomo beato, o vero felice, ne la loro operazione, sì come dice lo Filosofo nel primo de l'*Etica* quando difinisce la Felicitade, dicendo che 'Felicitade è operazione secondo virtude in vita perfetta.'" Cf. Aristotle, *NE* I, 9, 1099b10–30.
34 Aquinas, *ST* vol. 19, Ia2ae, 58, 3 ad 3.
35 Peter Brown, *Augustine of Hippo: A Biography* (Berkeley: University of California Press, 1950), p. 41
36 Letter quoted in Adele Fiske, "St. Augustine: Stages of Friendship," in *Friends and Friendship in the Monastic Tradition* (Cuernavaca, Mexico: Centro Intercultural De Documentacion, 1970), 2–3.
37 Augustine, *Confessions*, trans. William Watts (Loeb Classical Library. London: Heinemann, and Cambridge: Harvard University Press, 1989) IV, IV, p. 158: "amicitia mea, suavi mihi super omnes suavitates illius vitae meae."
38 Ibid., IV, IV, p. 160: "Quo dolore contenebratum est cor meum, et quid quid aspiciebam mors erat. et erat mihi patria supplicium, et paterna domus mira infelicitas."

39 Ibid., "Solus fletus erat dulcis mihi et successerat amico meo in deliciis animi mei"; p. 164: "et taedium vivendi erat in me gravissimum et moriendi metus."
40 Ibid., p. 166: "animam illius unam fuisse animam in duobus corporibus."
41 Aristotle, *NE* 9.9. 1170b5–8, p. 260: "The excellent person is related to his friend in the same way as he is related to himself, since a friend is another himself."
42 Augustine, *Conf.*, IV, IV, p. 156: "sed nondum erat sic amicus, quamquam ne tum quidem sic, uti est vera amicitia, quia non est vera, nisi cum eam tu agglutinas inter haerentes sibi caritate diffusa in cordibus nostris per spiritum sanctum, qui datus est nobis."
43 Ibid., IV, VII, p. 166: "O dementiam nescientem diligere hominess humaniter! O stultum hominem immoderate humana patientem! Quod ego tunc eram."
44 Ibid., IV, VI, p. 164: "miser eram, et miser est omnis animus vinctus amicitia rerum mortalium, et dilaniatur, cum eas amittit, et tunc sentit miseriam, qua miser est et antequam amittat eas."
45 Ibid., IV, IX, p. 172: "beatus qui amat te, et amicum in te, et inimicum propter te. Solus enim nullum carum amittit, cui omnes in illo cari, qui non amittitur ... te nemo amittit, nisi qui dimittit."
46 Ibid., IV, XII, p. 178: "si placent animae, in deo amentur, quia et ipsae mutabiles sunt et illo fixae stabiliuntur: alioquin irent et perirent."
47 Ibid., IV, XII, p. 180: "bonum, quod amatis, ab illo est: sed quantum est ad illum, bonum est et suave ... quia iniuste amatur deserto illo quidquid ab illo est."
48 Ibid., IV, XV, p. 190: "non enim noveram neque didiceram ... nec ipsam mentem nostram summum atque inconmutabile bonum."
49 Konstan, *Friendship in the Classical World*, p. 160; cf. Augustine, *City of God* 19.25. For the implicit contrast between civic virtue and Christian piety in Augustine see *Epistola* 86.1.
50 Karl Jaspers, *Plato and Augustine*, trans. Ralph Manheim (New York: Harcourt, Brace & World, Inc., 1962), pp. 96–7.
51 Marguerite Mills Chiarenza, "The Imageless Vision and Dante's *Paradiso*," in *Dante*, ed. Harold Bloom (New York: Chelsea House, 1986), pp. 86–7.
52 Rom 13:13–14: "Not in rioting and drunkenness, not in chambering and impurities, not in contention and envy, but put ye on the Lord Jesus Christ and make not provision for the flesh in its concupiscences." Cf. Augustine, *Conf.*, VIII, XII. Augustine understands this passage as a call to give himself to God and to be baptized.
53 Augustine, *Conf.*, I, I, p. 2: "tu excitas, ut laudare te delectet, quia fecisti nos ad te et inquietum est cor nostrum, donec requiescat in te."
54 Mazzotta, *Dante, Poet of the Desert*, pp. 163–4.
55 F.C. Copleston, *Aquinas* (Baltimore: Penguin Books, 1959), pp. 216–17.
56 Etienne Gilson, *Reason and Revelation in the Middle Ages*, pp. 16–17.

57 Vossler, *Medieval Culture: An Introduction to Dante and His Times*, p. 237.
58 Konstan, *Friendship in the Classical World*, p. 157.
59 Ibid., pp. 156–7.
60 Ibid., pp. 157–8. Cf. Paulinus, *Epistola* 13.2.
61 Konstan, *Friendship in the Classical World*, p. 160.
62 Philip H. Wicksteed, *Dante and Aquinas* (London: J.M. Dent and Sons, 1913), pp. 124–5.
63 Dante, *Conv.* Trattato Primo, Capitolo I, 1–2, p. 41. While echoing Aristotle, the beginning of the *Convivio* also echoes the *Contra Gentiles*, I, 4. Dante argues that by their very nature all men desire to know. Through the use of reason, an individual reaches both perfection and happiness. Cf. Wicksteed, *Dante and Aquinas*, p. 130.
64 Dante, *Monarchia, Epistole Politiche* (Turin: Edizioni RAI Radiotelevisione Italiana, 1966): II, vi, 5.
65 Wicksteed, *Dante and Aquinas*, p. 125.
66 Dante, *Conv.* Trattato IV, Capitolo III, 2. Cf. Wicksteed, *Dante and Aquinas*, p. 127.
67 See "Charity" in *The Catholic Encyclopedia*, ed. Robert C. Broderick (Nashville: Thomas Nelson Publishers, 1976), p. 108 cf. *ST* 2a2ae, q. 184, a3: "Essentially the perfection of the Christian life consists in charity, first and foremost in the love of God, then in the love of neighbor." (Aquinas quoted in *The Catholic Encyclopedia*).
68 See "Love," in *The Catholic Encyclopedia for School and Home* (New York: McGraw-Hill, 1965), p. 494.
69 Aquinas, *ST* vol. 34, *Charity* (New York: McGraw-Hill, 1967): 2a2ae. 25, 3, p. 86: "Sed caritas non est simplex amor, sed habet rationem amicitiae, ut supra dictum est."
70 Jn 15, 15; quoted by Aquinas, *ST* 2a2ae.23.1, p. 6: "Sed Contra est quod *Joan.* Dicitur, *Jam non dicam vos servos, sed amicos meos.* Sed hoc non dicebatur eis nisi ratione caritatis. Ergo caritas est amicitia."
71 Ibid.: "Cum igitur sit aliqua comunicatio hominis ad Deum secundum quod nobis suam beatitudinem comunicat, super hac comunicatione oportet aliquam amicitiam fundari. De qua quidem comunicatione dicitur I *Cor.*, *Fides Deus per quem vocati estis in societatem Filii ejus.*"
72 Ibid., 2a2ae.23.2, p. 8: "Ad primum ergo dicendum quod duplex est hominis vita. Una quidem exterior secundum naturam sensibilem et corporalem, et secundum hanc vitam non est nobis communicatio vel conversatio cum Deo et angelis. Alia autem est vita hominis spiritualis secundum mentem, et secundum hanc vitam est nobis conversatio et cum Deo et cum angelis"
73 Ibid.: "in praesenti quidem statu imperfecte, unde dicitur *Phillipp.*, *Nostra conversatio in coelis est*"; "Et ideo hic est caritas imperfecta, sed perficietur in patria."
74 Ibid.: "Ad secundum dicendum quod amicitia se extendit ad aliquem duplicitur. Uno modo respectu suipsius, et sic amicitia nunquam est nisi ad amicum. Alio

modo se extendit ad aliquem respectu alterius personae, sicut si aliquis habet amicitiam ad aliquem hominem, ratione ejus diligit omnes ad illum hominem pertinentes, sive filios sive servos sive qualiter-cumque ei attinentes."

75 Jaffa, *Thomism and Aristotelianism*, p. 134.

76 Aristotle, *NE* 2.2, 1103b31, p. 35; 2.6, 1107a1, p. 44.

77 Aquinas, *ST* 2a2ae.23.3, p. 16: "Unde sicut virtus moralis definitur per hoc quod est *secundum rationem rectam*, ut patet in *Ethic.*, ita etiam attingere Deum constituit rationem virtutis, sicut etiam supra dictum est de fide et spe. Unde cum caritas attingit Deum quia conjungit nos Deo, ut patet per auctoritatem Augustini inductam, consequens est caritatem esse virtutem."

78 Aquinas, *ST* 2a2ae. 23. 3, p. 14: "caritas est virtus quae, cum nostra rectissima affectio est, congiungit nos Deo, qua eum diligimus."

79 Aristotle, *NE* 8.1 1155a3.

80 Aquinas, *ST* 2a2ae.23.3, p. 16: "Ad primum ergo dicendum quod Philosophus non negat amicitiam esse virtutem, sed dicit quod est *virtus vel cum virtute*. Posset enim dici quod est virtus moralis circa operationes quae sunt ad alium, sub alia tamen ratione quam justitia ... Nec est simile de caritate, quae non fundatur principaliter super virtute humana, sed super bonitate divina."

81 Ibid., 2a2ae.23.4, p. 18: "proprium autem objectum amoris est bonum ... Bonum autem divinum, in quantum est beatitudinis objectum, habet specialem rationem boni. Et ideo amor caritatis, qui est amor hujus boni, est specialis amor. Unde et caritas est specialis virtus."

82 Ibid., 2a2ae.23.5, p. 20: "Et ideo, quia caritas habet pro objecto ultimum finem humanae vitae, scilicet beatitudinem aeternam, ideo extendit se ad actus totius humanae vitae per modum imperii, non quasi immediate eliciens omnes actus virtutum."

83 Ibid., "Praeterea, sub caritate includitur amicitia ad proximum ... Dicendum quod caritas, sicut dictum est, est quaedam amicitia hominis ad Deum."

84 Jn 4:21; quoted by Aquinas, *ST* 2a2ae.25.1, p. 82.

85 Aquinas, *ST* 2a2ae.23.6, p. 22: "Est etiam et una comunicatio beatitudinis aeternae super quam haec amicitia fundatur. Unde relinquitur quod caritas est simpliciter una virtus, non distincta in plures species."

86 Ibid.: "Hoc autem non est verum, sed Deus est principale objectum caritatis, proximum autem ex caritate diligitur propter Deum."

87 Ibid., 2a2ae.25.1, p. 82: "Ratio autem diligendi proximum Deus est: hoc enim debemus in proximo diligere ut in Deo sit. Unde manifestum est quod idem specie actus est quo diligitur Deus, et quo diligitur proximus. Et propter hoc habitus caritatis non solum se extendit ad dilectionem Dei, sed etiam ad dilectionem proximi."

88 Ibid., 2a2ae.25.3, p. 86: "Per amicitiam autem amatur aliquid dupliciter. Uno modo, sicut ipse amicus ad quem amicitiam habemus et cui bona volumus. Alio modo, sicut bonum quod amico volumus."

89 Ibid.: "Et hoc modo caritas per caritatem amatur, et non primo, quia caritas est illud bonum quod optamus omnibus quos ex caritate diligimus."

90 Ibid., 2a2ae.25.3, p. 86: "Ad primum ergo dicendum quod Deus et proximus sunt illi ad quos amicitiam habemus. Sed in illorum dilectione includitur dilectio caritatis; diligimus enim proximum et Deum inquantum hoc amamus, ut nos et proximus Deum diligamus, quod est caritatem habere."

91 John J. Sullivan, "Love," *The Catholic Encyclopedia for School and Home*, p. 491.

92 Ibid., p. 496.

93 Jaspers, *Plato and Augustine*, p. 96.

94 Etienne Gilson, *The Christian Philosophy of St. Augustine*, trans. L.E.M. Lynch (New York: Random House, 1960), p. 138.

95 Sullivan, "Love," *The Catholic Encyclopedia for School and Home*, p. 495.

96 Gilson, *The Christian Philosophy of St. Augustine*, p. 139.

97 Sullivan, "Love," *The Catholic Encyclopedia for School and Home*, p. 495.

98 Aristotle, *NE* 9.8 1168b19–23, p. 254: "Those who are greedy for these goods gratify their appetites and in general their feelings and non-rational part of the soul; and since this is the character of the many, the application of the term self-love is derived from the most frequent kind of self-love, which is base. This type of self-lover, then, is justifiably reproached." cf., 9.8 1168b29–1169a5, p. 255: "At any rate he awards himself what is finest and best of all, and gratifies the most controlling part of himself, obeying it in everything ... Moreover, his voluntary actions seem above all to be those involving reason ... Hence he most of all is a self-lover."

99 Ibid., 9.8. 1169a11–14, p. 256.

100 Mazzotta, *Dante, Poet of the Desert*, p. 119: "Friendship, to be sure, is an essentially earthbound value, but Ambrose, in a deliberate attempt to Christianize this most pagan human bond, speaks of friendship as a foretaste of the harmony of Heaven and a veritable experience of the Garden of Eden on earth." Cf. Ambrose, *Patrologia Latina* 16, cols. 73–4 and 178–84.

101 Jaspers, *Plato and Augustine*, p. 98.

102 See "Love," in *The Catholic Encyclopedia for School and Home*, p. 498.

103 Walter Farrell, *A Companion to the Summa* (New York: Sheed and Ward, 1942), p. 234.

104 Augustine, *Conf.*, IV, XII, p. 188.

105 Robert C. Broderick, *The Catholic Encyclopedia*, p. 108.

106 The scriptures encourage believers to seek the "friendship of God" (Ws 7:14); God is believed to be the most perfect friend (Prv 27:10); Jesus teaches that the greatest act of friendship is to sacrifice one's life for another (cf. Jn 15:13–23). The scriptures also presents charity as the greatest of the three theological virtues and as the greatest commandment (Mt 22:34–40). Charity is at once the love of God, the love of ourselves, and our neighbours for the love of God (cf. 1 Cor 13:8–13). For Aquinas, perfection is to be found in charity: "Essentially the perfection of the

Christian life consists in charity, first and foremost in the love of God, then in the love of neighbor" (*ST* Iia.Iiae, q. 184, a3, quoted in Robert C. Broderick, *The Catholic Encyclopedia*, p. 108).

107 Aquinas, *Super Evangelium Ioannis Lectura*, c. 15, 1.4, quoted by Yoshihisa Yamamoto, "Thomas Aquinas on the Ontology of Amicitia: Unio and Communicatio," *Proceedings of the American Catholic Philosophical Association* 81 (2007).

108 Aquinas, *ST* I, q.47, a.1: "God brought things into being in order that His goodness might be communicated to creatures, and be represented by them. And because His goodness could not be adequately represented by one creature alone, He produced many and diverse creatures, that what was wanting to one in the representation of the divine goodness might be supplied by another"; quoted by Yamamoto, "Thomas Aquinas on the Ontology of Amicitia."

109 Aquinas, *ST* I, q.106, a.4: "Every creature participates in the Divine goodness, so as to diffuse the good it possesses to others; for it is of the nature of good to communicate itself to others. Hence also corporeal agents give their likeness to others so far as they can. So the more an agent is established in the share of the Divine goodness, so much the more does it strive to transmit its perfection to others as far as possible." Quoted by Yamamoto, "Thomas Aquinas on the Ontology of Amicitia."

110 Aquinas, *ST* Ia.2ae, q.28, a1, p. 90: "Similiter cum aliquis amat aliquem amore amicicitiae, vult ei bonum sicut et sibi vult bonum: unde apprehendit eum ut alterum se, inquantum scilicet vult ei bonum sicut et sibi ipsi. Et inde est quod amicus dicitur esse *alter ipse*: et Augustinus dicit, *Bene quidam dixit de amico suo, dimidium animae suae*."

111 Ibid., Ia.2ae, q.28, a2, p. 94: "Potest autem et tertio modo mutua inhaesio intelligi in amore amicitiae, secundum viam redamationis, inquantum mutuo se amant amici, et sibi invicem bona volunt et operantur."

112 Ibid., Ia.2ae, q.28, a2, p. 94: "In amore vero amicitiae amans est in amato inquantum reputat bona vel mala amici sicut sua, et voluntatem amici sicut suam, ut quasi ipse in suo amico videatur bona vel mala pati, et affici. Et propter hoc, proprium est amicorum eadem velle, et in eodem tristari et gaudere, secundum Philosophum."

113 Aquinas, *Summa contra Gentiles*, I, c.43: "ex hoc ipso quod aliquid in actu est, activum est." Quoted by Yamamoto, "Thomas Aquinas on the Ontology of Amicitia."

114 Aquinas, *De Veritate*, q.1, a1: "A thing is said to be *aliquid* (something) as *aliud quid* (something other). Then, as a being is said to be as long as it is indivisible in itself, so it is said to be aliquid as long as it is separate from other things." Quoted by Yamamoto, "Thomas Aquinas on the Ontology of Amicitia."

115 Aristotle, *NE* 8.2 1155b20–8.3 1157a35, pp. 209–14.

116 Singleton, *Dante Studies 2: Journey to Beatrice*, pp. 102–3.

117 Copleston, *Aquinas*, p. 62.
118 Ibid.
119 Aquinas, *Scriptum super libros Sententiarium*, I, 19, 4, I, vol. 1, p. 486. Quoted by Armand A. Maurer, *Medieval Philosophy* (Toronto: Pontifical Institute of Medieval Studies, 1982), p. 185.
120 Maurer, *Medieval Philosophy*, p. 190.
121 Copleston, *Aquinas*, pp. 179, 193.
122 Maurer, *Medieval Philosophy*, pp. 180, 189.
123 Wicksteed, *Dante and Aquinas* (New York: E.P. Dutton, 1913), pp. 115–16.
124 *Summa contra Gentiles*, III, 19, 20, ed. C. Pera, P. Marc, P. Caramello (Turin: Marietti, 1961–7); cf. Wicksteed, *Dante and Aquinas*, pp. 115–16.
125 Vossler, *Medieval Culture: An Introduction to Dante and His Times*, p. 49.
126 Jaspers, *Plato and Augustine*, p. 98.
127 Ibid., *p*. 77.
128 Ibid., p. 79.
129 Wicksteed, *Dante and Aquinas*, p. 155
130 Gilson, *Methodical Realism*, trans. Philip Trower (Front Royal: Christendom Press, 1990), p. 72.
131 Copleston, *Aquinas*, pp. 109–10, 137.
132 Ibid., p. 64.
133 Gilson, *Reason and Revelation in the Middle Ages*, p. 69.
134 Ibid., p. 73.
135 Wicksteed, *Dante and Aquinas*, pp. 98, 132.
136 Ibid.; Copleston, *Aquinas*, p. 179.
137 Aquinas, *Summa contra Gentiles*, I, 7; cited in Wicksteed, *Dante and Aquinas*, p. 100.
138 Copleston, *Aquinas*, p. 193.
139 Vossler, *Medieval Culture: An Introduction to Dante and His Times*, vol. 1, p. 122.
140 Copleston, *Aquinas*, p. 193.
141 Vossler, *Medieval Culture an Introduction to Dante and His Times*, p. 124.
142 Jaspers, *Plato and Augustine*, p. 98.

5. The *Vita Nuova*: Dante's Friendship with Guido Cavalcanti and Others

1 Giuseppe Mazzotta, "Life of Dante," in *The Cambridge Companion to* Dante, ed. Rachel Jacoff (Cambridge: Cambridge University Press, 2000), pp. 5–6.
2 George Holmes, *Dante* (New York: Hill and Wang, 1980), p. 23.
3 Farinata twice expelled Dante's party, the Guelfs (1248 and 1260). Farinata's episode brings to light the political turmoil afflicting thirteenth century Florence:

the Guelfs were expelled in 1248, the Ghibellines in 1258. In 1260, at the battle of Montaperti, led by Farinata, the Ghibellines were once again victorious over the Guelfs. In 1264, Farinata died in Florence. In 1266, at the battle of Benevento, Manfred and the imperial forces were defeated, and the Uberti were exiled. Cavalcante, Guido's father, died in 1280. In 1289, at the battle of Campaldino (which Dante took part in), the Ghibellines were once again defeated by the Guelfs. In 1302, Dante was exiled.

4 See *Vita Nuova* III, 14; XXIV, 6; XXX, 3. At the fictive time of Dante's journey, Guido was still alive. However, Dante's mention of Guido's name might serve as a warning to his "materialist" friend that unless he mends his ways, he might join his father in Hell. Guido was one of the best lyric poets of his time. He was about ten years older than Dante. He was an independent-minded thinker and an aristocratic who had a reputation as a "materialist." Guido, like Dante, was a White Guelf. His loyalty to the White Guelfs was the cause of his fight with the leader of the Black Guelfs, Corso Donati. In the summer of 1300, during the period of Dante's priorate (June 15 to August 15), in an effort to end the disputes caused by opposing political loyalties, Guido and the leaders of both factions were banished from Florence. In his role as Prior, Dante may have played an instrumental role in the banishment of his friend.

5 John Freccero, "Epitaph for Guido: *Inferno* X," *Journal of Religion and Literature* 39, 3, (2007), pp. 1–3: "Its synthesis of theatricality and psychological depth has been admired by some of the greatest critics of modern times, among whom were Francesco De Sanctis, Antonio Gramsci, and Erich Auerbach. None of them discuss Guido, who appears in the canto by name only and who is supposed by the fiction to be still alive. Nevertheless, he is at the center of the text and of our attention ... but it is important that [the text] be revisited, because it represents the poet's last word on the life of his closest friend. Since in the fiction Guido is supposed to be still alive, able to change his ways, the mention of his name to his father in so ominous a context suggests that the verse, whatever it means, is in some sense an admonition, intended for a sinner."

6 *Inf.* 10, 58–60. The phrase "per altezza d'ingeno" (by virtue of your lofty genius) may bring to mind Dante's initial invocation: "O Muse, o alto ingegno" (O Muses, O lofty genius [*Inf.* 2, 7]). Cavalcante assumes that Dante's journey is in search of secular wisdom, a journey similar to the descent into the underworld made by Ulysses, Aeneas, Hercules, Theseus, and Orpheus, all of whom descended by their own power or by the power of their intellect. See Freccero, "Epitaph for Guido: *Inferno* X," p. 12: "He must assume that the pilgrim's journey is like the *descensus ad inferos* of the mythographic tradition, an allegory for the search for secular wisdom, of which Orpheus' descent was the prototype." For the four allegorical

ways of understanding the *descensus ad inferos* see, Bernardus Silvestris, *Commentary on the First Six Books of Virgil's* Aeneid, trans. Earl G. Schreiber and Thomas E. Maresca (Lincoln: University of Nebraska Press, 1974), 32–3.

7 At the fictive time of the poem Guido is still alive, though he will die in four months.

8 Some critics understand the passage to mean that Guido at some point distanced himself from the work of Virgil. Others understand it to mean that Guido rejected or disapproved of Dante's love of Beatrice, to whom Virgil is leading Dante (see *Inf.* 1, 122–3). Critics who understand Guido's scorn to be directed against Virgil are left to wonder why Guido would have experienced a change of heart regarding Virgil's work. Siro Chimenz and others understand Guido's "disdain" to be directed against Beatrice and Dante's loyalty to her. If understood in this sense, Dante is here thinking of Guido's scorn of Beatrice as an event that occurred at definite time in the past, as evidenced in a sonnet written by Guido for Dante, where he expressed his rejection of his friend. See Hollander's note to *Inf.* 10, 61: "Dante's words may reflect the Gospel of John (8:28) when Jesus says 'a meipso facio nihil' (I do nothing of myself), but only through the Father."

9 Freccero, "Epitaph for Guido: *Inferno* X," pp. 9–10: "... the exchange between the pilgrim and Cavalcante is far from muddled. It is a lucid and dispassionate representation of utter confusion. Just as the representation of the madness of Ophelia and Orlando required the consummate skill of their respective authors, so this representation of misconception and impasse demanded of the poet an astonishing control of linguistic subtleties. To understand the passage we must follow the logic not of the characters, the old man and the pilgrim, but of their creator."

10 Ibid., p. 8.

11 Ibid., p. 4. Cf. Inferno 19.5.

12 Ibid., pp. 3, 4.

13 Ibid. Cf. *Par.* 17 118. Freccero understands the line as a variation to the Aristotelian theme: *amicus plato, magis amica veritas.* See also *Conv.* III, xi, 8.

14 Giuseppe Mazzotta, "The Language of Poetry in the *Vita Nuova,*" *Rivista di studi italiani*, 1 (1983), p. 5: "The friendship between the two poets is a constitutive category of the *Vita Nuova*: Friendship comes forth as metaphor for an intellectual conversation, for a certain benevolence of minds on account of which the two friends, in goodwill, 'turn together,' exchange and communicate ideas, share the secrets of their craft, decipher and penetrate each other's fablings."

15 Ibid.: "From this point of view we must say that there is a drastic opposition in the *Vita Nuova* between on the one hand, Beatrice, the beloved, who eventually will not respond to or even acknowledge her lover, and in whose presence he will be unable to speak, and, on the other hand, Guido, the friend, with whom Dante will communicate thoughts and will probe the significance of things and words."

16 Ibid., pp. 1–16.

17 Aquinas, *ST* II, II, q. 24, a. 2, resp. "... caritas est amicitia quaedam hominis ad Deum fundata super communicationem beatitudinis aeterneae."

18 R.W.B. Lewis, *Dante: A Life*, p. 30: "Guido Cavalcanti was about ten years older than Dante and, astutely recognizing the remarkable talent of the eighteen-year-old, became as it were an older brother, both poetically and personally, to Dante. Their friendship flourished through continuing exchanges and conversations."

19 Mazzotta, "The Language of Poetry in the *Vita Nuova*," p. 5: "The friendship between the two poets is a constitutive category of the *Vita Nuova*. Friendship comes forth as a metaphor for an intellectual conversation, for a certain benevolence of minds on account of which the two friends, in good will, 'turn together,' exchange and communicate ideas, share the secrets of their craft, decipher and penetrate each other's fablings."

20 Ibid., p. 5. Cf. Guido Cavalcanti, *Rime*, a cura di M. Ciccuto (Milan, 1978).

21 Mazzotta, "The Language of Poetry in the *Vita Nuova*," p. 5.

22 See Mazzotta, "The Language of Poetry in the *Vita Nuova*," p. 5.

23 Mazzotta notes that Guido shifts to the present, in contrast to the past absolute used in reference to the dream. Guido's use of the present is a sign that he distorts Dante's subjective and finite experience into the world of abstractions and universals, the world of philosophical ideas: "Vedeste, al mio parere, onne valore / e tutto gioco e quanto bene om sente, / se foste in prova del segnor valente / che segnoreggia il mondo de l'onore, / poi vive in parte dove noia more ..." (Cavalcanti, *The Complete Poems*, p. 140). Cf. Mazzotta's note 6 in "The Language of Poetry in the *Vita Nuova*," p. 14: "The alternation between the past and present is the main technical feature of the sonnet."

24 Mazzotta, "The Language of Poetry in the *Vita Nuova*," pp. 5–6.

25 Ibid., p. 6.

26 Robert Pogue Harrison, "Approaching the *Vita Nuova*," in *The Cambridge Companion to Dante*, p. 40.

27 See Hollander's note 70 in "Dante and Cino da Pistoia," *Dante Studies* 110 (1992): p. 227. As Hollander reminds the reader, it is interesting that "... where Guinizelli is saved and, in his own language (*Purg.* XXVI, 127–132), utters the name of Christ and then suggests that the best form of 'poetic' utterance is now a paternoster ... *Inf.* X at the very least suggests that Guido was, like his father, an Epicurean, and, in Dante's eyes, almost certainly damned. For the view that Dante, like Boccaccio, wants to keep the door open for Guido's salvation, see Robert M. Durling, 'Boccaccio on Interpretation: Guido's Escape (*Decameron* VI.9),' in *Dante, Petrarch, Boccaccio: Studies in the Italian Trecento in Honor of*

Charles S. Singleton, eds. Aldo S. Bernardo and Anthony L. Pellegrini (Binghamton, NY: Medieval and Renaissance Texts Studies, 1983), pp. 273–304, esp. 283–4."

28 Hollander, *Dante: A Life in Works*, p. 21.

29 Robert Hollander, "Dante and Cino da Pistoia," *Dante Studies* 110 (1992), p. 214.

30 Paget Toynbee, *Dante Alighieri: His Life and Works* (Mineola, NY: Dover Publications, Inc., 2005), p. 51.

31 See Giorgio Padoan, "Il Canto degli epicurei," *Convivium* 27 (1959): pp. 12–39, esp. 34–6. Others who adhere to this view include Antonino Pagliaro, *Ulisse* (Messina-Florence: G. D'Anna, 1967), pp. 193–210; Leonardo Vitetti, *Il sonetto a Dante di Guido Cavalcanti* (Turin: Società editrice internazaionale, 1962), pp. 6, 21–2 (citing Pagliaro); Hollander, "Dante and Cino da Pistoia," p. 214.

32 See Mario Marti, "Guinizelli, Guido," *Enciclopedia Dantesca*, ed. Umberto Bosco, vol. 3 (Rome: Istituto dell'Enciclopedia Italiana), pp. 330–3. For Dante's relationship with his predecessors and companions, see Mario Marti, *Con Dante fra i poeti del suo tempo* (Lecce: Milella, 1966); Teodolinda Barolini, *Dante's Poets* (Princeton: Princeton University Press, 1984); Hollander, *Dante: A Life in Works*, p. 21 and note 30.

33 Charles S. Singleton, *An Essay on the Vita Nuova* (Baltimore: Johns Hopkins University Press, 1977), p. 37.

34 Ibid., p. 61.

35 Harrison, "Approaching the *Vita Nuova*," p. 41.

36 Ibid., p. 39.

37 Singleton, *An Essay on the Vita Nuova*, p. 60.

38 Ibid., p. 73.

39 Hollander, *Dante: A Life in Works*, pp. 21–2.

40 Singleton, *An Essay on the Vita Nuova*, p. 100: "And we understand, I think, by such a picture, why the *Vita Nuova* is written first of all for Guido Cavalcanti. The *Vita Nuova* takes a step which, in his doctrine of love, Cavalcanti would not take – a step by which the circle of a love which began in Heaven is completed. This is a new theory of love which should have interested a first friend."

41 It seems that at different points in time Cino both embraced and rejected Dante's friendship. He mourned Dante's death but later pointed out the "defects" in the *Commedia*. Upon the death of Beatrice and in an attempt to console Dante for his loss, Cino wrote a consolatory poem: "Avegna che el m'aggia piu' tempo." During the period of 1304–6, the fellow exiles (Cino exiled in Florence from Pistoia, Dante exiled somewhere in Italy from Florence) exchanged a total of ten poems, and Dante addressed his third epistle, "Exulanti Pistoriensi," to Cino. See Hollander, "Dante and Cino da Pistoia," p. 202.

42 See Dante, *De vulgari Eloquentia*, *Opere Minori*, ed. Pier Vincenzo Mengaldo (Milan-Naples: Ricciardi, 1979): "qui dulcius subtiliusque poetati vulgariter sunt." (I, x, 2); "Cynus Pistoriensis et amicus eius" (I, xvii, 3); "unum alium [Dante] ... et Cynum Pistoriensem" (I, xviii, 4); "Cynus Pistoriensis ... amicus eius" (II, v, 4); "Cynus de Pistorio ... amicus eius" (II, vi, 6); cf. I, xiii, 4.

43 See Teodolinda Barolini, *Dante's Poets*. Barolini's view is that Cino is absent from the *Commedia* because he was more of a friend and less of a poet: "He is not significant enough to be included in the *Comedy*'s poetic itinerary, precisely because he is too good a friend; poetically, Cino is Dante's mirror image, an elegiac version of Dante in his sweetest mode. Rather than exerting influence, Cino absorbed it, thereby guaranteeing his exclusion from the *Comedy*" (pp. 135–6).

44 See Domenico De Robertis: "Cino da Pistoia e le 'imitazioni' dale rime di Dante," *Studi danteschi* 29 (1950), pp. 103–77; "Cino e i poeti bolognesi," *Giornale storico della letteratura italiana* 128 (1951), 273–312; "Cino da Pistoia e la crisi del linguaggio poetico," *Convivium* 1 (1952), 1–35. See also: Vincenzo Pernicone, "Dante e lo stil novo di Cino,"*Studi danteschi e altri saggi*, ed. Matilde Dillon Wanke (Genoa: Università degli studi di Genova, Istituto della Letteratura Italiana, 1984 [1937], 1–6; Mario Marti, *Con Dante fra i poeti del suo tempo*, pp. 43–68, 69–121; Armando Balduino, "Cino da Pistoia, Boccacccio, e i poeti minori del Trecento," in *Atti del Colloquio Cino da Pistoia* (Rome: Accademia Nazionale dei Lincei, 1976), 33–85; Antonio Enzo Quaglio, *Lo stilnovo e la poesia religiosa* (Bari: Laterza, 1971), 146–7.

45 See Guglielmo Gorni, *Il nodo della lingua: studi su Dante e altri Duecenteschi* (Florence: Olsckhi, 1981). In this collection of essays, Gorni draws links between Cino's works and Dante's. See Guglielmo Gorni, "Cino 'vil ladro," pp. 134, 138–9. This is an accurate study of Cino's sonnet "Qua' son le cose vostre ch'io vi tolgo / Guido, che fate di me sì vil ladro?" (What are these things of yours I take from you, / Guido, that you make of me so vile a thief?). Cino composed this sonnet in 1300 in an attempt to defend himself against Guido Cavalcanti's accusations of poetic theft. Gorni argues that in composing the *Commedia*, Dante was well acquainted with Cino's sonnet. Gorni further suggests Cino's poetic influence in the *ladro* of verse 2 in *Inferno* 24, 138, and 25, 1–3, where Dante presents Vanni Fucci. Gorni's claim is shared by Rossi in "Una ricomposta tenzone," p. 63. Most importantly, Gorni asserts that "con disdegno" and "di basso 'ngegno" used in *Inferno* 10 are echoes from Cino (p. 134). Over a century ago, Isidoro Del Lungo made this same point in "Il disdegno di Guido," *Nuova Antologia* 24.3 (1889), 59–60. Also see Hollander, "Dante and Cino da Pistoia," pp. 201–31. Hollander argues "first, that Cino, even if he does not figure at all as a character in Dante's cast of vernacular poets in the *Commedia*, does serve significantly as a source for Dante ... second, that Cino was to have had a highly significant role in the Paradiso, but was finally not included because of a falling out between the two poets, a far more hypothetical argument." For the first of these two arguments, Hollander

points to the Cavalcanti episode in *Inferno* 10 and to Cino's sonnet addressed to Guido. In his poem, Cino denies Guido as an inspirational source, and asserts that the god of love is his sole inspirational source: "Ciò è palese: ch'io non sono artista, / né cuopro mia ignoranza con disdegno ... / ma son un uom cotal di basso 'ngegno / che vo piangendo, tant'ho l'alma trista ..." (That I am no artist is plain to see, / nor do I hide my ignorance behind contempt ... / for I am such a one, of lowly genius, / who go forth weeping, so sad a soul have I ...) (Cino trans. in Hollander). According to Hollander, Cino's sonnet was a source for various passages in the *Commedia* and particularly for *Inferno* 10, but also for *Inferno* 24 and 25, and *Purgatorio* 24, 52–4: "ma sono un uom ... che vo piangendo," echoing Dante's text "I'mi son un che ... significando."

46 John Ahern, "The New Life of the Book: The Implied Reader of the *Vita Nuova*," *Dante Studies* 110 (1992), pp. 1–16.

47 Teodolinda Barolini, *Rime giovanili e della "Vita Nuova"* (Milan: Rizzoli, 2009), p. 182: "Dante rende esplicito il legame tra fare poesia e fare amicizia. In *Guido, I vorrei* vediamo quindi le origini sia della 'primazia' di Guido sia del fortunatissimo connubio dantesco tra amicizia e poesia."

48 Ibid., p. 183.

49 In this sonnet addressed to Guido Cavalcanti and to their fellow Tuscan poet Lapo Gianni, a wizard sends the three Florentine poets on a magical journey away from human misery, somewhere where they would not "talk of anything but love."

50 Nelson, Lowry, Jr., ed. and trans., *The Poetry of Guido Cavalcanti* (New York: Garland Publishing, Inc., 1986), p. 116.

51 Domenico De Robertis, *Il libro della Vita Nuova*, 2nd ed. (Florence: Sansoni, 1970), pp. 183–7. Cf. John Ahern, "The New Life of the Book: The Implied Reader of the *Vita Nuova*," p. 3.

52 Brunetto Latini (1220–94) was an exile after the battle of Montaperti. He returned to Florence in 1266, shortly after the Guelf victory. His *Tresor* is a prose encyclopedia written in French. It traces the origin of Florence and its political disorder back to the Romans and to the envy, avarice, and pride of the people of Fiesole. His *Tesoretto*, an allegorical work written in Italian, tells the story of a spiritual journey in search of salvation. Latini translated Cicero's rhetorical treatise *De Inventione* and Aristotle's *Ethics* into Italian. In 1286, he served as one of the three priors. See Lewis, *Dante: A Life*, pp. 31–8.

53 What precisely did Brunetto teach Dante? In his *Tresor* II.cxx.I, Brunetto claims that the fame that is achieved through good works gives one immortality. In many ways the *Tresor* prefigures the *Convivio*. Both are philosophical treaties written in the vernacular. Both draw on classical and Christian sources and both echo Aristotle's classification of friendship for virtue, profit, and pleasure.

54 Aquinas, *Liber Super Ethicorum Aristotelis* VIII, lect. 12: "Filius est quodammo do pars patris ab eo separate. Unde haec amicitia propinquissima est dilectioni qua

quis amat sipsum, a quo omnis amicitia derivatur." Cf. Dante, *Conv.* I, xii, 4–6: "Tanto è la cosa più prossima quanto, di tutte le cose del suo genere, altrui è più unita: onde di tutti li uomini lo figlio è più prossimo al padre ... Perche, la prossimitade è seme d'amistà ..."

55 See the *tenzone* between Dante and his friend Forese written before Forese's death in 1296: "Bicci novel, figliuol di non so cui / (s'ì non ne domandasse monna Tessa), giù per la gola tanta roba hai messa / ch'a forza ti convien torre l'altrui" (Young Bicci, son of who I don't know who [short of asking my lady Tessa], you're stuffed so much down your gorge that you're driven to take from others) (Foster and Boyde, *Dante's Lyric Poetry*, I, p. 153). The sonnets exchanged between Dante and Forese were satiric and polemical in nature. In two of the sonnets, Dante accuses Forese of being a glutton, a thief, an illegitimate child, and servile toward others. Forese, in turn, accuses Dante of being "*ozioso*" (sluggish), one who lives off the charity of others and of his father's patrimony. See Teodolinda Barolini, "Dante and the Lyric Past," in *The Cambridge Companion to Dante*, ed. Rachel Jacoff (Cambridge: Cambridge University Press, 2000) p. 72. Cf. Lewis, *Dante: A Life*, pp. 66–7.

56 As verse 98 will make clear, Casella has been dead a bit more than three months. Dante seems surprised that Casella had to wait so long between death and his arrival in purgatory. The souls bound for purgatory are selected by the transporting angel, and some of the saved souls have to wait longer on earth, near Ostia, before being transported. Commentators, beginning with Poletto (1894) and Edward Moore in *Studies in Dante, First Series: Scripture and Classical Authors in Dante* (Oxford: Clarendon, 1969 [1896]), note a similarity between this scene and *Aeneid* VI, 315–6, where Charon selects only those shades who are eager to cross Acheron. As Hollander points out in his note to *Purgatorio* 2, 23, in the *Commedia* Charon transports the souls condemned to hell at once, while the souls of the saved who are destined for purgatory gather around the region of Ostia and await the transporting angel, who will select only some.

57 See Poletto and Hollander's note to *Purgatorio* 2, 94–105 and his notes to *Inferno* 1, 1–2, *Purgatorio* 1, 19–21. Hollander points out that the most likely date, 25 March 1300, for Dante's journey coincides with Casella's point of departure. Whether or not this is a coincidence, it is interesting that while Casella and Dante begin and arrive at different points in their journey toward salvation, their friendship survives death itself.

58 For the possibility that Casella had set Dante's song while on earth see Mario Marti, "Dolcezza di memorie ed assoluto etico nel canto di Casella (*Purg.* II)," in *Studi su Dante* (Galatina: Congedo, 1984), pp. 81–8; Fabio Bisogni, "Precisazioni sul Casella dantesco," *Quadrivium* 12 (1971), pp. 81–91.

59 The use of the word "fissi" (fixed) in *Purgatorio* 2 prefigures the episode in the Earthly Paradise, where the angels rebuke Dante for gazing at Beatrice "troppo

fiso" (too fixed [*Purgatorio* 32, 9]). In the Earthly Paradise, the angels notice that Dante still appreciates Beatrice as the beautiful woman with whom he fell in love, rather than as the blessed lady who wills and facilitates his journey toward salvation. Similarly, in the Casella episode Dante seems to be stuck on secular truth and beauty. The difference is that in the Casella episode it is the beauty of Lady Philosophy, rather than Beatrice (even the earthly Beatrice), that attracts Dante's attention and that of the other listeners.

60 For the Pauline reference see Paola Rigo, *Memoria classica e memoria biblica in Dante* (Florence: Olschki, 1994), pp. 93–4. For a reference to Colossians 2 and 3, see Robert Hollander, "*Purgatorio* II: Cato's rebuke and Dante's *scoglio*," *Italica* 52 (1975), p. 357; Hollander, "*Purgatorio* II: The New Song and the Old," *Lectura Dantis [virginiana]* 6 (1990), pp. 40–1; Hollander's note to *Purgatorio* 2, 118–21: "Cato's return sounds exactly like St. Paul, urging them all to 'put off the old man and put on the new' (Ephesians 4:22; Colossians 3:9)."

61 John Freccero, *Dante: The Poetics of Conversion*, ed. Rachel Jacoff (Cambridge: Harvard University Press, 1986), p. 189

62 Dante, *Conv.* III, xi, 13–15, pp. 191–2: "E sì come la vera amistade, astratta de l'animo, solo in sé considerata, ha per subietto la conoscenza de l'operazione buona, e per forma l'appetito di quella, così la filosofia, fuori d'anima, in sé considerata, ha per subietto lo 'ntendere, e per forma uno quasi divino amore a lo 'ntelletto. E sì come de la vera amistade è cagione efficiente la vertude, così la filosofia è cagione efficiente la veritade; e sì come fine de l'amistade vera è la buona dilezione, che procede dal convivere secondo l'umanitade propriamente, cioè secondo ragione (sì come pare sentire Aristotile nel nono de l'Etica), così fine de la filosofia è quella eccellentissima dilezione che non pate alcuna intermissione o vero difetto, cioè vera felicitade, che per contemplazione de la veritade s'acquista."

63 John Freccero, *Dante: The Poetics of Conversion*, p. 190. Freccero here argues: "Just as Boethius'*Philosophia* had cast out the Muses of secular poetry, she in turn is 'cast out' in Dante's text by Cato's rebuke. With the simile of the birds feeding, Boethius' figure is used against his own thesis."

64 See Daniello's commentary (1568), where he claims that it is precisely because of a "new law" in Purgatory that "one does not sing vain and lascivious things, but hymns and psalms in praise of God, and prays to Him." In the beginning of *Purgatorio* 2, the 113th Psalm sung by the souls who travel along with the angel stands in direct juxtaposition to the love song here sung by Casella.

65 Dante, *Conv.* I, i. 7, p. 42: "Oh beati quelli pochi che seggiono a quella mensa dove lo pane de li angeli si manuca! E miseri quelli che con le pecore hanno commune cibo!"

66 The first commentators believed that Dante here refers to the improper behavior, improper pleasures, or, to use Benvenuto's words, *delectabilia non honesta*,

that Dante and Forese shared in the course of their relationship. The more recent studies, in accordance with the first commentators, defend the opinion that in this passage, Dante refers to the actual relationship with Forese and to the improper pleasures they may have shared. See Hollander's note to *Purgatorio* 115–19, p. 524.

67 See Teodolinda Barolini, *Rime giovanili e della "Vita Nuova,"* p. 183.

68 See Hollander's note to *Purgatorio* 22, 19–24.

69 Niccolò Machiavelli, "Arte della guerra," in *The Essential Writings of Macchiavelli*, ed. and tr. Peter Constantine (New York: The Modern Library, 2007), p. 95: "I will be happy to tell you what I know about anything you ask, and will leave you to judge whether it is true or not. I will be grateful for your questions, because I wish to learn as much from you in what you ask as you will from me in what I answer. For often a wise questioner leads one to consider many things and to realize many others, things that would never have been realized had the question not been asked." Fabrizio's words to Ruccelai here are meant to underscore the importance of discourse and honesty in friendship. Friends arrive at the truth by means of discourse, by conversing, by asking and answering.

70 Ibid., p. 94.

71 According to Statius, it was Virgil who led him to a love of poetry and of God. Statius's Christian conversion continues to baffle readers, since there is no authoritative evidence to support Dante's fictional story. Virgil himself seems somewhat perplexed, as he found no evidence in Statius's works to support Statius's Christianity (*Purg.* 22, 53–63). See Scevola Mariotti, "Il cristianesimo di Stazio in Dante secondo il Poliziano," in *Letteratura e critica: studi in onore di Natalino Sapegno*, ed. Walther Binni et al., vol. 2 (Rome: Bulzoni, 1975), pp. 149–61; Massimiliano Chiamenti, *Dante Alighieri Traduttore* (Florence: Le Lettere, 1995). See also Robert Hollander, "Babytalk in Dante's *Commedia*," *Studies in Dante* (Ravenna: Longo, 1980), pp. 206–7. Hollander here argues that a passage in the *Thebaid* (II, 358–62) was a reference to Virgil's fourth *Eclogue*. In his note to *Purgatorio* 22, 64–73, years later in reference to his earlier argument Hollander notes: "He might have argued that there is an even more precise reference at V.461, the phrase 'iam nova progenies' (and now a new race) that matches exactly Virgil's key phrase in the *Eclogue* (IV.7)."

72 For a similar interpretation see Ettore Paratore, *Traduzione e struttura in Dante* (Florence: Sanzoni, 1968), pp. 72–3; Giorgio Padoan, "Il Canto XXI del *Purgatorio*," in *Nuove letture dantesche*, vol. 4 (Florence: Le Monnier, 1970), p. 354; Robert Hollander, "Baytalk in Dante's *Commedia*," *Studies in Dante*, pp. 123–4; William A. Stephany, "Biblical Allusions to Conversion in *Purgatorio* XXI," *Stanford Italian Review* 3 (1983), p. 151; Michelangelo Picone, "*Purgatorio* XXII," in *Dante's "Divine Comedy," Introductory Readings II: "Purgatorio,"* ed. Tibor Wlassics, *Lectura Dantis* [*virgiliana*], 12 (Charlottesville: University of Virginia, 1993), p. 330.

6. *Amor and Amicizia* in *Inferno* 2

1 *Inferno* 2 is filled with expressions that echo the language of friendship (line numbers in parentheses): *la pietate* (5), *m'aiutate* (7), *mi guidi* (10), *virtù* (11), *mi fidi* (12), *salvazione* (30), *di te mi dolve* (51), *l'amico mio, e non de la ventura* (61), *temo che non sia già smarrito* (64), *al soccorso levata* (65), *l'aiuta sì ch'i ne sia consolata* (69), *amor mi mosse, che mi fa parlare* (72), *m'aggrada il tuo comandamento* (79), *non ti guardi* (82), *non temo di venir qua entro* (87), *miseria non mi tange* (92), *si compiange* (94), *ha bisogno ... di te* (98–9), *io a te lo raccomando* (99), *nimica di ciascun crudele* (100), *soccorri* (104), *t'amò tanto* (104), *la pieta del suo pianto* (106), *lagrimando* (116), *venni a te* (118), *ti levai* (119), *ti tolse* (120), *curan* (125), *tanto ben ti promette* (126), *pietosa* (133), *mi soccorse* (133), *un sol volere è d'ambedue* (139).

2 Mazzotta, *Dante, Poet of the Desert*, p. 119: "Paulinus of Nola is even more explicit in stating that friendship is the means of raising oneself to God. Within this perspective one can understand, for instance, why it should be the act of friendship which brings the pilgrim out of his spiritual entanglement in *Inferno* 1." Cf. Paulinus of Nola, *Epistola* xi, 6, *Corpus Scriptorum Ecclesiasticorum Latinorum* xxix, 64; see also *Epistola* xxiv, 9, *Corpus Scriptorum Ecclesiasticorum Latinorum* xxix, 209. See also Aelred of Rievaulx, *De spiritali amicitia*, ed. Jean Dubois (Paris: Bayaert, 1948), ii, 671D–673A.

3 Dante, *Inf.* 2, 67–9. Cf. Amilcare A. Iannucci, "Beatrice in Limbo: an Metaphoric Harrowing of Hell" in *Dante Studies* 97, (1979), pp. 23–45. According to Iannucci, Beatrice's descent into Hell mirrors Christ's descent into Hell.

4 Dante, *Inf.* 2, 51. Cf. Jacoff and Stephany, *Lectura Dantis Americana: Inferno II*, p. 9.

5 Siro A. Chimenz, "Il Canto II Dell'Inferno," in *Letture Dantesche*, ed. Giovanni Getto (Florence: Sansoni, 1964), p. 27: "... insieme col primo costituisce, dirò col Tommaseo, 'la macchina del poema,' l'impostazione allegorica del mistico viaggio."

6 Antonino Pagliaro, *Ulisse*, p. 17. Cf. Francesco Mazzoni, "Il canto II dell'*Inferno*," in *Saggio per un nuovo commento alla "Divina Commedia": "Inferno"—Canti I–III* (Florence: Sansoni, 1967), p. 151. In his commentary to *Inferno* 2, Mazzoni notes a distinction between the first two cantos, "Questo canto, secondo una formula invalsa, è il 'prologo al cielo' dell'opera ...; ma è pur anche-sul piano strutturale – il prologo alla prima cantica (come il precedente lo era a tutta l'opera)" (Mazzoni quoted by Jacoff and Stephany, *Lectura Dantis Americana: Inferno II*, p. 95). In Silvio Pasquazi, "Il Prologo in Cielo,"*Critica letteraria*, 2 (Rome: Bonacci, 1974), p. 163, Pasquazi refers to *Inferno* 1 as a "proemio" to the *Commedia* and to *Inferno* 2 as "prologo" to the *Inferno*. In "Infernal Irony: The Gates of Hell," *Modern Language Notes* 99.4 (1984), pp. 772–3, Freccero considers the first two cantos as a unit, "Until we come to the entrance of Hell, things seem to exist in a double focus,

suffused with moral and allegorical intent so that their substantiality seems totally compromised" (Freccero quoted by Jacoff and Stephany, p. 95). And in "Dante's Prologue Scene," in *Dante Studies* 84, ed. Anthony Pellegrini (Cambridge, MA: Dante Society of America, 1966), pp. 1–25, Freccero notes that "mimetic fiction" begins in *Inferno* 3. Charles S. Singleton, *Dante Studies 1: Commedia Elements of Structure* (Cambridge: Harvard University Press, 1954), p. 7–13; Arguing against common opinion, in "The 'Canto of the Word' (*Inferno* 2)," p. 97, Hollander observes that "in this respect the separateness of the first two cantos from one another is underlined, since invocations occur in each of the first cantos of the succeeding *cantiche*. At the same time, their structural similarity tends to make them a unit." On this point, Hollander agrees with the argument presented by E.H. Wilkins in "The Prologue of the *Divine Comedy*," *Annual Report of the Dante Society* (1920), 1–7. Based on the characteristics of the prologues in the *Epistle to Cangrande* (*Epistle* XIII, 43–8), Wilkins argues that *Inferno* 1 and *Inferno* 2 form a unit as a prologue to the entire poem and to the *Inferno*.

7 Hollander, "The 'Canto of the Word' (*Inferno* 2)," p. 97.

8 Ibid. Hollander notes the similarity between the last verse of the second canto and the beginning of the first canto and a parallel of the three segments of speech divided by similes; In *Lectura Dantis Americana: Inferno II*, Jacoff and Stephany note a reversal of patterns: the first canto is set at dawn, and Dante is impeded by the three beasts; the second set at dusk and he is impeded by his own fears and doubts (p. 2).

9 Richard H. Lansing, *From Image to Idea: A Study of the Simile in Dante's "Commedia"* (Ravenna: Longo, 1977), pp. 128–31. Lansing notes a change from fear to hope and hope to fear in the two pairs of similes of the first two cantos; see Hollander, "The 'Canto of the Word' (*Inferno* 2)," note 9, p. 118. For a discussion of the parallel endings of *Inferno* 1 and *Inferno* 2, see Mazzoni, "Il canto II dell' *Inferno*," in *Saggio per un nuovo commento alla "Divina Commedia,"* p. 157.

10 Hollander, "The 'Canto of the Word' (*Inferno* 2)," pp. 96–7. As Hollander observes, 118 of its 142 verses (83 per cent) in *Inferno* 2 are spoken and only one other canto in *Inferno* (the eleventh canto) has a higher percentage of discourse: 106 of its 115 (92 per cent).

11 Ibid., p. 96.

12 For a summary of Ballerini's article on *Inferno* 2, see *Year's Work in Modern Language Studies* (1965), p. 306; Rachel Jacoff and William A. Stephany, "The 'Canto of The Word' (*Inferno* 2)," p. 4. Jacoff and Stephany juxtapose Ballerini's interpretation of *Inferno* 2 as the "canto of stasis" with the canto's extensive use of dialogue and motion.

13 Jacoff and Stephany, *Lectura Dantis Americana: Inferno II*, p. 4: The changes that occur between the beginning and the end of Canto 2 – changes in Dante's spiritual

state, in his relationship to Virgil, to nature, and to himself – are so great that rather than being a canto of stasis, Canto 2 must in fact be characterized as a canto of motion.

14 For a comprehensive list of words associated with motion, see Jacoff and Stephany, *Lectura Dantis Americana: Inferno II*, p. 97.

15 Hollander, "The 'Canto of the Word' (*Inferno* 2)," pp. 95–114. Hollander points to the link between language and motion, language and compassion, emotional and physical movement; cf. Jacoff and Stephany, *Lectura Dantis Americana: Inferno II*, p. 6. While the authors note the relation between love and motion, they fail to note the relation between *amor* and *amicitia*.

16 Jacoff and Stephany, *Lectura Dantis Americana: Inferno II*, pp. 4, 8.

17 Ibid., p. 8.

18 Chimenz, "Il Canto II dell'*Inferno*," in *Letture Dantesche*, pp. 28–9: "Quel tramoto si rileva come paesaggio spirituale: è tramonto di fede e speranza; è il riflesso dello stato d'animo del poeta, che 'sol uno' sulla terra si accinge a una impresa, sotto ogni aspetto, spaventosa come una Guerra."

19 Mazzoni, "Il canto II dell'*Inferno*," in *Saggio per un nuovo commento alla "Divina Commedia*," pp. 166–70. Cf. Jacoff and Stephany, *Lectura Dantis Americana: "Inferno" II*, p. 95. As Jacoff and Stephany note, Mazzoni discusses the symbolic significance of the canto's nocturnal setting in relation to Dante's distance from God.

20 Buti (1385): "si deve intendere che Virgilio non era con Dante se non quanto alla lettera, per seguitamento che Dante seguiva la sua poesia, et allegoricamente s'intende la ragione umana ... che non era altro che Dante" (Buti quoted by Robert Hollander); cf. Hollander, "The 'Canto of the Word' (*Inferno* 2)." Pointing to Buti's interpretation of the verse, Hollander rejects the common interpretation of Virgil in the *Commedia* as an allegory of Reason: "This misleading notion – that Virgil exists in the *Commedia* entirely (or even mainly) as an internalized rational capacity of the protagonist – lies at the heart of one of the most persistent basic misreadings of the text confronting students of the poem" (see Hollander's note 2, p. 117).

21 Hollander, "The 'Canto of the Word' (*Inferno* 2)," p. 101: "In this particular it should be clear that Dante intended to be understood as being 'alone' morally, despite Virgil's presence. Only *he* will or can experience Hell in a fully meaningful way, as his salvation is not yet achieved (despite the many promises offered throughout the poem of its likelihood). He is in *via*." See also Hollander, "Le opere di Virgilio nella *Commedia* di Dante," in *Dante e la "bella scola" della poesia: Autorità e sfida poetica*, ed. A.A. Iannucci (Ravenna: Longo, 1993), p. 256. Hollander looks to Virgil's *Aeneid* as a point of reference for Dante, who thought Aeneas to have been alone despite the presence of the Sibyl: "quando esso Enea sostenette solo con Sibilla a intrare ne lo Inferno" (*Conv.* IV, 26–9).

22 Hollander, "The 'Canto of the Word' (*Inferno* 2)," p. 101.

23 Erich Auerbach, "Figural Art" in *Dante*, ed. Harold Bloom (New York: Chelsea House, 1986), p. 27: "He was destined to be a guide, for not only was he a master of eloquent discourse and lofty wisdom but also possessed the qualities that fit a man for guidance and leadership, the qualities that characterize his hero Aeneas and Rome in general: *iustitia* and *pietas*. For Dante the historical Virgil embodied this fullness of earthly perfection and was therefore able of guiding him to the very threshold of insight into the divine and eternal perfection. The historic Virgil was for him a *figura* of the poet-prophet-guide, now fulfilled in the other world."

24 Dante is to be seen as the "new Aeneas" and the "new Paul." Jacoff and Stephany provide a thorough discussion on this subject in "Pilgrim and Poet," in *Lectura Dantis Americana: Inferno II*, pp. 57–72. In "Dante and the Pauline Modes of Vision," in *Structure and Thought in the Paradiso*, pp. 101–2, Mazzeo claims that, "the great parallel to St. Paul in the tradition of mystical thought was not Aeneas but Moses and that Dante creates a new typology and parallelism of his own. The two consummate seers are not the *Doctor Judaeorum* and the *Doctor gentium* but the *pater Romanorum* and the *Doctor gentium*" (quoted by Jacoff and Stephany in note 17, p. 113). According to Mazzoni in "Il canto II dell' *Inferno*," the parallel of Aeneas and Paul is created "col preciso scopo di affiancare all'esperienza tutta naturale di Enea quella soprannaturale del *Vas d'elezione*; ponendo così, fin dall'inizio dell'opera, due termini di conforto ben precisi, che valessero a indicare non solo il senso della duplice esperienza che Dante vive nella *Commedia,* ma anche precedenti, le fonti ideali (e le sole riconosciute esplicitamente) cui il poeta si richiamava (p. 230)" (quoted by Jacoff and Stephany in note 18, p. 114). Following Pascoli's footsteps, Mazzoni suggests that in the *Inferno* and the *Purgatorio*, Dante is like Aeneas, but in the *Paradiso* he is like Paul (p. 232). See Jacoff and Stephany's note 18, p. 114. For a rather recent study of the presence of Paul in Dante's works see Giuseppe Di Scipio, *The Presence of Pauline Thought in the Works of Dante* (Lewiston: The Edwin Mellen Press, 1995).

25 Chimenz, "Il Canto II dell'Inferno," in *Letture Dantesche*, p. 27: "Dante, incalzato dalle fiere, si è aggrappato a Virgilio apparsogli insperatamente, e ne ha, senza troppo rifletterci, accettato subito la proposta del viaggio oltremondano. Ma poi, quetata un pó la paura, pensa alla stranezza di un tal viaggio, dubita, teme, s'impunta, adduce le sue ragioni."

26 Jacoff and Stephany, *Lectura Dantis Americana: Inferno II*, p. 8.

27 Dante, *Inf.* 4, 52–4: "Io era nuovo in questo stato, / quando ci vidi venire un possente, / con segno di vittoria coronato." In 34 AD, about fifty-three years after his death, Virgil witnessed a "mighty one" (Christ) during the harrowing of Hell. See Hollander's note 52–4.

28 Jacoff and Stephany, *Lectura Dantis Americana: Inferno II*, p. 3: "Virgil responds to what is imagined as a personal crisis by invoking a "public" and universal solution

in his prophecy of the Veltro. However one reads this prophecy, it is clear that Virgil is talking about the salvation of "umile Italia" and not the pilgrim alone, understood as particular man in a specific moral crisis.

29 Giuseppe Mazzotta, *Cosmopoiesis: The Renaissance Experiment* (Toronto: University of Toronto Press, 2001), p. 94.

30 Augustine, *Conf.*, IV, IV.

31 Aristotle, *NE* 8.3 1156 b25: "Moreover, they need time to grow accustomed to each other; for, as the proverb says, they cannot know each other before they have shared the traditional peck of salt, and they cannot accept each other or be friends until each appears lovable to the other and gains the other's confidence."

32 Jacoff and Stephany, "Pilgrim and Poet," in *Lectura Dantis Americana: Inferno II*, p. 73: "When Dante calls Virgil 'poeta che mi guidi' at the beginning of *Inferno* II, he is still thinking of secular poetry and knowledge as the path to salvation."

33 Ibid., pp. 72–3: "In the address to Virgil in the beginning of Canto II, Dante seems still to be thinking of poetry as he had when he appealed for Virgil's aid in Canto I ... His praise of Virgil as the sole source of his own honor as a poet shows in retrospect how imperfectly he understands at the poem's beginning what he will come to learn during its course: the true nature of honor and of poetry, as well as the transformed role Virgil will come to play in his life and in his writing. One of the main objectives of Virgil's speech in *Inferno* II is to correct this misperception: Virgil did not come to rescue Dante as a reward for philological study or because his literary influence can somehow 'justify' Dante, but as an instrument of divine grace."

34 Ibid., p. 73.

35 On the continuing dispute concerning Statius's Christianity, see Giorgio Brugnoli, "Statius Christianus," *Italianistica* 17 (1988), pp. 9–15; Riccardo Scrivano, "Stazio personaggio, poeta e cristiano," *Quaderni d'italianistica* 13 (1992), pp. 175–97; Andreas Heil, *Alma Aeneis: Studien zur Vergil-und Statiusrezeption Dante Alighieris*, Inauguraldissertation zur erlangung der Doktorwurde der Philosophischen Fakultat der Ruprecht-Karl-Universitat Heidelberg (2001); Giorgio Padoan, "Il mito di Teseo e il cristianesimo di Stazio," in *Lettere Italiane* II (1959): pp. 432–57; Alessandro Ronconi, "L'incontro di Stazio e Virgilio," *Cultura e scuola* 13–14 (1965), pp. 566–71 (as a response to Padoan's discussion, Ronconi insists that the conversion of Statius is fiction); Giorgio Padoan, "Il Canto XXI del *Purgatorio*," *Nuove letture dantesche*, pp. 327–54.

36 Giorgio Padoan, "*Purgatorio* XXI," *Nuove letture danteschi*, p. 354: "Il poeta è riuscito a far vivere intensamente la commozione di Stazio di fronte a Virgilio, perché si potrebbe quasi affermare che dietro Stazio è Dante stesso che parla. Anche Dante, come Stazio, puó dire di Virgilio: 'per te poeta fui, per te cristiano,' perché la *Commedia* dà una illuminante rilettura dell'*Eneide* in chiave escatologica" (Padoan

quoted by Jacoff and Stephany); cf. Jacoff and Stephany, *Lectura Dantis Americana: Inferno II*, pp. 117–18, see note 44: "See Stephany's conclusion: 'Dante's *Commedia* is his attempt to do with his own writing what Statius had failed to do and what Virgil had accomplished, albeit unintentionally, with his. It is Dante's response to his own conversion' (1983, p. 162)."

37 Jacoff and Stephany, *Lectura Dantis Americana: Inferno II*, p. 72.

38 Ibid., p. 38. According to Jacoff and Stephany, Lucy's words recall the earthly Beatrice of the *Vita Nuova* and the heavenly Beatrice who reappears to Dante in *Purgatorio* 30: "Her cameo appearance in Canto II serves a double purpose: it both recalls the youthful Beatrice of the *Vita Nuova* and anticipates the transfigured Beatrice who will guide from *Purgatorio* XXX on. Lucy suggests an earlier narrative prehistory by reminding Beatrice (and the reader) of 'quei che t'amò tanto, / ch'uscì per te de la volgare schiera'; such a statement grants Beatrice a reality outside the poem and assumes a narrative continuity with the *Vita Nuova*."

39 Dante, *Purg.* 24, 57: "the sweet new style." See Robert Hollander's note to vv. 55–63. In an attempt to understand what Dante means by the phrase "dolce stil novo," Hollander provides "a series of hypotheses" that outline key points.

40 See Mazzoni, "Il canto II dell'*Inferno*," in *Saggio per un nuovo commento alla "Divina Commedia,"* pp. 289–93; Robert Hollander, "Dante's 'dolce stil novo' and the *Comedy*," in *Dante: mito e poesia*, ed. M. Picone and T. Crivelli (Florence: Cesati, 1999), pp. 263–81.

41 Chimenz, "Il Canto II Dell'Inferno," in *Letture Dantesche*, p. 35: "E` una beata che parla, e non ha bisogno di consolazione; ma, se la sua condizione è di beata, il tono della sua parola è patetico e umano."

42 Robert Hollander, *Allegory in Dante's* Commedia (Princeton: Princeton University, 1969), pp. 91–2. Hollander notes the Virgilian echo in Beatrice's tears. Like Beatrice, Venus also sheds tears of mercy in *Aeneid* I: "et lacrimis oculos suffusa nitentis" (I, 228) [her bright eyes dimmed and tearful]. Jacoff and Stephany (1989, p. 41) note the Biblical resonance in her tears – the salvation oracle of Jeremiah where the prophet describes Rachel's intervention on behalf of the Jews on their way to exile to Babylon.

43 Cicero, *DA* V, 20.

44 Francesco Mazzoni, "Il Canto II dell'*Inferno*," pp. 256–77.

45 Jacoff and Stephany, *Lectura Dantis Americana: Inferno II*, pp. 44–6.

46 Ibid., p. 44. Boccaccio interprets Beatrice's line as an attempt to enlist Virgil's assistance by appealing to his sense of compassion through a display of her own loyalty and compassion.

47 Ibid., p. 86.

48 Boethius, *De Consol.*, II, i, p. 54.

49 Ibid., p. 77.

50 Jacoff and Stephany, *Lectura Dantis Americana: Inferno II*, p. 86: "In his self-deception, he attributed what he thought was his good fortune to the conquest of Beatrice in his affections by her rival Philosophy, and yet through it all, *Inferno* II asserts, Beatrice's love remains unbroken ... What one might have taken to have been his good fortune proves only that at that time, despite appearances, he was not in reality Fortune's friend."

51 Cicero, *DA* VII, 23.

52 Jacoff and Stephany, *Lectura Dantis Americana: Inferno II*, p. 44. As Jacoff and Stephany note, Landino interprets the line to mean that Dante loves "dottrina" as an end, rather than as a means to gain earthly goods.

53 Ibid., p. 45.

54 Ibid. Jacoff and Stephany refer to Casella's invocation to Abelard and Saint Augustine who emphasize the contrast between true friends whose love is disinterested and false friends whose love is subject to fortune ("amici fortunae").

55 Benedetto Croce, *La poesia di Dante* (Bari: Laterza, 1921), pp. 13: "L'allegoria non è ... se non una sorte di criptografia ... Nella poesia e nella storia della poesia le spiegazioni delle allegorie sono affatto inutili, e in quanto inutili, dannose. Nella poesia l'allegoria non ha mai luogo" (quoted by Jacoff and Stephany, pp. 45–6).

56 Mazzoni, "Canto II dell' *Inferno*," in *Saggio per un nuovo commento alla "Divina Commedia*," p. 277.

57 Jacoff and Stephany, *Lectura Dantis Americana: Inferno II*, p. 45. Jacoff and Stephany note that, while Padoan (1976) rejects Casella's interpretation seeing it as a big mess ("un grosso pasticcio"), many recent scholars, including Mazzoni, accept Casella's argument as sound. As the authors continue to note, Mazzoni's acceptance of Casella's reading coincides with Domenico De Robertis's reading of the *Vita Nuova*, with its reference to the double theme of disinterested love and the poetry of praise. This reading seems to work well with the literary tradition that opposes the allegorical interpretation of Beatrice, a position which Mazzoni defends: "noi fermamente crediamo di dover rispingere ogni allegorizzazione astratta del personaggio di Beatrice, come di quello di Virgilio" (quoted by Jacoff and Stephany, p. 45).

58 Mazzoni, "Il canto II dell'*Inferno*," in *Saggio per un commento alla "Divina Commedia*," pp. 256–68.

59 Mazzotta, *Dante, Poet of the Desert*, p. 119

60 Jacoff and Stephany, *Lectura Dantis Americana: Inferno II*, p. 46.

61 Michele Barbi, "Ancora sul testo della *Divina Commedia*," *Studi Danteschi* 18 (1934), pp. 5–57. For a recent study of the allegorical interpretation of Beatrice, see Bruno Porcelli, "Beatrice nei commenti danteschi del Landino e del Vellutello" [1994], in his *Nuovi Studi su Dante e Boccaccio con analisi della "Nencia"* (Pisa: Istituti editoriali e poligrafici internazionali, 1997), pp. 57–78. See Robert Hollander's note to *Inf.* 2, 53–4, p. 39. Hollander refers to the presentation of Beatrice

in the *Vita Nuova* (ca. 1293) as a mortal woman, whose significance is linked with the Trinity and with Christ.

62 Jacoff and Stephany, *Lectura Dantis Americana: Inferno II*, pp. 43–4. The authors note the omission of the comma in all subsequent Italian editions, except that of Mattalia, stressing *virtù* as the means by which the human race surpasses all.

63 Mazzoni, *Saggio per un nuovo commento alla "Divina Commedia,"* pp. 276–7.

64 Jacoff and Stephany, *Lectura Dantis Americana: Inferno II*, p. 44. According to Jacoff and Stephany, Singleton's argument against Barbi's reading fell on deaf ears among Italian scholars. The authors believe that Maria Chiavacci Leonardi is the first Italian to consider Singleton's argument as solid. While Chiavacci focuses on Virgil's praise of Beatrice as a personification of revelation, Singleton focuses on Virgil's limited perspective. Cf. Anna Maria Chiavacci Leonardi, "Questioni di punteggiatura in due celebri attacchi danteschi (*Inf.* II, 76–78 e X, 67–69)," *Lettere italiane*, 36.1 (1984), p. 7.

65 Charles S. Singleton, "Virgil Recognizes Beatrice," *Annual Report of the Dante Society*, 74 (1956), pp. 29–38. cf. Jacoff and Stephany, *Lectura Dantis Americana: Inferno II*, p. 46: "Indeed, may we not see that Virgil's 'point of view' or perspective is respected by Beatrice herself, when in speaking to him she refers to the man to be rescued as 'amico mio e non de la ventura?' ... It is a language, a way of phrasing, which a Virgil could understand. In this way, Beatrice is already telling Virgil who she is."

66 Ibid. Cf. Jacoff and Stephany, "Tre Donne Benedette," in *Lectura Dantis Americana: Inferno II*, p. 44 and note 58, p. 107. The authors note the similarity between Singleton's reading of the lines and Biagioli's reading, from Virgil's vantage point: "figura il Poeta nella bellissima sua Beatrice quella stessa donna, che fu di Boezio consolatrice. Ella è dunque simbolo della Filosofia" (quoted by Jacoff and Stephany, p. 107, and see their note 55, p. 107). As Jacoff and Stephany note, Chiavacci Leonardi's understanding of the line is that Virgil praises Beatrice as a personification of revelation whose truth surpasses all secular wisdom. Singleton differs from Chiavacci by emphasizing the limits of Virgil's perspective and concludes that "in the *Commedia*, the capacity for the 'umana specie' to transcend its limits must be conceptualized in theological rather than philosophical terms, given the problematic of original sin (see *Paradiso* VII, 28–30)."

67 Mazzoni, "Il canto II dell'*Inferno*," in *Saggio per un nuovo commento alla "Divina Commedia,"* p. 278 (quoted by Jacoff and Stephany (1989), p. 46). Jacoff and Stephany note that Mazzoni ignores that the Boethian echoes in Virgil's response were noticed before Moore by Pietro di Dante himself.

68 For a full consideration of this verse, see Mazzoni, *Saggio per un nuovo commento alla "Divina Commedia,"* pp. 256–68.

69 Chimenz, "Il Canto II Dell'Inferno," in *Letture Dantesche*, p. 35: "Ora, Virgilio è un pagano che aveva esaltato appunto l'umana virtù: chiamando in questo senso Beatrice 'signora della virtù,' egli le fa la più alta lode che da parte sua potesse farsi."

70 Jacoff and Stephany, *Lectura Dantis Americana: Inferno II*, p. 46: "Once we think of Boethius we begin to see that the line 'amico mio e non de la ventura' cannot be understood apart from Virgil's response to it, his apostrophe to Beatrice 'donna di virtù, sola per cui.'"

71 Singleton, "Virgil Recognizes Beatrice," p. 34: "To see her so. To 'read' Beatrice so in the poem, has proved to be something of a major difficulty with the modern reader, and by modern I mean post-Renaissance ... It amounts, actually, to a reader's heresy (if we may conceive of such a thing, and with all due allowance made) not unlike one of the well-known heresies that denied one or the other of Christ's two natures" (quoted by Jacoff and Stephany, p. 47). Jacoff and Stephany argue that the elevation of Mary prepares the way for Beatrice's Christological analogy and that Singleton underestimates the importance of Mary: "Mary's own role is, of course, an imitation of Christ's salvific mediation for all mankind, but the emphatic feminization of the process of mediation at the poem's opening predisposes the reader to accept the extraordinary claims Dante will later make of Beatrice" (*Lectura Dantis Americana: Inferno II*, p. 29). For a discussion of the importance of the role of Mary, see Jaroslav Pelikan, *The Growth of Medieval Theology (600–1300)*, vol. 3 of *The Christian Tradition, A History of the Development of Doctrine* (Chicago: University of Chicago Press, 1978), pp. 158–74; cf. Jacoff and Stephany, note 19, p. 102.

72 Rachel Jacoff and William A. Stephany, *Lectura Dantis Americana*: *"Inferno" II*, p. 46: "For us, Beatrice as 'donna di virtù' recalls both the Beatrice of the *Vita Nuova*, 'regina de le vertudi' (X, 2) and the Boethian 'magistra virtutum,' Lady Philosophy, who is said to supplant Beatrice in the *Convivio*. The Beatrice of *Inferno* II subsumes both these figures in her new poetic incarnation." The earliest commentators tended to ignore Beatrice's historical identity. Her historical identity is first noted in Boccaccio and in Pietro di Dante's third redaction. Modern commentators including Hollander, Jacoff, and Stephany favor the historical identification of Beatrice.

73 Jacoff and Stephany, *Lectura Dantis Americana "Inferno" II*, pp. 40, 46–7. The authors interpret Beatrice's descent into Limbo as a sort of "condescension" of the Word. Later in the same chapter they note that while they differ in crucial details in their argument against Barbi's historical interpretation, both Singleton and Chiavacci Leonardi recognize Beatrice's dual nature, as historical and allegorical figure.

74 Iannucci, "Beatrice in Limbo: A Metaphoric Harrowing of Hell," pp. 23–45.

75 While focusing on Beatrice's humanity Boccaccio observes: "E in questo lagrimare ancore più d'affezione si dimostra, dimostrandosi ancora uno atto d'amante,

e massimamente di donna, le quali com'hanno pregato d'alcuna cosa la quale disiderino, incontanente lagrimano, mostrando in quello il disiderio suo essere ardentissimo." Jacoff and Stephany note that Padoan praises Boccaccio's admiring gloss "as an indication of Boccaccio's sensitivity to the 'umanità viva di Beatrice, solitamente ridotta dai commentatori trecenteschi a fredda e statica allegoria'" (Boccaccio quoted by Jacoff and Stephany, note 46, pp. 105–6). The same positive gloss of the lines is found in subsequent commentators who recognize and praise Beatrice's humanity. Momigliano notes: "Questo particolare costituisce l'ultima perfezione del motivo principale del canto: una fugace luce di lacrime in cui si tradisce appena l'umanità dell'anima beata che si allontana. Su questi occhi lucenti si chiude la visione; ma il resto del canto ne rimane tutto ravviato e commosso" (quoted by Mazzoni, p. 287, and by Jacoff and Stephany, p. 106, see note 47). See Chimenz, "Il canto II dell'*Inferno*," p. 39. While noting the beauty of the human pathos in the lines, Chimenz relates Beatrice's tears to Virgil's speedy flight to Dante's rescue: "Ma l'ultima parola è una lagrima che trema nei suoi occhi e li fa ancor più lucenti: una lagrima tutta umana, e soltanto umana, e di donna e di amante, ultimo sigillo di commozione impresso nell'animo di Virgilio ... Quello che segue è come il frutto raccolto da queste lagrime di Beatrice, il loro riflesso sentimentale."

76 Cicero, *DA* VII, 23.

77 Hollander, "The 'Canto of the Word' (*Inferno* 2)," p. 108. Hollander observes that "the question he poses is indeed an awkward one, emphasizing once again Virgil's inadequacy in matters of faith."

78 Christopher J. Ryan, "Virgil's Wisdom in the *Divina Commedia*," *Medievalia et Humanistica* 11 (1982), pp. 269–77. Ryan notes other limitations of Virgil's understanding in the *Commedia*. See also Hollander, "The 'Canto of the Word' (*Inferno* 2)," p. 108.

79 Mazzoni, "Il Canto II dell'*Inferno*," in *Saggio per un nuovo commento alla "Divina Commedia*," p. 282. As Mazzoni notes, the allusion to Aristotle's *Ethics* III.ix.349 has been noted since Boccaccio; cf. Jacoff and Stephany, *Lectura Dantis Americana: Inferno II*, p. 9.

80 Jacoff and Stephany, *Lectura Dantis Americana: Inferno II*, p. 16.

81 Ibid., p. 10: "... fear for one's own security can be debilitating, but acceptance of the concern for the other is empowering."

82 de Beauvoir, *The Ethics of Ambiguity*, pp. 72–3: "I concern others and they concern me. There we have an irreducible truth. The me-other relationship is as indissoluble as the subject-object relationship ... To will oneself free is also to will others free."

83 Hollander, "The 'Canto of the Word' (*Inferno* 2)," p. 190.

84 Giovanni Fallani, "Canto II" in *Lectura Dantis Scaligera* (Florence: Le Monnier, 1967), p. 44. Fallani notes the repetitive use of the word *perchè* (four times within the span of three lines).

85 Dante, *Inf.* 2, 142. Cf. Chimenz, "Il Canto II dell'Inferno, in *Letture Dantesche*, p. 40: "Allor si mosse, e io gli tenni retro, ci rappresenta Dante dietro Virgilio, senza entusiasmo, senza convizione ... La chiusa di questo pare, come dicevo identica: e poi che mosso fue, Entrai per lo cammino alto e silvestro. Quell'intrai; al principio del verso, dice la risolutezza con cui si mette in cammino, anche se il cammino è arduo e selvoso." See also Jacoff and Stephany, *Lectura Dantis Americana: Inferno* II, p. 96, note 9.

86 Guy P. Raffa, "A Beautiful Friendship: Dante and Vergil in the *Commedia*," *Modern Language Notes* 127.1 (2012): 72–80.

87 Aristotle, *NE* 9.9. 1170b5–8; 9.4 1166a32.

88 Augustine, *Conf.*, IV, VI.

89 Aquinas, *ST* Ia.2ae, q. 28, a1.

90 Dante, *Inf.* 2, 44. In the next verse, Virgil's magnanimity is contrasted with Dante's cowardice: "l'anima tua è da viltade offesa" ["your spirit is assailed by cowardice"].

91 Robert Hollander, *Il Virgilio dantesco: tragedia nella "Commedia"* (Florence: Olschki, 1983), pp. 69–70. For further clarification of the same line, Hollander points to Giorgio Brugnoli's article on *Inferno* 1, 63 in *Letteratura comparate: problemi e metodo: Studi in onore di Ettore Paratore*, vol. 3 (Bologna: Patron, 1981), pp. 1169–82.

92 J.H. Whitfield, *Dante and Virgil* (Oxford: Basil Blackwell: A.R. Mowbray & Co., 1949), p. 70.

93 Mazzotta, *Dante, Poet of the Desert*, p. 152.

94 Cicero, *DA* VII, 23; ibid., V, 20: "Namque hoc praestat amicitia propinquitati, quod ex propinquitate benevolentia tolli potest, ex amicitia non potest; sublata enim benevolentia amicitiae nomen tollitur, propinquitatis manet."

95 Dante, *Inf.* p. 18; cf. *Aeneid* I, 327–30.

96 Ernst Robert Curtius, *European Literature in the Middle Ages*, trans. Willard R. Trask (New York: Harper Press, 1963), p. 358: "The 'awakening' to Aristotle in the thirteenth century was the work of generations and took place in the cool light of intellectual research. The awakening of Virgil by Dante is an arc of flame which leaps from one great soul to another. The tradition of the European spirit knows no situation of such affecting loftiness, tenderness, fruitfulness. It is the meeting of two great Latins."

97 Hollander, Dante: A Life in Works, p.115.

98 Robert Hollander refers to the *Monarchia* I, xi, 1, where Dante's understanding of Virgil's virgin does not point to the blessed Mary, but to Aestrea (justice).

Hollander points to passages in the Commedia where Virgil behaves in ways that betray his fallibility as a pagan, such as in Inferno 21, when tricked by Malacoda he misinterprets his evil agenda. According to Dronke, early allegorical interpretations were grounded in fear for Dante's reputation and intended to escape accusations of blasphemy: "The early commentators on the Commedia, however, speak again and again of Dante's feigning – at times probably in order to shield the poet and his poem from accusations of hubris, indeed of blasphemy" (Dante and Medieval Latin Traditions, p. 3).

99 Hollander, *Dante: A Life in Works*, p. 116.

100 Jacoff and Stephany, *Lectura Dantis Americana: Inferno II*, p. 5. The authors point to the centrality of this *terzina* and to the relation of words to motion.

101 Hollander, *Studies in Dante*, p. 82. Hollander notes that the close relation of love, discourse, and motion in *Inferno* 2 is also stressed in *Purgatorio* 24, 52–4: "I' mi son un che, quando Amor mi spira, noto, e a quell modo ch'è ditta dentro vo significando." Hollander further points to the "theological" sense of these verses: "*Amore*" and "*spira*" iconographically understood in relation to Holy Spirit, and Dante's role understood as inspired poet, as *poeta theologus* and *scriba dei*.

102 Jacoff and Stephany, "The Canto of the Word," in *Lectura Dantis Americana: Inferno II*, p. 6: "These lines are the 'kernel of the canto and, in a sense, of the poem: the relationship between love and motion which is explicit here is played out repeatedly throughout the canto and will be recalled in cosmic terms in the poem's concluding line, when the pilgrim's desire and will are at one with 'l'amor che move il sole e l'altre stelle' (*Paradiso* XXXIII, 145) ... compassion leads to motion, which leads to words."

103 On this point see Robert Hollander's note to *Paradiso* 8, 55–7. I cite partially from Hollander's note: "... his use of the verb *amare* and the noun *amore* in this tercet, spoken by Charles in Venus, shows how the poet has reconceptualized the nature of love from Dido's kind to spiritual friendship (see note to *Inf.* II.61)." See Lino Pertile, "Quale amore va in Paradiso?" in "*Le donne, I cavalieri, l'arme, gli amori*": *Pema e romanzo: la narrativa lunga in Italia,* ed. Francesco Bruni (Venice: Marsilio, 2001), p. 60. As Hollander notes, Pertile is not alone in objecting that Charles is not present as a lover. For the relationship between Charles and Venus, see Patrick Boyde, *Perception and passion in Dante's "Comedy"* (Cambridge: Cambridge University Press, 1993), p. 285: "Perhaps we are meant to infer that the rays of Venus may dispose a 'gentle heart to disinterested friendship, as well as to *luxuria*" (quoted by Hollander). Hollander also points to Benvenuto da Imola who presents Charles as a "son of Venus."

104 Hollander, "The 'Canto of the Word' (*Inferno* 2)," p. 114: "It is my contention that, beginning with the second canto, Dante sets out the task of downgrading

the authority of Virgil overtly, if with delicacy. The phrase 'Tu dici ...' (13) is thus the first clear sign, one that requires only good sense to recognize that Dante has begun to distance himself from his own so very remarkable resuscitation of Virgil. He has come not only to praise Virgil, but to bury him. As unfair as this element in Dante's treatment of Virgil may seem to us, a clearer perception reveals its necessity in this poem which is striving to convince us of its accord with a higher truth than Virgil had managed to come to know."

105 Jacoff and Stephany, *Lectura Dantis Americana: Inferno II*, p. 84: "*Inferno* II begins the process of restablishing Beatrice's primacy in Dante's poetic life and of reconceptualizing the opposition between Beatrice and the *donna gentile*."

106 On the relation between Virgil and John the Baptist, see Hollander, "The 'Canto of the Word' (*Inferno* 2)," p. 114. In Virgil's line, Hollander hears the resonance of John's reference to Jesus: "Ipse est qui post me venturus set, qui ante me factus est; cuius ego non sum dignus ut solvam eius corrigiam calceamenti" (He it is, who coming after me, who was made before me, whose shoe's latche I am not worthy to unloose; John quoted and translated by Hollander). See also Andre Pezard, *Dante sous la pluie de feu* (Paris: Vrin, 1950), p. 343; Bruno Porcelli, "'Chi per lungo silenzio parea fioco e il valore della parola nella *Commedia*," *Ausonia* 19. 5 (1964), pp. 34–6; Hollander, *Allegory in Dante's* Commedia, pp. 261–3; Hollander, *Studies in Dante*, pp. 86–7, 193n; and Hollander, *Il Virgilio dantesco*, pp. 69–77.

107 Robin Kirkpatrick, *The Divine Comedy* (Cambridge: Cambridge University Press, 1987), p. 50: "The theme of this canto is the inadequacy of heroic and rational modes of conduct in the light of Christian humility and Christian faith" (see also Jacoff and Stepany, "Inferno II" in *Lectura Dantis Americana*, p. 117, see note 44).

108 Ibid., 2, 67. Cf. Mazzotta, *Dante, Poet of the Desert*, p. 157. Mazzotta explains that the phrase is "a rhetorical commonplace in the esthetic treatises of the twelfth century" and that it refers "to the order and design of the poetic text." Mazzotta quotes from Silvestris's *Commentum super sex libros* Eneidos, p. 2: "Ex hoc opere ex ornatu verborum et figura orationis ... quaedam habetur delectatio."

109 See Hollander's note to *Inferno* 2, 56–7, p. 40 in "The "Canto of the Word' (*Inferno* 2)," in *Lectura Newberryana*, p. 107. For Hollander, the distinction between "piana" and "ornata" brings to mind "the medieval categorizations of rhetorical styles, between the plain (*umile*) and the ornate (*alto*)" (p. 107). See also Mazzotta, *Dante, Poet of the Desert*, p. 158. For Mazzotta, Beatrice's language "exhibits rhetorical lures through the extended *captatio benevolentiae.*" See also Jacoff and Stephany, *Lectura Dantis Americana: Inferno II*, p. 99, note 27. According to Hollander, Jacoff, and Stephany, Beatrice's speech echoes the words spoken by Aeneas to Dido in his pledge of praise in *Aeneid* I, 605ff: "semper honos nomenque tuum laudesque manebunt" (I, 609) [ever your name and praise and honor shall last], a

pledge which, as the authors note, is ironic (Aeneas's words quoted by Jacoff and Stephany).

110 See Hollander's note to *Inferno* 2, pp. 56–7. Cf. Erich Auerbach, "*Sermo humilis*," in *Literary Language and Its Public in Late Latin Antiquity and in the Middle Ages*, trans. R. Manheim (Princeton: Princeton University Press, 1958), pp. 65–6; Mazzotta, *Dante, Poet of the Desert*, pp. 157–8; Hollander, *Studies in Dante*, pp. 217–18; Hollander, *Il Virgilio dantesco*, p. 153; Robert Hollander, "Dante's Pagan Past: Notes on *Inferno* XIV and XVIII," *Stanford Italian Review* 5 (1985), pp. 30–1.

111 The difference between Virgil's speech (ornate) and Beatrice's speech (piana) must be understood in relation to the medieval rhetorical distinction of the plain (low) style, and the ornate (high) style. Benvenuto da Imola was the first to make this point: "divine speech is sweet and humble, not elevated and proud, as is that of Virgil and the poets." For other discussions on this very same passage see: Erich Auerbach, "*Sermo humilis*," pp. 65–6; Mazzotta, *Dante, Poet of the Desert*, pp. 157–8; Robert Hollander, "The 'Canto of the Word' (*Inferno* 2)," p. 107.

112 Hollander, "The 'Canto of the Word' (*Inferno* 2)," p. 107.

113 Jacoff and Stephany, "The Canto of the Word," in *Lectura Americana Inferno II*, p. 17. The authors relate Virgil's "parola ornata" to the more encompassing question of language with its ability to represent truth or falsehood: "The question of the "parola ornata" is ultimately a question about literary language and its potential for both truth and falsehood, part of the poem's ongoing interrogation of the relationship between rhetoric and truth."

114 See Mazzotta, *Dante, Poet of the Desert*, p. 159: "But Dante knew well that there is a gap between the language of God and the language of men: for the language of men is prone to duplicity."

115 See Hollander, "Dante's Pagan Past," pp. 23–36. Hollander argues that the later use of "parola ornata" in retrospect undercuts the positive sense of the phrase as used about Virgil in *Inferno* 2.

116 See also Hollander's note on *Inferno* 2, 114, p. 43. Hollander understands "honest speech" as a reference to Virgil's moral greatness, to his nobility. He notes that the same observation is found in Sinclair's translation.

117 Aristotle, *NE* 8.1.1155a1–4. Cf. Cicero, *DA* VI, 20–1; XXII, 83; XXVII, 100; XXVII, 104.

118 Christopher J. Ryan, "The Theology of Dante" in *The Cambridge Companion To Dante*, ed. Rachel Jacoff (Cambridge: Cambridge University Press, 1993, p. 141.

119 Ibid., p. 144.

120 Augustine, *Conf.*, IV, VI, p. 164: "miser eram, et miser est omnis animus vinctus amicitia rerum mortalium, et dilaniatur, cum eas amittit, et tunc sentit miseriam, qua miser est et antequam amittat eas."

7. Friendship in *Purgatorio* 30 and *Purgatorio* 31

1 Foster, "The Mind in Love: Dante's Philosophy," p. 43: "What we enter, as readers of the *Comedy*, is the continuous spiritual movement of a mind seeking God."

2 Francesco De Sanctis, *Storia della letteratura italiana*, p. 217: "Quest'apoteosi di Beatrice, questo primo apparire della sua donna, ancora velata fra tanta Gloria, scioglie l'immaginazione dalla rigidità de' simboli e de' riti, e le dá le libere ali dell'arte. Il drama si fa umano; spuntano le immagini e i sentimenti ... L'apparire di Beatrice è lo sparire di Virgilio. Qui l'astrattezza del simbolo è superata. Ti senti innanzi ad un'anima d'uomo."

3 Dante, *Par.* 1, 70: "To soar beyond the human." Cf. Botterill, *Dante and the Mystical Tradition*, p. 231. Botterill traces the scholarly tradition of the term *trasumanar*, from medieval to modern times. Among those listed are Jacopo della Lana (1320s), Pietro Alighieri, Francesco da Buti, Benvenuto da Imola, Scartazzini, Poletto, Casini, Chimenz, Sapegno, and Bosco and Reggio. Notwithstanding differences in interpretation, all seem to underscore the relationship between *trasumanar* and contemplation while emphasizing the element of human fallibility. Scartazzini understands *trasumanar* as transcendence from humanity to divinity: "Trasumanar: divenire piú che umano, passare dall'umano al divino." Similarly, Poletto interprets *trasumanar* as a passing beyond humanity, without which the beatific vision of God would be impossible: "passare al di lá dell'umano, senza di che non è possible vedere Iddio." Casini also understands *trasumanar* as a passing from the human state to the divine state: "il passaggio dallo stato umano allo stato divino." Chimenz understands it as a means of assuming a superior and divine nature: "divenire di natura superiore all'umana." Sapegno understands *trasumanar* as a rising beyond human limitations: "innalzarsi verso i limiti dell'umano." For Bosco and Reggio *trasumanar* signifies a traveling beyond the limits of human nature: "oltrepassare i limiti della natura umana." According to Botterill, Benvenuto da Imola is the medieval commentator who provides "the fullest and most learned explication of word and concept alike." Benvenuto interprets *trasumanar* within the hermetic tradition while adding a "Neoplatonic twist to the contemplation." All the while, Benvenuto places *trasumanar* within the boundaries of a Christian mystical tradition, understanding it as a way, through grace, for man to become transhumanized in this world. (All quotes from Botterill.)

4 Edoardo Sanguineti, "Il Canto XXX del Purgatorio," in *Letture Dantesche*, ed. Giovanni Getto (Florence: Sansoni Editore, 1963), p. 1289: "il canto XXX del *Purgatorio* si pone come intermedio tra I primi 63 canti della *Commedia* e i restanti 36, è quasi algebricamente la sua concreta centralità strutturale (63 canti virgiliani, di contro a 36 canti sacri di Beatrice)."

5 Bruno Panvini, "Sul Primo Incontro Di Dante Con Beatrice Nel Paradiso Terrestre (*Purgatorio,* XXX e XXXI)," in *Filologia romanza,* vol. 5, (Turin: Loescher-Chiantore, 1958) p. 256: "L'incontro di Dante con Beatrice rappresenta il momento decisivo del viaggio del pellegrino di Dio, determinante delle sue future vicende. Tutto quanto gli è prima avvenuto è stato preordinato per quest'incontro; tutte le precedenti vicende sono la preparazione di questo momento supremo, che lo hanno portato e ferrato per una giusta e suprema decisione della sua volontà."

6 De Sanctis, *Storia Della Letteratura Italiana,* p. 217: "L'apparire di Beatrice è lo scomparire di Virgilio. Qui l'astrattezza del simbolo è superata. Ti senti innanzi ad un'anima d'uomo. Quella donna è la sua Beatrice, l'amore della sua prima giovinezza; e Virgilio è il dolcissimo padre che sparisce, quando piú ne aveva bisogno, quando era proprio come un fantolino in paura che si volge alla mamma; e si volge, e non lo vede piú, e lo chiama tre volte per nome nella mente sbigottita. Il mistero liturgico si trasforma in un dramma moderno." Cf. Edoardo Sanguineti, "Il Canto XXX Del Purgatorio," in *Letture Dantesche* (1964), p. 1294: "quella che additavamo come la centrale dialettica delle figure di Virgilio e di Beatrice; ché la vita del canto si riassume appunto nella presenza di questa e nella assenza (assenza da codesta stessa presenza implicata e imposta) di quello, nel drammaticamente violento apparire della donna e nel drammaticamente violento disparire del maestro (le sue simmetriche occasioni del 'pianger' del poeta)."

7 Sanguineti, "Il Canto XXX Del Purgatorio," in *Letture Dantesche,* p. 1289: "ché qui agisce, in effetti, il rovesciamento prospettico che l'alunno di Virgilio farà il devoto di Beatrice ... il poema ritrova, in un certo modo, nuova inaugurazione, ritrova almeno, in termini reali, l'avvio alla sua maggiore vicenda."

8 Giorgio Petrocchi, *L'Ultima Dea* (Rome: Bonacci Editore, 1977), p. 135: "La serie delle esperienze morali e degli atti esteriori ... si svolge attraverso trapassi analoghi dell'*iter* purificatorio e del lento riprendesi dei rapporti umani tra la donna e il poeta, diremmo d'un normalizzarsi di questi rapporti sullo *standard* d'un'amicizia riconquistata e ormai indistruttibile perché celestiale, nutrita dai carismi straordinari acquisiti nell'*altro viaggio.*"

9 Panvini, "Sul primo incontro di Dante con Beatrice nel Paradiso Terrestre (*Purgatorio,* XXX e XXXI)," p. 256: "onde l'incontro di Dante con Beatrice nel Paradiso terrestre rappresenta simbolicamente l'incontro dell'anima umana con la Grazia divina, vale a dire il momento supremo dell'anima umana, quando essa deve riconoscere e accettare la Grazia come l'esclusivo e indispensabile fattore di tutti i propri meriti terreni, della propria salvazione e della propria possibile futura beatitudine."

10 Mazzotta, *Dante, Poet of the Desert,* p. 114: "in the garden the pilgrim's journey under Virgil's guidance ends and the new journey led by Beatrice starts; moreover, this is the place where the Pauline *rite de passage* from the condition of the old man occurs and, at the same time, it appears as a veritable garden of love where the fall of man took place."

11 Singleton, "The Goal at the Summit," in *Dante Studies 2: Journey to Beatrice*, p. 107: "In which case we have again the familiar sequence: justice as the disposition or preparation for what then follows, be it Christ, or Sapientia, or Contemplation, or Light of Grace. Beatrice, in fact, can mean more names than one in the allegory of the poem." For a study of the allegorical interpretation of Beatrice, see Bruno Porcelli, "Beatrice nei commenti danteschi del Landino e del Vellutello," in *Nuovi studi su Dante e Boccaccio con analisi della 'Nencia,'* pp. 57–8. See also Hollander's note to *Inferno* 2, 53–4, p. 39. In the *Vita Nuova* (1293) the meaning of Beatrice is linked with the Trinity, and more particularly with Christ.

12 Panvini, "Sul primo incontro di Dante con Beatrice nel Paradiso Terrestre (*Purgatorio*, XXX e XXXI), in *Filologia romanza*, p. 257: "Beatrice è stata vista soprattutto come simbolo della teologia, o della fede, o, meglio, della rivelazione. A me sembra invece che la funzione di Beatrice intendendola come il simbolo delaa grazia operante e santificante e della rivelazione insieme, in quanto anche la rivelazione è un atto della Grazia."

13 Ibid., p. 258: "Come per Tommaso, anche per Dante la Grazia è un dono dell'amore divino, il qualegiunge all'uomo in un modo inaspettato e non richiesto."

14 Ibid., p. 257: "... che Dante voglia dire che solo esclusivamente mediante la Grazia, signora (*donna*) delle virtù, l'umana specie puó vincere d'eccellenza e trascendere ogni altra cosa terrena, in quanto è esclusivamente la Grazia che rende l'uomo partecipe della Divinità." Panvini cites Aquinas, *Summa Theologiae*, tomus II, Pars prima secundae, Quaesto CX, Articulus 1, p. 561: "... est dilectio (Dei) specialis, secundum quam trahit naturam rationalem supra conditionem naturae, ad participationem divini boni"; and quaestio CXI, Art. 1, p. 565: "... gratia ... per quam ipse homo Deo congiungitur ... vocatur gratia gratum faciens."

15 Mazzotta, *Dante, Poet of the Desert*, p. 122. Mazzotta applies the two types of baptisms administered to Christians (baptism as a preparation to grace, and baptism as the descent of grace) to the moral structure of the *Commedia*, particularly as it is analogous to Dante's movement through Purgatory as preparation and in the Garden as the arrival of grace itself in the figure of Beatrice.

16 See Hollander's note to *Purgatorio* 27, 139–41, p. 616: "Virgil gives over the instructional task that has been his since *Inferno* I, presiding over the correction and perfection of Dante's will." See also Hollander, "The Invocation of the *Commedia*," *Yearbook of Italian Studies* 3 (1976): 235–40.

17 Dante, *Purg.* 27, 140: "libero, dritto e sano è tuo arbitrio"; ibid., 30, 139: "Non aspettar mio dir più ne' mio cenno."

18 Giovanni Gentile, *Studi su Dante*, p. 26: "La condizione del *sapiens* spinoziano è quella di Virgilio nella *Commedia*, perchè Virgilio è il saggio dantesco; è la condizione degli spiriti del Limbo"; ibid., p. 27: "Che se Virgilio è il *sapiens* spinoziano, Beatrice è quell'altra sapienza, quell'altra via, che secondo Dante si può trovare veramente all'eterna pace."

19 Sanguinetti, "Il Canto XXX del Purgatorio," in *Letture Dantesche*, p. 1295: "Il canto XXX del *Purgatorio* esprime il concreto emergere della vita religiosa dinanzi alla coscienza del poeta (in figura di Beatrice, 'regalmente ... proterva'), dinanzi alla sua vita morale (in figura di Virgilio, 'dolcissiomo padre'), e il necessario cedere di questa a quella."

20 Sanguinetti, "Il Canto XXX del Purgatorio," in *Letture Dantesche*, p. 1295: "Che questa vita morale sia però immediatamente, in qualche modo, compresa e assunta nella vita religiosa stessa, che essa sia, in ogni modo, giustificata, nella nuova dimensione di esperienza ('Virgilio a cui per mia salute diè mi'; e confermerà solennemente Beatrice: 'colui che l'ha qua su condotto'), è conclusione che appartiene alla sicurezza di fedė, tutta medioevale ancora, che è propria del poeta."

21 Gentile, *Studi su Dante*, p. 25: "Anche per Dante il processo teorico dello spirito è processo etico, e l'emendazione dell'intelletto, che trae dall'errore a Dio, libera dai dolori della vita, elevando alla vera e sola felicità compartita dalla visione dell'assoluta verità. La *Commedia* potrebbe dirsi un'*Ethica* sovrannaturale, come l'*Ethica* potrebbe a sua volta dirsi una *Commedia* naturalistica."

22 Dante, *Purg.* 30, 41; ibid., 30, 140. Cf. See Sanguinetti, "Il Canto XXX del Purgatorio," in *Letture Dantesche*, p. 1296: "E Virgilio ottiene precisamente il suo luogo e il suo significato: egli sarà colui che riconduce il poeta dalla colpa alla sua vocazione originaria."

23 Panvini, "Sul primo incontro di Dante con Beatrice nel Paradiso Terrestre (*Purgatorio*, XXX e XXXI)," p. 258: "E pertanto Virgilio è sì il simbolo della retta ragione mossa dalla Grazia, ma è anche e pur sempre il Virgilio storico, l'immortale poeta di Roma, che Dante ha amorosamente studiato e ammirato."

24 Erich Auerbach, *Studi su Dante*, p. 81: "Virgilio, l'annunciatore di Cristo e il cantore dell'impero romano, diventò la sua guida, il sesto libro fu per lui verità autentico-poetica."

25 Hollander, *Dante: A Life in Works*, p. 117: "if Virgil is allowed an honorable afterlife in Dante's pages, his standing is nonetheless frequently undercut in ways that point up the distance from him of even his greatest admirer."

26 Dante, *Inf.* 1, 122, p. 10. Cf. Hollander, "The 'Canto of the Word' *(Inferno 2)*," p. 114. Hollander notes an echo of John 1:27 in Dante's line. "So far as I have been able to ascertain, no one has heard the echo of John 1:27 in that verse: 'Ipse est qui post me venturus est, qui ante me factus est: cuius ego *non sum dignus* ut solvam eius corrigiam calceamenti' ('He it is, who coming after me, who was made before me, whose shoes's latched I am not worthy to unloose'; italics added)" (p. 114). Virgil harps on his own unworthiness.

27 Hollander, *Dante: A Life in Works*, p. 118. Hollander notes instances when Virgil's authority is undermined and his fallibility emphasized: "he is denied entrance to the city of Dis by the rebellious forces that guard it (VIII); he gives a confused

and Empedoclean explanation of the Crucifixion (XII, 37–45); he offers several incorrect interpretations of the wicked intentions of the *Malebranche* and subsequently experiences annoyance at having been tricked by them (XXI–XXIII). In *Purgatorio*, Virgil is chastised by Cato, along with the saved souls who lent their ears and hearts to Casella's song (II and III); we find him indirectly but unmistakably compared to the loser in the simile that opens the sixth canto, in which Dante is like a winner in a game of dice; we observe the difficulty he has in understanding how Statius, who is accounted as a Christian by none but Dante, could have been saved (XXII)." By means of these examples his readers are to understand that as a Christian poet Dante is faithful to Christian dogma.

28 Dante, *Purg.* 6, 43–8, p. 120, cf. Gentile, *Studi su Dante*, p. 27.

29 Gentile, *Studi su Dante*, p. 27: "Beatrice ride; Virgilio no. Beatrice ride perché essa è lume tra il vero e l'intelletto, è la vera scienza."

30 Dante, *Purg.* 18, 46–8, p. 390, cf. Gentile, *Studi Su Dante*, p. 28. For Gentile, Virgil is to be understood as reason and philosophy and Beatrice as faith: "Beatrice, insomma, è la fede e Virgilio è la ragione; quella la teologia e questo la filosofia." Gentile refers to other definitions of Beatrice in the *Commedia – Inferno* 10, 131: *quella, il cui bell'occhio tutto vede; Paradiso* 15, 54: *colei ch'a l'alto volo mi vestì le piume*; Par. XVIII, 4: *quella donna ch'a Dio mi menava;* Par. XXVIII, 3: *quella che imparadisa la mia* mente; *Par.* 30, 75: *il sole degli occhi miei.* In all the passages above, Beatrice is defined in relation to ultimate light and heavenly vision. While recognizing that Virgil leads through the light of natural reason and Beatrice through the light of grace, it is both erroneous and limiting to understand Virgil and Beatrice as mere symbols of reason and faith respectively. First and foremost the identity of Virgil in the *Commedia* is historical; he is the ancient Roman poet from whom Dante took his own poetic style. And, Beatrice is both the Florentine girl with whom Dante fell in love and the blessed lady who descends from Heaven for the sake of her friend's salvation.

31 See Dante, *Par.* 4, 118–32; 5, 1–9: "S'io ti fiammeggio nel caldo d'amore / di là dal modo che 'n terra si vede, / sì che del viso tuo vinco il valore, / non ti maravigliar, ché ciò procede / da perfetto veder, che, come apprende, così nel bene appreso move il piede. / Io veggio ben sì come già resplende / ne l'intelletto tuo l'etterna luce, / che, vista, sola e sempre amore accende."

32 For passages in the *Commedia* when Virgil's authority is fallible, see *Purgatorio* 6, 43–8; 15, 76–8; 18, 46–8; 27, 128–49.

33 Barolini, *Dante's Poets*, p. 239.

34 Ibid.

35 See variations of the use of the words *dolce* and *padre*: "lo dolce padre" (*Inf.* 8, 109–10); "Lo più che padre" (*Purg.* 23, 4); "dolce padre" (*Purg.* 15, 25); "O dolce padre mio" (*Purg.*15, 124); "Dolce mio padre" (*Purg.* 17, 82); "dolce padre caro"

(*Purg.* 18, 13); "O dolce padre" (*Purg.* 23, 13); "Lo dolce padre mio" (*Purg.* 25, 17); "Lo dolce padre mio" (*Purg.* 27, 52); "dolcissimo patre" (*Purg.* 30, 50).

36 Teodolinda Barolini, *Dante and the Origins of Italian Literary Culture* (New York: Fordham University Press, 2006), p. 157.

37 Cicero, *DA* XXVII, 102: "Mihi quidem Scipio, quamquam est subito ereptus, vivit tamen semperque vivet; virtutem enim amavi illius viri, quae exstineta non est."

38 Cicero, *DA* VI, 23: "Quocirea et absentes adsunt et ergentes abundant et imbecilli valent et, quod difficilius dictum est, mortui vivunt; tantus eos honos memoria desiderium prosequitur amicorum, ex quo illorum beata mors videtur, horum vita laudabilis."

39 Barolini, *Dante's Poets*, p. 240.

40 Aristotle, *NE* 8.7 1159a29–33, pp. 22–3.

41 Gustav Heylbut, *Aspasii in Ethica nicomachea quae supersunt commentaria* (Berlin: CAG 19, 1889) 179.28–180.5.

42 Barolini, *Dante's Poets*, p. 241: "... while, theoretically, we must acknowledge that Vergil [*sic*] is not irreplaceable, emotionally he is perceived as such."

43 Cicero, *DA* VIII, 26: "Amor enim, ex quo amicitia nominate est, princeps est ad benevolentiam coniungendam."

44 Michele Barbi, *Problemi di critica dantesca*, seconda serie 1920–1937 (Florence: Sansoni, 1975), p. 69: "Dante segue San Tommaso nel valutare l'importanza degli studi profani e l'utilità di essi anche in rapporto con una più vera e profonda conoscenza di Dio. Questo è il pensiero animatore del *Convivio*, e non subisce cambiamento nella *Divina Commedia*." Cf., *Conv.* III, xiv, 2–15.

45 Panvini, "Sul primo incontro di Dante con Beatrice nel Paradiso Terrestre (*Purgatorio*, XXX e XXXI), p. 257: "Invero le virtù cardinali sono le precorritrici della Grazia, quelle che sostengono nel bene l'uomo non ancora infuso della Grazia e lo preparano ad essa; esse erano le sole virtù dell'umanità prima della Redenzione, in quanto prima di allora l'uomo in genere non poteva fruire della Grazia per l'impedimento del peccato originale. Dopo la Redenzione, superata la barriera che divideva l'uomo da Dio, la Grazia è stata restituita all'uomo e in primo modo mediante la rivelazione evangelica."

46 Dante, *Purg.* 30, 51, p. 668: "Virgilio a cui per mia salute die' mi."

47 Barbi, *Problemi di critica dantesca*, p. 73: "e la separazione delle due autorità e del loro compito e dominio è, ripeto, fondamento, nel Poema, d'ogni invenzione ... il 'savio gentil che tutto seppe' guida D. con piena indipendenza Beatrice ha rimesso a lui pienamente la scelta dei mezzi: 'l'aiuta s` chì ne sia consolata;' ed egli sa di suo la via per cui condurlo e la meta: il paradiso terrestre, cioè lo stato di vita unamente perfetto, quella felicità che l'uomo è in grado di conseguire in questo mondo col suo mezzo della propria virtù"

48 Panvini, "Sul primo incontro di Dante con Beatrice nel Paradiso Terrestre (*Purgatorio,* XXX e XXXI)," p. 261: "Dante, perfezionando S. Tommaso, pur ritenendo con l'Aquinate che la salvazione umana sia un atto della grazia divina, vuole anche che sia un merito della retta volontà dell'uomo, una conquista della verità divina che l'uomo attua con l'ausilio della *Gratia gratum faciens,* la quale fa *ut anima ad gloriam perveniat.*"

49 Barbi, *Problemi di critica dantesca,* pp. 75–6: "In D. si osserva sempre – nella *Commedia* come nelle altre opere, e in ciò che sappiamo della sua vita – un perfetto equilibrio delle facoltà morali ed intellettuali, che lo fa rifuggire instintivamente da ogni esagerazione, ed in virtù del quale egli è sempre disposto ad apprezzare quel che pur v'è di buono nell'uomo e nelle sue cose, anche come bene in sè. Per questo il poeta non spregia l'umano sapere, ma lo ricerca con sete insaziabile."

50 Mazzotta, *Dante, Poet of the Desert,* p. 119.

51 Charles T. Davis, *Dante and the Idea of Rome* (Oxford: Clarendon Press, 1957), p. 137. Cf. Mazzotta, *Dante, Poet of the Desert,* p. 150.

52 Panvini, "Sul primo incontro di Dante con Beatrice nel Paradiso Terrestre (*Purgatorio,* XXX e XXXI)," p. 260: "Virgilio, cioè la retta ragione mossa dalla Grazia, gli è sempre a fianco fino a che la complessa esperienza del male e della purificazione lo ha portato alla quasi perfezione della sua natura umana, alla libertà spirituale, alla possibilità, cioè, di rettamente giudicare e risolversi." As Panvini observes, the complete perfection of Dante's human nature is achieved only after he is babptized in the waters of Lethe to be reborn in Christ.

53 Dante, *Purg.* 27, 142. See Hollander's note to verse 142. As Hollander notes, Virgil is metaphorically crowning Dante with the authority to rule himself morally. Now Dante is in command of his own will. See also Michelangelo Picone, "*Purgatorio* XXVII: passaggio rituale e *translatio* poetica," in *Medioevo romanzo* 12 (1987), pp. 400–1. Picone understands the crown and miter as allegories for the laurel of the modern poet and the Christian truth that completes and fulfils Virgil's pagan wisdom. Hollander points to Remo Fasani, "Canto XXVII," in *Lectura Dantis Turicensis: Purgatorio,* ed. Georges Guntert and Michelangelo Picone (Florence: Cesati, 2001), p. 432. Fasani observes that, while modern criticism has understood the two terms (crown and miter) as synonyms, as far back as Ottimo (1333) and Francesco da Buti (1385) they were understood as separate. See also Theophil Spoerri, "Il Canto XXXI Del Purgatorio," in *Letture Dantesche,* ed. Giovanni Getto (Florence: Sansoni, 1964), p. 1302: "Quindi Virgilio lo ha insignito delle più alte corone ('per ch'io sovra te corono e mitrio')."

54 Panvini, "Sul primo inconto di Dante con Beatrice nel Paradiso Terrestre (*Purgatorio,* XXX e XXXI)," p. 260: "A questo punto, quando Dante stà per lasciare alle spalle il regno del contingente e del transitorio per quello del reale e dell'eterno,

Virgilio, cioè la *Gratia gratis data*, scompare per far posto alla *Gratia gratum faciens*, cioè a Beatrice, lasciando Dante solo arbitro di se stesso e del suo futuro destino." Cf. Robert Hollander's note to vv. 49–51. Hollander notes an echo of Orpheus's three-verse farewell to Euridice in Dante's three-verse farewell to Virgil; few twentieth-century commentators have heard this echo. See also Hollander, *Il Virgilio dantesco*, pp. 132–4. A few centuries earlier, Bernardino Daniello (1568) noted this very same echo.

55 See Hollander's note to verse 134, p. 686.

56 Spoerri, "Il Canto XXXI del Purgatorio," p. 1302: "La donna amata indossa vesti che hanno i medesemi colori di un tempo, del tempo in cui Dante la vide, fanciulla di nove anni, per la prima volta."

57 Erich Auerbach, *Studi su Dante*, p. 56: "Per quanto evanescenti e appena sfiorate, la vita e la passione terrena di Beatrice esistono; noi sentiamo il profumo della sua persona umana, che era giovane e meravigliosa; aveva sofferto ed era morta; assistiamo al suo incielarsi, e nella trasfigurazione dell'aldilà vediamo mantenuta e potenziata la sua contingente figura terrena." Auerbach later observes "Beatrice non cessa mai ciò che era al principio, e cioè una creatura particolare e un'esperienza contingente e personalissima" (p. 90).

58 Hollander, *Dante: A Life in Works*, p. 114–21.

59 Auerbach, *Studi su Dante*, p. 81: "L'aver conservato e definitivamente fissato l'unità della figura umana nell'aldilà è quello che distingue fondamentalmente la *Commedia* da tutte le precedenti visioni dell'oltretomba."

60 Ibid., pp. 90–1: "sono le forze dell'incanto dei sensi che vengono messi al servizio della redenzione, è Amore in persona che guida in alto l'uomo alla vista di Dio; nella sorte eterna il fenomeno non è distinto dall'idea, ma è contenuto e trasformato in essa."

61 Panvini, "Sul primo incontro di Dante con Beatrice nel Paradiso Terrestre (*Purgatorio*, XXX e XXXI)," p. 258: "Ma Dante ci mostra il fallimento del proprio tentativo, in quanto da buon tomista ritiene che l'uomo non possa con le sole sue forze liberarsi dal male e conseguire il sommo bene, perché a ciò è indispensabile l'intervento della Grazia." Cf. Aquinas, *Op. cit.*, tom. Cit., Pars cit., Quaestio CIX, Art. 7, p. 553: "requiritur auxilium gratiae ad hoc quod homo a peccato resurgat, et quantum ad abituale donum, et quantum ad interiorem Dei motionem"; Quaestio cit., Art. 2, p. 547; 'natura humana indiget auxilio divino ad faciendum vel volendum quodcumque bonum"; Quaestio cit., Art. 5, p. 551: "... sine gratia homo non potest mereri vitam aeternam" (Aquinas quoted by Bruno Panvini). As a personification of Grace, Beatrice moves Dante through Virgil, the personification of reason. Along these lines, Virgil and Beatrice are to be understood in relation to an individual's two ends: earthly and celestial happiness.

62 Aquinas, *Op. cit.*, tom. Cit. 6, pp. 55–6: "Voluntatis autem causa nihil aliud esse potest quam Deus. Et hoc patet dupliciter. Primo quidem, ex hoc quod voluntas est potentia animae rationalis, quae a solo deo causatur per creationem ... Secundo vero ex hoc patet, quod voluntas habet ordinem ad universale bonum. Unde nihil aliud potest esse voluntatis causa nisi ipse Deus, qui est universale bonum ... Deus movet voluntatem hominis, sicut universalis motor, ad universale obiectum voluntatis, quod est bonum" (Aquinas quoted in Bruno Panvini). Cf. Panvini, "Sul Primo Incontro Di Dante Con Beatrice Nel Paradiso Terrestre (*Purgatorio* XXX e XXXI)," p. 259: "In sostanza, così per S. Tommaso come per Dante, la Grazia può considerarsi l'atto con cui Dio riconduce a Sè le creature muovendo la loro volontà e determinando i loro pensieri e le loro azioni."

63 Dante, *Inf.* 2, 67–9: "Or movi, e con la tua parola ornata / e con ciò c'ha mestieri al suo campare, l'aiuta sì ch'i' ne sia consolata."

64 Gentile, *Studi su Dante*, pp. 30–1. That Beatrice needs the assistance of Virgil for Gentile is a sign of the subjugation of theology to reason. "Beatrice non può correre essa incontro a Dante sulle spiaggia deserta; e fa capo a Virgilio, alla ragione ... E questa non è più trascendenza, ma vero e proprio razionalismo: quel razionalismo tomistico che riesce in certo modo a sottomettere la teologia alla ragione. Questo accade, avvertiva Tommaso, *propter defectum intellectus nostri*; qui Beatrice direbbe che ha bisogno, essa, la beatrice, di Virgilio, pel difetto di Dante; ma certo è, che senza Virgilio ella non sarebbe beatrice, perché non beerebbe Dante, ne potrebbe beare nessuno."

65 Hollander, *Dante: A Life in Works*, p. 122: "This does not make philosophizing unnecessary but makes it relatively less valuable."

66 Ibid., p. 122.

67 Barbi, *Problemi di critica dantesca*, p. 69: "Dante segue San Tommaso nel valutare l'importanza degli studi profani e l'utilità di essi anche in rapporto con una più vera e profana conoscenza di Dio. Questo è il pensiero Animatore del *Convivio*, e non subisce cambiamento nella Divina Commedia."

68 Ibid., pp. 71–2: "Appunto perché egli sente bene salda la sua fede ed è disposto a riconoscere i limiti della ragione, prova – ora come al tempo del *Convivio* – l'impulso ad indagare, con speranza di merito più che con timore di peccato, anche le verità inaccessibili all'intelletto umano: *fides quaerens intellectum*." Cf. Barbi, *Studi danteschi* 18 (1934), p. 22.

69 Singleton, *Dante Studies* 2: *Journey to Beatrice*, pp. 101–2: "Then, at the summit where Beatrice comes to this man, speaking to him at first so sternly, her words again point to the same *other* meaning of the mountain ... here at the top of the mountain is found nothing less than Eden itself, where our first parents lived so briefly in perfect happiness ... Happiness must surely be the allegorical meaning of this summit, the goal of this mountain climb."

70 De Sanctis, *Storia della letteratura italiana*, p. 208: "Ne nasce un mondo idillico, che ricorda l'età d'oro, dove tutto è pace e affetto, e dove tutto si manifestano con effusione le pure gioie dell'arte, I dolci sentimenti dell'amicicia."

71 Ibid. p. 114: "nel Purgatorio si sale sino al paradiso terrestre; immagina terrena del paradiso, dove l'anima è monda del peccato o della carne e rifatta bella e innocente ... Il purgatorio è il centro di questo mistero o commedia dell'anima; è qua che il nodo si scioglie."

72 Aristotle, *NE* 9.9 1169b2–70b19.

73 Dante, *Purg.* 27, 115–17. cf. Singleton, *Dante Studies 2: Journey to Beatrice*, p. 102. Singleton interprets Virgil's promise of "that sweet fruit" as the promise of happiness to be attained at the summit of the mountain.

74 Singleton, *Dante Studies 2: Journey to Beatrice*, pp. 104–5.

75 Ibid., p. 115. For Singleton, at the summit of the mountain Dante regains the Earthly Paradise and that moral innocence which was the inner state of Adam before the Fall.

76 Dante, *Purg.* 30, 49–51: "Ma Virgilio n'avea lasciati scemi / di sé, Virgilio dolcissimo patre, Virgilio a cui per mia salute die' mi." See Hollander's note to vv. 49–5. Dante's triple farewell to Virgil echoes Orpheus's three-verse farewell to Eurydice. According to Hollander, Bernardino Daniello (1568) heard the same echo.

77 Ibid., 56–7: "non pianger anco, non piangere ancora; ché pianger ti convien per altra spada." See Hollander's note to vv. 56–7. The thrice-utterance of the word *pianger* by Beatrice echoes the thrice-utterance of Virgil's name by Dante in verses 49–51.

78 See Hollander's note to *Purgatorio* 30, 73–5, p. 683. Tommaseo perhaps was the first to note this echo: "That Beatrice speaks the word *ben* (here meaning "really," but also carrying its root sense, "good" or "well") three times in order to echo the triple iteration of "Virgil" (vv. 49–51) and of "weep" (vv. 56–7) was first noted by Tommaseo (1837)."

79 Singleton, *Dante Studies 2: Journey To Beatrice*, p. 116.

80 Barbi, *Problemi di critica dantesca, p.* 72: "Il presupposto che la ragione è sufficiente a raggiungere la conoscenza di certe verità indipendentemente dalla rivelazione induce D. a pensare e a dimostrare – e non tanto nel *Convivio* quanto nella *Monarchia* e nella *Commedia* – che come duplice è il fine dell'uomo, uno per la vita terrena e uno per la vita eterna, così al raggiungimento del primo sia mezzo sufficiente la ragione, a quello del secondo occorra la fede. La ragione viene in tal modo ad essere considerata, per quanto attiene alla vita terrena, indipendente dalla fede." In contrast to Pietrobono, who believes that Dante's insistance on the independence of reason is exclusive to the *Convivio*, Barbi notes how the independence of reason is a concept that he becomes more passionate about as time progresses and is represented in his later works including in the *Commedia*: "la ragione si muove

di per sè ed opera secondo le proprie forze. Questo concetto non è, come pensa il Pietrobono, proprio esclusivamente del *Convivio*, nè viene ad essere temperato o sconfessato nelle opere più tarde: anzi Dante se ne persuade sempre più quanto più sente il bisogno di trovare una base per sostenere l'indipendenza del potere imperiale dal potere religioso" (p. 72).

81 Ibid., p. 66: "Accanto a Beatrice dà luogo a Virgilio, che rappresenta la ragione e la filosofia, ed è guida alla felicità terrena. Anche nella *Commedia*, come già nel Convivio, appar dunque chiaro com'egli tenga in gran conto tanto la verità rivelata quanto la scienza umana, e come miri costantemente a conciliare l'una con l'altra, armonizzando insieme il fine celeste col fine terreno della vita."

82 Aquinas., *Op. cit.*, tom. Cit., Quaestio CXI, Art. 1, pag. 566, "gratia gratis data, per quam unus homo cooperatur alteri ad hoc quod ad Deum reducatur." cf. Panvini, "Sul Primo Incontro Di Dante Con Beatrice Nel Paradiso Terrestre," in *Filologia romanza* (Aquinas quoted by Panvini)

83 Barbi, *Problemi di critica dantesca*, p. 71: "Che Dante non abbia anche nella *Commedia* sentito vivamente, al pari di tanti altri pensatori cristiani, in contrasto fra ciò che insegna la fede e ciò che soltanto appare credibile alla ragione, nessuno potrebbe asserirlo."

84 Dante, *Monarchia* III, xvi, 7; cf., Singleton, *Dante Studies 2: Journey to Beatrice*, p. 265.

85 Singleton, *Dante Studies 2: Journey to Beatrice*, p. 266.

86 Ibid., p. 32: "Virgil as guide can and does represent a first movement toward God by the natural light, even though 'contemplation of invisible things' is not a significant or prominent part of that movement. Virgil ... guides toward a condition of justice at the summit of the mountain."

87 Barbi, *Problemi di critica dantesca*, p. 73: "ad ogni modo il 'savio gentil che tutto seppe' guida D. con piena indipendenza. Beatrice ha rimesso a lui pienamente la scelta dei mezzi ... ed egli sa di suo la via per cui condurlo e la meta."

88 Singleton, *Dante Studies 2: Journey to Beatrice*, p. 16.

89 Ibid., pp. 31, 33. For Singleton, Beatrice "is *lumen gratiae,* and the vision by such a light does indeed serve to kindle the kind of love which is 'true' because its other name is charity"; "Virgil, then, when urged by Beatrice to rescue the wayfarer from his struggle ... takes on a function as guide which, allegorically, is that very light itself: *lumen naturale*."

90 Aristotle, *NE* 8.3.1156b6–30.

91 Singleton, *Dante Studies 2: Journey to Beatrice*, p. 31.

92 Ibid., p. 269: "To come to Beatrice and to move with her is to move beyond the human. To move with Virgil means to move within the proportion of man's nature, as Thomas Aquinas liked to express it. To journey with Virgil is to journey by that natural light which may not extend beyond such confines."

93 Francis X. Newman, "St. Augustine's Three Visions and the Structure of the *Commedia*" in *Dante*, ed. Harold Bloom (New York: Chelsea House Publishers, 1986), p. 72: "The passage from Hell to Purgatory is an entry into the light and thereby into a realm which calls for a different kind of vision. The culminating action of *Purgatorio* is not a vision of *corporalia*, but of *spiritualia*, in Augustine's sense of the term." Newman studies Dante's journey toward salvation as a hierarchical progression toward light. The progression through the three canticles is studied in relation to the Augustinian schema of three visions. With the appearance of Beatrice in *Purgatory*, Dante leaves behind the *gravitas* of the sinner, the *pondus* of evil, and the *visio corporalis* of Hell to be introduced to a *visio spiritualis*.

94 Ibid., p. 75.

95 Ibid.: "Purgatory is the realm in which the pilgrim begins to see the heavenly Light, but his eyes are not yet ready to look upon it directly. He still requires media to shield him from its full brilliance. In Paradise Dante will see God face to face; here in Purgatory he still sees *per speculum in aenigmate*: through a glass and in a sign." Beatrice is the sign and the glass.

96 Dante, *Par.* 1, 64–9, p. 6: "Beatrice tutta ne l'etterne rote / fissa con li occhi stava; e io in lei / le luci fissi, là sù rimote. / Nel suo aspetto tal dentro mi fei, / qual si fé Glauco nel gustar de l'erba / che ' l fé consorto in mar de li altri dei." Through Beatrice, Dante experiences *trasumanar* – he passes beyond humanity and approaches divinity. See Hollander's notes to vv. 64–6, 67–72, pp. 23–4.

97 Singleton, pp. 79–81. Singleton interprets the return of Beatrice in *Purgatorio* 30 as an analogy for the coming of Christ, an advent, and more specifically, as three advents of Christ: "But, until we came across the pattern of it in Bernard and again in Thomas, we had not thought to look upon the advent of Beatrice for the resemblance which it might reveal to *three* advents of Christ ... Now, we do see, being aware of the pattern. Beatrice comes as Christ *came*; the signs of that are unmistakable. Beatrice comes as Christ *shall* come – in glory, to judge ... Beatrice comes as Christ *comes* ... *in mentem* ... Beatrice's other names in this advent in the present are the same as Christ's other names when His advent is *now*: Wisdom and Grace " (pp. 79–81). Since grace comes as light, the advent of Beatrice is an advent of light. Cf. Aquinas, Opusc. 53, *De Humanitate Jesu Christi*: "Grace is caused in men by the presence of the Divinty, even as light in the air by the presence of the sun; whence it is said in Ezachiel 43 that 'the glory of the God of Israel came forth out of the East ... and the earth shined with His glory" (quoted by Singleton, p. 82).

98 Dante, *Inf.* 2, 116–17. For possible influencial sources of Beatrice's tears see Hollander's note to verse 116, p. 43. See also Robert Hollander, *Allegory in Dante's* Commedia, pp. 91–2. In Beatrice's tears, Hollander finds an echo of Venus, who weeps for her burned son in *Aeneid* I, 228. Also see Rachel Jacoff, "The Tears of Beatrice," *Dante Studies* 100 (1982), p. 3. The authors understand Beatrice's tears in relation to Rachel's tears for the loss of her children (Jer 31:15).

99 Dante, *Par.* 1, 65–6. See Hollander's note to vv. 64–6. It is presumed that Dante and Beatrice have passed the sphere of fire that circles the earth below the sphere of the Moon. Through Beatrice's eyes, Dante's eyes are guided toward the heavenly spheres.

100 Dante, *Purg.* 30, 142–5. See Hollander's note to vv. 142–5.

101 Ibid., 5–6. Beatrice demands that Dante confesses with reference to the list of accusations she directed against him in *Purgatorio* 30, 124–32.

102 Ibid., 31, 13–21: "Confusione e paura insieme miste / mi pinsero un tal "sì" fuor de la bocca, / al quale intender fuor mestier le viste / ... sì scoppia' io sottesso grave carco, / fuori sgorgando lagrime e sospiri, / e la voce allentò per lo suo varco."

103 Ibid., 34–6. Dante confesses and identifies his trangressions as having loved false goods. He is rather vague in identifying the precise nature of these pleasures. See Hollander's note to *Purgatorio* 31, 34–6. I cite partially from Hollander's note on page 703: "It does seem clear that they are presented in so vague and encompassing a way as to allow two primary interpretations, that is, both carnal and intellectual divagations from the love he owed God, awakened in him by Beatrice."

104 Spoerri, "Il Canto XXXI del Purgatorio," pp. 1301–2: "La confessione di Dante è il nucleo vero del *Purgatorio*, anzi il nucleo ed il centro di tutta la *Commedia*."

105 Gilson, *Mystical Theology of Saint Bernard*, pp. 72–3.

106 Holmes, *Dante*, p.74.

107 Bernard of Clairvaux, "On the Canticle of Canticles," in *On the Love of God and Other Selected Writings*, ed. Charles J. Dollen (New York: Alba House, 1996), p. 66: "No one can be saved without that self-knowledge that leads to humility, the mother of salvation."

108 Gilson, *Mystical Theology of Saint Bernard*, pp. 73–4: "My history is also my history; my state is also your state. When a man knows himself miserable, guilty, under condemnation and deserving to be so, then he knows also by that very fact that all men are in the same condition. To know the truth concerning oneself is therefore to know the truth concerning one's neighbour, and it is indispensable to know it, not this time to pass judgement, as we have to do in our own case, but that we may have compassion."

109 Ibid., p. 77.

110 Spoerri, "Il Canto XXXI del Purgatorio," p. 1301: "La confessione è la forma di comunicazione attuale, personale, della conoscenza. È del pari il legame della comunità, un uscire dalle barriere dell'io, un aprirsi per gli altri. La purificazione penetra sin nella zona più intima, più occulta dell'anima. L'uomo diviene limpido e trasparente a se medesimo e agli altri ... Ciascuno parla del proprio errore. Nessuno si cela dinanzi all'altro." Spoerri notes that Dante's poetry has the unique ability to overcome the subjective and personal "I" of the poet to encompass the universal "you": "Perciò questa poesia non è come molta altra poesia: soggettiva – un mero accadimento interno dell'anima, nell'io esclusivo del poeta; ma oggettiva:

rivelazione, dialogo, impetuoso passaggio dalle proiezioni dell' 'io' alla realtà dell'incontro col 'tu'" (p. 1301).

111 Panvini, "Sul primo incontro di Dante con Beatrice nel Paradiso Terrestre (*Purgatorio*, XXX e XXXI)," p. 263: "E nel pentimento si risolve il contrasto fra la libera volontà dell'uomo e la libera volontà di Dio."

112 Botterill, *Dante and the Mystical Tradition*. Cf. Jacopo della Lana, *La Commedia di Dante degli Allagherii col "Commento" dì Jacopo della Lana Bolognese*, ed. Luciano Scarabelli, vol. 3 (Bologna, 1866).

113 Dante, *Par.* 1, 65–6: "fissa con li occhi stava; e io in lei / le luci fissi, di là sù rimote." See Hollander's note to vv. 64–6. In fixing his gaze on Beatrice, Dante is transmuted from the earthly sphere to the heavenly spheres.

114 Botterill, *Dante and the Mystical Tradition*, p. 231. According to Botterill, Jacopo della Lana undermines the element of change in "*trasumanar.*"

115 See Francesco da Buti in Steven Botterill, *Dante and the Mystical Tradition*, p. 231. Buti conceives of contemplation as an activity of this world and understands *trasumanar* as a consequence of grace: "trasumanar, cioè passare dall'umanità a più alto grado, che non può essere se none Iddio: imperò che nulla natura è più nobile dell'umana se non la divina ... sé come li santi omini che sono nel mondo si trasumano per grazia, stando in vita contemplativa, che sono quanto a l'anima risplendenti come è lo Sole nel cospetto di Dio." Focusing on the importance of change in *trasumanar*, Buti draws attention to the Glaucus episode: "E questo esemplo ha indutto l'autore, a dimostrare com'elli fu trasformato, secondo l'anima, dell'umanità alla divinità" (quoted by Botterill). In the same way that Glaucus the fisherman is transformed into a god after eating a magic herb and throws himself in the sea, Dante is transformed through Beatrice. The analogy underscores the miraculous nature of Dante's transformation and the importance of Beatrice in relation to this transformation. Through Beatrice, Dante transcends humanity and joins divinity.

116 Auerbach, *Studi su Dante*, p. 85: "Egli comincia con l'uomo smarrito, in aiuto del quale viene mandata la ragione – non Aristotole ma Virgilio – ed essa lo conduce alla verità rivelata che gli fa vedere Dio."

117 Hollander, *Dante: A Life in Works*, p. 120: "For Dante, Virgil is the most welcome of sources, the most needed of poetic guides. It is simply impossible to imagine a *Comedy* without him. And no one before Dante, and perhaps very few after, ever loved Virgil as he did."

118 See Hollander, *Allegory in Dante's* Commedia, p. 261: "At Dante's beginnings we do well to have in mind his endings, and vice versa. It is Beatrice, the figure of Christ, who brings Dante to salvation; it is Virgil who brings Dante to Beatrice. Dante does not (and did not in the *Vita Nuova*) use the word *salute* lightly. His last words

to Virgil give him the highest function anyone less than Christ can perform, and that is to bring another to Christ." See also Hollander's note to *Paradiso* 31, 79–81.

119 *Purg.* 30, 49–51. See Hollander's note to *Purgatorio* 30, 43–8. Hollander notes the reversal of roles between Virgil and Beatrice. He juxtaposes Virgil's feminine demeanor, his motherly and nurturing role, with Beatrice's masculine demeanor, like an admiral. While the use of the word *mamma* does indeed emphasize Virgil's nurturing role, the fact is that on various occasions Virgil also fulfils a fatherly role. In *Purgatorio* 30, 50, for instance, in addressing the pagan poet Dante says "Virgil, sweetest of fathers" (50). Whether as father (*patre*) or mother (*mamma*), what is emphasized is Virgil's tender affection for Dante.

120 Dante, *Purg.* 30, 55–7. See Hollander's note to *Purgatorio* 30, 55, p. 681. For Hollander this moment is "the climax of the poem. Everything before it leads here ... And, once Dante is named, his new mission begins to take form, first as Beatrice has him cleanse himself of his past crimes and misdemeanors. (His 'vacation' in the garden of Eden is over)." Also see Hollander's note to *Purgatorio* 30, 63.

121 See Hollander's notes to *Purgatorio* 30, 63, pp. 682–3. Dante's self-nomination echoes the *Convivio* (I, ii, 12–14) and Virgil's only self-nomination in *Georgic* (IV, 563, "Vergilium"). Also see Trifon Gabriele's commentary, *Annotazioni nel Dante fatte con M. Trifon Gabriele in Bassano*, ed. Lino Pertile (Bologna: Commissione per i testi di lingua, 1993).

122 Dante, *Purg.* 30, 62–3. Cf. John Freccero, *Dante The Poetics of Conversion*, (1986), p. 2.

123 Hollander, *Il Virgilio dantesco*, p. 133.

124 Dante, *Conv.* I, ii, 12–16, pp. 48–9: "... per necessarie cagioni due sono più manifeste. L'una è quando sanza ragionare di sè grande infamia o pericolo non si può cessare ... E questa necessitate mosse Boezio di se medesimo a parlare ... L'altra è quando, per ragionare di sè, grandissima utilitade ne segue altrui per via dottrina; e questa ragione mosse Agustino ne le sue Confessioni a parlare di sè, chè per lo processo de la sua vita ... ne diede esemlo e dottrina ... Movemi timore d'infamia, e movemi desiderio di dottrina dare, la quale altri veramente dare non può ..."

125 See Hollander's note to *Purgatorio* 30, 63, p. 682. Hollander is cognizant of his own oversight in *Il Virgilio dantesco* (p. 133, n. 24) where he failed to note "that his self-nomination echoed the only self-nomination found in the extended works of Virgil, indeed in the very *Georgic* (IV, 563, 'Vergilium') that Dante had cited a few lines earlier (vv. 525–7 at *Purg.* XXX. 40–51)." Hollander points to Trifon Gabriele's commentary as an "earlier commentator who had made the same discovery ... where he says that, in naming himself, Dante wished to imitate

Virgil's self-nomination ('volendo imitar Virgilio ... *illo Vergilium me tempore*')." In the *Commedia*, the fear of infamy as one of the two justifications for his self-nomination takes us back to the conflict between the donna gentile and Beatrice. Dante's self-nomination would seem to be another attempt to defend himself against accusations of infamy, betrayal and fickleness in matters of love. In calling out his name, Beatrice confirms the solidarity of their friendship, a union grounded in divine wisdom and love. It is worth noting that the idea of the late-naming in an epic or romance of the protagonist or hero is by no means unique. In Chretien's *Perceval*, the hero discovers his name, or who he actually is, only rather late, for instance, and in Wolfram's *Parzival* the same technique is adopted as an illustration of the impact of the hero's destiny.

126 See Hollander's notes to *Purgatorio* 30, 55, p. 681.

127 Cicero, *DA* XIII, 44, p. 156: "... consilium verum dare audeamus libere, plurirum in amicitia amicorum bene suadentium valeat auctoritas, eaque et adhibeatur ad monendum non modo aperte, sed etiam acriter, si res postulabit, et adhibitae pareatur."

128 Dante, *Purg.* 30, 125–6. As Dante reports in the *Vita Nuova* (chapters XXXV–XXXIX), after the death of Beatrice he devoted himself to at least one other lady (as Hollander notes, *altrui* can be either singular or plural in Dante). In the *Convivio,* this other lady is presented as an allegory of philosophy, Lady Philosophy. See Hollander's note to *Purgatorio* 30, 124–6 and to *Purgatorio* 33, 85–90.

129 Dante, *Purg.* 30, 16–18. As the saved souls will arise on Judgement Day, one hundred angels rise up ready to welcome Beatrice, who soon will enter the scene. See Hollander's note to verse 16–18. One notes, as Hollander does, the connection between this scene and the scene in *Vita Nuova* XXIII, 7, where Dante imagines the death of Beatrice and sees a group of angels escorting Beatrice up to heaven upon a cloud singing "Osanna in altissimi." Charles Singleton in *Commedia Elements of Structure* (1954) was perhaps the first to make this connection. In both scenes, "Hosanna" associates Beatrice with Christ triumphant as he enters Jerusalem. I cite partially from Hollander's note: "'Hosanna' associates her with Christ's triumphal entry into Jerusalem: in the *Vita Nuova,* the New Jerusalem that is life eternal in the Empyrean; here, a triumphant descent to earth modeled on Christ's return in judgement." The association between Beatrice's entrance with Christ's entry into Jerusalem and with Christ's return on Judgement day serve to confirm and defend the position affirmed in the present study, that is, Beatrice is a perfect friend in Christ. Through Beatrice, Dante is transmuted from flesh to spirit.

130 Dante, *Purg.* 30, 20. See Hollander's note to v. 20. There has been a tradition among commentators, since the time of Daniello (1568), to associate this line with the scattering of palms as Jesus entered on Palm Sunday.

131 Ibid., 19–21. See Hollander's notes to vv. 19, 21. In his note to verse 19, the author focuses on the clause "Blessed are you who come." Dante gives the masculine ending of the adjective instead of the feminine, which would seem to be a more appropriate description of Beatrice. Since the feminine rendering "benedicta" would interfere neither with rhyme nor meter, Hollander concludes: "It seems clear that the poet wants his reader to realize that her meaning, her eventual identity, is totally involved in Christ. And thus she comes as Christ, not as herself." "Benedictus qui venis" is derived from the scene of Christ's entry into Jerusalem described in Mark 11:9–10: "And they that went before, and they that followed, cried, saying, 'Hosanna; Blessed be the kingdom of our father David, that comes in the name of the Lord: Hosanna in the highest' (*Hosanna in excelsis*)" (quoted by Hollander). Hollander observes that "While Matthew (31:9) and John (12:13) also report the "Hosanna" and the blessedness of him who comes in fulfilment of the prophesy in Zechariah 9:9, only Mark has the words almost exactly as Dante has them in this passage and in *Vita Nuova* XXIII, 7." See Hollander's note to vv. 16–18 and also to v. 21, where he notes the Virgilian echo (*Aeneid* VI, 883): "Give lilies with full hands." Also see Hollander, "Dante's Use of the Fiftieth Psalm," in *Dante Studies* 91 (1973), p. 146.

132 The olive branch crown associates Beatrice with wisdom: the olive is associated with the goddess of wisdom, Minerva. The colors she wears link her to faith (white), hope (green), and charity (red), the three theological virtues. It is rather interesting that in her apparel, Beatrice at once is associated with the classical and Christian worlds. The olive branch, the classical symbol of Minerva, acquires a higher level of significance through the colors Beatrice wears. Beatrice is associated with a wisdom that is more perfect and more complete than the wisdom of Minerva.

133 Jacoff and Stephany, *Lectura Dantis Americana: Inferno II*, p. 42: "Beatrice is seen from the very beginning of the poem as *mediatrix* both in the Christological and in the ecclesiological sense ... The duality of Beatrice's role, at once courtly and erotic, maternal and mediatory, necessitates the conflation of stilnovistic language and biblical resonance ... the duality is there in her appearance at the top of the mountain of Purgatory."

134 Petrocchi, *L'Ultima Dea*, p. 130: "... in quanto negli occhi di Beatrice si rispecchiano le due nature dell'unico Verbo."

135 I cite here from Hollander's note to *Purgatorio* 31, 115–17, p. 708: "The four virtues prepare Dante to do something that will become, very quickly, the standard way of learning for the protagonist in this new Beatricean realm of the poem: gaze into her mirroring eyes."

136 *Purg.* 31, 119–23. Traditionally the griffin is understood as Christ. See Hollander's note to *Purgatorio* 31, 123, p. 708. Hollander points out that the modern Italian

sense of the word *reggimenti* (regiments, goverments, regimes) seems to support those who argue against the traditional understanding of the griffin as Christ. The author continues to note that beginning with Venturi (1732), commentators have understood the word to mean *atteggiamento* (as bearing or self-presentation), while Daniello (1568) had understood the word to mean that the griffin acted "now as man, now as God" (quoted by Hollander).

137 Singleton, "The Three Lights," in *Dante Studies 2: Journey to Beatrice*, p. 31: "Beatrice's eyes do in fact become the symbol of seeing by a new kind of light (new, following upon Virgil's guidance) is clearly marked." For Singleton, Beatrice is *lumen gratiae.*

138 Singleton, *Dante Studies 2: Journey to Beatrice*, p. 28. Also see Robert Hollander's note to verse 123.

139 Singleton, *Dante Studies 2: Journey to Beatrice*, p. 30: "Thus, man's nature may be raised above its own natural proportion and powers to a dignity that is *transhuman.* Beatrice is in fact the *lumen gratiae* by which this takes place, and the grace in question can be none other than that here defined by Thomas ... Virgil as guide can and does represent the first movement toward God by the natural light, even though 'contemplation of invisible things' is not a significant or prominent part of that movement."

140 Petrocchi, *L'Ultima Dea*, p. 130: "L'accusatrice dei canti XXX e XXXI diventerà, sul finale di questo secondo canto del processo alla giovinezza del poeta, *isplendor di viva luce etterna*, riverbero e rivelazione di dio Verità somma, trasfigurata."

141 Dante, *Purg.* 31, 79–81: "e le mie luci, ancor poco sicure, / vider Beatrice volta in su la fiera / ch'è sola una persona in due nature." See Hollander's note to verse 81. As Hollander notes, the phrase "one person in two natures" makes it difficult to argue that the griffin is not a symbol of Christ. Cf. *Purg.* 118–23, p. 700. See also Peter Armour, *Dante's Griffin and the History of the World: A Study of the Earthly Paradise ("Purgatorio" XXIX–XXXIII)* (Oxford: Clarendon, 1989). Armour does not think that the griffin is not a symbol of Christ.

142 Petrocchi, *L'Ultima Dea*, p. 130: "in quanto negli occhi di Beatrice si rispecchiano le due nature dell'unico Verbo."

143 *Purg.* 31, 128–9. Scartazzini is perhaps the first commentator to have found the likely influential source of this passage in Ecclesiasticus 24:29: "He who eats of me will hunger again, who drinks of me will thirst again." The speaker is Wisdom, the second person of the Holy Trinity according to Christian faith. Hollander notes that while Scartazzini's claim is shared by a number of twentieth century commentators, they neither credit nor acknowledge him. That the speaker is Wisdom strengthens the association between Beatrice and Christ as Sapience. This is an association also favored by Singleton in *Dante Studies 2: Journey to Beatrice*, pp. 122–34. See Hollander's note to vv. 128–9.

144 Hollander, *Dante: A Life in Works*, p. 124.

145 Ibid., p. 126.

146 Dante, *Par.* 31, 85: "Tu m'hai di servo tratto a libertate." See Hollander's note to vv. 79–90. The first commentator to have noticed Dante's switch from *voi* to *tu* was Grabher (Hollander's note to vv. 70–93). Porena also notes the switch, but in terms of ending the distance between the two, though it remains a distance since she is a saint. Chimenz (Hollander's note to vv. 79–84), Giacalone (Hollander's note to vv. 79–84), and Bosco and Reggio (note to vv. 82–4) support Porena's interpretation. Singleton (see note to v. 80) understands the use of the *tu* as a sign that Beatrice the guide has resumed her individuality. Cf. Hollander, *Dante: A Life in Works*, pp. 126–7. As in the *Vita Nuova,* Beatrice is adressed with the familiar *tu* only when she is united with God in heaven, as Hollander notes, "where and when there are no human hierarchies."

147 Dante, *Conv.* III, ii, 8–9, p. 151: "E però che ne le bontadi de la natura si mostra divina, vèn[e] che naturalmente l'anima umana con quelle per via spirituale si unisce, tanto più tosto e più forte quanto quelle più appaiono perfette; lo quale apparimento è fatto secondo che la conoscenza de l'anima è chiara o impedita. E questo unire è quello che noi dicemo amore, per lo quale si può conoscere quale è dentro l'anima, vegendo di fuori di quello che ama."

148 Mazzotta, *Dante, Poet of the Desert*, p. 187: "As Virgil disappears, the poem actually seems to take on what might be called an Augustinian literary form ... Cantos XXX and XXXI enact precisely a confessional experience. The pilgrim voices his contrition and goes into a brief recapitulation of his past from the 'vita nuova' (*Purgatorio* 30, 115) to the new encounter with Beatrice."

149 Augustine, *Conf.*, XIII, viii, p. 232: "Our rest is our place. Love lifts us up to it, and your good spirit raises our lowness from the gates of death. In your good will is our peace. A body tends to go of its own weight to its own place, not necessarily downward toward the bottom, but to its own place! Fire tends to rise upward; a stone falls downward. Things are moved by their own weights and they go toward their proper places ... Put them back in order and they will be at rest. My weight is my love; wherever I am carried, it is my love that carries me there. By your gift we are set on fire and are carried upward ... we are red hot with your fire and we go; for we are going upward toward the peace of Jerusalem"

150 Mazzotta, *Dante, Poet of the Desert*, pp. 163–9. Mazzotta applies Augustine's theory of love in the *Confessions* to the moral structure of the *Inferno.*

151 I cite here from Robert Hollander's commentary to *Purgatorio* 32, 1–3, p. 726: "Dante would seem to be looking back in time, seeing Beatrice now, in 1300, as she was in Florence in 1290 (the year in which she died). That his eyes are so 'fixed' will be noted by the theological virtues at verse 9 – and not with approval." See also Hollander's note to *Purgatorio* 32, 9: "How can Dante love Beatrice too

much? Only if he does not love her in God. And that, we should realize, is why he is rebuked here by the theological virtues (not the least of them being Charity), who understand that his gaze is fixed on the image of the young woman he loved and lost rather than on the saved soul who has made his journey possible. (See the note to *Purg*. XXX. 58) The problem is as old as Plato's *Phaedrus*. How do we love physical beauty in such a way as to see it as only the manifestation of a higher beauty (in Dante, of the *etterno piacer* [*Purg*. XXIX.32])?" See also Mazzeo's "Dante and the Phaedrus Tradition of Poetic Inspiration" in *Structure and Thought in the "Paradiso,"* pp. 1–24. The virtues chide Dante because they understand that he is still stuck on Beatrice's physical beauty, rather than appreciating her spiritual beauty (p. 726).

152 Mazzeo, *Structure and Thought in the Paradiso*, p. 2. Dante had no direct knowledge of Plato's *Phaedrus*. Nonetheless, as Etienne Gilson and Joseph Mazzeo assert, although Plato was absent in Western Europe during the Middle Ages, platonism was present everywhere in the fathers of the Church, in Cicero, in the Arab philosophers, and in Aristotle.

153 Ibid., p. 7: "The *philokalos* as well as the *philosophos* reach the supreme reality which Plato calls the plain of truth (*to pedion aletheias*) and which Dante calls God."

154 Ibid., p. 132.

155 Beatrice's friendship never altered. She remained constant and loyal in her love. Beatrice words takes us back to the narrative of the *Vita Nuova*, when for a period of sixteen years (1274–90) she attempted to guide Dante to God. See Hollander's note to vv. 118–23, p. 686.

156 See Hollander's note to verse 134, pp. 686–7. The Siren in *Purgatorio* 19, 7–32 is an example of the type of negative dream Beatrice asked God to send Dante about his affection for the *donna gentile*. Regarding the "inspirations" Beatrice was granted in order to divert his attention back to her even after her death, Hollander points to Scartazzini (1900) who "offers a simple and compelling hypothesis." The gist of the argument is that while Dante is asleep, God sends him dreams of the unworthiness and baseness of his love for the *donna gentile*; while Dante is awake He sends positive images of Beatrice.

157 See Hollander's note to vv. 139–41. Beatrice who sought out Virgil's help does not mention his name, but refers to him as "colui" (the one who). At the summit of the mountain, it is Dante's name that Beatrice calls out and not Virgil's. Perhaps, as Hollander suggests, as one who is condemned to eternal damnation, Virgil cannot be refered to by name. Virgil is not a member of the community of Christ. One cannot help but feel empathy for the pagan poet, who as Hollander points out, "has done the Christians sixty-four cantos' worth of service, guiding their great poet to his redemption and vision" and now is most likely headed once again

resume his place in Limbo. Virgil's name will be heard twice more (*Paradiso* 17, 19 and 26, 118) and never again from Breatrice, who uses it only once in verse 55, to chide Dante for his tears when Virgil disappears.

158 Mazzeo, *Structure and Thought in the Paradiso*, p. 128.

159 Ibid.

160 See Hollander's commentary on *Par.* 33, 98 and *Purg.* 32, 9. In *Purg.* 32, 9, Dante is rebuked by the angels for looking at Beatrice "troppo fiso!" (too fixed), or for appreciating her in a carnal sense. Instead, in *Par.* 33, 98 Dante's mind is "fissa" (fixed) on God and rightly so since, as Hollander explains, fixed contemplation of God is the eternal condition of the blessed in heaven. Cf. Bernard, *On the Love of God and Other Selected Writings*, p. 35: "In the presence of God he will lay aside all the cares of self and the flesh and be wholly absorbed in the glory of God, alone."

161 Mazzeo, *Structure and Thought in the Paradiso*, p. 7: "For Dante, the spirit of love matures the soul and illumines truth. Thus when, in the sphere of Mercury, Dante is puzzled about the Redemption, Beatrice speaks to him as follows: This decree, brother, lies buried from the eyes of everyone whose mind is not matured in the flame of love."

162 Ibid., p. 13.

163 Ibid., p. 113. According to Mazzeo, in their notion of love, Dante and Plato unite the personal and particular love with the transcendent love that encorporates it. The relationship between Dante and Beatrice from the *Vita Nuova* to the *Commedia* exibits this movement from the particular and temporal to the eternal.

164 Bernard of Clairvaux, *Sermones in canticum canticorum, Sermo* XXV; *P.L.*, 183: cols. 901D-902A; cf. Mazzeo, *Structure and Thought in the Paradiso*, p. 81.

165 Mazzeo, *Structure and Thought in the Paradiso*, p. 135.

166 Gilson, *Mystical Theology of Saint Bernard*, pp. 73, 75.

167 Ibid., p. 77. Gilson calls to mind Jesus as the most complete example of humility and compassion: "For we have but to call Jesus to mind and we behold the perfect image of humility, and understand that the end of humility is compassion."

168 Ibid., p. 9.

169 Ernesto Livorni, "Charity," in *The Dante Encyclopedia*, ed. Richard Lansing (New York: Garland Publishing, 2000), p. 156.

170 Bernard of Clairvaux, "Letter to Guy, the Carthusian Prior (12)," in *On the Love of God and Other Writings*, p. 112: "... neither can turn the soul to God; only charity can do this because it alone can render a soul disinterested."

171 Gilson, *Mystical Theology of Saint Bernard*, pp. 8–13. Gilson notes the influence of Cicero on the Cistercian theology. More particularly, he focuses on Cicero's doctrine of disinterested friendship grounded in the love of virtue and on the identification of friendship with *benevolentia*, as wishing the good of the friend for himself (*DA* Cap. VI). Gilson continues to explore Cicero's influence on St.

Bernard. He argues that Bernard's "fructus ejus, usus ejus" echoes Cicero's doctrine that the fruit of friendship lies in the love and good will we have toward our friend: "... sic amicitiam, non spe mercedis adducti, sed quod omnis ejus fructus in ipso amore inest, expetendam putamus" (*DA*, Cap. IX). Cf. Cicero, *DA*, Cap. XIV. Gilson also notes the resemblance between Cicero's "Nam cum amicitiae vis sit in co, ut unus quasi animus fiat ex pluribus..." (*DA*, Cap. XXV) and the *unitas spiritus* that is essential to the mystics. (Cicero and St Bernard quoted by Gilson)

172 Bernard of Clairvaux (1090–1153). In 1111, Bernard entered the monastic life at Citeaux. Then in 1115, he found another monastery at Clairvaux. While being a firm supporter of the Second Crusade, he was known for his devotion to the mystical contemplative life, and for his devotion to the Virgin Mary. While deeply involved in the Christian fight, his writings reveal his mystical side. His most important works include: *De diligendo Deo, De laudibus novae militiae, De gratia et libero arbitrio, In laudibus Virginis Matris, Sermones super cantica Canticorum,* and *De consideratione.*

173 Hollander, *Dante: A Life in Works*, pp. 127–9. The author notes: "If the schema for Dante's growth as protagonist proposed earlier (correction and then perfection of the will followed by correction and then perfection of the intellect) does indeed correspond to the intentions of Dante the writer, then Bernard occupies the most elevated and crucial position among Dante's several guides." Bernard disappears after his last smile in *Par.* 33, 50.

174 Ibid., pp. 127–9. According to Hollander, as a Christian Saint, the role of St Bernard as guide in a fourteenth-century Christian poem would seem more plausible than that of Virgil or Beatrice.

175 See Etienne Gilson, *Dante et la philosophie* (Paris: J. Vrin, 1939), pp. 278–9. Gilson here argues that Dante chose Bernard as his guide for the concluding part of his journey because he recognized Bernard as a leading figure in mystical theology. Gilson's view finds support in Manselli and others. Modern commentaries tend to attribute Dante's choice to Bernard's devotion to the Virgin Mary. For this view, see Auguste Valensin, *Le christianisme de Dante* (Paris: Aubier, 1954), pp. 132–5, and Botterill. Others believe that Dante acquired an indirect knowledge of St Bernard from the Franciscans (such as Bonaventure and others) and other mystical thinkers (such as Joachim of Flora). For this view see Raoul Manselli, "Bernardo di Chiaravalle, santo," in *Enciclopedia Dantesca*, ed. Umberto Bosco, vol. 1 (Rome: Istituto dell'Enciclopedia Italiana, 1970), pp. 601–5. See Hollander's note to verse 164. More recent studies on Bernard's importance for Dante are to be found in "Dante e la tradizione mistica: San Bernardo di Clairvaux" in *Atti del Seminario dantesco internazionale I*, pp. 147–278, by Steven Botterill, Francesco Mazzoni, and Lino Pertile. See also Giorgio Petrocchi, "Dante e san Bernardo," in *L'ultima*

dea (Rome: Bonacci Editore, 1977), pp. 137–55; Botterill, *Dante and the Mystical Tradition*.

176 Botterill, "St. Bernard," in *The Dante Encyclopedia*, ed. Richard Lansing (New York: Garland Publishing, 2000), p. 100.

177 For this interpretation, see Bosco and Reggio (commentary to *Par.* 32, 40–75). Bosco and Reggio explain Dante's violation of the norm as artistic freedom, Bernard as an old man being more believable than a young one. Hollander cites Carroll (commentary to *Par.* 32, 1–48), who discusses the babes seated in the lower half of the Rose: "Further, as we saw in the case of Bernard himself, Dante appears to ignore the doctrine of Aquinas that in the Resurrection the saints will rise at the age of thirty. Bernard, himself an old man, draws his attention to the child faces and voices of the lower ranks (*Par.* 32, 46–8)" (quoted by Hollander). See Hollander's note to *Paradiso*, 31, 59.

178 Hollander notes the differences in length and tone between the two scenes. This scene is much briefer and less tragic than the earlier one. While in *Purgatorio* 30, 43–54, Virgil disappears never to be seen again, in *Paradiso* 31, 55–8 Beatrice disappears to then reappear in the Rose (see v. 71, p. 766): "e vidi lei che si facea corona."

179 See Hollander's note to *Paradiso*, 31, 63. The other paternal figures in the *Commedia* are Virgil, Brunetto Latini, Cacciaguida, Statius, and Guinizelli.

180 Hollander, *Dante: A Life in Works*, p. 127.

181 See Hollander, "The Invocations of the *Commedia*," in *Yearbook of Italian Studies*, pp. 235–40. See also Hollander's note to *Purgatorio* 27, 139–41 and his note to *Paradiso*, 33, 127–32.

182 Bernard of Clairvaux, "On the Love of God," in *On the Love of God and Other Selected Writings*, pp. 34–5: "First, therefore, man loves himself for his own sake; for, he is flesh and he can have no taste for anything except in relation to himself. And when he sees that he cannot subsist of himself, he begins to seek God through faith as something, as it were, necessary for him (cf. Heb 11:6) and to love Him. Thus he loves God according to the second degree, but for his own sake, not for Himself ... and thus by tasting how sweet the Lord is (cf. Ps 34:9), he passes to the third degree so that he loves God now, not for his own sake but for Himself ... and I know not if the fourth degree is attained, in its perfection, by any man in this life so that, indeed, a man loves himself only for the sake of God. But it will be so, beyond a doubt, when the good and faithful servant has been brought into the joy of his lord (cf. Mt 25:31) and 'inebriated with the plenty of God's house' (Ps 36:9)."

183 Bernard of Clairvaux, "On the Canticle of Canticles," in *On the Love of God and Other Selected Works*, p. 51: "As to the way in which our Redemption was accomplished, God's emptying of Self, there are also three points which I commend

to your attention. For that emptying out was not a simple matter or limited. 'He emptied Himself,' even to the extent of becoming flesh, of enduring death, even 'the death on the cross' (Philippians 2:7–8)."

184 Dante, *Par.* 33, 131. See Hollander's note to *Paradiso*, 33, 127–32, p. 934. I cite partially from his note: "It took centuries until a commentator (Scartazzini [comm. to verse. 131]) realized that this image contained a reference to St Paul (Philippians 2:7), 'but made himself nothing, taking the form of a servant, being born in the likeness of men.' This is currently a fairly widespread perception, but the only other writer in the DDP to observe it is Grandgent (comm. to verse 131)" (p. 934). See also Hollander's note to *Paradiso* 33, 131, p. 934. For an echo in *Paradiso* 33, 131 of the fourth mode of loving God in St Bernard's *De diligendo Deo*, see Hollander, "The Invocation of the *Commedia*," p. 35. In *De diligendo Deo* in *Sancti Bernardi Opera*, ed. J. Leclercq and H.M. Rochais, vol. 3 (Rome: Editiones Cistercienses, 1963), p. 142, St Bernard makes reference to the same Pauline passage in a similar context, describing the highest form of mystical love: loving oneself in God. For Bernard's four modes of love and their possible influence on the stages in the *Commedia*, see Hollander's note to *Purgatorio* 27, 139–41. According to Hollander, this suggestion was first made by Donald J. Mathison, a student at Princeton, in 1968. For more recent discussions that agree with the above, see Francesco Mazzoni, "San Bernardo e la visione poetica della *Divina Commedia*," in *Seminario Dantesco Internazionale: Atti del primo convegno tenutosi al Chauncey Conference Center, Princeton, 21–23 ottobre 1994*, ed. Z.G. Baranski (Florence: Le Lettere, 1997), p. 176, as well as Christian Moevs, *The Metaphysics of Dante's "Comedy"* (Oxford: Oxford University Press, 2005), p. 81. Also see Edmund G. Gardner, *Dante and the Mystics: A Study of the Mystical Aspect of the Divina Commedia and its Relations with Some of its Medieval Sources* (New York: E.P. Dutton and Co., 1913), p. 118, for the link between the *De diligendo Deo* X, 27–8 and Dante's spiritual preparation for the final vision of God.

185 Gilson, *Mystical Theology of Saint Bernard*, p. 86.

186 Bernard of Clairvaux, "On the Love of God," in *On the Love of God and Other Selected Writings*, p. 25: "The substance, indeed, will remain, but in another form, another glory, another power. Man's human nature and individual identity will remain, transfigured."

187 Ibid., p. 26: "... let the soul hope to apprehend the fourth degree of love, or, rather, to be apprehended in it (cf. Philippians 3:12–13), for in truth, it is within the power of God to give it to whomsoever He wishes, not for human diligence to procure by its own efforts."

188 Ibid., p. 31: "Therefore charity is rightly called both God and the gift of God. And so charity gives charity, the substantial gives what is the accident." Cf. Bernard of Clairvaux, "Letter to Guy, the Carthusian Prior (12)," in *On the Love of God*

and Other Selected Writings, pp. 112–13: "... but I say that charity is the Divine Substance itself. There is nothing new or strange about this, for St. John himself has said, 'God is love' (1 Jn 4:8). It follows that love (charity) can be correctly said to be both God and the gift of God; that charity gives charity; the substance of charity, the quality of charity."

189 Bernard of Clairvaux, "Letter to Guy, the Carthusian Prior (12)," in *On the Love of God and Other Selected Writings*, pp. 111–12.

190 Bernard of Clairvaux, "On the Canticle of Canticles," in *On the Love of God and Other Works*, p. 30: "... for it is charity alone which is strong enough to convert a soul from love of self and of the world and direct it to God."

191 Bernard of Clairvaux, "Letter to Guy, the Carthusian Prior (12)," in *On the Love of God and Other Selected Writings*, p. 114: "Because we are flesh and blood born of the desire of the flesh, our desire or love must start in the flesh, and it will then, if properly directed, progress under grace by certain stages until it is fulfilled in the spirit for 'that was not first which is spiritual, but that which is natural; afterwards that which is spiritual' (1 Cor 15:46). We must first bear the image which is earthly and afterwards that which is heavenly."

Bibliography

Aelred of Rievaulx. *De spiritali amicitia*. Ed. Jean Dubois. Paris: Bayaert, 1948.

Ahern, John. "The New Life of the Book: The Implied Reader of the *Vita Nuova*." *Dante Studies* 110 (1992): 1–16.

Ambrose, St. "On the Duties of Ministers." *De Officiis* (391). Ed. J. Davidson. Vol. 10 (1963): 77–125

Annas, J. "Plato and Aristotle on Friendship and Altruism." *Mind* 86.344 (1977): 532–54.

Aquinas, Thomas. *Commentary on the Nicomachean Ethics*. Trans. C.I. Litzinger. 2 vols. Notre Dame: Dumb Ox Books, 1993.

— *De moribus divinis. On the Ways of God*. Trans. B. Delaney. London: Burns and Oates, 1926.

— *Questiones disputatae de veritate*. Trans. Robert W. Mulligan, S.J. Chicago: Henry Regnery Company, 1952.

— *Scriptum super libros Sententiarium*. Ed. P. Mandonnet and M.F. Moos. 5 vols. Paris: Lethielleux, 1929–56.

— *Sententia libri Ethicorum* in *Opera Omnia*. Ed. R.A. Gauthier. Vol. 47, Kpts. 1–2 (2 vols.). Rome: Leonina, 1969.

— *Summa contra Gentiles*. Ed. C. Pera, P. Marc, P. Caramello. Turin: Marietti, 1961–7.

— *Summa Theologiae*. Trans. Thomas Gilby, et al. 61 vols. New York: McGraw-Hill, 1964–80.

— *Super Evangelium S. Ioannis Lectura*. 5th ed. Raphaelis Cai. Rome: Marietti, 1951.

Aristotle. *The Complete Works of Aristotle: The Revised Oxford Translation*. Ed. Jonathan Barnes. 12 vols. Princeton: Princeton University Press, 1984.

— *Eudemian Ethics*. Trans. H. Rackham. Ed. T.E. Page. Cambridge: Harvard University Press, 1974.

— *Nicomachean Ethics*. Trans. Terence Irwin. Indianapolis: Hackett Publishing Company, 1985.

Armour, Peter. *Dante's Griffin and the History of the World: A Study of the Earthly Paradise ("Purgatorio" XXIX–XXXIII)*. Oxford: Clarendon, 1989.

Armstrong, David. *Horace*. New Haven, CT, and London: Yale University Press, 1989.

Armstrong, Hilary A. "Platonic Eros and Christian *Agape*." *Downside Review*, 79.255 (Spring 1961): 105–21.

Ascoli, Albert Russell. "The Unfinished Author: Dante's Rhetoric of Authority in *Convivio* and *De vulgari eloquentia*." *The Cambridge Companion to Dante*, 45–66. Ed. Rachel Jacoff. Cambridge: Cambridge University Press, 1993.

Auerbach, Erich. *Dante: Poet of the Secular World*. Trans. Ralph Manheim. Chicago: University of Chicago Press, 1969.

— "Figura" (1944). *Scenes from the Drama of European Literature*. Trans. Ralph Manheim. New York: Meridian, 1959. 11–76.

— "Figural Art." *Dante*. Ed. Harold Bloom. New York: Chelsea House, 1986. 290–3.

— *Mimesis: The Representation of Reality in Western Literature*. Trans. Willard R. Trask. Princeton: Princeton University Press, 1953.

— "*Sermo Humilis*." *Literary Language and Its Public in Late Latin Antiquity and the Middle Ages*. Trans. Ralph Manheim. Princeton: Princeton University Press, 1958. 25–82.

— *Studi su Dante*. Trans. Maria Luisa De Pieri Bonino. Milan: Giacomo Feltrinelli, 1966.

Augustine. *The Complete Twenty-Two Books of the City of God*. Eds. Rev. Marcus Dods and Rev. J.F. Shaw. Trans. Gerard O'Daly. Oxford: Oxford University Press, 1999.

— *Confessions*. Trans. William Watts. Loeb Classical Library. London: Heinemann, and Cambridge: Harvard University Press, 1989.

— *De Fide Rerum Quae non Videntur, 1–2* in *Trilogy on Faith and Happiness*. Trans. Roland Teske, S.J. New York: New City Press, 2010.

— *On Christian Doctrine*. Trans. James Shaw. Oxford: Benediction Classics, Oxford University Press, 2010.

— *On the Trinity*. Trans. Stephen McKenna. Ed. Gareth B. Matthews. Cambridge: Cambridge University Press, 2002.

— *Sermons 20–50*. Trans. E. Hill. New York: New York City Press, 1990.

Balduino, Armando. "Cino da Pistoia, Boccaccio, e i poeti minori del trecento." *Atti del Colloquio Cino da Pistoia*. Rome: Accademia Nazionale dei Lincei, 1976. 33–85.

Ball, Robert. "Theological Semantics: Virgil's *Pietas* and Dante's *pietà*." *Stanford Italian Review* 2 (1981): 59–71.

Ballerini, Carlo. "Il canto del ricordo (II dell'*Inferno*)." *L'Albero*, 12 (1962): 26–42.

Barbi, Michele. "Ancora sul testo della *Divina Commedia*." *Studi Danteschi* 18 (1934): 5–57.

— *Life of Dante*. Trans. Paul G. Ruggiers. Berkeley and Los Angeles: University of California Press, 1966.

— *Problemi di critica dantesca*. Seconda serie (1920–1937). Florence: Sansoni, 1975.

Barolini, Teodolinda. "Dante and the Lyric Past." *The Cambridge Companion to Dante*. Ed. Rachel Jacoff. Cambridge: Cambridge University Press, 2000. 14–33.

—*Dante and the Origins of Italian Literary Culture*. New York: Fordham University Press, 2006.

— *Dante's Poets*. Princeton: Princeton University Press, 1984.

— *Rime giovanili e della 'Vita Nuova.'* Milan: Rizzoli, 2009.

— *The Undivine Comedy: Detheologizing Dante*. Princeton: Princeton University Press, 1992.

Bergin, Thomas, ed. *From Time to Eternity*. New Haven and London: Yale University Press, 1967.

— *Perspectives on the Divine Comedy*. New Brunswick, NJ: Rutgers University Press, 1967.

Bernard of Clairvaux. *Cantica Canticorum: Eighty-six Sermones on the Song of Songs*. Trans. and ed. Samuel J. Eales. London: Elliott Stock, 1895.

— *De consideratione*, in *Tractatus et Opuscula*, S. Bernardi Opera, vol. 3. Eds. Jean Leclercq and H.M. Rochais. Rome: Editiones Cistercienses, 1963.

— *De diligendo Deo*. In *Sancti Bernardi Opera*. Ed. J. Leclercq and H. Rochais. Vol. 3. Rome: Editiones Cistercienses, 1963.

— *De diligendo Deo liber seu tractatus ad Haimericum S.R.E. Cardinalem et Cancellarium. Patrologia Latina* 182, cols. 973–1000.

— *Epistolae. Patrologia Latina*, vol. 3. *Life and Works of St. Bernard Abbot of Clairvaux*. Ed. Dom. John Mabillon. Trans. Samuel J. Eales. London: Burns and Oates Limited, 1889: 580–1.

— *Five Books on Consideration, Advice to a Pope*. Trans. John D. Anderson and Elizabeth T. Kennan. Kalamazoo, MI: Cistercian Publications, 1976.

— *On the Love of God and Other Selected Writings*. Ed. Charles J. Dollen. New York: Alba House, 1996.

— *The Steps of Humility*. Trans. and ed. George Bosworth Burch. Cambridge: Harvard University Press, 1950.

Beyenka, Mary M., trans. *Saint Ambrose: Letters*. Fathers of the Church 26. Washington, D.C.: Catholic University of America Press, 1954.

Bisogni, Fabio. "Precisazioni sul Casella dantesco." *Quadrivium* 12 (1971): 81–91.

Bloom, Allan. *Shakespeare on Love and Friendship*. Chicago: University of Chicago Press, 1992.

Bloom, Harold, ed. *Dante*. New York: Chelsea House Publishers, 1986.

Bobik, J. "Aquinas on Communicatio, the Foundation of Friendship and Caritas." *Modern Schoolman* 64 (1986): 1–18.

Boethius, Anicius Manlius Severinus. *The Consolation of Philosophy*. Trans. Richard Greene. Indianapolis: Bobbs-Merrill, 1962.

— *The Consolation of Philosophy*. Trans. V.E. Watts. New York: Penguin Books, 1969.

— *The Tractates and The Consolation of Philosophy*. Ed. E. Rand and H.F. Stewart. London: Heinemann, and New York: Putnam, 1918.

Bolotin, David. *Plato's Dialogue on Friendship: An Interpretation of the* Lysis. Ithaca: Cornell University Press, 1979.

Bond, L.M. "A Comparison between Human and Divine Friendship." *Thomism* 3 (1941): 54–94.

Bosco, Umberto, dir. *Enciclopedia dantesca*. Ed. Giorgio Petrocchi. 6 vols. Rome: Istituto dell'Enciclopedia Italiana, 1970–8.

Botterill, Steven. *Dante and the Mystical Tradition: Bernard of Clairvaux in the "Commedia."* Cambridge: Cambridge University Press, 1994.

Bourbeau, Marguerite. "Aristotle in Dante's *Paradiso*." *Laval Theologique et Philosophique* 47.1 (1991): 53–61.

Boyde, Patrick. *Perception and passion in Dante's "Comedy."* Cambridge: Cambridge University Press, 1993.

Bradley, Francis Herbert. "Selfishness and Self-sacrifice." *Ethical Studies*. 2nd ed. Ed. Oskar Piest. Oxford: Clarendon Press, 1927.

Broderick, Robert C., ed. *The Catholic Encyclopedia*. Nashville: Thomas Nelson Inc., 1976.

Brown, Peter. *Augustine of Hippo: A Biography*. Berkeley: University of California, 1950.

Brugnoli, Giorgio. "Chi per lungo silenzio parea fioco." *Letterature comparate: problemi e metodo: Studi in onore di Ettore Paratore*. Vol. 3. Bologna: Patron, 1981. 1169–82.

— "Statius Christianus." *Italianistica* 17 (1988): 9–15.

Bruno, Brunella, and Elisabetta Ferrarini. "XXX Canto del *Purgatorio*." *Lectura Dantis* (2000): 68–87.

Brunt, Peter. "'Amicitia' in the Late Roman Republic." *Proceedings of the Cambridge Philological Society* 191 (1965): 1–20.

— *The Fall of the Roman Republic and Related Essays*. Oxford: Oxford University Press, 1988.

Busnelli, Giovanni, and Giuseppe Vandelli, eds. *Il Convivio*. Vols. 1, 2. Florence: LeMonnier, 1934, 1937.

Cahill, Thomas. *Mysteries of the Middle Ages and the Beginning of the Modern World*. New York: Anchor Books, 2008.

Casella, Mario. "L'amico mio e non della ventura." *Studi Danteschi* 27 (1943): 117–34.

— "Le guide di Dante nella DC." *Atti e Memorie dell'Accademia Fiorentina di Scienze Morali La Columbaria*, n.s., 1 (1943–6): 3–51.

— "Interpretazione III. Tre donne intorno al cor mi son venute." *Studi Danteschi* 30 (1951): 5–22.

Cassell, Anthony K. *Dante's Fearful Art of Justice*. Toronto: University of Toronto Press, 1984.

— *Lectura Dantis Americana: Inferno I*. Philadelphia: University of Pennsylvania Press, 1989.

Cassidy, Eoin. "The recovery of the classical ideal of friendship in Augustine's portrayal of *caritas*." *The Relationship between Neoplatonism and Christianity*. Eds. Thomas Finan and Vincent Twomey. Dublin: Four Courts Press (1992): 127–40.

Cavalcanti, Guido. *The Complete Poems*. Trans. Marc A. Cirigliano. New York: Italica Press, 1992.

Cervigni, Dino. "Dante's Lucifer: The Denial of the Word." *Lectura Dantis* 3 (1988): 51–62.

Chadwick, Henry. *Boethius: the Consolations of Music, Logic, Theology and Philosophy*. Oxford: Clarendon Press, 1981.

Chaucer. *Translation of Boethius de Consolatione Philosophiae*. Ed. Richard Morris. London: Early English Text Society, Extra Series V, 1868.

Cherchi, Paolo, and Antonio Mastrobuono, eds. *Lectura Dantis Newberryana*. Vol. 2. Evanston: Northwestern University Press, 1990.

Chiamenti, Massimiliano. *Dante Alighieri Traduttore*. Florence: Le Lettere, 1995.

Chiarenza, Marguerite Mills. "Boethian Themes in Dante's Reading of Virgil." *Stanford Italian Review* 3.1 (1983a): 25–35.

— "The Imageless Vision and Dante's *Paradiso*." *Dante*. Ed. Harold Bloom. New York: Chelsea House Publishers, 1986. 83–95.

Chiavacci Leonardi, Anna Maria, ed. *La Commedia*: *Inferno I-V*. Pavia: Tip. Del Libro, 1979.

— *La Guerra de la pietate*: *saggio per una interpretazione dell'Inferno di Dante*. Naples: Liguori, 1979.

— "Questioni di punteggiatura in due celebri attacchi danteschi (*Inf*. II, 76–78 e X, 67–69)." *Lettere italiane* 36.1 (1984): 3–24.

Chimenz, Siro A. "Il canto II dell'*Inferno*." *Letture dantesche*. Ed. Giovanni Getto. Vol. 1. Florence: Sansoni, 1964. 27–41.

Cicero. *De Amicitia*. Trans. William A. Falconer. Cambridge: Harvard University Press, 1992.

— *De Officiis*. Trans. William A. Falconer. Cambridge: Harvard University Press, 1992.

— *De Oratore De Fato, Paradoxa Stoicorum, Partitiones Oratoriae*. Trans. E.W. Sutton and H. Rackham. 2 vols. Cambridge: Harvard University Press, 1942.

— *Epistulae ad Familiares*. Ed. D.R. Shackleton Bailey. Vol. 1. Cambridge: Cambridge University Press, 1977.

— *Letters of Cicero.*Trans. Evelyn S. Shuckburgh. Vol. 1. London: George Bell and Sons, 1908.

— *Letters to Atticus*. Ed. and trans. D.R. Shackleton Bailey. Vol. 1. Cambridge: Harvard University Press, 1999.

Cioffari, Vincenzo. *The Conception of Fortune and Fate in the Works of Dante*. Cambridge: Dante Society of Cambridge, 1940.

Constantine, Peter, ed. *The Essential Writings of Machiavelli*. New York: The Modern Library, 2007.

Contini, Gianfranco. *Un'idea di Dante: saggi danteschi*. Turin: Einaudi, 1976.

— ed. *Poeti del Duecento*. 2 vols. Milan-Naples: Ricciardi, 1960.

Cooper, John M. "Aristotle on Friendship." *Essays on Aristotle's Ethics*. Ed. Amelie O. Rorty. Berkeley: University of California Press, 1980. 301–40.

— "Forms of Friendship." *Review of Metaphysics* 30 (1977): 619–48.

Copleston, F.C. *Aquinas*. Baltimore: Penguin Books Inc., 1959.

Corti, Maria. *Dante un nuovo crocevia*. Florence: Sanzoni, 1981.

— "L'amoroso uso di sapienza nel *Convivio*." *La felicità mentale*. Turin: Einauidi, 1983. 72–145.

— "La filosofía aristotélica e Dante." *Letture classensi* 13 (1984): 111–123.

Crabbe, Anna. "Literary Design in *De consolatione philosophiae*." *Boethius: His Life, Thought and Influence*. Ed. Margaret Gibson. Oxford: Basil Blackwell, 1981. 237–74.

Croce, Benedetto. *La Poesia di Dante*. Bari: Laterza, 1921.

Curtius, Ernst Robert. *European Literature in the Latin Middle Ages*. Trans. Willard. R. Trask. New York: Harper, 1963.

Dante Alighieri. *Il Convivio*. In *Opere di Dante*. Vols. 4–5. Ed. G. Busnelli and G. Vandelli. Florence: F. Le Monier, 1964.

— *Convivio*. Ed. Giorgio Inglese. Milan: Biblioteca Universale Rizzoli, 1999.

— *Dantis Alagherii Epistolae*: *The Letters of Dante*. Ed. and trans. Paget Toynbee. Oxford: Clarendon Press, 1966.

— *The Inferno*.Trans. Robert Hollander and Jean Hollander. New York: Anchor Books, 2002.

— *Monarchia, Epistole Politiche*. Ed. Francesco Mazzoni. Turin: Edizioni RAI Radiotelevisione Italiana, 1966.

— *Paradiso*. Trans. Robert Hollander and Jean Hollander. New York: Anchor Books, 2007.

— *Purgatorio*. Trans. Robert Hollander and Jean Hollander. New York: Anchor Books, 2004.

— *Vita Nuova*. *Opere minori*. Vol. I, pt. I. Ed. Domenico De Robertis. Milan-Naples: Riccardo Ricciardi, 1984.

— *Vita Nuova e Rime*. Ed. Fredi Chiappelli. Milan: Mursia, 1965.

— *De Vulgari Eloquentia*. Trans. A.G. Ferrers Howell, L.L.M. London: Rebel Press, 1973.

— *De Vulgari Eloquentia. Opere Minori.* Vol. I, x, 2. Ed. Pier Vincenzo Mengaldo. Milan-Naples: Ricciardi, 1979.

— *De Vulgari Eloquentia.* Ed. Steven Botterill. Cambridge: Cambridge University Press, 1996.

Davis, Charles Till. *Dante and the Idea of Rome.* Oxford: Clarendon Press, 1957.

de Beauvoir, Simone. *The Ethics of Ambiguity.* Trans. Bernard Frechtman. New York: Citadel Press, 1948.

Del Lungo, Isidoro. "Il disegno di Guido." *Nuova Antologia* 24.3 (1889): 59–60.

De Matteis, Maria C. "Aristotele." *Enciclopedia dantesca.* Ed. Umberto Bosco. Vol. 1. Rome: Istituto della Enciclopedia Italiana, 1970. 373.

De Robertis, Domenico. "Cino da Pistoia e le 'imitazioni' dale rime di Dante." *Studi danteschi* 29 (1950): 103–77.

— "Cino e i poeti bolognesi." *Giornale storico della letteratura italiana* 128 (1951): 273–312.

— *Il Libro della "Vita Nuova."* 2nd ed. Florence: Sansoni, 1970.

Derrida, Jacques. *Politics of Friendship.* Trans. George Collins. London and New York: Verso, 1997.

De Sanctis, Francesco. *Storia della letteratura italiana.* Ed. Benedetto Croce. Vol. 1. Bari: Laterza, 1965.

— "The Subject of the *Divine Comedy.*" *Critical Essays on Dante.* Ed. Giuseppe Mazzotta. Boston: G.K. Hall, 1991. 77–8.

Di Scipio, Giuseppe. *The Presence of Pauline Thought in the Works of Dante.* Lewiston: The Edwin Mellen Press, 1995.

Dodek, J.F. "Friendship with God." *The New Catholic Encyclopedia*, vol. 6 (1967): 207–8.

Dronke, Peter. *Dante and Medieval Latin Traditions.* Cambridge: Cambridge University Press, 1986.

— *Dante's Second Love: The Originality and the Context of the Convivio.* Exeter: Society for Italian Studies, 1997.

Durling, Robert M. "Boccaccio on Interpretation: Guido's Escape (*Decameron* VI.9)." *Dante, Petrarch, Boccaccio: Studies in the Italian Trecento in Honor of Charles S. Singleton.* Eds. Aldo S. Bernardo and Anthony L. Pellegrini. Binghamton, NY: Medieval and Renaissance Text Studies, 1983. 273–304.

Fabre, Pierre. *Saint Paulin de Nole et l'amitiè chrestienne.* Paris: Bibliotheque des Ecoles francaises d'Athenes et de Rome, 1949.

Fabricotti, C.A. "L'incontro di Dante e Beatrice sulla cima del *Purgatorio.*" *Saggi Danteschi.* Florence, 1916. 49–125.

Fallani, Giovanni. "Canto II dell'Inferno." *Lectura Dantis Scaligera.* Florence: Le Monnier, 1967. 25–45.

Farrell, Walter. *A Companion to the Summa.* New York: Sheed and Ward, 1942.

Fasani, Remo. "Canto XXVII." *Lectura Dantis Turicensis: Purgatorio*. Eds. Georges Guntert and Michelangelo Picone. Florence: Cesati, 2001.

Ferrante, Joan. "The Relation of Speech to Sin in the *Inferno*." *Dante Studies* 87 (1969): 33–46.

Fiske, Adele. "St. Augustine: Stages of Friendship." *Friends and Friendship in the Monastic Tradition*. Cuernavaca, Mexico: Centro Intercultural De Documentacion, 1970. 2–3.

Foster, Kenelm. "The Mind in Love: Dante's Philosophy." *Dante: A Collection of Critical Essays*. Ed. John Freccero. New Jersey: Prentice Hall, 1965: 43–60.

Fowlie, Wallace. *A Reading of Dante's Inferno*. Chicago: University of Chicago Press, 1981.

Freccero, John, ed. *Dante: A Collection of Critical Essays*. Englewood Cliffs, NJ: Prentice-Hall, 1965.

— "Dante's Prologue Scene." *Dante Studies* 84. Ed. Anthony Pellegrini. Cambridge, MA: Dante Society of America, 1966, 1–25. Reprinted in *Dante: The Poetics of Conversion*. Ed. Rachel Jacoff. Cambridge: Harvard University Press, 1986. 55–69.

— *Dante: The Poetics of Conversion*. Ed. Rachel Jacoff. Cambridge: Harvard University Press, 1986.

— "Epitaph for Guido: Inferno X." *Journal of Religion and Literature* 39.3 (2007): 1–29.

— "Infernal Irony: The Gates of Hell." *Modern Language Notes*, 99.4 (1984): 769–86.

— "Introduction to *Inferno*." *The Cambridge Companion to Dante*. Ed. Rachel Jacoff. Cambridge: Cambridge University Press, 2000.

— "The River of Death: *Inferno* II, 108." *The World of Dante*. Ed. S. Bernard Chandler and J.A. Molinaro. Toronto: University of Toronto Press, 1966. 25–42.

Gabriele, Trifon. *Annotationi nel Dante fatte con M. Trifon Gabriele in Bassano*. Ed. Lino Pertile. Bologna: Commissione per i testi di lingua, 1993. 1525–7.

Gardeil, H.D. *Introduction to the Philosophy of St. Thomas Aquinas*. Trans. John Otto. St. Louis: B. Herder Book Co., 1967.

Gardner, Edmund G. *Dante and the Mystics: A Study of the Mystical Aspect of the Divina Commedia and its Relations with Some of its Medieval Sources*. New York: E.P. Dutton and Co., 1913.

Gentile, Giovanni. *Studi su Dante*. Florence: Sansoni Editore, 1965.

George, J.W. *Venantius Fortunatus: A Latin Poet in Merovingian Gaul*. Oxford: Oxford University Press, 1992.

Getto, Giovanni. "Dante e Virgilio." *Il Veltro* 3 (1970): 11–20.

Giamatti, A. Barlett, ed. *Dante in America*. Binghamton: Medieval and Renaissance Texts and Studies, 1983.

Giglio, Raffaele. "Il prologo alla *Divina Commedia*." *Critica letteraria* 1 (1973): 131–59.

Gilson, Etienne. *The Christian Philosophy of St. Augustine*. Trans. L.E.M. Lynch. New York: Random House, 1960.

— *Dante et la philosophie*. Paris: J. Vrin, 1939.

— *Dante the Philosopher*. Trans. David Moore. London: Sheed and Ward, 1952.

— *History of Christian Philosophy in the Middle Ages*. New York: Random House, 1955.

— *Methodical Realism*. Trans. Philip Trower. Front Royal, VA: Christendom Press, 1990.

— *The Mystical Theology of Saint Bernard*. Trans. A.H.C. Downes. New York: Sheed and Ward, 1955.

— *Reason and Revelation in the Middle Ages*. New York: Charles Scribner, 1938.

Gilson, Simon A. "Dante and the Science of 'Perspective': A Reappraisal." *Dante* Studies 115 (1997): 185–219.

— "Medieval Lore and Dante's *Commedia*: Divination and Demonic Agency." *Dante Studies* 119 (2001) [published 2003], 27–66.

— *Medieval Optics and Theories of Light in the World of Dante*. Lewiston, NY: Edwin Mellen Press, 2000.

— "Medieval Science in Dante's *Commedia*: Past Approaches and Future Directions." *Reading Medieval Studies* 27 (2001): 39–77.

— "Rimaneggiamenti danteschi di Aristotele: gravitas e levitas nella *Commedia*." *Le culture di Dante. Atti del quarto seminario Dantesco internazionale*. Ed. Michelangelo Picone et al. Florence: Cesati, 2004. 151–77.

Goldhill, Simon. *Reading Greek Tragedy*. Cambridge: Cambridge University Press, 1986.

Gorni, Guglielmo. *Il nodo della lingua: studi su Dante e altri Duecenteschi*. Florence: Olschki, 1981.

Haden, J. "Friendship in Plato's Lysis." *Review of Metaphysics* 37 (1983): 327–56.

Hardie, W.F.R. *Aristotle's Ethical Theory*. Oxford: Oxford University Press, 1968.

Harrington, John H., ed. *The Catholic Encyclopedia for School and Home*. 12 vols. New York: McGraw Hill, 1965.

Harrison, Robert Pogue. "Approaching the *Vita Nuova*." *The Cambridge Companion to Dante*. Cambridge: Cambridge University Press, 2000. 34–44.

Hawkins, S. Peter. "Dante and the Bible." *The Cambridge Companion to Dante*. Ed. Rachel Jacoff. Cambridge: Cambridge University Press, 2000.

Heath, Malcolm. *The Poetics of Greek Tragedy*. Stanford, CA: Stanford University Press, 1987.

Hegel, G.W.F. *Phenomenology of Spirit*. Trans. A.V. Miller. Oxford: Oxford University Press, 1977.

Heylbut, Gustav. *Aspasii in Ethica nicomachea quae supersunt commentaria*. Commentaria in Aristotelem Graeca, vol. 19.1. Berlin: Reimer, 1889.

Hollander, Robert. *Allegory in Dante's* Commedia. Princeton: Princeton University Press, 1969.

— "Babytalk in Dante's *Commedia*." *Studies in Dante*. Ravenna: Longo, 1980: 115–29.

— "The 'Canto of the Word' (*Inferno* 2)." *Lectura Dantis Newberryana*. Evanston: Northwestern University Press, 1990. 95–119.

— *Dante: A Life in Works*. New Haven and London: Yale University Press, 2001.

— "Dante and Cino Da Pistoia." *Dante Studies* 110 (1992): 201–31.

— "Dante's 'dolce stil novo' and the *Comedy*." *Dante: mito e poesia*. Atti del second Seminario dantesco internazionale. Ed. M. Picone and T. Crivelli. Florence: Cesati, 1999. 263–81.

— *Dante's Epistle to Cangrande*. Ann Arbor, MI: University of Michigan Press, 1993.

— "Dante's Pagan Past: Notes on *Inferno* XIV and XVIII." *Stanford Italian Review* 5 (1985): 23–36.

— "Dante's Use of the Fiftieth Psalm." *Dante Studies* 91 (1973): 145–50.

— "The Invocation of the *Commedia*." *Yearbook of Italian Studies* 3 (1976): 235–40.

— "Le opere di Virgilio nella *Commedia di Dante*." *Dante e la "bella scola" della poesia: Autorità e sfida poetica*. Ed. Almicare A. Iannucci. Ravenna: Longo, 1993.

— "*Purgatorio* II: Cato's Rebuke and Dante's *scoglio*." *Italica* 52 (1975): 348–63.

— "*Purgatorio* II: The New Song and the Old." *Lectura Dantis [virginiana]* 6 (1990): 28–45.

— *Studies in Dante*. Ravenna: Longo, 1980.

— *Il Virgilio dantesco: tragedia nella "Commedia."* Florence: Olschki, 1983.

Holmes, George. *Dante*. New York: Hill and Wang, 1980.

Horace. *Odes*. Trans. David Ferry. New York: The Noonday Press, 1997.

— *Satires, Epistles and Ars Poetica*. Ed. and trans. H. Rushton Fairclough. Loeb Classical Library. Cambridge: Harvard University Press, 1966.

Iannucci, Amilcare A. "Beatrice in Limbo: A Metaphoric Harrowing of Hell." *Dante Studies* 97 (1979): 23–45.

Jacoff, Rachel, ed. *The Cambridge Companion to Dante*. Cambridge: Cambridge University Press, 1993.

— "Shadowy prefaces: an introduction to the *Paradiso*." *The Cambridge Companion to Dante*. Cambridge: Cambridge University Press, 2000.

— "The Tears of Beatrice." *Dante Studies* 100 (1982): 1–12.

Jacoff, Rachel, and William Stephany. *Lectura Dantis Americana: Inferno II*. Ed. Robert Hollander, Anthony L. Pellegrini, Aldo D. Scaglione, and Joan M. Ferrante. Philadelphia: University of Pennsylvania Press, 1989.

Jaffa, V. Harry. *Thomism and Aristotelianism*. Chicago: University of Chicago Press, 1952.

Jaspers, Karl. *Plato and Augustine*. Trans. Ralph Manheim New York: Harcourt, Brace & World, Inc., 1962.

Joachim, H.H. *Aristotle: The Nicomachean Ethics.* Ed. D.A. Rees. Oxford: Oxford University, 1951.

Keats, John. "Ode on a Grecian Urn." *The Bedford Introduction to Literature.* Ed. Michael Meyer. Boston: Bedford Books of St. Martin Press, 1996.

Kelly, Henry A. "Dating the Accessus Section of the Pseudo-Dantean *Epistle to Cangrande.*" *Lectura Dantis [Virginiana]* 2 (1988): 93–102.

Kenny, Anthony. *Aristotle on the Perfect Life.* Oxford: Clarendon Press, 1992.

Ker, W.P. *The Dark Ages.* London: Heinemann, 1923.

Kirkpatrick, Robin. *The Divine Comedy.* Cambridge: Cambridge University Press, 1987.

Konstan, David. *Friendship in the Classical World.* Cambridge: Cambridge University Press, 1997.

Kwasniewski, Peter A., Thomas Bolin, and Josephine Bolin, trans. *On Love and Charisty: Readings from the Commentary on the Sentences of Peter Lombard.* Washington, D.C.: The Catholic University of America Press, 2008.

Lana, Jacopo della. *La Commedia di Dante degli Allagherii col "Commento" di Jacopo della Lana bolognese.* Ed. Luciano Scarabelli. Vol. 3. Bologna, 1866.

Lange, K. "Geistliche Speise." *Zeitschrift fur deutsches Altertum* 95 (1966): 81–122.

Lansing, Richard H., ed. *The Dante Encyclopedia.* New York: Garland Publishing, 2000.

— "Dante's Intended Audience in the *Convivio,*" *Dante Studies* 110 (1992): 17–24.

— *From Image to Idea: a Study of the Simile in Dante's "Commedia."* Ravenna: Longo, 1977.

Latini, Brunetto. *Li Livres dou Tresor.* Ed. Francis J. Carmody. Berkeley and Los Angeles: University of California Press, 1948.

— *The Book of the Treasure (Li Livres dou Tresor).* Trans. Paul Barrett and Spurgeon Baldwin. New York: Garland Publishing Inc., 1993.

— *Il Tesoretto.* Ed. and trans. Julia Bolton Halloway. Vol. 2, series A. New York: Garland Publishing, 1981.

— *Il Tesoretto. Poeti del Duecento.* Ed. Gianfranco Contini. Vol. 2. Milan-Naples: Ricciardi, 1960: 175–277.

Lewis, C.S. *The Allegory of Love: A Study in Medieval Tradition.* Oxford: Oxford University Press, 1936.

— *The Discarded Image.* Cambridge: Cambridge University Press, 1964.

Lewis, R.W.B. *Dante: A Life.* New York: Penguin Books, 2001.

Lowry, Nelson, Jr., ed. and trans. *The Poetry of Guido Cavalcanti.* New York and London: Garland Publishing, Inc., 1986.

Mabillon, John, ed. *Life and Works of Saint Bernard.* Trans. Samuel J. Eales. Vol. 2. London: Burns and Oates Limited, 1889: 580–1.

Macierowski, E.M., trans. *Thomas Aquinas's Earliest Treatment of the Divine Essence: "Scriptum super libros Sententarium," Book I, Distinction 8*. Binghamton, N.Y.: Center for Medieval Studies, Binghamton University, 1998.

Manselli, Raoul. "Bernardo di Chiaravalle, santo." *Enciclopedia Dantesca*. Ed. Umberto Bosco. Vol. 1. Rome: Istituto dell'Enciclopedia Italiana, 1970. 601–5.

Mariotti, Scevola. "Il cristianesimo di Stazio in Dante second il Poliziano." *Letteratura e critica: Studi in onore di Natalino Sapegno*. Ed. Walther Binni et al. Vol. 2. Rome: Bulzoni, 1975. 149–61.

Marti, Mario. *Con Dante fra i poeti del suo tempo*. Lecce: Milella, 1966.

— "Dolcezza di memorie ed assoluto etico nel canto di Casella (*Purg*. II)." *Studi su Dante*. Galatina: Congedo, 1984. 81–99.

— "Guinizelli, Guido." *Enciclopedia Dantesca*. Ed. Umberto Bosco. Vol. 3. Rome: Istituto dell'Enciclopedia Italiana, 1970–8. 330–3.

Masciandaro, Franco. *The Myth of the Earthly Paradise and Tragic Vision in the Divine Comedy*. Philadelphia: University of Pennsylvania Press, 1991.

Maurer, Armand A. *Medieval Philosophy*. Toronto: Pontifical Institute of Medieval Studies, 1982.

Mazzeo, Joseph A. "Light Metaphysics in the Works of Dante." *Dante in America*. Ed. A. Bartlett Giamatti. New York: Medieval & Renaissance Texts & Studies, 1983: 293–324.

— *Medieval Cultural Tradition in Dante's Comedy*. New York: Greenwood Press, 1968.

— *Structure and Thought in the Paradiso*. Ithaca: Cornell University Press, 1958.

Mazzoni, Francesco. "Il canto II dell'*Inferno*." *Saggio per un nuovo commento alla "Divina Commedia": "Inferno"—Canti I–III*. Florence: Sansoni, 1967.

— "*Purgatorio* Canto XXXI." *Lectura Dantis Scaligera*. Florence: LeMonnier, 1965.

— "San Bernardo e la visione poetica della *Divina Commedia*." *Seminario Dantesco Internazionale: Atti del primo convegno tenuotosi al Chauncey Conference Center, Princeton, 21–23 ottobre 1994*. Ed. Z.G. Baranski. Florence: Le Lettere, 1997.

Mazzotta, Giuseppe, ed. *Cosmopoiesis: The Renaissance Experiment*. Toronto: University of Toronto Press, 2001.

— *Critical Essays on Dante*. Boston: G.K. Hall & Co., 1991.

— *Dante, Poet of the Desert*. Princeton: Princeton University Press, 1979.

— "The Language of Poetry in the *Vita Nuova*." *Rivista di Studi italiani* 1 (1983): 1–16.

— "Life of Dante." *The Cambridge Companion to Dante*. Cambridge: Cambridge University Press, 2000.

McGuire, Brian Patrick. "Friendship and Community: The Monastic Experience 350–1250." *Cisterian Studies* 95 (1998): 95–128.

McNamara, M.A. *Friendship in Saint Augustine*. Staten Island, NY: Alba House, 1958.

Millett, Paul. *Learning and Borrowing in Ancient Athens*. Cambridge: Cambridge Cambridge University Press, 1991.

Moevs, Christian. *The Metaphysics of Dante's "Comedy."* Oxford: Oxford University Press, 2005.

Moleta, Vincenzo. *Guinizzelli in Dante*. Rome: Edizioni di Storia e Letteratura, 1980.

Moltmann, Jurgen. "Open Friendship: Aristotelian and Christian Concepts of Friendship." In *The Changing Face of Friendship*, ed. Leroy S. Rouner, 29–42. London: Routledge, 1994.

Montaigne, Michel de. *Essays*. Trans. J.M. Cohen. New York: Penguin Classics, 1983.

Moore, Edward. "The Reproaches of Beatrice." *Giornale Dantesco* 20 (1912): 189–97.

— *Studies in Dante, First Series: Scripture and Classical Authors in Dante*. Oxford: Clarendon Press, 1969 [1896].

Morris, R., ed. *Chaucer's Translation of Boethius de Consolatione Philosophiae*. London: N. Trubner & Co., published for the Early English Text Society, 1868.

Musa, Mark. *Essays on Dante*. Bloomington: Indiana University Press, 1964.

Najemy, M. John. "Dante and Florence." *The Cambridge Companion to Dante*. Cambridge: Cambridge University Press, 2000.

Nardi, Bruno. "Dal *Convivio* alla *Commedia*." *Dal Convivio alla Commedia*. Rome: Istituto storico italiano per il medio evo, 1960. 37–150.

— *Dante e la cultura medievale*. Bari: Laterza, 1942.

— *Dante e la cultura medievale*. Ed. Paolo Mazzantini. Rome: Laterza, 1983.

— *Nel mondo di Dante*. Rome: Edizioni di "Storia e Letteratura," 1944.

— *Saggi di filosofia dantesca*. Florence: La Nuova Italia, 1967.

— *Saggi e note di critica dantesca*. Milan-Naples: Ricciardi, 1966.

Newman, Francis X. "St. Augustine's Three Visions and the Structure of the *Commedia*." *Dante*. Ed. Harold Bloom. New York: Chelsea House Publishers, 1986. 65–81.

Nietzsche, Friedrich, *Daybreak*. Trans. R.J. Hollingdale. Cambridge: Cambridge University, 1982.

— *Thus Spake Zarathustra. The Portable Nietzsche*. Ed. and trans. Walter Kaufmann. New York: Penguin Books, 1976.

— *Human All Too Human*. Trans. R. Hollingdale. Cambridge: Cambridge University Press, 1986.

Oppenheimer Paul. *Evil and the Demonic*. New York: New York University Press, 1996.

Österberg, Eva. *Friendship and Love, Ethics and Politics: Studies in Medieval and Early Modern History*. Budapest: Central European University Press, 2010.

Padoan, Giorgio. "Il Canto degli epicurei." *Convivium* 27 (1959): 12–39.

— "Il canto II dell'*Inferno*." *Letture classensi* 5 (1976): 41–56.

— "Il Canto XXI del *Purgatorio*." *Nuove letture dantesche*. Vol. 4. Florence: Le Monnier, 1970. 327–54.

— "La 'mirabile visione' di Dante e l'Epistola a Cangrande." *Il Pio Enea, l'empio Ulisse: Tradizione classica e intendimento medievale in Dante.* Ravenna: Longo, 1977. 30–63.

— "Il mito di Teseo e il cristianesimo di Stazio." *Lettere Italiane* 2 (1959): 432–57.

Pagliaro, Antonino. "Il Canto II dell'*Inferno*." *Nuove letture dantesche.* Vol. 1. Florence: Le Monnier, 1967. 17–46.

— *Ulisse.* Messina-Florence: G. D'Anna, 1967.

Pakaluk, Michael. "Friendship and the comparison of Good." *Phronesis* 37.1 (1992): 111–30.

Panvini, Bruno. "Sul primo incontro di Dante con Beatrice nel Paradiso Terrestre (*Purgatorio* XXX e XXXI)." *Filologia romanza.* Vol. 5. Turin: Loescher-Chiantore, 1958. 256–66.

Pasquazi, Silvio. "Il canto II dell'*Inferno*." "*Inferno*": *Letture degli anni 1973–76.* Ed. S. Zennaro, Casa di Dante in Roma. Rome: Bonacci, 1977. 35–65.

— "Il Prologo in Cielo." *Critica Letteraria.* Vol. 2. Rome: Bonacci, 1974. 163–4.

Patch, H.R. *The Tradition of Boethius: A Study of His Importance in Medieval Culture.* Oxford: Oxford University Press, 1935.

Paulinus of Nola. *Epistola* 13.2 in *Letters of St. Paulinus of Nola.* Eds. Rev. Johannes Quasten, Rev. Walter J. Burghardt, and Rev. Thomas Comerford Lawler. New York: Paulist Press, 1966.

Pelikan, Jaroslav. *Eternal Feminines.* New Brunswick: Rutgers University Press, 1923.

— *The Growth of Medieval Theology (600–1300). Vol. 3, The Christian Tradition, A History of the Development of Doctrine.* Chicago: University of Chicago Press, 1978. 158–74.

Pellegrini, Flaminio. "Canto Secondo," *Lectura Dantis Genovese.* Vol. 1. Florence: Le Monnier, 1904. 83–109.

Pellegrini, Silvio. "*Inferno,* II. 59–60." *Studi di varia umanità in onore di Francesco Flora.* Ed. Arnoldo Mondadori. Milan: Mondadori, 1963. 278–82.

Pernicone, Vincenzo. "Dante e lo stil novo di Cino." *Studi danteschi e altri saggi.* Ed. Matilde Dillon Wanke. Genoa: Università degli studi di Genova, Istituto della Letteratura Italiana, 1884 [1937].

Pertile, Lino. "Quale amore va in Paradiso?" "*Le donne, I cavalieri, l'arme, gli amori*": *Poema e romanzo: la narrativa lunga in Italia.* Ed. Francesco Bruni. Venice: Marsilio, 2001. 59–70.

Peterson, Erik. Der Gottesfreund: Beiträge zur Geschichte eines religiösen Terminus. *Zeitschrift für Kirchengeschichte* 42 (1923): 161–202.

Pétré, Hélene. *Caritas: Ètude sur le vocabulaire latin de la charité chrétienne.* Spicilegium sacrum Lovaniense, 22. Louvain, 1948.

Petrocchi, Giorgio. "Dante e San Bernardo." *L'Ultima dea.* Rome: Bonacci Editore, 1977.

— ed. *La Commedia secondo l'antico vulgato.* 4 vols. Milan: Mondadori, 1966–7.

— *L'Ultima dea*. Rome: Bonacci Editore, 1977

— *Vita di Dante*. Bari: Laterza, 1983.

Pezard, Andre. *Dante sous la pluie de feu*. Paris: Vrin, 1950.

Phelan, G. B. "Verum Sequitur Esse Rerum." *Mediaeval Studies* 1 (1939), 11–22.

Picone, Michelangelo. *"Purgatorio XXII." Dante's "Divine Comedy," Introductory Readings II: "Purgatorio."* Ed. Tibor Wlassics. *Lectura Dantis [virginiana], 12,* supplement. Charlottesville: University of Virginia, 1993: 321–35.

— "*Purgatorio* XXVII: passaggio rituale e *translatio* poetica." *Medioevo romanzo* 12 (1987): 389–402.

Pieper, Josef. *The Silence of Saint Thomas*. Chicago: Henry Regnery Co., 1957.

Pizzolato, L.F. "L'Amicizia nel Sant'Ambrogio e il Laelius di Cicerone." *Archivio Ambrosiano* 27 (1974): 53–67.

Plato. *Lysis*. Trans. David Bolotin. Ithaca: Cornell University Press, 1979.

— *Phaedrus: The Collected Dialogues*. Trans. R. Hackforth. Princeton: Princeton University Press, 1978.

Porcelli, Bruno. "Beatrice nei commenti danteschi del Landino e del Vellutello." *Nuovi Studi su Dante e Boccaccio con analisi della "Nencia."* Pisa: Istituti editoriali e Poligrafici internazionali, 1997.

— "Chi per lungo silenzio parea fioco' e il valore della parola nella *Commedia*." *Ausonia* 19.5 (1964): 34–7.

Powell, J.G., ed. *Cicero: Laelius, on Friendship and the Dream of Scipio*. Warminster: Aris & Phillips, 1990.

Pretor, Alfred, ed. *The Letters of Cicero to Atticus*. Cambridge: Deighton, Bell, and Co., 1873.

Price, A.W. *Love and Friendship in Plato and Aristotle*. Oxford: Clarendon Press, 1989.

Proust, Marcel. *A la recherche du temps perdu*. Eds. P. Clarac and A. Ferre. Paris: Gallimard/Bibliotheque de la Pleiade, 1954.

Quaglio, Antonio Enzo. *Lo stilnovo e la poesia religiosa*. Bari: Laterza, 1971.

Quinones, Ricardo J. *Dante*. Boston: Twayne Publishers, 1979.

Raffa, Guy P. "A Beautiful Friendship: Dante and Vergil in the *Commedia*." *Modern Language Notes* 127.1 (2012): S72–S80.

Reeve, C.D.C. *Practices of Reason: Aristotle's* Nicomachean Ethics. Oxford: Clarendon Press, 1992.

Reynolds, Barbara. *Dante the Poet, the Political Thinker, the Man*. United Kingdom: Shoemaker Hoard, 2006.

Rigo, Paola. *Memoria classica e memoria biblica in Dante*. Florence: Olschki, 1994.

Rand, E.K. "On the Composition of Boethius; *Consolatio Philosophiae*." *Harvard Studies in Classical Philology* 15 (1904): 1–28.

Rogers, B.J. "The Poems of Venantius Fortunatus: A Translation and Commentary." Dissertation. New Brunswick, NJ: Rutgers University, 1970.

Ronconi, Alessandro. "L'incontro di Stazio e Virgilio." *Cultura e Scuola* 13–14 (1965): 566–71.

Rorty, Amelie, ed. *Essays on Aristotle's Ethics*. Berkeley and Los Angeles: University of California Press, 1980.

Ross, David. *Aristotle*. London: Methuen and Co., 1968.

Rossetti, Maria. *A Shadow of Dante*. New York: Kennikat Press, 1901.

Ryan, Christopher J. "The Theology of Dante." *The Cambridge Companion to Dante*. Ed. Rachel Jacoff. Cambridge: Cambridge University, 2000.

— "Virgil's Wisdom in the *Divina Commedia*." *Medievalia et Humanistica* 11 (1982): 1–38.

Sanguineti, Edoardo. "Il canto XXX del Purgatorio." *Letture dantesche*. Ed. Giovanni Getto. Vol. 1. Florence: Sansoni, 1964. 1279–97.

Scott, John A. "Dante's Other World: Moral Order." *Dante Alighieri*. Ed. Howard Bloom. New York: Infobase Publishing, 2011. 149–76.

Scrivano, Riccardo. "Stazio personaggio, poeta e cristiano." *Quaderni d'italianistica* 13 (1992): 175–97.

Sedley, D. "Is the *Lysis* a Dialogue of Definition?" *Phonesis* 34 (1989): 107–8.

Seely J.R. *Ecce Homo: A Survey of the Life and Work of Jesus Christ*. London: E.P. Dutton and Co., 1910.

Shaw, James E. *The Lady "Philosophy" in the Convivio*. Cambridge: Dante Society of Cambridge, 1938.

Sherwin, Michael. *By Knowledge and By Love: Charity and Knowledge in the Moral Theology of St. Thomas Aquinas*. Washington: Catholic University of America Press, 2005.

Silvestris, Bernardus. *Commentary on the First Six Books of Virgil's* Aeneid. Trans. Earl G. Schreiber and Thomas E. Maresca. Lincoln: University of Nebraska Press, 1974.

Sinclair, John D. *The "Divine Comedy" of Dante Alighieri: Italian Text with English Translation and Comment*. 3 vols. Galaxy Edition. New York: Oxford University Press, 1961.

Singleton, Charles S. *Dante Studies 1: Commedia Elements of Structure*. Cambridge: Harvard University Press, 1954.

— *Dante Studies 2: Journey to Beatrice*. Cambridge: Harvard University Press, 1958.

— *An Essay on the Vita Nuova*. Baltimore: Johns Hopkins University Press, 1977 [1949].

— *"Inferno" 2 Commentary*. Princeton: Princeton University Press, 1970.

— "*Inferno* X: Guido's Disdain." *Modern Language Notes* 77 (1962): 49–65.

— "Virgil Recognizes Beatrice." *Annual Report of the Dante Society* 74 (1956): 29–38.

Solomon, Robert C. *In the Spirit of Hegel*. Oxford: Oxford University, 1983.

Spiazzi, R.M., ed. *Decem Libros Ethicorum Aristotelis ad Nicomachum Expositio*. Turin: Marietti, 1964.

Spoerri, Theophil. "Il canto XXXI del *Purgatorio.*" *Letture dantesche*. Ed. Giovanni Getto. Vol. 1. Florence: Sansoni, 1964. 1301–10.

Stephany, William A. "Biblical Allusions to Conversion in *Purgatorio* XXI." *Stanford Italian Review* 3 (1983): 141–62.

Stern-Gillet, Suzanne. *Aristotle's Philosophy of Friendship*. New York: State University of New York Press, 1995.

Stewart, H.F. *Boethius – An Essay*. London: Heinemann, 1981.

Stewart, J.A. *Notes on the Nicomachean Ethics of Aristotle*. Oxford: Clarendon Press, 1892.

Strayer, Joseph R., ed. *Dictionary of the Middle Ages*. 13 vols. New York: Scribner, 1982–9.

Syme, Ronald. *The Roman Revolution*. Oxford: Oxford University Press, 1939.

Taylor, C. *Party Politics in the Age of Caesar*. Berkeley: Berkeley University Press, 1949.

Tessitore, Aristide. *Reading Aristotle's Ethics*. Albany: State University of New York Press, 1966.

Toja, Gianluigi. "La Fortuna." *Studi Danteschi* 42 (1965): 247–60.

Took, J.F. *Dante Lyric Poet and Philosopher*. Oxford: Clarendon Press, 1990.

Toynbee, Paget. *Dante Alighieri: His Life and Works*. Mineola, NY: Dover Publications, Inc., 2005.

Ungaretti, Giuseppe. "Il canto I dell'*Inferno*." *Letture dantesche*. Ed. Giovanni Getto. Vol. 1. Florence: Sansoni, 1964. 5–23.

Valensin, Auguste. *Le christianisme de Dante*. Paris: Aubier, 1954.

Vallone, Aldo. "Interpretazione del Virgilio dantesco." *L'Alighieri* 10.1 (1969): 14–40.

Villani, Filippo. *Commento al primo canto dell' "Inferno."* Ed. G. Cugnoni. Città di Castello: Lapi, 1896.

Virgil. *The Aeneid*. Trans. James H. Mantiband. New York: Frederick Ungar Publishing Co., 1969.

— *The Aeneid*. Trans. H.R. Fairclough. Cambridge: Harvard University Press, 1994.

Vitetti, Leonardo. *Il sonetto a Dante di Guido Cavalcanti*. Turin: Società editrice internazaionale, 21–2.

Vlastos, Gregory, ed. *Plato: a Collection of Critical Essays*. Vol. 2. New York: Doubleday and Company, 1971.

— *Platonic Studies*. Princeton: Princeton University Press, 1973.

Vossler, Karl. *Medieval Culture: An Introduction to Dante and His Times*. Trans. William C. Lawton. Vol. 1. New York: Harcourt, Brace and Company, 1929.

Waddell, Helen. *The Wandering Scholar*. London: Penguin Books, 1954.

Wallace, William A. "Aristotle in the Middle Ages." *Dictionary of the Middle Ages*. Ed. Joseph Strayer. Vol. 1. New York: Charles Scribner's Sons, 1982. 456–69.

Walsh, P.G. Introduction. *The Consolation of Philosophy*. Boethius. Trans. Walsh. New York: Oxford University Press, 1999.

Wasserman, Earl. "Ode on a Grecian Urn." *The Finer Tone: Keat's Major Poems*. Baltimore: Johns Hopkins University Press, 1967 [1953].

White, C. *Christian Friendship in the Fourth Century*. Cambridge: Cambridge University Press, 1992.

Whitfield, J.H. *Dante and Virgil*. Oxford: Basil Blackwell, A.R. Mowbray & Co., 1949.

Wicksteed H. Philip. *Dante and Aquinas*. London: J.M. Dent and Sons, 1913.

Wilkins, E.H. *A Concordance to the Divine Comedy of Dante Alighieri*. Cambridge: Harvard University Press, 1965.

— "The Prologue of the *Divine Comedy*." *Annual Report of the Dante Society* (1920): 1–7.

Williams, Charles. *The Figure of Beatrice: A Study in Dante*. New York: Boydell & Brewer, 1994.

Yamamoto, Yoshihisa. "Thomas Aquinas on the Ontology of Amicitia: Unio and Communicatio." *Proceedings of the American Catholic Philosophical Association* 81 (2007): 251–62.

Index